# POLITICAL THEORY AND THOUGHT

# POLITICAL THEORY AND THOUGHT

Madan G. Gandhi

PRAGATI PUBLICATIONS
2007

First published January 2007
Second Revised Edition October 2007



Published by
PRAGATI PUBLICATIONS
4382/4B, Ansari Road, Darya Ganj
New Delhi 110 002
E-mail: pragati1@ndf.vsnl.net.in

ISBN: 81-7307-122-5

Printed in India
Printed and published by
Vikas Kapoor for Pragati Publications,
4382/4B, Ansari Road, Darya Ganj,
New Delhi 110 002

# Contents

# Preface to the Second Edition

The moment of fulfillment for an author is one when his/her work is well-received and acclaimed. The response to the first edition of Political Theory and Thought has been so overwhelming that within six months there arose a demand for a reprint. Instead of hastening to do that, it was thought opportune to update and revise the whole text in the light of informed reviews and comments as well as feedback from a large number of students and teachers.

It is worth keeping in mind that Political Theory and Thought was not written in a hurry. Rather it was the ripened fruit of the author's life-long tending the field of Political Theory and Thought.

In the present edition, changes have been made wherever deemed necessary. But in doing so the broad thematic structure and the original content has been retained. In the new edition the text at many places has been rewritten to achieve better readability and comprehension. By employing an easy to understand language, even abstruse ideas, paradoxes and arguments have been invested with clarity and coherence.

Our grateful thanks to all whose comments and advice have benefited us in revising this work.

Any suggestion that may help to improve the present work will be welcome.

31 August 2007

MADAN G. GANDHI

# Preface to the First Edition

The terms political science, political theory, political thought and political philosophy are generally used interchangeably in common day usage, but the fact is that each one has its specific meaning and connotation. Political theory is concerned with systematized reflections on political reality and all political matters. It provides theoretical explanation of the key features of state, society and government; the question of natural good, political obligation, good government and good society; political behaviour and political capabilities of human beings.

Political thought, in contrast, is a wider term than political theory. It encompasses the entire subject-matter of society and politics, state and government, rights and duties, citizenship, liberty, equality, justice and democracy. It includes the study of political behaviour, political institutions and political realty in all its dynamic aspects. It contains the ethical, moral, philosophical, cultural, social, economic, political dimensions of politics. It is concerned with the theories, approaches and perspectives on the study of man as natural political animal in societal setting and the role of politics in human well-being and good life. Political thought indeed is the net-result of centuries of spirited dialogue among thinkers of every country and age on all those perplexing questions which have agitated the advanced minds of their generations.

The present book, *Political Theory and Thought*, written chiefly to help students, strictly conforms to the restructured syllabus of BA programme of Delhi University. The topics dealt with in the book include the nature and relevance of political theory, what is politics, state, citizenship, civil society, identity, rights, liberty, equality, property and democracy. The book also contains an in-depth study of some select concepts by prominent thinkers, both Western and Indian. In the closing section of the book there is discussion on some topics of common interest such as protective discrimination, democracy versus economic growth, how fair is censorship or state interference in the family and so forth.

Though strictly designed as text book for BA programme of Delhi University, it will be found useful for Post Graduates students and All India Services and Civil Services examinations. For, an attempt has been made here to make the treatment as comprehensive and contemporaneous as possible.

Despite all efforts to keep the book error-free, some errors might have crept in, for which I look upto my learned readers to offer their valuable suggestions for improving the book in the second edition.

There is a long tradition of books on political theory and political thought and I have drawn on them in writing this book. My grateful acknowledgment of them all. The bibliography at the end of the book includes the names of some prominent writers and their books as suggested readings.

MADAN G. GANDHI

# PART I

# Introducing Political Theory and Politics

# 1

# WHAT IS POLITICS?

The much discussed, very often criticized, seldom admired, reluctantly accepted concept of modern times is politics. The meaning, nature, and function of politics has been interpreted differently by different people. Politics for an ordinary man means election, poster war and slogan shouting. It means motivating and mobilizing people by any means at regular time intervals and educating them that there is a wide gap between promises and performance by the political parties after their coming to power. So there are divergent perceptions of politics for different segments of the population. The student of Political Science, means by politics, what he studies in college and university. Political Theory is also not the same as it may be found in practice. The academicians who teach Political Science, the specialists, who investigate and do political analyses, the leaders of political parties—they all give different viewpoints on what politics is all about.

The meaning of politics also varies with the different social structures like caste, class, gender, geographical locations, occupations, income groups, age groups, urban/rural sectors. So statements like, 'the young people are more interested in politics than the Old People', 'the middle class people are more influenced by politics than the rich and the poor, because while the poor fail to understand, the rich have no interest/time for the same'—are but mere simplifications as explanatory statements. Perhaps this explains Aristotle's argument and justification of his middle class democracy.

There are two divergent views of politics on the basis of its degree of understanding and the extent of influence:

1. The narrow view of politics
2. The broad view of politics

The people who have the narrow perception of politics, very often take the partial view by mixing it with the business of political parties and end with statements such as these: 'politics is the dirty game and noble people should not play it'. The broader view of politics is about all-inclusive nature of politics. It denotes the institutional arrangements like parliament, executive, judiciary and bureaucracy etc. It also explains that as methods and approaches it is both science and art of government. Politics embraces the relationship between the individual and the state, of state with local bodies of state with state and the international socioeconomic, cultural bodies as also the relation among the nations through foreign policy. In this sense, politics can be domestic, national, federal, municipal, local or international.

## Politics: Traditional and Modern Meanings

On the degree of fact and value, scientific techniques and philosophical speculations, politics has been explained and understood both traditionally and scientifically.

### (a) Traditional Meaning of Politics

Historically, Politics has been regarded as a study of the state. The Dictionary of Political Science describes it to mean a systematic study of the state and of the processes governing, its internal and external relations. Politics thus connotes the traditional meaning of the politics. The supporting scholars regard state as synonym of politics. Garner says that politics 'begins and ends up with the state.' Bluntschlli holds that politics "is concerned with the state which endeavours to understand and comprehend the state in its fundamental conditions, in its essential nature, in its various forms of manifestations,. Its development." Gettell views, politics as "the historical investigation of what the state has been, an analytical study of what the state is and a political and ethical discussion of what the state ought to be."

Some of the traditional scholars also regard politics as the study of government. Seeley states that politics "investigates the phenomena of government as Political Economy deals with wealth; Biology, with life; Algebra, with numbers and Geometry, with space and magnitude." Leacock describes politics as a study concerning government only. Macmillan's *Modern Dictionary* defines politics as something "dealing with the organization and administration of government."

The traditional scholars also regard politics as the study of both the state and government. For Gilchrist and Gettel politics is the study of the state and government. David Easton defines politics 'as authoritative allocation of values'. For him it is 'the science of authoritative distribution of values in a society'. This is, more or less, akin to the view that equates politics with the science of the state and government.

Politics, as the study of the state or the government or of both, does contain the whole truth, because the study of politics is all-inclusive. It tells that the political principles, processes and purposes of the state and government are its subject matter. Politics has been considered as the organization of the state, its nature, purpose and functions.

Politics as the study of political community—state or government—conceals more than what it reveals about politics. It does not so much focus on the institutional arrangements of the state or the government but the dynamics of its functions, its activities, the underlying focus which enable the state to work in a particular way. Since politics is both an institutions and an organization, the incomplete meaning of traditional view of politics results into raw approaches, concepts and views of politics.

### (b) Modern Meaning of Politics

Like the traditional meaning of politics and its inadequacy as the study of the state or government or of both, the modern meaning of politics mostly under the influence of science, as the study of power is also equally incomplete. It attempts to give politics a meaning in which it is described as an activity. Hobbes, Max Weber and most modern political scientists like Merriam, Lasswell, Shils, Catlin, Dahl, Easton and others describe politics as the study of power. They define and explain politics as power and as a relation among actors in which one actor induces other actors in some way to act what they would not otherwise act (Robert Dahl) or politics denotes the 'ability to produce intended effects as directly involve other persons' (Lasswell) or politics is 'a relationship in which one person or group is able to determine the actions of another in the direction of the former's own ends' (Easton).

Again, as Robert Dahl states: "The government is any government that successfully upholds a claim to the exclusive regulation of the legitimate use of physical force in enforcing its rules within a given territorial area. The political system made up of the residents of that territorial area and the government of the area is a state". And to Lasswell and Kaplan politics is 'an empirical inquiry in the study of the shaping and sharing of power.' In conclusion, as Dahl says, politics 'deals with power, rule or authority'.

**Basic Characteristics of Politics:**

(a) Politics can be an activity, performed by individual in public life. It is related with the activity of an individual with other individuals in a group and as interaction among them all.

(b) Politics is related with what is political and how the nonpolitical dimensions like economics, history, sociology influence it. In that sense, politics as a study is interdisciplinary in its approach.

(c) Politics is not only the institutional arrangement of the type and form of government but also the government acting in an environment. Politics is also the study of political process, purpose, policy and how these are influenced by both domestic and international factors.

(d) Politics deals with the study of individual rights and the state authority and how the two are balanced in achieving individual good and common good. State is an arbitrator, coordinator, regulator in defining the common good and promoting the same.

(e) Politics as a part of the social system, it (politics) can never be separate from the social system. Stephen Wasby, argues that, though political system is developed to perform the political functions, and to study politics, it is to take the social whole in order to examine one part of its structure and operations. When we do this, we need to know and understand, what the politics does for the society. This justifies the interrelationship and influence of political system and the social system as a whole and the role of political system in changing the social system.

## Dormant Meaning of Politics

With changes of historical development, the structure, nature, function of the state and government, its (state) relationship with individuals, with other states, also drastically undergoes change. The laissez-faire state, the positive welfare state, and the present liberal state with minimum state functions should be analyzed in the course of studying the different views of politics, of state activity and of government.

Different views of politics involve different underlying postulates and bases on which politics has grown and developed. They are: basis of objectivity, centralization of political power in the hand of few and many, the class character of the power holder, the realization of power as a means of maintenance of law and order and performance of social good. The politics, the nature of the state etc. can also be classified into: *liberal view of politics, Marxist view of politics, politics as common good* and *politics as power.* These different views of politics have originated, developed and applied by different sections of people in different states to fulfill their political aims and aspirations.

### (i) The Greek View of Politics

The aim of politics as it originates in the ancient Greek city-states is to maintain a good community life. Plato and Aristotle, the pioneers of the then civil society go to the extent of identifying politics with the 'Master Science' and participation of citizens in politics as a precondition for human self-realization. According to Aristotle, 'man is a social animal' and 'he who lives without society (which means city-state and community) is either a god or a beast'. Politics in the Greek city-state is all–embracing because of its geographical size, community life, and means of public life and private life. The aim of politics is to create essential conditions by which the individual can achieve the concrete ethical goal *i.e.,* the self-realization of man. So the Greek concept of politics is very comprehensive. It is a guide to political power, a course of civic training, a moral philosophy. It is a historical metaphysics—all social sciences, all branches of human knowledge coalescing into one.

The decline of city state and separation of public life from private life, the difference of political aspect of life from the religious, economic, cultural life results in not only delimiting the scope and sphere of politics but also allowing the individuals to become the members of other communities (religious, cultural and social). As an outcome of this change in the politics and loyalty of the citizens and their division into multiple communities the decline of politics has been at all levels.

### (ii) Politics as a Study of State and Government

The emergence of city-state either in western world or eastern, 'Janpada and Mahapada' result in the primacy of politics. The eastern authors, thinkers, very often use the term statecraft in place of politics. The character of the state, its purpose, its relation with individual citizen, with other nations can trace back its historicity to Manu and Kautilya. So, the science and art of the subject dealing with the ruler, his actions, decisions and also just dispensation—they all are included in the study of politics. In contrast the relatively modern political thinkers like Garner and Gettel hold that, 'politics begins with the state and ends with the state', 'it is the study of state in the past, present and future'.

Historically, the emergence of nation-state also justifies the supremacy of the state as a political organization exercising sovereignty over the individuals residing within its territory and securing their protection from foreign attacks. The nation-state is supreme for exercise of its internal sovereignty and external sovereignty.

The state has a monopoly of coercive power and the right to obedience. The state exercises its monopoly by negative enforcement and also positive functions:

(1) Protecting the life, liberty and estate; promoting the common good; creating the condition essential for the realization of the good of the individual itself through its positive functions.

(2) Enforcing law and order through police, Jail and judiciary to implement its decisions *i.e.,* by means of negative enforcement. Both the functions are carried out by the government. So, the study of the state actually means the study of government and its institutional performance to support the government in implementation of its policies, programmes and purposes. The study of different forms of governments like parliamentary, presidential, monarchy, aristocracy, federalism and democracy, the notion of government in different governments and its influence by external environment i.e political processes, public opinion, pressure groups, the foreign policy of other states etc. They all constitute the subject matter of politics.

### (iii) Liberal View of Politics

The liberal view of politics emerged in western Europe. Its chief objective was individual well-being, his liberty and self-dignity. It was advocated by number of liberal thinkers such as Thomas Hobbes, John Locke, Adam Smith, Bentham, J.S. Mill, T.H. Green, Laski, Barker, MacIver and many others. Its concern was not so much the institutional infrastructure of the state, but the individual, his happiness, his freedom, rights and privileges.

Liberal thinkers believe that all conflicts are seen to flow from the diversity in society in terms of diversity of religion, race, language, nationality, colour, identity etc. of interest in the society. These conflicts are social, cultural, religious, economic, and partly political.

Man as a social creature not only strives to fulfill all the essential conditions but also to be his best self. But also when he strives for the same he comes in contact as well as conflict with the other individuals. Since the conditions, opportunities, privileges are not in abundance, this perception of the scarcity results in social conflict. The self-interests tend to clash, and the attending conflict in turn results in social disorder, indiscipline, insecurity, and chaos, jeopardizing thus the orderly civilized activity.

The diversity of the society may also result in conflicts which intensify the demand for political liberation. The state may seek to resolve these into conflicting interests of the individuals, groups and organizations to maintain law and order in exercising the sovereign power of the state.

The other view also states that, politics facilitates rule of law and justice. It protects the weak against the strong, the individual against the mass. In this way the state guarantees the life, liberty and prosperity of the individual and finally the common good/general interest as well.

Since politics is the major aspect of man's social activity, it is evident that, it must be viewed in the social context. The analysis of politics begins with the beginning of the society when man has his first relationship with the bare necessities of life along with basics of politics.

Hobbes postulates the concept of 'self preservation' which means continuance of biological subsistence as the primacy of politics in his book *Leviathan*.

## Politics and the Roots of Human Conflict

It is well experienced that, there is a perpetual conflict between animality versus humanity within the human self. It may be co-related with the Rousseau's real will and actual will, Hobbes self-preservation thesis, Marx's concept of negation of negation (every positive thing produces its equal and opposite thing and contradicts it) and Gandhi's selfishness vs. selflessness. The fundamental nature of human being is to preserve his own interest, his enterprise, his advancement, progress, growth, and above all his desire for happiness. The individual judged narrowly according to the liberal view of politics, is not a moral, spiritual, social being but only as the self-directed owner of his body and mind. Thomas Hobbes sketches out the individual behaviour based on the fundamental principles of self-preservation, which means continuance of biological subsistence. Here Hobbes explains the human nature and human being in self-interest, egoistic, independent, and atomistic terms. The concept of rationality, as pointed out by Rousseau, very often makes him self-centered. So in this situation, to maintain law and order and to protect the weak against the strong, the state has to play the role of an arbitrator, mediator and reconciler of conflicts among the individuals.

Like the pervasiveness of conflict within, the conflict is also without *i.e.*, human individual (s). This conflict may be among the individuals, the groups (in form of interest groups), organizations (on the basis of function, purpose) and socio-religious communities. It is to fulfill the objectives of the groups that are continuously in conflict with each other, the state intervenes to resolve the conflict. The notable exponents of this view are Maclver, Harold Laski, G.D.H. Cole, Arthur Bentley and Jamman. They hold that if the individual is concerned with pursuing his own interest, and society is the meeting place of conflicting interests, then the politics is the activity to resolve conflicts and maintain social order.

Liberalism believes that, there is no automatic unity in the society. Politics is an activity through which conflicts are converted into cooperation. Therefore unity and harmony among conflicting individuals and groups are to be continually maintained in the society. As the political scientist Wolin writes, "Politics as a mode of creativity seeks to resolve conflict and promote readjustment". Politics by resolving conflict in the society makes clear the path for peaceful social change.

The early liberal view and later liberal view are distinguished on the basis of the degree of freedom enjoyed by the individual. The former upholds the theory of Laissez Faire which means 'let alone'. It believes that, the state should allow the individuals to do whatever they like and it should only put such restrictions as are strictly necessary for the better social good. The task of politics is only to define the rules of the game. For society is governed by the invisible market forces. This results in the concentration of wealth, services, profit, power and privileges in minority groups. It creates a reaction and gives birth to positive liberal state with interference in the activities of the individual for the greater good. The activity of the early liberal state was chiefly confined to maintenance of law and order whereas the new positive liberal state extended its activity to planning, protection, coordination and government policy, touching on almost every aspect of human life.

With the emergence of welfare states, the state activity has got further broadened. It includes protection and promotion of minority and interests of the weaker section of the people. Besides it aims at creation of structure for coordination of government policies for the welfare of some of its consequences. This view has been supported by political scientists like Miller in his book *The nature of politics* (1965). Maurice Duverger in his book *The idea of politics* (1964), Adrain Leftwich in his book *What is politics*? (1984).

According to Miller, politics is the rational reflection of disagreements among the members of the society. Socially these disagreements may be on economic aspects like scarcity, social groups at positions of advantage and disadvantage, countries endowed with unique resources but victims of poverty, men who may be differing in intelligence, skills etc. Such disagreements may produce social tensions which find many political expressions. Politics thus occurs because of the diversities in society and men themselves feeling disagreements on them and striving for new conciliations. Politics is the application of government to social situations which will not settle of themselves. Politics keeps on happening because changes in social situation and opinion never move uniformly towards agreement. But instead they continue to generate new conflicting situations. However thinkers like Bernard Crick beheve that politics is the activity by which different interests within a given unit of rule are conciliated. This object is secured by giving them a share in power in proportion to importance to the welfare and survival of the whole community. This conflict, when personal, creates the activity called ethics and such conflict when created in the level of public domain is called politics.

Politics is needed because the problems of order can be solved better by conciliation rather than by coercion or violence. Politics allows various types of power within a community to find some reasonable level of mutual tolerance and support. It is said that, politics arises out of diversity. Neither does it try to reduce all to a unity, nor allow the pluralism to continue. It is a way of ruling the divided societies where the conciliation is preferred to coercion or any violent activity among the normal peace loving people. Since most technological societies are divided societies, they consider pluralistic and peaceful rule as always better than the violent rule. In this sense, politics based on minimum interference is not a necessary evil but a necessary good. Maurice Duverger, opines that, politics plays the role of integrator. Politics resolves the conflict through integration of interests and the extent to which any society resolves conflicts, it is far away from politics. 'Politics tries to replace fists, knives, guns with the weapon of discussion, dialogue, debate, replacement of bullets by ballots'. The central theme of politics is to create unity among the diversified interests.

## Politics-- the Craft of Reconciling Conflicting Interests

The individual interests, group interests and organizational interests which are competitive, conflictual are integrated, reconciled by the following ways:

(1) statutory laws,
(2) political institutions,
(3) social welfare,
(4) cultural traditions,
(5) principles of nationalism, national character,
(6) communitarian ethics,
(7) acceptance of the political sovereignty etc.

Statutory laws are the final arbiters between conflicting social interests. These are the most effective means within a society and are usually backed by the fear of punishment. They include any form of law that defines the rights and duties of state with another state, and of individual with the state, that is, international law, and the constitutional law, by which politics are governed. They give direction to politics, shape, and reshape, politics. They along with ordinary laws made by the parliament define the limits within which individuals and groups are allowed to compete. The ideological framework, *i.e.*, liberalism has created a long history of its political process: participation, political institutions like democracy, political parties, universal suffrage, civil and political rights including right to life and property, creation of different groups, communities, organizations and associations. These organizations, institutions resolve the conflict among the individuals within the group, outside the groups and with the help of groups by which the people are integrated into the social and political process.

The state after the growth of positive state and positive liberalism comes to express its domain of duties and functions by intervening in the social and economic life. Through the intervention in the market society, the welfare state, regulating and coordinating and at last adopting some socialistic principles for human welfare such as free education, health insurance, social security measures etc. reduces the social conflicts. The children, from the very childhood are socially indoctrinated into political culture and ideology. This is done to develop allegiance and respect to the political authority, political culture, political tradition and ideology. The political parties, pressure groups/interest groups also promote/use the ideological means like education, mass media, propaganda to create consensus among the society. It encourages pessimism, debate/discussion and this results in harmony and persuasion.

So, the liberal view of politics, centrally revolves around the individual freedom, liberty, justice and human dignity. In it politics as a social process resolves conflicts, maintains law and order, brings unity and cooperation by serving the individual interest and the common interest through peaceful manner, application of the rule of law, political participation and so forth. But, the liberal view of politics in supporting the concept of private property, private ownership of the means of production puts a question mark before not only the socialists but all the political scientists about the future of this institution. For any striving for maximizing liberty at the cost of equality many times end with increase of disparity, gap between the poor and rich. It may result in social discord, conflict, tension and fissiparous tendencies.

### (iv) Marxist Views of Politics

Like liberalism Marxism starts with the premise of conflict of interests. But while liberalism believes that the conflict arises out of the competition among the individuals and group of people, it is natural at all stages of human development. It can, if properly handled, be converted into cooperation and harmony. Marxism sees this conflict in the process of fulfilling the physical and mental needs of the man living in the society.

While the liberals opine that the conflicts are natural and at the same time they can be resolved through cooperation and harmony, the Marxists consider conflicts as man-made. They depend upon the productive relations and modes of production. The conflicts in the society shall continue so long as specific groups control the mode of production. They believe in the concept of total uprootment of the causes of conflicts. This can be achieved by abolishing the class and finally the state which is identical with the class and which controls the means of production as well as determines the production relations.

Marxists hold that the common interests for all practical purposes are reflected in the dominant class. Politics too is seen to be the instrument to promote the class interests. Politics, according to Marxists, arises in a class-divided society. It remains there until mutually antagonistic classes are seen to exist in the society. The class society is represented by class politics. Here mutually opposing classes may continue to remain in the state of perpetual struggle against each other. It is only in the classless society, that politics in the form of state would disappear, wither away, as Marx had envisioned.

### (i) Man, Society and the Natural World

Marxists advocate that the individual is a social being. His essence lies within the aggregate of social relations. It is social, because all his powers are socially guided, influenced, and shaped. His creative activities also satisfy the needs, necessities of the society. The individual as a factor of production, a labour force, is mutually related with others. The development of individual also takes place in the society. For he is both an object and subject of the society. If he is influenced by the social conditions, he also has the power to change the society and social conditions by organized revolutions. The society, according to Marxism, is not the aggregate of the individuals, an artificial institution but a product of man's reciprocal mutually integrated living organisms. Marxism does not separate society from nature, as man is a part of the natural world which is the basis of real activity. The entire social relationships are based on the concept of production and reproduction of material life. Society, to strengthen itself, requires material production while production in turn depends upon the factors of production like land, labor, capital, technology and management based on entrepreneurship. The factors of production result into relations of production and modes of production, between the owners of production and non-owners. Throughout the history of human development, the society is shaped and reshaped on the basis of production relations, among the non-owners and owners of the means of production.

According to Marx, all history is essentially a history of class struggle. In the classical age, we see pitted against each other the antagonistic classes, masters and slaves; in feudalism, the nobles and the peasants; and in capitalism, the capitalists and the workers. The interests of the dominant class and the subordinate classes are antagonistic to each other. The major reason for this antagonism is that, the surplus value provided by the working class are appropriated by the dominant class. In the *Communist Manifesto* Marx explains phenomena of class struggle. Depending upon the level of production forces and the relations of production, freemen and slaves, lord and serf, bourgeoisie and proletariat in the Marxian terminology, are always in a state of conflict; the ruling class in control of means of production is always the oppressor. The exploited and oppressed have carried out their struggle all through the history which shall be ended with a classless and stateless society, free from exploitation, free from haves and have nots, rich and poor.

So, Marxism considers the society as reflecting the class divisions based on ownership of production and control by the dominant ruling class as against the non-owing, have-nots as the ruled. Marxism, though does not deny other causes and other forms of social conflicts as are based on religion, ethnicity, culture, social status etc. but, the fundamental basis of class conflict is what remains primarily and predominantly related with the economic factor and all other forms of conflicts are but the reflections of the same.

### (ii) Role of Politics: From Status Quo to Revolutionary Change

Marxism sees the basis of Political Philosophy in the principles of dialectics *i.e.*, thesis, antithesis, synthesis, unity of opposites, regulation of negation and quality transformation. Politics explained thus is the logical outcome of the economic systems of production and relations of production.

The state as it has emerged in its present form is not the same in matters of production relations. Marx clearly distinguishes economics and politics as two factors of social life. He sees them related to each other in mutual interdependence and inseparable unity. The economic system is the base, or the substructure, upon which stands the superstructure, called the politics, state, law, culture, ideology and the political power. Politics and ideology being the essence of dominant class character, they try to justify the status of the particular economic class.

Marxism insists that, the politics can not be studied in isolation. For, the nature, character of politics depends upon the productive relations. The order of Political Theory, according to Marxism is that, as the state and society come into being and start serving the class interests, the coercive apparatus of the state comes into play to subserve the end of the dominant class. In this context, the Political Theory has a role in putting to an end the politics of class interest in the state. So must it end this maintenance of status quoism in politics through the political manipulation of the ideology and complimentary culture. Instead it must need transform the whole society through revolutionary action.

Marxism classifies the conflict between the antagonistic classes into three forms:

(a) Economic Conflict, (b) Political Conflict, and (c) Ideological Conflict.

(a) **Economic Conflict:** The capitalists try to earn more and more profit by paying less wages (*i.e.*, the surplus value), therefore the labor/workers trying to secure the economic equality, put up demand of higher wages, and shorter hours of work. Besides they try to build their organizations so as to create and strengthen their struggle and solidarity.

(b) **Political Conflict:** The political conflict revolves around the capture of political power. It is commonly observed phenomena that each class is trying to capture the political power: The workers are trying to capture the same through both parliamentary means if possible and through armed struggle, if necessary; the capitalist are seen to be devising strategies to retain the political power through the capture of state machinery, coloring the same thorough capitalist ideology and culture to subjugate the workers. The capitalist class is also using its coercive state apparatus like police, jail, law, statutory rules etc. to regulate and control the state and not allow any change of their status quoism.

(c) **Ideological Conflict:** Ideology is a frame of planning applied in the practical field to serve a particular class character. The ideology of the capitalist society is the role of the few over the majority. The ideology of the working class which is called socialism is based on the principle of equality, justice and democracy. It represents the oppressed class character and tries to abolish the former (capitalism) to establish the latter (socialism).

The mode of production, class antagonism, class solidarity, class interest and domination are central to the Marxist view of politics. As the state originates at a particular point of human history to represent a particular class of people, it is by overthrowing the same and building a classless society that the end of politics can be realized. The end of the class signifies not only the end of the state but also end of the politics.

In addition to the above, the Marxist view of politics has the following aspects:

(a) Man is a social being; the economic aspect of man plays a very important role to fulfill the biological needs like food, shelter, clothing. Man by nature and necessity lives in the society.

(b) The society is primarily based on the principle of production relation, and mode of production. Society has been divided into classes on the basis of ownership of the means of production.

(c) The interest of the classes are conflictual in character, in their purpose. The continuance of the class compositions are antagonistic. The interest of the antagonistic classes result in class struggle, class conflict. This shall finally end with ending of classes and the state as the handmaiden of the dominant class. So the final state in Marxism shall be classless, stateless and exploitation-free society.

(d) The state originates in a particular point of historical development. That politics is the statecraft of capitalist classes. Politics, for the Marxists, emerges to resolve the conflicts between the classes but not of the individuals, groups, organizations, as the liberals argue.

(e) The mode of production, the ideology, the culture which emerges out of the particular way of production also justify the class character and the pattern of its continuous domination over the rest.

(f) The politics cannot serve the whole society. Rather politics serves the particular society that works the forms of production and political power. So, according to Marx, the deprived people, the exploited ones when they get organized, shall determine their future.

(g) The concept of the state as the representative of the dominant class shall be continued. For in a class-divided society there is little possibility that the concept of equality, justice, democracy etc. can be realized. This may be possible only in a classless society. So long as classes exist in society, the communist society will not be achieved. Nor shall the state wither away. Marx maintains that through the use of politics *i.e.,* the revolution, the capitalist politics shall be eliminated.

(h) The capitalist state character is also not confined to the particular state but it expands into other states through its policy of expansionism.

The private property is the accumulation of surplus value of the labour appropriated by the capitalist class. The latter (capitalist class) sometimes uses the different tactics to disunite the working class by the method of co-option, motivation, influence, repression. The history stands testimony to many such instances.

Marxism poses some crucial problems to the working class, involving its applicability. A clear gap between the theoretical paradigm and praxis is seen to exist. The critics very often term it as a deterministic theory and its law of applicability restricts it to its own time and place.

**(a) Politics as Political Power**

Machiavelli and Hobbes may be taken as the pioneers of the interpretations *i.e.*, the politics is nothing but a power concept. The supporters of this concept may be philosophers like Vilfrado Pareto, G. Mosca, George Catlin, Charles Marriam and Harold Lasswell. Their central argument is that politics revolves around power. According to Hobbes, "There is a general inclination of all mankind for a perpetual and restless desire for power which ceased only in the death". Machiavelli, the realist philosopher and protagonist of modern state in the name of nationalism also argues on the basis of power that the whole of international politics, the balance of power, the influence of one state over other, the domination, the dependence etc., all are based on the power equation.

Robert Dahl, defines power in relation to other actors in which one actor influences the achievement of others and makes us do what we want to be done with the help of others.

Lasswell defines politics as a power concept. Politics, to him, is 'who gets what, when and how'. It is through use of power that the intended objectives are achieved.

David Easton, defines political power as a relationship with which one person or group is able to determine the actions of another in the direction of former's own end.

The arguments of this power theory of politics point to the fact that by exercise of political power, the state, the government can maintain law and order in the society. It can exercise power, authority over the individuals for obedience to the law and voluntary compliance. Its justification of this theory consists in that it is the instrument of force. That state government exercises control over the whole territory, distinguishes itself from the other associations, organizations, and individuals. The states not only make laws only for the individuals for voluntary compliance but also ensure that the violation of law is punishable by the court of law. The violation of any rules/principles of any organization do not necessarily result in punishment but in case of the state it is an exception. The state also serves to have political power as well as the government. The coercive part of the state always is in conflict with the other groups, associations etc. and the power is sought to be retained through use of influence, domination control and force.

Harold Lasswell and Abraham Kaplan in the book *Power Society* (1950) also make a detailed analysis of power. The concentration of power detracts from efficient governance. They argue that for better governance the power should be distributed and delegated in all the units from top to bottom and those located horizontally in interactive relation with each other.

Michael Foucault, in *The Contemporary Society* conceptualizes the concept of power in the more radical terms. He gives a new dimension to the concept of power. He explains how the same is influenced by the tradition, custom, norms, morality etc. He advocates that, the decision-makers are also influenced by the peoples' power. Their choice is also influenced and preconditioned by the multiple factors like traditions, customs, and cultures. The human knowledge and the individual consciousness are subject to the environment settings and the present specialized knowledge as it is provided to the experts seeking to shape the behaviour of others.

The forms or types and nature of power is dynamic. It can be classified into the political, economic and ideological on the basis of its usefulness, degree of exercise, purpose, instrumental capacity to bring out the desired results.

The political power is the power which is exercised through the legitimate political authority rather than the coercive one. It is exercised through the institutional frameworks of the state and binding in the prescribed area. The central theme of exercise of this political power is that it operates through the organs of government like legislation, executive and judiciary, law making, law executing and law interpreting bodies. The primary function and purpose of exercise of political power is the maintenance of law and order, justice through reward and punishment.

Marx's view of political power is the logical extension of economic power. He emphasizes the class character of the state. He explains how the minority of people having ownership of the means of production control the majority class to serve their own class interest. The liberalists of the Gandhian and the contemporary political statesmen believe in the method of decentralization, delegation and devolution of power. But contrasted with them the Marxists believe in the abolition of the capitalist state with a view to establish the communist state in which the state as a class organization shall be liquidated on its own and stateless, classless society come into being.

### (b) Politics as Economic Power

The economic power is derived from the holding of means of production. It results in the extension of the benefits to all those who are the owners of means of production, the rest of the people who are not so placed, are denied the benefits. Through the economic reward and punishment, those who hold economic power are able to win the minds of the people. The power theorists rejecting the unity of the economic and political power, advocate that, the economic power is relatively decentralized. But the fact is that instead of the clear-cut distinction of economic power and political power, there is convergence of the two throughout in all cases. The propertied class by controlling economic power and trying to build up its own ideology, be it of consumerism through the media, by commercial ads on TV channels, use their wealth for influencing the political behavior of the people.

### (c) Politics as Ideological Power

Liberal writers like Sydney Verba, Max Weber, relate the ideological power with the religion, education, culture, literature and history, philosophy, ethics, the traditional wisdom etc. In the developed society, the ideas, thoughts, values of the masses are shaped, controlled, revisited in a fashion that it will be in conformity with the state power as well as the political power. This symmetry is promoted through the mass media, means of education, propaganda, socializing agencies etc.

According to the Marxists, the political power of the dominant class continues because of the convergence of and the making of intellectual force with the ruling material force. The class which owns the means of production also controls at the same time, the means of mental production. Marx calls the ideological power as "factor consciousness" and describes its role as binding. The economic factor in order to make it work as the deterministic factor, proceeds to justify the class exploitation as legitimate.

Different ideological people can thus perceive a different definition of the political power. But politics as a power connotes invoking the help of the state machinery to maintain law and order, integrate the society through law and punishment. The state of nature and the human values in all situations are not expected to be the same. Nor do the modifications of the behaviour of the individual to cope up with the intractable problems of society. It is in such a situation that the requirement of power is felt necessary.

### (d) Politics as Common Good

The politics as a common good has been advocated by the political theorists after 1980s. To them, the state is nothing but one of a political community. They favour the idea of attending the community along with protecting the individual liberty. They lament that equality between the values of the community has not been properly distinguished by the liberal-individualistic theorists of politics. In contrast the communitarians believe that the individual can develop his best self only in a community. It provides him an ample space to reflect upon the personal choices, tastes, temperaments, as individualistic factors integrated with the community. The task of politics is to encourage the people to adopt a concept of good that conforms to the community's way of life. It should discourage the concept of good which is not acceptable, or in conformity with community's belief-system. They hold that state should provide cultural structure which should be built by the community, not either by individual or the market. The cultural structure should be based on the community's values as a whole. The individual good should be evaluated by the cultural evaluation and replaced by the same. The political legitimacy, the governmental exercise of power over the individuals/associations should also necessarily be related with the common good of the community.

The duty of the state is to protect and promote the community life. It is expected to protect traditions, philosophy, way of life, value judgments etc., and community life encouraging to individuals participate in it. The following are the central points of the "politics as a common good":

1. According to Garner, state is nothing but the collection of large number of organizations, associations with distinct ideologies, purposes. Each member of the same organization is integrated as the interest of the individual as a member and the community that are not in conflict but are in congruence with each other. The state always should strive to achieve the common good which is the majoritarian good where the individual good is duly adjusted.
2. The emphasis here is not on the individual but the community. The individual interest has to develop in the community. It should develop in such a manner that the common good of all is duly emphasized.
3. The early Greek tradition as also the idealistic tradition emphasizes the whole organized social order wherein the duty conferred on each individual can be clearly defined. But in reality the politics as a common good in the early societies is the protection and justification of the position, privileges of a few rulers, masters over the subjects and slaves.
4. The concept of common good presupposes a state that serves and not one that orders. Benn and Peter say that, the establishment of social order ends up with serving all.
5. The negative liberalists allow the state minimum functions and maximum individual liberty. The positive liberalists also put emphasis on protection of right, liberty, equality etc. But they do so along with fulfillment of the common needs of the individual such as education, health care, pension, proper distribution of resources and welfare achievements.

In Gandhian concept of *Sarvodaya*, which means good of all and welfare through all is based on principle of *Samnavaya* where the individual is related with the community as a drop of ocean in the oceanic circle and where each community and group are also converging with the bigger circle without losing its identity.

### (e) Functional View of Politics

Rather than mainly focusing on state institutions as the sole center of political activity, contemporary political scientists prefer to take a functional view of politics. They look upon politics as the process by which policies are formulated and executed for the society. They think that political life takes place within a system by which they mean that its different parts are dependent upon each other and its each part affects the operation of the other parts and thus the whole. Accordingly, the changes in one or more parts set up pressures for changes in the other parts. The concept of system, therefore, implies interaction, interrelation and interdependence among the parts. Here one may ask the question: What constitute the parts of a political system? There are at least five components of a political system *viz.* (a) cultural values (b) rules (c) structures (d) electors and (e) policies.

**(a) Cultural values:** These denote general concept of the desirable values such as liberty, equality, fraternity, individualism, and democracy.

**(b) Rules:** The general values referred above may be realized through more specific rules and regulations. While some of these rules are formal, others are customary and written. This also includes formal rules like laws embodied in a society's constitution which regulate the operation of the political institutions. Other formal rules specify the ways to implement policies. Social security laws fall in this category.

**(c) Structures:** These refer to pattern of interaction among two or more individuals. A distinction is also made between concrete and analytic structures:

(i) Concrete structures have parts that can be physically separated. For instance society is the most general concrete structure and the family and the Indian parliament are two specific examples of concrete structures. Within the family group, the parents are physically separable from children, the mother is separable from the father, the brother is separable from the sister. Similarly in case of parliament, different parts which are physically separable parts include the Lok Sabha and Rajya Sabha, the various committees, the committee chairman and the committee members, the majority and opposition leaders etc.

(ii) Analytic structures: In contrast to concrete structures the parts of analytic structures cannot be physically separated. Role is the most widely used analytic structure. Each person may play several roles as a father, husband, brother, union leader, director of a firm etc. Although it is possible to distinguish between such diverse roles—each one having different rights and obligations, these cannot be physically isolated. Thus concrete structures refer to things, analytic structures denote aspects of things.

**(d) Political Actors:** Political actors play a pivotal role in political life. One can distinguish between two types of actors—the leader and the citizen. The leader exercises the power to make and carry out the binding decisions for the society and rules over the governing structures. In contrast, the citizen does not have the major responsibility for making the public decisions. If politically active, the role of the citizen is to organize resources either to make demands upon the leaders or to offer his support.

**(e) Policies:** Finally policies and decisions form a crucial part of the political system. Its formulated content depends upon the other parts of the political system mentioned above. Cultural values, rules, structures and personal factors tend to limit the policies chosen from the alternatives. When making decisions, political leaders are as much influenced by values, rules and structural conditions as by their own personal goals, motivations, perceptions and attitudes. Thus, the political process involves choosing from among the alternative courses of action. After a policy has been made and executed, political scientists often try to assess its effects on individuals, groups and the society. In short, they study not only the causes of a policy but also its consequences.

Political life when viewed from the perspective of a process leads us to certain postulates about the nature of politics which are summed up as follows:

1. Politics is an analytic concept.
2. Politics deals with policy issues and binding decisions.
3. Politics is a process of making and carrying out these decisions. This involves change, conflict and cooperation.
4. Politics focuses on issues which affect the whole society.

To elaborate these points we may point out that the functional interpretation of political life takes analytic view of system and process of politics. It views politics as an analytic concept. It seeks to separate the diverse aspects of political behaviour for purposes of investigation. It presumes that in the analytic sense political activity can take place in any concrete structure.

The political aspect of social life involves the formulation and implementation of binding decisions. But a specific behaviour or activity may contain both political and economic aspects. Economic decisions are made by a government which also allocates goods and services in the form of agricultural subsidies. Likewise large corporations engage in political decisions and in that process try to influence tax policy which otherwise is made by the government regularly. Families also carry on several type of activities—political, social, economic, religious etc. However, in the modern nation state there exist many specialized institutions which are devoted to political issues and are known as political structures.

Thus policies represent a programme of action and are designed to reach a goal. However, a policy decision is binding only when people feel that they ought to obey that decision.

**Why do People Obey?**

It is argued that fear of punishment ensures obedience. But in stateless societies and even in the modern nation-state, there are other bases besides fear, for securing obedience which may be as follows:

1. Some obey because they want reward or benefit.
2. Others wish to avoid disapproval of those in higher positions and thus obey.
3. Still others obey as a result of habit, convention and tradition and thus learn to respect the decisions of higher authority.
4. Some people obey out of a respect for the rules or law rather than for persons in authority.
5. Some people are endowed with a high moral sense and may formulate some internal principles having universal validity. In such cases, voice of conscience lies behind their obedient behaviour.

Since not in all cases do citizens accept policies as binding, therefore, while identifying politics with binding decisions, we must examine the potential capacity of leaders to make and execute their policies. Apart from this, we must examine actual use of capacitics by leaders to make the decisions binding upon them.

However, the notion of binding decisions does not necessarily imply a static concept of politics. The process of making and carrying out decisions denotes change, conflict and cooperation. In this sense it is a dynamic process. It implies that when people make policy, they interact to convert their demands and resources into political decisions. And the process of implementing these decisions also involves change and intense political activity. When policies are being formulated and carried out, several groups find it necessary to cooperate in order to realize their demands. Group leaders enter into alliances, bargain and negotiate with each other. They try to reconcile and adjust their initially incompatible demands. All these cooperative activities may result in some changes in policies.

Another important factor of change is the phenomena of conflict visible in political life. This is caused due to the fact that the policy-making process, demands and resources must be converted into decisions. Since the demands of different groups often come in conflict due to scarce resources, political leaders as well as citizens have different ideas about how resources ought to be used and about which demands ought to be recognized as morally good. Thus, if politics deals with 'who gets what, when, how', then some groups may get little, while others may succeed in getting the maximum political gains.

In so far as some segments of the population refuse to accept policies as binding, political leaders when faced with this situation may employ several strategies which may be listed as follows:

1. They may decide to change the content of policies in order to satisfy some dissatisfied groups.
2. They may change some of the government personnel.
3. The top leaders may even resign when under fire or may be removed from office by a military coup.

4. The leaders may change the laws or governing structures.
5. The leaders may allow the dissidents to set up a new political system as it was decided in Britain in 1921 to allow the Irish people to establish a separate state.
6. Alternatively, the leaders may decide to ignore or reject demands to make or change particular policies.

If a sizeable portion of the population with considerable resources refuses to accept the existing policies as binding the leaders may be forced to resort to coercion to secure obedience. But when the established leadership lacks the necessary will, resources and skills to meet the discontent with either change or coercion and dissident groups possess these capacities, then a drastic change in political system becomes likely.

The difficulty with Dahl's concept of politics as power, rule or authority is its failure to distinguish between societal and sub-societal concrete units. True, Churches, Trade Unions and the like, make binding decisions but these decisions are binding only on the members of these sub-societal organizations. Therefore, to understand the nature of politics, we should make a distinction between policies binding on the whole society and decisions binding on only a part of society.

Therefore, we may conclude that most modern political scientists choose to analyze the interaction between the polity, the society and the individual. As regards, the questions like: how do social organizations influence the making and carrying out of binding decisions? What are the effects of public policies on the society and on the individual? What relationship exist between political life and social changes? Most political scientists while examining all these interactions tend to take an essentially analytic or functional view of politics.

# 2

# POLITICAL THEORY: NATURE, CHARACTERISTICS, RELEVANCE

## Meaning and Definition

Theory is derived from the Greek word '*Theoria*', Theory connotes a well-focused attention at something in a state of contemplation with the intent to grasp or comprehend it in its totality. The word 'theory', in its broader sense, means a thinker's entire teaching on a subject (including description of facts, thinker's explanation, his conception of history, his value judgments, and his proposals of goals, policy and principles), whereas in the narrower sense, 'theory' points to explanatory thought only or at least primarily.

Theory is often confused with its related concepts like philosophy and thought, for their boundaries overlap. But theory is not philosophy, as theory is about 'something', while philosophy is about 'everything'. Theory is also not thought because theory is a thought about thought and not a fulsome thought itself. However, there is much common between theory and reason because both claim to be scientific. Yet theory has its gaze fixed beyond reason, even beyond science.

Accordingly, theory is an attempt to explain, order and relate disjointed data. It identifies what is relevant and also what is missing in any phenomenon. It makes predictions on the basis of observable facts. Theory, in this sense is, therefore, a guide to practice. It adds much to what is merely described as also clarifies hypothesis. In addition, as a part of philosophy, theory explains an issue which meets the requirements of both reason and vision.

Political Theory, therefore, in being a theory about what is 'political'. It is the science and philosophy of something that is 'political'. To elucidate the meaning, nature and scope of Political Theory, a few definitions of Political Theory may be given below:

1. A body of thought that seeks to evaluate, explain and predict political phenomena. As a subfield of Political Science, it is concerned with political ideas, values and concepts, and the explanation on prediction of political

behaviour. In this broad sense, it has two main branches: one is Political Philosophy or Normative Theory, with its value, analytic, historical and speculative concerns. The other is Empirical Theory, with its efforts to explain, predict, guide, research and organize knowledge through the formulation of abstract models, and scientifically testable propositions. (Political Science Dictionary)

2. Political Theory is a combination of a disinterested search for the principles of good state and good society on the one hand, and a disinterested search for knowledge of political and social reality on the other. (Andrew Hacker)
3. Broadly it means as anything about politics or relevant to politics and narrowly as the disciplined investigation of political problems. (Sabine)
4. Political Theory is an explanation of what politics is all about, a general understanding of the political world, a frame of reference. Without one we would be unable to recognize an event as political, decide anything about why it happened, judge whether it was good or bad or decide that was likely to happen next. (Bluhm)
5. Political Theory is a network of concepts and generalizations about political life involving ideas, assumptions and statements about the nature, purpose and key features of government, state and society and about the political capabilities of human beings. (David Held)

The above definitions bring out certain essential aspects of Political Theory which are as follows:

1. Political Theory has as its area of operation, the realm of politics. It includes political life of a citizen, his political behaviour, his political ideas, the government he establishes and the tasks that government performs.
2. The methods, which Political Theory applies, include description, explanation, and investigation of any political phenomenon, chiefly with an intent to grasp or comprehend all about what is 'political'. But in doing so it attempts to understand 'political' in relation to moral, historical, social, economic, psychological, ecological, dimensions and the like.
3. The ultimate objective of Political Theory is to build a good state in a good society. In the process it also attempts to create processes, procedures, institutions and structures, historically tested and rationally attuned.
4. As a systematized body of thought, Political Theory seeks to explain, evaluate and predict political phenomena. In the process it also builds scientifically testable models as well as values as rules of human conduct.
5. As explained above, Political Theory is both prescriptive and explanatory. It is an overview of what the political order is about and it is also a symbolic representation of what is 'political'.
6. Political Theory, so far as it is a formal, logical and systematic analysis of the processes and consequences of political activity, it is analytical,

expository and explanatory. Viewed thus, Political Theory seeks to give order, coherence, and meaning to what is described as 'political'.

Political Theory is not static but dynamic. It is dynamic in a sense that it changes with change of political behaviour *i.e.,* voting behavior, the change of policy of governments, the expansion of the activities of the state, the interrelationship among political factors and nonpolitical factors and the verification of political facts with the help of scientific approaches. The scope of Political Theory expands with the concept of regulative state (*i.e.,* the only duty of the state is to maintain law and order (giving place to positive welfare state (*i.e.,* it touches almost every aspect of human life). The propelling factors are located in the geography, climate and culture, milieu, and development of strategies which result in subjugation of some over many. With state intervention through specific policies, programmes and projects, uniformity in the developmental patterns is sought to be achieved.

The human history has witnessed that the disequilibrium, disturbances, disorder in critical aspects of social life leads to state intervention and growth of its scope of activities. The great depression in 1930's in USA resulted in state's market regulation functions. The Second World War and its aftermath also brought changes not only in the political sphere at the international level but also in internal spheres of state activities as well. So did the birth of United Nations as a peacekeeping machinery, the measures taken for abolition of socioeconomic disparity and restructuring of economic and cultural relations which not only changed the scope of Political Theory but also its content and nature. The understanding of a particular theory is made possible better in comparison than in isolation, so does derivation of logical conclusions.

The Classical Political Theory has been concerned with what ought to be. It held the ground till there emerged the Behavioural Revolution in USA. As against the classical political thinkers it set standards of prescriptive norms in respect of what is factual empirical analysis today. In contrast, the Classical School of Thought has been primarily based on what "ought to be" rather than "what is".

The Behavioural Revolution not only introduced the principles of biological sciences to understand the social reality but also statistical and mathematical tools to reach the concrete conclusion. With the introduction of System Theory and Structural Functional Analysis, an effort was made to integrate and coordinate the political with the nonpolitical and hence, expand the scope Political Theory to embrace what it constitutes, its environment, its periphery and beyond.

## Nature of Political Theory

The nature of Political Theory is closely related to nature of the state, the authority-liberty relationship, the structure of the state, the interaction of the state with its environment *i.e.,* both political and nonpolitical. The nature of Political Theory is subject to the change in meaning suggesting disagreement and any disagreement in its meaning would result in disagreement about the nature of Political Theory.

There are some who equate Political Theory with the works of political thinkers. But, this tends Political Theory to mean more of Political Thought. Some equate Political Theory with Political Philosophy. Undeniably Political Theory constitutes a part of Political Philosophy, but a part is but a part of a whole and never the whole. The modernists, by incorporating 'science' in Political Theory, prefer to call it Political Science. But Political Science as the Science of Politics is different from Political Theory in a sense that, it is excluded from the History of Politics, or a Culture of Politics, or even a Philosophy of Politics.

The fact is that Political Theory is much more, rather a combination of all these. Political Theory is usually used interchangeably with Politics. But the difference between the Politics and Political Theory is just like the difference—between theory and practice: The phrases like a politician, a political scientist, a political theorist, or a political philosopher, have not the same connotation. Each one conveys a different meaning. None of them can be considered inclusive.

### (a) Political Theory: As History

Men like George Sabine have described Political Theory as History in a sense that, it developed with the development of human history and it has its historical developments. Contemporary issues can be properly understood by understanding its historical evolution, growth, dynamics and change. The Political Science as a science has been advocated by scientists like Robert Dahl and David Easton. But their view is not tenable since all science is not Political Theory. Political theorists like Leo Strauss describe Political Theory as a philosophy but the fact is that all philosophy is not scientific. Likewise, all history is not political, all science is not political, all theory is not political and all philosophy is not political and scientific. Therefore it cannot be justified that, Political Theory is excluded from history, science or philosophy.

Political Theory has the same relationship with history as a structure having a base. Through a study of History of Politics or Political Theory we come to understand what is a political tradition, and how men and societies have behaved in the past, how the institutions have grown, through what vicissitudes have they passed. Politics is therefore, the study of history and its development. By studying history, we learn that evolution of human civilization has been much more than the tale of the dead and buried. Rather it has been the product of centuries of experience and wisdom of the wisest and best among leaders of thought.

### (b) Political Theory: As Science and Philosophy

There is a strong affinity between Political Theory and Science. If theory is seen to provide an explanation of a phenomenon, as Brecht says, the phenomenon, without the element of science, would make it a matter of mere faith, a conviction, a supposition or a belief without scientific validity, reliability and prediction. Theory does have a 'science' in it, but only what theory should need. There is no scope of too much scientism in Political Theory.

Political Theory depends on Political Philosophy in many respects. For Political Philosophy, as the sum-total of general laws (morals, norms, values, ends and purposes etc. etc.), has served Political Theory well through the ages. Philosophy, Kant observes, has answered three questions: "What can I know?" "What must I do?" and "What can I hope for?" *i.e.,* consciousness, action and aspiration. This is what makes the philosophy a lodestar of life. Without Philosophy, no Political Theory can ever hope to exist as it sets directions, goals to be accomplished.

Science and Philosophy, though poles apart, it is theory that combines the two *i.e.,* Philosophy as well as Science. Viewed thus, a political theorist is both a political philosopher and a political scientist. The Political Philosophy and Political Science or Politics are inadequate to take the place of Political Theory. In this context Brecht aptly notes: "Political Philosophy, Political Theory and Political Science are no longer interchangeable terms." With focus on Science as distinct from Political Philosophy, Political Science now refers to efforts limited by the use of scientific methods. But Political Philosophy is free to transcend these limits. Likewise, Political Theory, as distinct from Political Philosophy, now usually refers to scientific theory only. When it is opposed to scientific theory, it comes to usually mean a mere philosophy.

Isaiah Berlin aptly puts it: "Neo-Marxism, Neo-Thomism, Nationalism, Historicism, Existentialism, Anti-existential Liberalism, and Socialism, trans-portation of doctrines of Natural Rights and Natural Law into empirical terms, discoveries made by skillful application of models derived from economic and related techniques to political behaviour and the collusions, combinations, and consequences in action of these ideas indicate not the death of a great tradition, but, if anything, new and unpredictable developments."

The true nature of Political Theory has its roots within the nature of the individual citizenship and its logical extension of political organization which means that the state changes itself with the change of human nature, role, character and objectives of both life and livings.

## Changing Content and Scope of Political Theory

If the area in which Political Theory works is the domain of 'political', then its subject-matter too is bound to vary from time to time. From the early Greeks to about the end of the eighteenth century, the major focus of Political Theory mostly has been with what politics "ought to be." However, during the nineteenth century and the first half of the twentieth century the focus of Political Theory mainly shifted to the nature and structure of government as a decision-making body. It was then followed by a period when some American political scientists, under the influence of scientism, announced the death of Political Theory. This was despite the fact that the British traditionalists were seen advocating the value and usefulness of Political Theory as a guide to political action. As a result a virulent debate about the decline and resurgence of Political Theory ensued. While it was reaching its climax the two sides came to realize the true process and purpose of political activity as well as the nature and proper ends of government.

Since Political Theory, as David Held puts it, is concerned with "what is really going on" in the political world and, thereby, with the nature and structure of political practices, then a theory of politics today must come to grips with the polity within geopolitical and market processes, that is, within the system of nation-states, international law and global political economy.

Now, in seeking to address the concerns and the challenges of today's world, Political Theory has now broadened itself to include in its contents such pressing human interest issues as:

(a) social justice;
(b) expanding network of welfare activities;
(c) varying democratic systems with emphasis on mass participation;
(d) feministic challenges having a profound bearing on the whole of Political Theory today;
(e) environment problems;
(f) post-modernism;
(g) terrorism and its global dimension;
(h) new social movements of liberation and self-determination; and
(i) equal and just world order, feminism and gender justice, life-giving ecology and sustainable environment.

If group and not so much an individual is the real basic concept in Political Theory, as Arnold Brecht suggests, then it is quite natural that any clash of interests has not only be among the individuals, but also among the numerous groups. As a result, equilibrium or reconciliation of opposing interests should be an important component of Political Theory.

(i) Obviously the focus on group life, their concerns and anxieties, power, influence, control, legitimacy, justice and the like, must also influence both individual and group choices along with decision-making.
(ii) Other areas of concern for Political Theory today, should include: resolution of peoples' ever-recurring conflicts and disagreements, problems of war, peace and the like.
(iii) Nature and proper ends of the state and government and political system.
(iv) Politicization, political socialization, political culture, political development, political communication, impact of social movements and of revolution, etc.
(v) Social justice, equality, freedom, democratic participation, social movements relating to gender, environment and pollution-free society.

The scope of Political Theory may be summarised as follows:

(a) It undertakes the study of the classical thinkers, their relative contributions to their respective school of thought, how do they find out the truth and justify the same in their writings. Plato justifies the Ideal State based on the principles of Philosopher King in his book *The Republic*. Aristotle's quest in his *Politics* leads him to a model government in polity, Hobbes finds his absolute sovereign in *leviathan* and Rawls just dispensation is to be found in his *Theory of Distributive Justice*.

(b) It provides an understanding/explanation of human society, history and relationship of man with the society, and of the individual goal and social goal. Along with these, it tells the sources of social conflict and its development.

(c) Political Science as a discipline indicates that even as the problems various political scientists, thinkers confront are the same, their approaches are different.

(d) The subject matter of Political Theory consists of the principles, policies, ideologies, the nature and structure of political parties. Why a political ideology is adopted and why it suits some countries like the liberal, communist, and mixed economy mode ones?

## Classical Political Theory and Modern Political Theory Points of Divergence

Contrasted with the Classical Political Theory, Modern Political Theory encompasses diverse trends like the institutional- structural, scientific, positivistic, empirical, behavioural, post-behavioural and even the Marxist. All these trends, are seen to dominate the greater part of the 20th century. If the Classical Political Theory is philosophical, normative, idealistic and to some extent, historical, Modern Political Theory largely is seen split into two opposing divisions—the Liberal Tradition and the Marxist. While the Liberal Traditions include the individualist, the elitist and the pluralist, the Marxist Political Theory, is dialectical-materialist in nature.

Besides, Modern Political Theory, with its institutional, behavioural and post-behavioural trends deplores the historical-normative-evaluative tradition of the Classical Political Theory. Instead, it emphasizes the scientific empirical-behavioural study in seeking to understand the intricacies of politics. It seek to develop an objective rather than subjective, analytic rather than philosophic, explanatory rather than descriptive, process-oriented rather than purpose-oriented; scientific rather than theoretical model. In short, it attempts to build a science of politics, with sole emphasis on objective, clinical, value-free, observational, measurable, operational, dimensions of study.

Historically stated, Modern Political Theory denies the early Classical Political Theory the status of a legitimate form of knowledge and enquiry. According to the positivists and empiricists, all knowledge is found in sensory observation, concepts and generalizations. They are seen to represent only the particulars from which these have been abstracted. They hold that values can not play any role in the formation of knowledge. Being directly tied to empirical observations, value-judgments therefore are not accorded the status of knowledge. So is the case with the normative statements of Political Theory which are characterized as mere declarations. Though positivism and empiricism do not lived long, its legacy in the form of scientism thrived and had its influence on the emerging behaviouralism and post- behaviouralism.

Modern Political Theory has the following essential features:

1. Human behaviour can be scientifically studied and regularities of human behaviour expressed in generalizations.
2 Facts and data and not philosophical speculations constitute the basis of study. Facts are to be accumulated, explained and used to test hypothesis.
3. Facts and values are required to be separated. While in the behavioural phase the values have no place in research, yet in the latter post-behavioural phase values come to make the facts as relevant as possible.
4. The quantitative methods are to be adopted for research as they would make the study scientific and empirical.
5. The shift of focus has to be from subjectivity to objectivity; philosophical interpretation to analytical explanation; purposive to procedural; descriptive to observational; and normative to scientific.
6. Political activity involves numerous other activities representing religious, moral, psychological, social, economic, ecological, and the like. Hence, to study the complete interrelated nature of political reality inter-disciplinary focus is best suited to yield better results.
7. Values and facts, substance and forms, and theory and research, are inseparable. This is the theme of post-behaviouralism.

To conclude, Modern Political Theory combines the merits of empirical, formal and normative studies and accords adequate importance to both facts and values, description and prescription, explanation and valuation.

## Various Schools of Political Theory

Political Theory has been developing throughout the ages. Its development has been linked with the development of science, technology and the change of production forms, production relations, development of human knowledge, concept of freedom of individual and rationalization of political power. The centrality of Political Theory depends upon the individual freedom, liberty and state authority. On the basis of purposes of the state, sources of political authority, its legitimacy and state-citizen relationships, political thinkers have divided the development of Political Theory on the basis of the following five schools of thought:

(a) Classical Political Theory
(b) Liberal Political Theory
(c) Marxist Political Theory
(d) Behavioural Political Theory

(e) Contemporary Political Theory

**(a) Classical Political Theory:** On the basis of modern science and absence of it, the schools of Political Theory have been distinguished into Classical and Modern. In the Classical Political Theory, the predominance of philosophical abstraction, perspective suggestions play a very vital role. Political Theory in its classic form is seen to emerge in Ancient Greek culture, in the writings of Socrates, Plato, and Aristotle, and it is continued till the nineteenth century.

The following are the fundamental features of the Classical Political Theory:

(i) Its basis is philosophical and it refers to explanation, description, prescription and evolution of achievement on the basis of 'ought to be', as the principle of judgment.

(ii) The autonomy of Political Theory, its chief preoccupation with theological and philosophical issues.

(iii) The practice of systematic enquiry to acquire reliable knowledge about critical public issues concerning the common good. Greek *Polis,* the Roman *Res Publica* and thc usage of Commonweal during the medieval times was indicative of a sharing of what is common. Since the basic unit of analysis in Classical Political Theory has always been the political whole, therefore, the *Polis*, the *Res Publica* or the Commonweal and other connected components are seen to function with an eye on the quality of life in the Political Whole--the State.

(iv) The Classical Political Theory has tended to view the state as composed of, and dependent upon, various inter-related structures. They all cumulatively denote the triple aspect of activity, relationships and belief such as ruling, warfare, education, religious practices, production of commodities; (activity); what exists between social classes, the authorities and the subjects; (relationships); what concerns gods, justice, equality, natural law and the like. (belief)

(v) The notion of the Political Whole, *i.e.,* the State, gives way to an idea of System, or an Order. This, in turn, gives rise to the resultant conceptions of balance, equilibrium, stability and harmony. It is with the help of these concepts that the Classical Political Theory has tried to analyze the sources of conflicts, anarchy, instability, anomie and revolution. So has the principle of justice seen to form a guide for the discharge of duties in the *Polis*, the political community.

The Classical Political Theory enriches itself with the help of comparative studies. Aristotle employs the comparative method to provide a more comprehensive explanation and a wider range of alternatives of polity. This way he not only develops a comprehensive classification for political forms *e.g.,* monarchy, aristocracy, democracy, their variants but also a set of concepts like law, citizenship, justice and participation, to explain differences or similarities.

(vi) The Classical Political Theory has been essentially ethico-moral in its nature and views the world in terms of ideal types. Plato, for example, envisions the Ideal State, Aristotle, a State capable of achieving the best possible common good and good life and St. Augustine, the City of God. Through appraising the various constitutional forms, in a comparative perspective, the Greek Political Theory seeks to determine the best suited form of government for a particular set of circumstances, possibly even an absolutely best form.

**(b) Liberal Political Theory**–Political Theory further develops with the development of the state after the introduction of industrialization, renaissance, reformation, modern science and modern philosophy. This emergent political state creates a philosophy of liberalism with thrust on freedom. The liberalism as a Political Philosophy, its central theme, pertains to maximization of individual freedom and lessening of state interference in their personal activities. This new Political Philosophy finds its expression through the writing of Grotius, Thomas Jefferson, Thomas Paine, Hobbes, Locke, Bentham, J.S. Mill and Herbert Spencer.

While the Classical Political Theory, lays emphasis on the moral development of the individual and evolution of community life, the Liberal Theory centres around individualism, absolute value of individual personality, autonomy of each individual and spiritual equality. The individual freedom and its various kinds—political, social, cultural, economic, intellectual and religious freedoms—rest on the belief that every individual is endowed right from his creation with certain inalienable rights. Since man and his rights *i.e.,* life, liberty and property, exist before the foundation of the state, no such rights shall be encroached upon after the establishment of the state.

The Liberal Political Theory is different from classical Political Theory in the following respects:

1. The Classical Political Theory accepts the state as a natural institution but the Liberal Political Theory accepts the contractual basis of the origin of the state.
2. The sole purpose of the state according to the liberalists is protection of life, liberty and property by the state and if the state fails to discharge the same, then the individual has the right to revolt against the state and establish in freedom a new government.
3. The Classical Political Theory believes in the community. It is organized round and rooted in nature but the focus of liberals is on the individual. They advocate the principle of least governing and freeing of individuals from the restraints of social and economic life.
4. The Classical Political Theory believes in the subordination of individual to the state because the individual can realize his best self only in living in a state which is prior to individual and natural. This view is countered by the liberals on the basis of artificial creation of the state by the consent of the individuals. The view that consent is the basis of delimiting the power of the state creates a scope for revolt and change of the government with a

desired substitute if it fails to keep the covenant. This theory provides a more rational view of the origin of the state, its basis, the proper balancing between individual rights and state authority.

The renaissance, reformation, enlightenment and scientific development, not only contribute to clearly defining the sphere of different activities of the individuals, but also clearly distinguish the political authority *i.e.,* King, from the religious authority *i.e.,* Pope.

(c) **Marxist Political Theory:** This Theory is also called the dialectical materialist, and scientific socialist. It is founded on the general law of motion which has a role in the development of all phenomena. The centrality of Marxist Political Theory is inexorable progression of thesis, antithesis, and synthesis. It means every valid logical proposition has its contradictory proposition which is the synthesis that combines what is best in thesis and its opposite, antithesis. The second premise of this theory is the unity of the opposites. The third premise refers to quality, quantity, transformation. The change of quantity results in the change of quality and vice-versa.

Marxist Political Theory not only provides a scientific basis of understanding the whole historical development of the society in terms of productive forces and productive relations but also provides enormous scope for changing it.

The exponent of this Political Theory, Karl Marx states:

"The salvation is to be found in this society itself. So they lay down the revolutionary reconstruction of the present society which is based on poverty, inequality, exploitation into a socialist world order where no man is to be exploited by others, a society where every man will have full opportunity to develop their potentiality and personality, a classless stateless society where the development of each is related with the development of all."

The Marxist Political Theory is based on the principles of mode of production, class division, class struggle, property relations and state as an instrument of exploitation. That propertied people exercise the political power of the state and the real liberty and equality cannot be realized in a class-divided society *i.e.,* haves and have-nots.

While the Liberal Political Theory gives primacy to individual liberty and freedom, the Marxist Political Theory puts emphasis on the equality. It asserts that unless the equality is ensured the political liberty is meaningless. Thus, while the primary objective of Liberal Political Theory is to establish a modern liberal capitalist democratic state, the Marxist Political Theory strives for establishment of a socialistic state through revolutionary action.

Marxist Political Theory and Practice is derived from the works of Marx and Engles. The Theory has been acclaimed by a number of revolutionaries, philosophers, academicians and political activists belonging to different countries of the world. It has also been subjected to various interpolations and adaptations among the socialists themselves. Its applicability has been variously interpreted in different geographical locations, contexts, situations and also its changing possibilities with change of time. The approach, methodology and strategy followed in USSR, China and, of course in India, are quite different in regard to different social classes. There is divergence of views on the stage of development, the nature of the class structure, the division of the society into classes on the basis of property, income, wealth and exercise of political power. The history of Marxist Political Theory points to the fact that upto first world war the philosophy in practice was quite deterministic for socio-political changes and its culmination was the USSR revolution. But after the USSR revolution, during the interwar period, Marxism acted as a critique of the prevailing socioeconomic conditions rather than a philosophy of revolutionary action

Some of the pronounced characteristics of the Marxist Political Theory can be summarized as under:

1. That all matter, every phenomenon is in a state of flux. For, it is in the nature of every phenomenon to realize its utmost development. As such, the movement is from lower to the higher stage of development.
2. The development proceeds through a dialectical method which is a triad and what Hegel calls: thesis, anti-thesis and synthesis. Marx terms them as: relations of production, productive forces, and a new mode of production.
3. Between mind and matter, matter comes first and propels and dictates forces of production and relations of production. It is matter that essentially produces while mind merely reflects.
4. In the course of historical development matter evolves because of its own law of evolution inherent in it.
5. On the material base which consists of the forces of production and relations of production is built the superstructure comprising social, political, economic or educational components. As is the base, or the foundational structure, so is the superstructure.
6. Politics, is a class phenomenon. Its basis is in the class character of a particular society. As and when class division in the society is abolished, politics or state, as an instrument of domination and exploitation would lose all significance and wither away.
7. Politics serves a dual purpose. It not only destroys the fabric and values of the earlier society, but also builds those of the new society.
8. Politics, as the Dictatorship of the Proletariat, is an instrument of social and political transformation. By abolishing the capitalist society it helps build the socialist society.
9. Socialism then develops into Communism *i.e.,* Classless Exploitation-free Social Order and with it Politics, as State, would wither away.

**(d) Behavioural Political Theory**: The Behavioural Political Theory is developed in liberal democracies to justify its continuance by bringing changes in the political setup. The end of Second World War brings out multiple changes in the economic, political, socio-psychological spheres of individual's life. The role of emerging labour party, the concept of positive welfare state and political upheavals result in study of political formations through the psychological parameters of the political actors. The central theme of Behavioural Political Theory has been individual behaviour and how the same acts in electoral process *i.e.*, political representation.

The Beharioural Political Theory advocates the justification of scientific method based on facts rather than philosophical principles or values. The social scientists like Max Weber, Graham Wallas and Arthur Bentley have advocated scientific methodology. They have tried to integrate the Political Theory and its analysis through concepts and methods of other social sciences like sociology, psychology, anthropology and social anthropology. The Chicago school of thought which has such famous names as Charles Merriam, Harold Lasswell, Gosnell, David Easten and David Apter, separate the study of Political Theory from the ideals, institutions, values to the role and interrelatedness of individual and group behaviour in the political process.

The Classical Political Theory differs from the Behavioural Political Theory in respect of the following points:

1. The Behavioural or Scientific Political Theory strives to maintain order. It explains and predicts the phenomenon but not evaluate it by setting the utopian standards. The former is based on the principles of science rather than the philosophical propositions.
2. The Political Behavioural Theory frees itself from values and centres around facts, *i.e.*, from who rules to how does one rule and how?
3. The Behavioural Political Theory is different from the Classical Political Theory in a sense, that it is not concerned with the study of institutional framework *i.e.*, state but also the political process.
4. Behavioural Political Theory does not believe in the critical function. Far from questioning the validity of the state, it supports the maintenance of status quo, stability, harmony and equilibrium in the society.
5. Behavoural Political Theory is also influenced by biological views and introduces the concepts like system, structure, function, decision-making and policy-making.

The Behavioural Political Theory has attracted criticism because of its claim of complete value-free judgment, its failure to study the present social, political issues. The debate in 1970's, resulted in reaching the conclusion that the values, purposes, missions, visions should be related with the political structure. The core issues of Political Theory like liberty, equality, justice are taken up once again by the Post-behavioural School and political scientists like John Rawls, Robert Nozick, Habermas and many others.

So, the Behavioural School of Political Thought which initially gives primacy to empirical facts is seen to end with a convergence of fact and values and according ethical norms and values preeminence in political analysis.

**(e) Contemporary Political Theory**: The failure of Marxism in many parts of the world on the one hand and the Scientific Empiricist School like Behavioural School and its too much emphasis on facts, pure sciences and its failure to understand the present socio-political reality on the other, gives shape to the Contemporary Political Theory.

The dominating era of Behavioural Political Theory is now to be seen overpowered by Scientific Theory which derives its legitimate status through scientific enquiry and knowledge. But, the mixing of social facts and understanding of the social facts with the help of natural sciences/pure sciences cannot last long. The political scientists like Thomas Kuhn challenge the whole model of what is science of society and politics. Also others are led to believe that understanding social science and social issues cannot be studied by a model of unified science.

Soon, it was realized that Political Theory is more than a Philosophy and also more than a Science as it has both vision and relevance. To this may be ascribed the revival of interest in Political Theory since 1960s and 1970s in Europe, U.S.A. and in other parts of the world.

According to David Held the Contemporary Political Theory has the following characteristics:

(a) philosophical, because it is based on normative as well as conceptual framework,
(b) empirical, because it is based on explanation of the concepts,
(c) historical, because it interprets and understands the concept in historical situation/context, and
(d) strategic and future perspective, because it says not only where we are today but also wherefrom we have started and how far we should travel and at what velocity.

Held lists the following as the major essential reasons for this resurgence of Political Theory:

(i) break-up of the post-war consensus,
(ii) the consequential clash of values, and
(iii) changes in the humanities and social sciences, particularly a renaissance in Political Thought.

The principal task of Contemporary Political Theory is to give us an in-depth knowledge of the political phenomenon, through explanation, investigation and ultimately comprehension of what relates to politics, its concepts, principles and institutions. As John Rawls states that Contemporary Political Theory entails not only a continuous search for truth, but also the pursuit of scientific-empirical methods. R. Nozick is convinced that Political Theory can solve many political problems by combining the classical ends with empirical means. John Plamenatz pointing to consensus, holds that the empirical analysis and reflections of a logical and moral character can co-exist in Political Theory.

The other major tasks of the Contemporary Political Theory are given below:

1. To renew, as the history of Political Thought, and examine the significance of political texts in their historical context.
2. To revitalize the discipline as a form of conceptual analysis and in the process Political Theory as a systematic reflection upon, and classification of, the meanings of the key forms and concepts such as sovereignty, democracy, justice and the like.
3. To develop as the systematic elaboration of the underlying structure of our moral and political activities: the disclosure, examination and reconstruction of the foundations of political value.
4. To revitalize as a form of argument concerned with abstract theoretical questions and particular political issues.
5. To provide as a critique of all forms of foundationalisms, post-modernists and the liberal defenders alike, and accordingly, to present itself as a stimulant to dialogue and conversation among human beings.
6. To elaborate as a form of systematic model-building influenced by theoretical economics, rational choice theory and game theory, and in the process aim to construct formal models of political processes.
7. To develop as the theoretical enterprise of the discipline of Political Science and thus attempt to construct Theory on the basis of observation and modest empirical generalizations.

The post-1970s developments in Political Theory, gave rise to broadly four distinct perspectives:

1. Political Theory, as branch of moral philosophy is essentially normative. Accordingly, it aims to develop not only general principles for evaluating the social structure, but also to design appropriate institutions, procedures and policies.
2. Viewed primarily as a contemplative and reflective enquiry, its concern is to understand human existence in general as it is understood, in its older form. But the fact is that Political Theory is neither a branch of moral philosophy nor exclusively normative in its orientation.
3. The prime task of Political Theory is to articulate the self- understanding of a particular community, and so understood, it is essentially municipal in its scope and interpretive in its orientation.
4. Political Theory must retain its tentative, exploratory, conversational, open-minded, ironic of sensitive nature. This view finds inspiration from post-structuralist and post-modernist contents of thought.

On the basis of above discussion the major essential characterists of Contemporary Political Theory are as follows:

1. Every situation differs from the other and is autonomous, independent in respect of its own issues.
2. Political Theory should not delimit its scope to the natural sciences and should also perform a critical role.
3. Contemporary Political Theory disapproves any dissociation of Political Theory from history. So, the origin, genesis, the developmental aspect should again be attached with the Political Theory.
4. There is need to analyze the conceptual findings of the Political Theory as a systematic reflection of classification, in respect of the key concepts such as sovereignty, democracy, equality, justice, etc.
5. There is need to lay emphasis on the importance of subjective interpretation and arrival of different conclusions. The truth of a particular problem may be many and the degree of truth also may vary from person to person and time to time. Political Theory attaches value to subjective interpretation to find out the objective truth.
6. It relates to the study of historical tradition in the process of understanding the truth. The historical understanding of tradition and development justifies that the process of history and its progress in giving substance to that truth is final. Interpreting "Post-modern Theory" one writer emphasizes that there is no crux and everything is in flux. In this context the Indian tradition and its concepts Anekantvad and Sayadvad may be referred for a proper understanding of truth and its many-sidedness.
7. It has been elaborated as a form of systematic model building based on economic theory, rational choice theory and game theory. Its aim is to construct formal models of political process.
8. It has developed a theory building based on normative elements with the importance given to justification and explanation of factual structures, political activities, examination and construction of principal political values.

## Political Theory: Changing Analytical Perspectives

The development of Political Theory has been marked by changing analytical perspectives which are seen to shift at least in five directions. These are:

1. From human nature to power relations
2. From discussion to analysis
3. From behavioural studies to development models
4. From sociology of politics to political sociology
5. From political sociology to political economy

### 1. From Human Nature to Power Relations

The speculation about politics starts from the premise: What is man? What is human nature? This question has agitated the minds of the ancients in Greece, Palestine, China and India. Many thinkers have sought to establish general postulates about human nature and then to erect on that basis a theory about man-in-politics. Plato, Hobbes, Locke, Rousseau, Spinoza, Bentham, Green etc. have followed this path.

Aristotle, however, is the originator of a new trend. He regards man as basically a political animal who lives in political societies and ecologically adjusts himself to the environment.

Following Aristotle, Sophocles' *Antigone* too speaks of the clever man and his unique position in nature gained by virtue of his gifts for language and social organisation. While the advocates of the first school start from man or human nature, the focus of those belonging to the latter is human behaviour in political situation. The Roman concept of imperium, *viz.* supreme authority as a bundle of legal powers, conferred by the people on a legitimate order falls in this category.

In the definitions of politics given by scholars the concept of power has invariably crept in directly or otherwise. For example, Aristotle defines his *polis* or political association as the most sovereign and inclusive association. A polity or constitution, for Aristotle, is the organisation of a *polis*, in respect of its offices generally but especially in respect of that particular office which is sovereign in all issues. Thus Aristotle presumes the existence of authority or rule in a *polis* or political association.

Among the moderns, Max Weber, for example, considers an association as political if and in so far as the enforcement of its order is carried continually within a given territorial area by the application and threat of physical force on the part of the administrative staff. Thus, while stressing territorial aspect of political association, Weber too specifies that a relationship of authority or rule is an essential feature of political association.

Harold Lasswell while defining Political Science as an empirical discipline, calls it the study of the shaping and sharing of power. He describes a political act as one performed within power perspectives.

David Easton defines political activity as the authoritative allocation of values. Thus, power perspective in political analysis has been the dominant trend and has the largest following in the discipline even today.

## 2. From Discussion to Analysis

Discussions about ideologies and forms of Governmental institutions have been replaced by a thoroughgoing analysis of the political process. Some think that anyone who professionally debates issues about political authority with major premises drawn from legal, historical, philosophical, and/or theological is a political scientist.

As against this, the other view refers those who write as if they seek to be naturalists, classifying political phenomena and generalizing from their own observations and those of others.

Thinkers like Plato, Augustine, Acquinas, Hobbes, Locke, Rousseau, Spinoza and Hegel may be roughly placed in the first category whereas Thucydides, Polybius,

Machaiavelli, Montesquieu, de Tocqueville and Bagehot qualify themselves for the second. Aristotle like Karl Marx in modern times, has his feet planted in both camps. The behavioural approach in political science is an extension of the second perspective and uses the comparative method in the study of politics.

It is Herodotus who at first uses the historical confrontation of Greek-atics and Asiatic empires to make a number of significant points about government and the combination of discipline and freedom. About a century after him, Aristotle undertakes to work on analyzing the 158 Constitutions, mainly of Greek city states. But only one of these documents (that of Athens) has come down to us. The politics contains not much of evidence to enable us to see how strictly Aristotle handles the logic of comparison.

A comparative study of politics has to pass through various stages:

1. Collection of a number of examples of the category of object to be investigated, as is done in the case of Greek city states, and smaller European democracies.
2. To divide and separate them into a number of factors or areas which can be documented in each case, and which have a bearing on the subject of investigation. Now, if the examples are alike in respect of a pretty large proportion of these factors, they are comparable. One can then proceed to experiment mentally with the small number of remaining factors which lie within a field of special interest of inquiry, and which show differences in cases alike in other respects.

As an example of the application of comparative method, one may cite the case of the smaller European democracies. They are ideal samples, because they are tolerably similar in size, with comparable indicators such as economic development, literacy rate, standard of living as well as their history of religious divisions. But there do exist certain sharp differences even in these states and their underlying causes can be discovered through the comparative perspective.

Thus, comparative analytic framework involves two phases:

(a) that of hypothesis formulation, which involves a search for correlations such as to suggest explanations in general terms;
(b) that of search for disproof by contrary example.

### 3. From Behavioural Studies to Development Models

As a result of the new behavioural and empirical mood the discipline of Political Science gets enriched by a number of studies that come to be classified under the rubric of sociology of politics. While Political Science is emerging as a separate field, the early sociologists, both in Europe and America continue to show considerable interest in politics. In their efforts to generalize about institutions and social behaviour, they can not ignore as important a set of institutions as the political, nor can they be indifferent towards the formation of attitudes and group norms in politics. Thus sociologists like Max Weber, Robert Michels, Wilfred Pareto, and Emile Durkheim involve themselves in political analysis as part of their sociological concerns.

Under the influence of behaviouralism, political analysts seek to apply the various concepts and methods of sociology to the study of political behaviour and institutions. Not only they try to explain voting behaviour, but also apply the analysis of bureaucratic structures (developed in the work of Max Weber and Robert Michels) to a variety of institutional structures ranging from government agencies to trade unions, political parties, and economic institutions. Simultaneously the theoretical and methodological approaches of sociology and psychology with inter-disciplinary focus are also adopted by the political analysts to the study of political phenomena.

A new impetus to the development of sociology of politics comes to be the sudden arousal of interest in the new nations, particularly of Asia and Africa, especially after second world war. An attempt is made to study the conditions under which new societies come to being, formed out of cultures placed under one political authority. The major focus of new studies has been on the question how new political systems come to acquire legitimacy and incorporate or mobilize a previous population within the polity. An attempt is also made to pinpoint the conditions under which relatively poor agrarian societies advance economically and to link all these changes to the concomitant adjustments in various social relationships. *e.g.*, kinship system, social stratification, mechanisms of social control and the like.

From the behaviour studies like that of voting behaviour and political attitudes, the focus now shifts on to development studies. Consequently the political analysts start thinking in terms of developmental frameworks which would include the polity, economy, society, and personality. In this way they are seen moving towards a social science rather than social sciences.

It is assumed that all forms of social behaviour are intrinsically interrelated. Therefore, changes incorporated at one dimension—whether social, economic, political or psychological—are bound to have an impact on the other dimensions. This makes it necessary to have a concept of the social system in which all its aspects hang together. The theoretical framework of structural-functionalism which is devised first by anthropologists and sociologists is later developed and adopted in political studies by political analysts like David Easton and Gabriel A. Almond.

### 4. From Sociology of Politics to Political Sociology

The sociological perspective in Political Science is as old as Political Science itself. What is new has been a shift in recent years from the sociology of politics to political sociology. To quote Gabriel Almond, the Classical Political Theory itself is more of political sociology and psychology than a theory of the political system and its consequences are inferred from the ways in which the social structure is represented in it. The Platonic, Aristotelian, and later Roman classifications of the type of political systems are far more explicit on the consequences of varieties of social stratification and their representation in political systems for their forms and their performance than they are regarding the varieties of political decision-making processes. That is to say, the bases of political classification are sociological rather than political. In essence, the Greek and Roman theory of political development is a socio-psychological theory,. They treat the pure forms of rule (Monarchy, Aristocracy or Democracy) as inherently unstable because of their susceptibility to corruption which stem from sociological and psychological processes.

The phrase, sociology of politics, signifies a sub-field or a sub-division of the overall field of sociology–like the sociology of religion, sociology of leisure, and the like. The term sociology of politics denotes that the framework, the approach or the focus of the inquiry is sociological. It means an attempt at analyzing the political process in terms of the unit-ideas of sociology, *viz.* community, authority, status, the sacred, and alienation. The assumption behind it is that the formal theory of the social system leaves off where the formal theory of the political system begins. But political sociology is no synonym for sociology of politics. It is one of the connecting bridges between sociology and politics. Sartori calls political sociology as an interdisciplinary hybrid attempting to combine social and political explanatory variables, *i.e.,* the inputs suggested by the sociologist with the inputs suggested by the political scientist. The sociology of politics is instead a sociological reduction of politics.

According to Bendix and Lipset, the chief impetus in the voting behaviour studies stems from an interest theory of political behaviour and it goes back ultimately to the Marxian theory of class consciousness. The authors hope that ultimately a theoretical framework for political sociology as an integral part of sociology sans phrase will be established. But later Lipset and Rokkan come to suggest a different emphasis focusing on the question: how are conflicts and cleavages translate into a party system? This they find useful for causal explanations and understanding of the political reality.

According to Sartori, this new perspective has two advantages:

1. It gives equal attention to any kind of conflict and cleavage—race and ethnicity, region and locality, culture and tradition, religion and ideology—all point to the dimension of class and these may be as important as its class dimension. To quote Sartori, "Conflicts are not only economic and related to the class structure, but also regional, ethnic, linguistic, religious, and ideological". To assume that these latter sources of conflict are destined in the long run to give way to objective economic factors, amounts to a naïve view of the complexity of human nature at least in politics.
2. The inquiry is now correctly focused on the real problem *viz.* the translation of conflicts into politics. While previously in 1957 the essence of the essay of Bendix and Lipset is seen to equate politics to the strategy of conflict management, the new perspective of Lipset and Rokkan in 1967 treats politics as the study of conflicts and cleavages surpassing the old-style sociology of politics. It unquestionably inaugurates the new political sociology

where politics is not viewed as a mere projection of political and social conflicts.

Lewis A. Coser has rightly attributed the emergence of Political Sociology to the sense of dissatisfaction against the traditional Political Science and Classical Democratic Theory for their too narrow a focus and inability to examine fully the many-faceted social process that determines the behaviour of political actors, be they ordinary citizens, or members of a decision-making process. In contrast Political Sociology claims that political views are not arrived at through dispassionate study or in insolation. These are regarded as the outcome of the associations, most of them not even formal political associations. In fact it is the family, the school, neighbourhood and peer group which form and mould the personality of the child. It is in such groups that the child learns to define himself in relation to the world that surrounds him. It is believed that his attitudes and values, including his political views are powerfully shaped in these early encounters with others.

Thus, at the risk of over simplification, one may say that Political Science has tended to concentrate on the visible part of the political iceberg whereas, Political Sociology has paid greater attention to the submerged portions. One has to admit, however, that in the course of its long evolution spanning several centuries, the discipline of Political Science has moved closer to science, consequently it can now rightly boast of greater precision, integration and wiser perspective incorporating the methods, approaches and frameworks of other disciplines.

**5. From Political Sociology to Political Economy**

With the decline of System Theory, a new enthusiasm is noticed for the application of economic theory to politics. The revival of economic analysis in the study of politics can be attributed to two major factors:

1. It is being increasingly accepted that the mathematical or statistical models are the best way to formulate patterns and processes and that social sciences must follow the lead of economics in defining their propositions. They should do so in ways which can be specified in formal models and frameworks the like of which are in vogue in economics. It is argued, if social science seeks to be scientific, its underlying assumptions must be spelt out in clear, rigorous terms.
2. The policy problems faced by the social science, have undergone a change. As a result the dominant issues of today are poverty, race, gender, environment and the problem of urban government. These involve efforts to decide how to allocate resources in an optimum way to attain certain agreed upon objectives, within the system. Thus, many political scientists have to turn to economics to find a suitable model for political enquiry. This entails the new direction of Political Science as a shift towards the integration of politics with economics and sociology. They see it again heading

towards political economy which once was one of the dominant trends in Political Science during the nineteenth century.

## The Relevance of Political Theory

The relevance of Political Theory can be well understood from the purpose it serves and the task it performs. Political Theory may be seen as a system of values, norms and ideals on forming an organization—social, political, cultural etc. They help us to understand the political reality. They provide necessary perspective to change it if deemed necessary. It enables us to speculate about the nature of good life, the appropriate political institutions needed to realize it. It offers a vision on what the end of the state is and what steps be taken to achieve those ends. The relevance of Political Theory could be tested in relation to (i) a description of the political phenomena (ii) a nonscientific (based upon philosophy or religion) speculation or a scientific (based upon empirical studies) analysis or explanation (iii) political goals and political action, and (iv) ethico-normative and moral judgment. Normative-philosophical speculations in essays on Political Theory propounded in Plato's *Republic*, Isiah Berlins *Liberty* or Rawls' *A Theory of Justice* or Nozick's *Anarchy, State and Utopia* can be cited as some examples.

The fundamental question facing human beings is how to 'live and let live'. Politics is an activity of legislating, managing and administering of the collective affairs of society. The relevance of Political Theory lies in evolving and explaining various doctrines, methods, approaches etc. regarding the nature and purpose of the state : the nature, types and dimensions of political authority, vision of an ideal polity, state or government, relations between the state authority, law and the individual liberty and issues like justice, rights, liberty, equality, property, common good etc. Further it seeks to explain the interrelation between such core issues of politics as liberty and equality, equality and property, justice and property etc. With it peace, order, harmony, stability and unity in the society remain abiding concerns. In fact peace, order and harmony or for that matter, unity and stability in the society are very much dependent upon how the values of liberty, equality and justice etc. are interpreted and implemented.

Contemporary states face a number of problems such as poverty, overpopulation, corruption, racial and ethnic tensions, global terrorism, environmental pollution etc. Political Theory undertakes an in-depth study and analysis of these issues with a view to suggesting practical solutions and an alternative course of action as well as the extent to which they have the potential to deliver.

David Held views the task of political theorist as really demanding. He sees a danger that, politics will be left to the ignorant and self-seeking whose concern is only pursuing it as power rather than instrument of selfless service. In short, the relevance of Political Theory consists in the following :

(i) It provides systematic thinking about the nature and purpose of state and government relationship of individual, authority and state.

(ii) It helps us to establish a correlation between socio-political ideals and the socio-political phenomena.

(iii) It makes the individual conscious of his rights and duties in a state or a society.

(iv) It helps us to know the nature and ends of the socioeconomic system and the stages of its evolution through the ages.

(v) It helps us to find solutions to problems like poverty, violence, corruption, ethnicity etc.

(vi) As Karl Marx rightly explains, the task of Political Theory is not only to understand and explain the social reality but also to change it. Viewed in this light Political Theory helps us to evolve ways and means to change society either through reform or revolution.

(vii) If Political Theory performs its desirable function, then the people will be equipped with the instruments of struggle for their advancement. The correct political theories may make us choose right goals and means so as to avoid the roads that end in darkness of despair.

In sum, the relevance of Political Theory lies in its striving to explain the political facts, the political upheavals, set of political goals and objectives. It helps us to find out the means and methods of solving the political problems through recruitment of political actors and solving the political problems through political leaders. It seeks to provide interest and initiative to the common people to participate in political process and integrate themselves with the political society. It equips the people to exercise their political power by fixing the standards and principles for both the government and governed. It teaches them how the political systems acts, interacts and reacts with its environment.

Finally, it establishes the vision of the ideal state before the people and suggest ways as to how it could be realized from time to time through political idealism, thought and philosophy.

# 3

# WHY STUDY THE HISTORY OF POLITICAL THOUGHT?

## What is Political Thought?

The terms Political Science, Political Theory, Political Thought and Political Philosophy are quite often used interchangeably, though each one has its specific meaning and connotation. Political Theory implies systematized reflection on politics. It is the study of 'who gets, what when, how and why'. It reflects on the nature and purpose of state and government. David Held defines Political Theory as "a network of concepts and generalizations about political life involving ideas, assumptions and statements about the nature, purpose and key features of government, state and society, and about the political capabilities of human beings". George Catlin includes in Political Theory both Political Science and Political Philosophy. While Political Science refers to the phenomena of control in many forms over the process of whole social field, it is concerned with means. In contrast, Political Philosophy is concerned with the end or final value, when man asks 'what is the natural good' or 'what is good society'. Gould and Kolb define Political Theory as "a subfield of Political Science" which includes:

(i) Political Philosophy as a moral theory of politics and a historical study of political ideas,
(ii) a scientific criterion,
(iii) a linguistic analysis of political ideas,
(iv) the discovery and systematic development of generalizations about political behaviour.

Contrasted with these explanations the term Political Thought is much wider. It is open-ended, time-bounded, culture-specific and a continuum. Political Thought encompasses theories, beliefs, values and assumptions. It includes valid and not valid hypotheses of all those sensitive minds who have thought on the basic questions agitating human mind. Their reflections range from day-to-day activities, to policies and decisions on the problems of the day and great issues of politics, as of state and government, poverty, human rights and justice. The creators of Political Thought may be philosophers, thinkers, writers, journalists, poets, political commentators etc. They may be culture-bound, time-bound, yet transcending all bounds they participate in a continuing dialogue, no body knows when it started and when will it end.

Political Thought refers to systematic reflection about political life, its institutions, processes and practices. It is an orderly reflection on political authority; why do people obey or resist it; how does political life relate to and is influenced by the external world. Its concern is also on how does political authority operate within a political system, or how does the latter relate to subsystems that exist within the political system as also outer systems.

Political Thought is based on Great Texts of Political Thought such as Plato's *Republic,* Aristotle's *Politics*, Hobbes *Leviathan* and Marx's *Das Capital*, *Communist Manifesto* etc. These classics while undertaking broad-ranging exploration of politics also attempt to understand the general conditions of life and experience.

Political Thought provides us a base upon which is raised the structure of the political concepts and institutions. Studying Political Thought, we learn to understand political tradition, a concrete manner of behaviour, experience and time-tested wisdom.

A study of Political Thought as political tradition is the study of the thought of the whole society of a particular period. It is reflective of the political vision of a whole people about politics and political institutions.

Political Thought explains, speculates, narrates, enquires, speaks, sketches; and evaluates political life, institutions, processes, concepts, all at once, while seeking to understand a part along with the whole.

As a historical narrative, Political Thought is descriptive to a considerable extent besides at the same time observational, empirical, operational, comparative and scientific. Viewed thus, Political Thought is both History and Politics.

Political Thought is the aggregation of the numerous philosophical speculations and explorations of political philosophers who among themselves have theorized on political issues confronting their peoples, and times. As the child of their own age they have grown discussing and enriching political ideas of their time.

In brief Political Thought has the following major essential ingredients:

1. Political Thought is about politics or political life or political institutions. It is also about ideas and theories of political philosophers, their speculations about politics, about the government that ought to be. Political Thought in essence is normative and value-laden.
2. Political Thought is the political commentary by political philosophers on their time and circumstances, the society they lived in, political life, political structures and institutions that they confronted in the course of their living.
3. Political Thought very much deals with the theories and concepts about

politics and political life. It concerns concepts such as types of polity, common good, state, division of power, legal frameworks, citizenship, law, justice, rights, political obligation and the like.

4. Political Thought refers to a body of thought as contained and expressed through the writings and reflections of political thinkers, publicists and writers. It is through its concepts and categories that it helps us understand the subject matter.
5. Political Thought is a treasury of knowledge and wisdom. It consists of political concepts and explanatory frameworks which enable us to formulate new models and theories suited to the newer times and social contexts.
6. While attempting to understand the political life and institutions of their times, political philosophers have given them fresh meanings and have suggested ways of altering them. Taking cue from them, subsequent philosophers have introduced alterations in the institutions wherever needed, but maintaining continuity.

Political Thought is a generic term. It can appropriately encompass the entire subject matter of society and politics, state and government, rights and duties, citizenship and political obligation, justice and common good and so forth. In short it includes the whole discipline of Political Science in its broadest sense. It may include concepts and approaches to the study of political behaviour, political institutions, cycles of revolutions, changing forms of government, nature, origin and purpose of state, law, government, constitutions, the study of political reality in all its dynamic aspects, the ethical, moral, philosophical, cultural, social, economic, political theories, approaches and perspectives on the study of man as a political animal in societal setting, the role of politics in human well-being and good life.

Among all animate beings man is the only one in whom rational faculty is most developed whereby he can know about himself, his boundaries, his environment, the values and norms of the system of which he is a part. All disciplines and branches of learning are the outcome of his insatiable curiosity to know about the essence and existence, fact and value, science, metaphysics, self, world and the truth behind it all.

Political Thought is as old as human society. Each generation has its own perplexing questions on which it has been reflecting to find appropriate answers. This is equally true of every country and every age. Over the centuries mankind has been a witness to an interminable dialogue on both the topical and the perennial issues of human existence. They include the purpose for which state, government and various institutions and organizations have come into being and the extent to which they are able to achieve their object. Speculation has also focused on man and his relationship with the universe and his place in the cosmos.

Political thinkers like Plato, Aristotle, Kautilya, Confucious, St. Augustine, St. Thomas Acquinas, Hegel, Green, Marx or Gandhi, offer a wide range of views on man and society, on family, civil society, state, justice, good society, good governance and finally good of all. There have been a continuing debate on all the above topics. Even on so central a topic like the state there has been a diversity of views, in particular on the nature, origin, purposes and functions of the state. For Plato, the State is 'man writ large'; for Aristotle, the state is 'prior to man'. For Sophists, the state is 'an artificial institution' designed to achieve certain set goals. For Medieval thinkers the state is 'a divine institution'. Later Liberals find the origin of the state in 'contract, pre-social or pre-political'. Marx views the state as 'an instrument of class domination'. Anarchists advocate the total disappearance of the state with all its coercive apparatus. They find the state as 'an unnecessary evil'. In order to have a total picture to arrive at the correct perspective, the study of Political Thought of all those thinkers who have dealt with the above questions concerning the state can be highly fruitful.

Some questions have been recurring age after age. They have been seen constantly agitating the minds of political philosophers and Man per se. Much of the theorizing and philosophizing that constitute the corpus of Political Thought is the outcome of their efforts at seeking appropriate answers to all such questions: Why should people obey? Who is a good ruler? What is good governance? What is the purpose of state? How much there be state interference in family? Should there be unlimited freedom of expression and action or some restrictions be imposed on this right? How is censorship justified? etc. etc. During the last two thousand years there have been spirited debates on these questions as well as on the others like law and liberty; liberty and equality; law, justice and ultimate good; citizenship, political obligation and state, and so forth.

Not only on the substantive issues of politics, but there has also been a continuing debate on approaches to the study of political reality. The thinkers like Plato and Aristotle, St. Augustine and Thomas Acquinas, Hobbes, Locke and Rousseau, Bentham and Mill, Green and Bosanquet, Marx, Gandhi, Rawls and Nozick–have all studied the same questions, each one, from his own perspective. They are all guided by reason and good sense that inhere in every being and they have produced some acknowledged classics in the History of Political Thought. For instance, Plato's *Republic*, Aristotle's *Politics*, St. Augustine's *The City of God*, Machiavelli's *Prince*, Hobbes's *Leviathan*, Locke's *Two Treatises on Government*, Hegel's *Philosophy of Rights*, Karl Marx's *The Communist Manifesto*, Rawl's *A Theory of Justice*, and so forth. In all these there are some central concepts, problems, methods, approaches, paradigms etc. that need be studied from different perspectives with a view to bringing out the many hidden facets of the problem under study.

It would be wrong to view History of Political Thought as a study of kingship, their conduct in peace and war, their policies and decisions. It is about the structure and function of social system, socioeconomic organizations, the causes behind the emergence of various institutions,– governmental and non-governmental—the concepts like political power, authority and conditions of obedience; conflictual relationship between caste, class and power. There has been a continuous interaction and process of evolution in regard to institutional structures, laws and procedures.

One finds a dynamic, constantly evolving relationship between man, society and state; tradition and modernity; continuity and change in political institutions, political processes, belief systems, values and ideas.

A deep study of the Classics on Political Philosophy and reflection on their concepts, methods, approaches and ideas can guide our footsteps into the future. It can throw a fresh light on the problems we face in the present and suggest appropriate solutions of them. It can teach us that all great works of Political Thought as we know them today have been built on the substantive issues of human existence that constitute the subject-matter of the great political texts of the masters who preceded them. Absorbing the vocabularies and the language of political discourse in these texts, they have expanded, developed and enriched them in the process of their actual theorizing on the issues before them. This is how mankind has advanced in the realm of ideas, values and culture. A deep study of the great texts of Political Thought provides us a comparative perspective to formulate fresh policies and programmes for human welfare. By putting imaginative, creative and purposeful use of the insights and ideas of political thinkers we can evolve new explanatory tools to interpret our present concerns and anxieties and find appropriate ways to cope with them in order to build a better future.

The study of the History of Political Thought offers us a peep into our past, an in-depth understanding of the present and a glimpse of the future. It gives us a perspective to judge what will suit us best in our situation. It will help sharpen our analytical faculty, refine our judgement on men and affairs, and offer a clear view of the situations in which they are involved. This can enable us to know better how institutions and systems of beliefs arise, how they evolve, how they develop to their full potential in a particular socioeconomic setting and how in course of time they decline and fade from our racial memory.

By studying the past Classics of Political Philosophy we come to have a standard and a touchstone applying which we judge every new development in society and polity. The application of the comparative method provides us a sense of history and a sense of fact. It gives us a range of awareness, expansive and all-embracing. It lets us comprehend the mystical shades of human behaviour, how it manifests in the working of social political institutions. This offers a better understanding and perspective of the human endeavour that have gone into the making of our culture and civilization. It also tells us how there has been an intimate relation between Political Theory and Practice and how jointly they have gone to shape man's actions and movements in the past and how they are likely to do so in our present times and the future times as well.

All political ideas grow in a particular soil and not in vacuum. They bear the imprint of their times. They reflect the social and political concerns of their people, their despairs and dilemmas. The solutions that were suggested by the most advanced sections of the society to the problems they then faced, find reflected today in great bodies of Political Philosophy. While this is certainly relevant in their times, it may have some relevance for our times as well and may prove useful in addressing some of our crucial problems and concerns.

Since every age has its specific political issues, this is what is reflected in the political tradition which embodies the dialogue of political thinkers of each age.

David Miller identifies the issues peculiar to our times which Contemporary Political Thought is seized with at present and which, in brief, can be mentioned as under:

1. *Social Justice:* The issue of social justice as indicative of the economic and social inequalities can be seen to be the product of an unfettered market economy. This issue is very much reflected in the writings of the Marxists as also of Rawls and Dworkin, with their distinct versions and emphasis. As against them, there are dissentient voices like those of Hayek and Nozick.
2. *Feminism:* Feminism has emerged as a major movement in our times. Its chief aim is to remove conventional liberal disparities between public and private spheres. While voicing the need for effecting fundamental changes, in men and women relationships, Feminists have advocated affirmative action policies.
3. *Identity:* The issue of cultural identity demands, in an environment of multiculturalism, modifications in political institutions so that they should reflect and express distinctive characteristics of numerous cultures. Everywhere we are witness to virulent debate about political identity, ethnicity and self-determination.
4. *Environmentalism:* Environmentalism has emerged as a crucial issue of our times having its basis in universal concern for environmental degradation. Today all over the world environmental movements are seen addressing urgent environmental dangers to our planet and are seen advocating green democracy, sustainable environment and environmental ethics.

A political thinker, in so far as he is a creature of his race and a product of his time-spirit, he stands in interactive relationship with his environment. He also bears the imprint of other factors that have gone to shape his personality, and his thought. They all combine to lend a meaning and significance that extends far beyond his race, milieu, environment and time-spirit. The transformative alchemy is the creativity of his personality. It is indeed a crucial factor in making of his thought. The fact that it partakes of the human essence is what makes it relevant for all times.

Political philosophers, both ancient and modern, have dealt with a variety of issues, ofcourse, from each one's own standpoint. Even though they have disagreed on the solutions, the continuity of issues is what is seen to capture their imagination. By trying to deliberate on these key issues with a view to finding appropriate solutions suited to their people and times they have given Political Thought, both a direction and unity of thought-processes, to ensure for an orderly discourse.

The vocabulary of Political Philosophy is nothing but the legacy accruing from the historical activity of political philosophers. In this connection, Sheldon Wolin refers to the power relations between government and subject, the nature of political authority, the problems created by social conflicts, purposes and objectives of political activity, and the character and utility of political knowledge.

Referring to the value of the teaching of Political Thought, Wolin points out that the theorist is engaged in an act of political unitization, that is of introducing new generation of students of politics and of developing the capacity for discriminating judgment in them. He is seeking to cultivate that sense of significance which is vital to political enquiry but cannot be furnished by scientific methods. His major concern is to the ways in which new theoretical vistas are opened. The benefit from studying classics and celebrated political texts is that with the aid of knowledge and experience derived from them we can construct our life experience as well as enrich our own experience in ways, unthought-of.

Admittedly, political philosophers while dealing extensively with the major contradictions and dimensions of the political process, not only transcend their localism but also develop a framework of analysis that would illumine and enrich other periods as well. They are able to do so by providing insightful and thoughtful reflections on perennial issues of politics such as state, power, authority, legitimacy and order. The Classics, as masterpieces, are timeless treasure of mankind in so far as the themes they touch are relevant in all ages.

Commenting on 'why should we study the History of Political Thought', Ashirvatham aptly points out: "It (Political Thought) gives precision and definiteness to the meaning of political terms. It is conducive to clarity and honesty of thought. It is an aid to the interpretation of History. A knowledge of past Political Thought is an invaluable help in understanding present day politics and international relations." Political Thought, so far as it represents a high type of intellectual achievement, is wisdom-rich, and therefore edifying, illuminative and educative.

We study the masters of Political Philosophy because their thought embodies universal, permanent values. In many respects their thought bears a timeless aspect. It enhances our understanding of our present as well as our future. They are beacons standing above the din and roar of their times. They blaze path to all the stranded and forlorn as the lodestar does in the all-pervading darkness. They stimulate and inspire our imagination to continue the quest. They encourage us never to feel disheartened by the odds and with courage to face and overcome all hurdles in the way.

The great political thinkers of the past offer us a vision of good life. They want to see it translated into practice. Each generation has to make fresh reflection on what can be the best model of living for them and what would suit their conditions. The achievements of the past have a practical value for us today since a study of ancient thought shows us how the present is an outcome of the past and how a better future is always seen to be muscling out of the womb of the present. We instantly learn about the modernization of tradition and the presence of transfigured tradition in what passes for modernity today. Every society and civilization has its distinct History as also its distinct Political Thought. If West has its Western Political Thought, India has its Indian Political Thought and Egypt and Persia have their own glorious political traditions.

## Conclusion

The above discussion throws up the following salient points on the issue of the relevance of the Study of the History of Political Thought:

1. The study helps to identify certain political issues together with their solutions as have remained the same in different times and climes. The ongoing debate among philosophers can act as a beacon to us. Taking cue from them we can restate and redefine them to suit our context.
2. The study of the same issues repeatedly helps us to view and understand them from varying perspectives. We see the great political philosophers joined in a dialogue and through their texts. We too can commune with the makers of our political tradition and common heritage. Every time we converse with them, we enrich ourselves.
3. Each political philosopher is a child of his times. He writes about the society he lives in. His Political Philosophy is but the history of his times, how he views and reviews it and in the process, he provides a fresh peep into it.
4. Political Thought contributes to a great evolution of concepts in the course of their interpretation by different political philosophers. The concepts of Justice, Liberty, General Will, Civil Society and the like, are some examples. Their meaning has not been the same as the concept was first conceived and expressed.
5. Political Thought contributes to specialized language of discourse through the use of new words, ideas, symbols, concepts and the like. The new vocabulary helps crystallize new concepts, meanings and interpretations, in effect the entire political corpus.
6. Political Thought, as an aid to thinking lets us think of other possible alternatives to solve our problems. Viewed thus, Political Thought is diagnostic, suggestive and inspirational in regard to its ends and purposes.
7. Through the study of political philosophers we gain an access to a range of political institutions and structures, forms of governments and of states.Out of these we can choose those institutions and structures or types of governments and political systems which would be suited to our social milieu and circumstances.
8. The study of Political Thought invests us with a penetrating insight, power of discrimination and discernment and a sound judgment. The comparative perspective clarifies our doubts and misgivings, enriches our knowledge and experience, trains and refines our sensibilities, broadens our vistas and visions, responses and responsibilities.

In fine, the thought of each and every society and civilization has certain unique features along with certain common characteristics. In our globalized world of today each society, culture and civilization has valuable lessons to teach to the entire human race. Despite the uneven stages of development through which various peoples have passed and may be passing even today, they shall all meet one day at one level in the confluence of culture of the whole humanity. Thus the study of Political Thought is a very rewarding enterprise having great significance for the whole mankind.

# PART II

# Concepts

# 4

# STATE

## The Term and the Concept

The concept of the modern state emerged in the sixteenth century. The pioneer of modern state was Machiavelli (1469–1527). The modern states are different from the ancient Greek city-states, Janapadas (as appeared in Indian political vocabulary), river valley civilizations, and political organizations. Unlike the modern states the ancient Greek city-states are more like city community. The Roman used the term 'civitas' which means a community who enjoys full civil rights. But some political philosophers also justify the concept of slave-master relationship. Admittedly the concept of modern state is seen to be nonexistent for the greater part of middle ages. The modern state as defined and designed by Machiavelli, comes in particular socioeconomic conditions. It comprises the spirit of nation state, trade and commerce, technological development and scientific inventions and discoveries.

The term state means condition: when somebody says, what is the mental state, what is the state of nature, what is the state of health, or what is the state of economy. But, the state, in Political Science Dictionary though backed by its various conditions, like (under what conditions the rights and authorities are related, in what conditions citizens should obey and when defy etc.) means a particular group of people organized together under a common goal with obedience to well defined principles.

Garner defines state as "a community of persons, more or less numerous, permanently occupying a definite proportion of territory, independent or nearly so, of external control and possessing an organized government to which the great body of inhabitants render habitual obedience".

According to MacIver, "the state is an association which, acting through law as promulgated by a government endowed to this end with coercive power, maintains within a community territorially demarcated, the universal external conditions of social order".

The Roman writers and also the Medieval lawyers use terms such as *status*, *civitatus*, or *status regni*, referring to the condition of the ruler, the fact of possessing stability. The English word "state" is in fact, a contraction of the word "estate". It is similar to the French word "*estute*" and modern French "*etat*". Both of them imply a profession or social status. The Spanish "*estudo*" gives the same idea of state, stability, or status.

## Components of the State

The fundamental components of the state are as follows:

(a) *Population:* The most important and human element of the state is population or say people. There cannot be any organization without the human dimension *i.e.,* people. Plato, the political philosopher of the early Greek political tradition delimited the population of the city-state to 5040. He excluded the slaves who constituted the bulk of the population in those times. Rousseau thought that, the population should not exceed 10,000 people. However it is very difficult to fix up the population for a particular state. But as compared with family and its components *i.e.,* members, the population should be as per the available natural resources, sufficient to support political organization. The ideal ratio between the ruler and the ruled should be as per the available conditions for their development. It should not be too large in number to support, taken care of, and too small to protect itself from foreign aggression. It should have a voice of its own and be able to express itself through political sovereignty.

(b) *Definite Territory:* The territory is also equally important like population to form a state. The migratory nomadic tribes shifting from one place to another cannot form the state. The Jews did not form the state until they were finally settled in Palestine. The territory may be large or small, but it has to be confined with a territorial dimension.

There is also a contrary view to what would be states and that why a moving tribal community with an organized set of rules *i.e.,* government cannot be treated as a state? The organized community though does not have any distinct territory it has its own distinctiveness, independence, autonomy and capability of interacting with other communities. The political scientist, who supports this view, named Seeley, says, 'what holds a state together is not territory but the principles of government'. This view is rejected by Bluntschli who states that population is 'the personal boundaries of the state' whereas 'the territory is the material basis of the state'. The concept of the territorial sovereignty of the state is co-terminus with the concept of the territory. The topography, the climatology, the soil conditions may differ from one place to another but there must be a definite demarkable territory. The territory of the state should include land, water, air, sky, over it.

However, territorial limit of the sea has ever been a controversial issue in international law. Traditionally it was three miles from the coast but now some of the countries are claiming more and India has extended its territorial jurisdiction to twelve miles from the coast.

Like the size of the population there is no ideal size of the territory. But there should always be an ideal ratio between the population and territory. That means the state should not be that densely populated to which the natural resources available may not be able to support nor should it be so badly populated as to have its own identity under threat of extinction or seem helpless to express itself in international situations.

(c) *Government:* The population, with permanent inhabitant of a particular territory cannot form a state. The people need to express themselves by their representatives, solve their day-to-day problems, establish relationship with other people, have international relationship with the help of an agency which is called the government. The government carries the administration of the state, determines the common policies, regulates the common affairs, extends its relations with the international community. The form, nature, typology of the government has been defined on the basis of the number of people holding the governmental machinery, the relationship between the individual rights and state autonomy, the priority of individual or community, the degree of freedom allowed and public interference, the applicability of law either through persuasion or coercion. But the government as a generic entity is deemed very essential from the times of the early Greek city-states. The state has to carry out its day-to-day functions through institutional arrangements like legislature, executive and judiciary, supported by a set of bureaucratic people.

(d) *Sovereignty:* Sovereignty means the absolute supreme power of the state. The word sovereignty has been derived from the Latin word "*Superanus*" which means free. India was not a state till 15th August 1947, because till that date it has the other three elements but not sovereignty. The sovereignty is the power of the state which goes with the constitution of the country. It has been classified into internal sovereignty and external sovereignty. Internal sovereignty means the state exercises absolute control over the associations and individuals who reside within the limits of that state and external sovereignty means it is completely free from foreign domination.

The sovereignty of the state distinguishes itself from other organizations and no organization / individual can appeal against the state. That means the decision of the state is final.

There can be only one state over the same territory and same people, though some immunities / privileges are granted to the embassy by the concerned state where the embassy is located. The embassy is subject to the law of the land, where the office is situated and the immunities granted should not be treated as the limitations of the sovereign state.

Both pluralists and internationalists very often criticize the national state and absolute sovereignty of the state. The pluralists believe that like any other organization state is a plural organization, so the sovereign power should not be exclusively enjoyed by the particular organization *i.e.,* the state. They see, that importance of other organizations, associations, their relations with citizens as members contribute no less towards the development of the individual and the state. Hence, the decentralization of the sovereignty.

The internationalists also argue that the absolute sovereignty of the state is a dangerous concept. It is the root cause of international disturbances, including wars. The states should surrender their absolute sovereign power for the promotion of international peace, international law, brotherhood and humane values of civilization.

The development of international understanding, the fast developing information and communication devices have challenged the clear-cut boundaries of the nationstate and nationalism. With the coming of globalization, the whole world is designed to be integrated in the economic network through international trade policy justifying the concept of internationalism above and beyond nationalism through the same.

## Nature of the State

Since the very conception of the state, its nature, functions, purposes and perspective have undergone a change. Several conflicting ideas have been presented in this respect. The idea of the state as an organized society goes back to the Greek city-states. Aristotle, while emphasizing the social nature of man, refers to the state as a kind of community. It is a union of unlike persons to satisfy their needs. The state is the natural growth of family and village and is prior in nature, family being older in time. Just as an acorn grows into an Oak, the nature of state is contained in its seed. It is natural for family and community to find its fulfillment in the Sate.

The Romans are seen to borrow the idea of state from the Greeks but apply it to a bigger geographic unit. The Roman term *Status Rei Publicae* means the State of Public Concern. In its modern sense, the term is first used by Machiavelli during the 16th century as a general term for a *body politic*. Hobbes, Locke and Bentham come to see the state as an artificial creation. As the result of our conscious will, design and planning, state is a human contrivance intending to fulfill certain utilitarian ends. In Hobbe's state of nature, prior to civil society, the life of man is 'solitary, poor, nasty, brutish and short', whereas in Locke's state of nature, men are equal and free and enjoy rights to life, liberty and property. In view of the insecurity and the need for an executive authority, men make a contract to form a civil society and government. For Locke's limited government the contract is both pre-social and pre-political. But for an absolute state of Hobbes it is pre-political. This contract to forming a civil society and limited government for Locke and an absolute state for Hobbes is the outcome of man's reason and will.

For Bentham, the utilitarian thinker, the state is an artificial creation, aiming at the promotion of human happiness or pleasure. Hegel identifies the idea of state with the world spirit and gives it a place of divinity among human institutions. For Hegel, the state is not utilitarian institution providing services, but the very incarnation of God. Being the divine will, it is absolutely rational. Hegel wields a great influence on political developments in recent times.

Among moderns, Maclver, Laski, and Max Weber require special mention. Maclver's contribution to Political Theory consists in his view of the state as an agency of human purpose. The essential attributes of the state, according to Maclver, are association, law, government, coercive power, a community territorially demarcated, and the regulation of the external conditions of social order. Maclver asserts that the state provides a link between political structure and social values. He maintains that being creature of society, the state reflects its value-systems as well.

The two important characteristics of the state, according to Laski, are its social basis and sovereign character. The state provides the necessary balance between demands and satisfactions on the largest possible scale. While conceding coercive power to the state Laski provides a large number of safeguards as a check against misuse of power. He proposes measures like decentralization, group consultations and restrictive governmental action.

C. L. Weyper divides the theories of the state into three broad categories viz.

1. the state as organism;
2. the state as machine; and
3. the state as class.

The classification is by and large rational and Weyper gives us an overview of the idea of the state as it has progressed from one phase to another.

### 1. The State as Organism

This theory starts from the premise that the individual is to the state what a bodily organ like the leg is to the human body. The bodily organ can exist and function only in relation to the whole human body. Similarly the citizens by themselves are insufficient and can have real existence, and function only in relation to a state. In other words the state is prior to the individual and that the individual as a part has any meaning only in relation to the whole *i.e.,* the state. So a man is not man unless he is attached to a state and therefore, it is the state that gives man his existence and makes him what he is. In short, state is the creator of social man.

Plato and Aristotle are mainly responsible for developing the organic theory of the State. Later, the stoics apply it to include humanity as a whole. Then this theory is adopted by the Christian forefathers and continues to reign supreme throughout the middle ages. But due to scientific revolution of the seventeenth century, the theory receives challenge from the newly developed mechanistic theory of the state which comes to dominate the scene during the period of enlightenment. However, assault on the theory comes from Rousseau and the German Romantics during the Nineteenth century. They reject the concept that the state is a machine. They reiterate and reemphasize the vitality of the organic theory as against the bloodless and soulless mechanist theory of the state. Influenced by nineteenth century biological and twentieth century totalitarian practices, the organic theory of the State becomes very popular with political leaders.

Thus state as an organism implies three things: (a) a close relationship of parts to the whole, (b) that the organism develops from within and (c) that the organism is an end in its own self or in the organism produced by it.

Hegel compares the state with the Spirit, the Divine Idea on its way to Self-Knowledge. He believes that the Spirit progresses from the inorganic world to the organic world of plants, animals and finds its ultimate evolution in man and state.

T. H. Green, the idealistic thinker, supports this concept and regards man as partial and the state as the fullest embodiment of the Divine Spirit.

### 2. The State as Machine

According to this theory the State is nothing but a creation of man. It is made as a machine to subserve human social ends. State is viewed as a contrivance or mechanism and man is the artist who creates this machine. To understand the state, we need understand its maker, Man.

The mechanistic theory of the state assumes that the individual is sovereign over himself. He can and does exist in his fullness without the state which is his handiwork. Some of the key questions asked by its theorists are: Why and how does men create the state, and what is the nature of the state that is created by man?

The chief exponents of the concept of the state as a machine are Thomas Hobbes, John Locke and Bentham. But this theory is as old as the Greek Political Thought itself. We find it reflected in the sophists who believe that there are no ideal models to copy down and that justice is made by man himself. Cicero too subscribes to it. He emphasizes that the state is not a divine inspiration guiding man's footsteps to Eternal Truth, but only a device of man's own making. It is meant to enable him to put up with one of life's major inconveniences *viz.* the existence of other people. The same view also underlies the Roman concept of *Lex* or Law, as well as the Hebrew and Christian conceptions of divine will and creation. This view is represented by St. Augustine in fifth century and later nominalists like William of O'cam, Duns Scotus, and Marisilius of Padua continue it in their writings. These thinkers view society as artificial, as a mere contrivance, devised by men to ensure peace, order, and justice.

But it is only with the dawn of the machine age in the seventeenth century does the mechanistic theory of the state rise to its full stature. Hobbes, one of its strongest proponents, holds that there exists a state of nature prior to the civil society in which the life of man is 'solitary, poor, nasty, brutish and short'. Haunted by an acute sense of insecurity, man is willing to pay any price to get out of this hell-like state guided by his reason and will which man retains even in the state of nature. Despite all deficiencies, Hobbes, therefore, decides to enter into perpetual and irrevocable contract to form a civil society and an absolute state.

Contrasted with Hobbesian state of nature, Locke's state of nature is inhabited by men who are equal, free and enjoy rights to life, liberty, and property. But owing to the insecurity and the need for an executive authority, men make a contract to form a society and a government. For Bentham, the state is an artificial creation. Its aim is to promote happiness or pleasure of most of its citizens and fulfill the possible utilitarian needs. In his view societal institutions are the result of ever conscious will, design and planning. The state is the product of genuine agreement. It is created to provide law and order to human beings.

### 3. The State as Class

The state as class or class theory of the state is based on the Marxian conception of history. The latter treats human progress as the outcome of a confrontation of opposites in a series of thesis, anti-thesis and synthesis. For Marx, 'the history of all hitherto existing society is the history of class struggles'. This is the opening sentence of *Communists Manifesto* and provides the best summing of the class theory of the state. According to Marx and Engels, at every stage of history following the stage of the primitive communism, a particular class gets control and exploits the rest. "Freeman and slave, patrician and plebeian, lord and serf, guildmaster and journeyman, in a word", says the *Manifesto*, "oppressor and oppressed, stood in constant opposition to one another, carried on an uninterrupted, now hidden, now open fight, a fight that each time ended either in a revolutionary reconstitution of society at large or in the common ruin of the contending classes".

According to the *Communist Manifesto*, the nature of the state is as follows:

1. The state is the executive committee of the bourgeoisie.
2. Political power is merely the organized power of one class oppressing the other class or classes. Oppression is there because state is controlled by one class. This fact is as true of monarchy as of democracy.
3. The state is product of the class struggle. It will wither away when there are no classes, the state being a condition of class exploitation. Where there are no classes, there is no state.
4. Through an inherent law of historical development the oppressed and the exploited proletarian class will overthrow the oppressing exploiting bourgeoisie. The proletariat will establish a socialist society by destroying private ownership of the means of production and thus prepare the way for the emergence of communist society. And once communism becomes the established order, the whole machinery of the state will be consigned to the scrap-heap. The mode of production relation in communist society will be: 'to each according to his needs, and from each according to his abilities.'
5. The State belongs to the superstructure which is created by the productive forces. The need for the state arises because the division of labour increases as a result of which society is divided into various classes. This development breaks up the old social order. The new phenomenon produces groups whose

divergent interests lead to disputes which can only be settled by the state. In the course of time, these groups or classes come to acquire different property rights. Consequently, the nature of the state undergoes a change due to the emergence of property and property rights. Thus, the state becomes a class institution, an instrument of class rule and class exploitation.

6. The state as a class rests on the premise that man is both a creature of needs and the creator of needs as well. He must eat in order to live. Production is viewed as the most important of all activities. Since men in association produce more than men in isolation, society becomes necessary to secure the necessities of life. But no society is perfect. In this respect every society has been subject to internal stresses and strains. It gives rise to an over-arching authority over men and things to subserve the ends of the class controlling the means of production.

Thus class theory of the state is an invitation to man to discover himself as a creature as well as creator of needs. It aims at wiping out human misery by establishing a perfect economic system, and perfect human being by realizing all his innate potentialities.

## State as Political System

Sociologically the state cannot be defined in terms of its ends. There is hardly any task which is not handled by some political association or the other. Conversely one cannot also pinpoint any task which may be performed exclusively by those associations which are designated as political ones. Consequently it is not easy to define the modern state sociologically, but only in terms of specific means peculiar to it, as is done to every political association, whether by the use of physical force or allocation of values or common good etc. Yet state as political system aims at a comprehensive definition, having several subsystems with set boundaries and various subsystems standing in interactive interrelationship.

Weber equates politics with the activities of the State. He defines the state as a human community that claims the monopoly of the legitimate use of physical force within a given territory. He considers the state as the sole source of the right to use violence. Hence, politics, to Weber, becomes a striving to share power or to influence the distribution of power, either among states or among groups within a state. Thus the state may be defined in terms of the means *i.e.,* physical force used to enforce obedience and viewed thus that the state is a concrete administrative structure or organization.

In terms of Weber's definition, a state has many political administrative characteristics which can be summarized as follows:

1. It consists of several specialized structures *i.e.,* officers, roles and institutions. These administrative structures are clearly defined, formal, complex and permanent.

2. The state has a monopoly of coercive powers: Its officials have the right to take away life and seize property, a power which does not belong to the private individuals.
3. The state exercises legitimate authority or sovereignty, the absolute legal right to make final decisions binding on the society.
4. The state structures are contained within clearly defined territorial boundaries.

This notion of the state as the embodiment of force originates mainly in Western Europe and flourishes there from fourteenth to seventeenth century. Machiavelli (1469–1527) in Italy and Bodin (1530–1596) in France write about a centralized monarch who embodies the State. With the decline of absolute monarchies in the west, the concept becomes less applicable.

In the contemporary western countries, the power and authority are dispersed rather than concentrated in one sovereign. Hence, it becomes difficult to locate the source of authority. For example, in a federal system where shall we find the ultimate authority? So, in contemporary writings, less attention is given to legal sovereignty and coercive power as the crucial element of political life.

In non-western areas, the concept of the state had even less validity. Some of these societies had been marked by the existence of highly egalitarian, segmentary stateless societies in ancient times. A few examples worthy of note were the Pygmies, Bushman and Ibo in Africa, thc Eskimos in North America, the Aborgines in Australia and Kalinga and Saine societies in Asia. The people of these areas maintained very simple economic and political systems. They hunted animals, herded cattle or raised crops. In keeping with their simple, small-scale economies, the political systems of these people did not show the commonly designated four aspects of State organization *viz.* Population, Territory, Government and Sovereignty. In these societies there existed very few specialized structures and even their administrative structures were vaguely defined: simple, highly informal and ad hoc. Among a few basic structures, family in particular handled a wide variety of functions: economic, political, religious and recreational. The political leader being simultaneously the elder in the family organized the allocation of land, and looked after the welfare and security of the tribe. There existed no clear distinction between social and political roles. Besides the family, the other concrete structures were councils of elders. Most often the people settled conflicts in these informal structures.

Thus such segmentary societies did not have certain structures that exercised a monopoly of coercive power. There were some controls over behaviour, but these were mainly in the form of moral and psychological sanctions. No military or police force controlled human conduct. And the individual always had the freedom to leave the community customs. Thus rule in these societies rested on consensus and not coercion.

Anthropologists have found it difficult to locate the source of sovereignty in such societies. If by sovereignty was meant the absolute right to make final binding decisions, then these societies lacked sovereignty. Here the power and authority were dispersed throughout the society. Several different groups such as class, lineages, kin groups, territorial units and village elders exercised legitimacy.

Likewise no clearly demarcated boundaries existed there. For example, those people herding their cattle moved freely from one area to another in search of water and fertile land for grazing their cattle. Also if one group became dissatisfied with the decisions of the ruling council of elders, then that group moved to another area.

However, the notion of the state as a concept of politics pertaining to all societies and times, does not hold true when applied to the international society. There exists no world government with coercive power. The United Nations does not have sovereignty; it has rather the power, not the legal right, to make final binding decisions on its members. Power and legal authority are all dispersed among the nation states. Many disputes are settled not through permanent specialized structure, but rather through ad hoc gatherings.

But despite the absence of coercive powers, it will be erroneous to assume that the world societies like U.N. lack political life. Both so-called stateless and world societies reveal political structures to regulate political life of their people. But nonetheless they lack concrete structures having binding authority over the whole society.

There are also some other political philosophers who are not in conformity with any of the above three categories of the conception, origin, functions of the state. The idealist like Rousseau, Kant, Hegel, Green, like Plato and Aristotle regards the state as an ethical institution which is indispensable for the full moral development of the man. According to Hegel, "the state is the world, the spirit made for itself". The individualists hold the view that the state limits the natural freedom of the individual and therefore is a necessary evil. Herbert Spencer and Bentham uphold this point of view. They argue that though it is necessary because of maintenance of law and order, still it is evil because it is antithetical to human freedom.

Many other writers like Tritschke and Machiavelli interpret the state as a power system. The thinkers like Hugo Grotius and Bodin regard the state as a welfare system–that is like a public utility company. Herbert Spencer says that the state is like a joint stock company for mutual assurance whose membership should be optional and voluntary. The anarchists like Prodhon and Kroptkin regard the state as an evil and plead for the immediate removal of the state. The pluralists like Laski and MacIver view the state as one of the organizations and that there are number of other organizations which are equally important to groups like church, family and trade union.

The totalitarians view the state as all-inclusive in which the individual can express his best self by complete subordination before the state. The Fascists and Nazis support this philosophy. The central theme of the totalitarian state is that everything is within the state, nothing is outside the state and nothing is against the state.

The structural functionalists and the system theorists also view the state from a different angle. Comparing Political Science with the subject matter of biological science, for purposes of a proper theory of political behaviour, and political sociology, the study of state has been replaced as the study of political system. The scholars of the system theory address the problems of political behaviour very adequately and much more accurately than the theorists of the state. They do not study the state believing that it has evolved historically or is a historical entity but like to study it empirically *i.e.,* in terms of the basic facts of the present day politics. Two contradictions of the state are between its basis of origin and the nature and function of the state. It concerns what exactly the state is. The common agreement that, the state is a political entity or primarily a historical entity along with thè nature, function and dynamics of the state has undergone a change with the change of time.

## The Historical Evolution and Growth of the State

The state is the growth of an evolving process and not a product of a movement. Several social factors like social instinct in man, religion, kinship, war, political consciousness and economic activities contribute in this regard. The modern state as found today has undergone the following stages of development:

(a) The Primitive State
(b) The River Valley Civilization
(c) The Greek City-State
(d) The Roman Civilization and Large Empire
(e) The Feudal State
(f) The Modern National States
(g) The Newly Emerged States of the Developing World
(h) The Communist States

To have a clear idea of each stage of development, it will be worthwhile to analyze one by one the various stages of development.

### (a) The Primitive State

Social anthropologists like Sir Henry Maine and MacIver have rightly emphasized that people live in different segments as tribes. The relations among the tribes are not so well defined as in case of family. Social relations governing the family life in the tribal unorganized state in course of time result in the birth of organized life. The Matriarchal family becomes the basis of the family life where the mother plays a more dominant role than the father. The Matriarchal family also gets converted into the Patriarchal family system where the importance of male members in the family is felt very often to be greater than the female. Blood relationships become a strong tie for people to live together. A group of families develop into a clan and members of clan ultimately emerge as a tribe. But, at every stage the clan is controlled by a chief who commands obedience from his members. The law of succession though based on the principle of heredity, sometimes results in superior physical force or mutual consensus among the members of the organization.

The tribal societies are organized on the basis of their homogeneity and guided by customs and superstitions. The tribal society creates an essential condition for the emergence of the state. Still today in some pockets the tribal societies are in existence. Though not mixed with the state they continue to provide an environment for the emergence of modern state.

### (b) The River Valley Civilization

It has been a common experience to see the empires developed around the valleys because of the fertility and other essential conditions available there. The earliest known empires have been the Nile, the Ganges, the Indus, the Tigris, the Yellow River and the Yangtse. These semi-civilized empires have been arbitrarily controlled by some outstanding war lords or mighty kings. The kings would rule over their respective areas by exclusively depending upon their personal chivalries and with the help of local customs and traditions, *i.e.,* the so-called laws. The command of the monarchs are very often regarded as laws and the monarchs are seen to act as the true representative of the God, commanding complete obedience from their people.

The rule by the monarchs have been subject to instability due to common command over the vast area and the tendency among kings to continue fighting against each other for victory, glory and expansion of the territory. According to Marriot and MacIver, these valley civilizations have been at best "a loose congeries of semi-independent states". The imperial scepter in their cases has been shifting "not only from dynasty to dynasty, but also from city to city". But the difference between the tribal primitive organizations to valley civilization may be seen to be more territorial life than nomadic life. In all these a systemic development of obedience to authority, property and concept of family are seen to become deep rooted. Because of the large number of population and areas coming under a common banner, a greater realization of law and order dawns in the society. The Harappa and Mohanjodaro civilizations bear testimony to the above facts.

### (c) The Greek City-State

The geographical settings of Greece contributes to development of city-states which are of course very small in respect of size as well as population. The natural climate and geographical settings provide opportunities to the people to contact with the outside world by trade and develop autonomous activities of the city-states. The city-states as a unity of villages emerge into one political unit. The important city-states have been Athens, Sparta, Syracuse, Orinth, Argos, Thebes and Attica. The form of governance have not been the same in all the city-states. Sparta has been the only city-state which is seen to maintain a perfect conservative existence, autocratic tradition and perfect discipline throughout its existence. In contrast Athens provides an ideal platform for direct democracy, experiencing myriad turmoils.

The Greek city-states are seen to ensure citizenship to only certain sections of people whom they allow to participate in the political process while debarring the slaves and foreigners from it. The main philosophy of the Greek city-states has been that the state is a natural institution and it is only in the city-state that the people can achieve their highest perfection. Thus, the Greek city-states are seen to reach a very high level of political development and personal liberty.

The shortcomings of Greek city-states pose a great threat to their survival. The shortcomings include:

(i) the wrong intermixing of state with society,

(ii) large number of people who are not citizens *i.e.,* slaves, foreigners are denied political participation. Slavery is supported as if it were any material possession. Aristotle maintains that, like any material possession slave is a human possession,

(iii) the practice of communism of property and family is highly impracticable in modern society,

(iv) finally, the small Greek city-states have been lacking in any common vision and purpose.

Their continuous fight with each other would not let them unite to face the outside invasion. An instance of this is that the Greek city-states fighting among each other make them so weak that they are unable to face the attacks of Macedon and Rome. This is how city-states comes to an end, inviting their own downfall.

The greatest mistake of Greek city-states has been that they view society and state as one without distinction and differentiation. To them law, custom and convention have been one and the same. The city-state has been state, religion, culture and economy, all in one. MacIver points out that, "under such a theory, no form of life is safe, no religion, no opinion, unless its adherents control the government".

### (d) The Roman Civilization and Large Empire

The city-state of Rome is formed by the union of several tribes occupying seven easily defensible hills on the fertile plains of the Tiber. Because of its location near the only navigable river and its central position it acquires prominence. In 510 B.C. monarchy gives way to Aristocratic Republic. The struggle between the plebeians and patricians results in the introduction of popular sovereignty. The Roman empire is proclaimed under the emperorship of Augustus in 27 B.C., which is characterized by effective centralized administration.

The Romans have always differentiated between the civil rights and political rights. Civil rights means rights to equality before law and political rights means right to participate in the political power, the sovereign body. The empire is maintained by well-knit civil servants, hierarchically organized. They would ensure the freedom of trade and travel with advanced form of communication. Though slavery does exist, they are allowed to possess property duly protected by law. The Roman empire under emperor Augustus is seen trying to rejuvenate society by admitting to it the best elements of the society and putting them in highest circles and the most important positions.

Augustus, the founder of the empire is called the 'first citizen'. It is claimed that he derives power from the senate (assembly) and people. Initially laws are made by the senate but later transferred to the emperor and what he alters becomes the rule. The elements of the Roman empire are, the reasonable taxation, professional army, formation of Diets in the provinces. The provinces are free to develop their life in their own way. Subsequently under Diocletian, the empire is made aristocracy. The empire is unified and provinces become equal to Rome. The civil and military is separated in each province of the great empire to avoid any discontent or rebellion in its any part.

The following era witnesses the disintegration of the Roman empire. For the sake of national unity the individual liberty is completely sacrificed. In fact, unity cannot be extended after a particular point. As MacIver points out, "the soulless efficiency which characterized Roman administration, the depravity of the upper class, the unsound economic basis of the empire, the failure to provide the suitable successor, the religious disintegration and the invasion of barbarian hordes contributed to the downfall of the Roman empire". Getell says, "the Greek had developed democracy without unity; the Rome secured unity without democracy". Despite their statesmanship and intellectual capabilities the Romans fail in their efforts to develop a sound basis of political organization.

Inspite of the above shortcomings, the Roman civilization has left imperishable imprint in the development of Political Theory in general and the concepts of state, law and sovereignty in particular.

### (e) The Feudal State

The downfall of Roman empire results in the erosion of the position of the king and his powers. The powers now begin to be enjoyed by the feudal chiefs. Feudalism provides a transition from highly centralized Roman empire to modern nation state. The feudalism which means the power of the landlords, who possess vast tracts of land and people in their respective areas come under their direct control. These landlords are otherwise known as feudal chiefs. The king's control over the feudal lords is superficial. The feudal system is hierarchical, king is at the top, and at bottom is the serf. In between come the feudal lords, barons etc. who are assessed on the basis of their possession. There is no sovereign authority. Powers are delegated from the top to the authorities below down. With the central authority getting weak in the absence of uniform law and common citizenship, decline of political organization sets in.

The king in the feudal state is challenged by the church as it is able to amass considerable wealth and landed property. The Pope as the head of the state claims superiority over the king. The king also is challenged by the feudal lords who individually act as sovereign in their respective areas. They sometimes join together and dispute with the king's authority. The challenge to the King comes also from the local commons in the town. They assert political authority in their local municipal governments. Barker points out that since the political authority is divided, the king is incapable of enforcing law and order in the society. The organization comes into existence on the basis of religion, class or profession, each having its own law and thus the authority of the state is sidelined.

Feudalism which emphasizes the local customs, traditions and practices rather than uniform, impartial law indirectly contributes to the power and position of the people. This contributes, if not substantially, towards the development of the modern concept of the state and society based on different elements.

### (f) The Modern National States

The modern state first comes into existence in England and hence it expands to Europe, Germany and Italy in the later part of the nineteenth century. The following are the causes of emergence of the modern state:

During the fourteenth and fifteenth centuries Europe witnesses the revival of ancient Greek knowledge based on reason and justice which has been neglected in the Medieval period of feudalism. The reason replacing the beliefs and superstitions results in rationalism. Besides, the monopoly of Latin language is replaced by English, Italian and French. The people start questioning the church and individual rights are given more importance than ascriptive principles. The nationalist feeling based on the common language, history, religion and culture thus results in the development of a modern state. The deepening of ideas of individualism and nationalism, further contribute, in the sixteenth century Europe, to the promotion of modern nation state.

The eighteenth century witnesses a slow transition of monarch to constitutional monarchy and even democracy in large parts of Europe. In the opinion of MacIver, the very influence which has had exalted the king, as they expand, works for his downfall and reduction to the status of "constitutional monarch".

The invention of democracy in the vocabulary of political dictionary, the basic principles of liberty, equality, popular sovereignty and rule of law etc. have been established in large number of nation states in the world at large.

The advent of nation state results in the rise of colonialism, imperialism by colonizing the Afro-Asian states. The second world war, the public opinion, the international law, the concept of human rights, the national sovereignty with peaceful co-existence—they all result in the independence of the colonized states. With the achievement of independence, the sovereign power of the states contributes enough for the international political system.

### (g) The Newly Emerged States of the Developing World

The newly independent states, owing to their long period of struggle for independence come to develop some kind of state consciousness. These states which are basically from Afro-Asian subcontinent, under the leadership of their respective leaders do come to realize that the forms of governments, the western societies are following, are not of much help to their problems. So, these states introduce new forms of governments *i.e.,* military, socialist, mixed economy. They do so to address the problems like poverty, illiteracy, health problems, population control and unemployment rather than personal liberty, popular sovereignty or judicial supremacy etc.

The independence of third world states from the imperialist powers of the European countries with regard to the formulation of constitutions, defining the principles of the states, objectives to be achieved, spirit of nationalism, solidarity among groups and communities to fight for the common causes like independence, poverty and literacy contribute enough perspective to understand the nature of the state, its origin, development after independence and at last the potential of each of its member in the international bodies.

### (h) The Communist States

Marxists refute the concept of nation state because it is based on the class character which holds that all power resides in those who own the means of production. They believe that, the economic factor has been the dominant factor. It is this factor which has been the cause of the changes in history resulting from interplay of material forces. The democracy which passes for peoples power, participatory government, popular sovereignty, in essence is bourgeois democracy. In it the state power is used for exploitation and oppression of the weaker section in the society. Marxists therefore are in favour of complete overthrow of capitalist democracy. Their goal is to replace it by socialist state, which is a transitional state. It will finally result in communism where state shall be liquidated.

The socialist revolution is seen to take place in Russia in 1917. It is followed by many other countries like Poland, Hungry, Cuba, Romania, East Germany, North Korea and China. Based on the total control of economic activity for the people, political power is denied to the people. The socialist state also functions like a nation-state where all the powers are concentrated in the hands of a few people in the name of the socialist party. The people do not appreciate to sacrifice their political freedom for economic emancipation and the economic progress of these states is not impressive. This factor results in the decline of the Soviet Union and change of the socialistic form of government in other parts of the socialistic countries as well.

So, the modern democratic state which is the central theme of politics is not evolved in one day or at a particular point of time or even the development has also not been unidimensional. In fact the state has emerged from different parts of the globe differently depending upon elements such as the geographical locations, the historical facts, the culture, traditions and customs, the preference of life and also the various personality factors incorporated with ideology, plan of action etc.

So, all the variety and versatility of the state emerges in different phases of history in different geographical locations with their peculiar demographic dimensions, contributing thereby enough to serve the present state in its present form.

## Theories of the Origin of the State

It is impossible to trace the origin of the state to a single cause or to a single moment in history. The state has emerged out of primitive communities in different parts of the world in different times. It has developed into several forms over time including its present-day form.

Various writers have tried to explain the origin of the state with the help of different speculative theories which include the following:

(a) The Theory of the Divine Origin of the State.
(b) The Theory of Force.
(c) The Patriarchal and Matriarchal Theory.
(d) The Social Contract Theory.
(e) The Historical or Evolutionary Theory.

The above theories regarding the origin of the state have been discarded as fallacious, although there is some residuum of truth in all of them. One regards the state as a divine creation. Another looks upon it as a child of force. Another considers the state as an expansion of the family, patriarchal or matriarchal. Another finds the contract as the basis of the state, whether the contract is pre-social or pre-political or both. Yet another sees the origin of the state as an evolutionary process, from hoary beginnings to its present day form.

### (a) The Theory of the Divine Origin of the State

The oldest theory regarding the origin of the state is the Divine Origin Theory. The theory receives support from all religions in early times. For instance, Mahabharata enjoins that people request God to save them from anarchy and God appoints Manu to rule over them. The basic assumptions of this theory are as follows:

(a) The state is the creation of God and not a creation of man's will.
(b) King represents God on earth and whosoever resists. His power, resists the ordinance of God.
(c) Kings are answerable for their actions to the Almighty and not to their subjects.

### (b) The Theory of Force

The theory of force has been advanced to explain both the origin and basis of the state. It is based on the old maxim "war begot the king" which is the basic idea behind this theory. A strong member of the tribe asserts his authority over the weaker members. Under his leadership the tribe conquers other tribes. Gradually, the leader establishes his sway over a considerable territory. The warlord becomes the king. The tribe, the kingdom, the empire—this is the chain forged by force.

### (c) The Patriarchal and Matriarchal Theory

According to Henry Maine, society originates in separate families, held together by the authority and protection of the eldest male member. The aggregation of families forms a house. The aggregation of houses makes a tribe. The aggregation of tribes constitutes the commonwealth.

Maine finds the genesis of the state in the patriarchal family *i.e.,* the family in which the eldest member who holds authority is male. Maine unfolds the sequence of development: "First a household, then a patriarchal family, then a tribe of persons of kindred descent and finally a nation". This sequence bears a close resemblance to Aristotle's conception of the origin of the state.

Matriarchal theory is a variation of the patriarchal theory. It has been developed mainly by Mclennan and Morgan. For them, primitive society is marked by promiscuity in which a woman usually marries more than one man. As such kinship is traced through the mother and not through the father. Mclennan illustrates his doctrine with facts concerning the natives of Australia and Malay Archipelago.

### (d) The Social Contract Theory

The social contract theory explains the origin, nature and basis of modern sovereign nation state. It has exercised a profound influence on Modern Political Theory. The theory postulates that state is the product of a deliberate and voluntary agreement. This agreement that people make is in the nature of a contract with one another.

The theory assumes that human history can be divided into two periods—the one that precedes the establishment of the state and the other one that follows it. The period antecedent to the institution of civil society is called "state of nature".

Views vary about the condition of men in the state of nature. Hobbes depicts it as a state of wild savagery in which 'might is right' and the 'life of man, solitary, poor, nasty, brutish and short'. Locke's state of nature presents both a pre-political and a pre-social condition. Far from being a state of anarchy it is governed by law of nature. Macpherson interprets this state of Locke as an "ambiguous state of nature". On the one hand there is peace, order and rule of laws of nature and on the other there is uncertainty and lack of order in the absence of law-executing and law-adjudicating authority. But Locke is in no two minds. For him, it is a state of insecurity, though not of savagery. Rousseau pictures the state of nature as a life of ideal innocence and idyllic happiness. It is a society of natural man, his noble savage, free, equal, independent, self-sufficient and thoroughly contented.

Writers agree that at some stage, people decide to put an end to the state of nature and establish civil society. This is done by means of a covenant. Human laws replace the laws of nature and their violation is made punishable. Thus, under the protection of man-made law, which people agree to obey, they enjoy their social rights. In this way while each loses the natural liberty enjoyed by him in the antecedent state of nature, he gains in return the security, which is now guaranteed to him by the covenant of all his fellows.

While there is complete agreement that the state is a human creation and the result of a contract, the views differ considerably in their answer to the question: what are the terms of this contract and who are the parties to it? Most writers refer to a single contract (Hobbes and Rousseau), while others allude to two contracts (Locke). The first social contract establishes civil society. The second, the governmental contract, creates the government (Locke).

Some writers regard the contract as an historical fact. Others call it fiction or an "idea of reason". For some the state of nature is pre-social and for some others it is pre-political. While some assume that individuals surrender all their natural right available to them in the state of nature to a sovereign authority (Hobbes and Rousseau), others hold that the sovereign is made the guardian or trustee of these natural rights and freedoms (Locke).

### (e) The Historical or Evolutionary Theory

The historical or evolutionary theory rejects the idea that the state is suddenly created at some stage in human history. The state, to quote Burgess, is a product of 'gradual and continuous development of human society'. The state, as Garner puts it, is "neither the handiwork of God, nor the result of superior force, nor the creation of revolution or convention, nor a mere expansion of family". It develops from crude and simple forms into improved and complex ones under the influence of a number of factors.

To sum up, the state is a "growth not a make". Kinship, religion, force and political consciousness coupled with urbanization, class divisions of society, race and nationality, development of science and above all, social nature of man—all these factors, some more prominent than the others, have contributed to the evolution of the state in its present-day form. Aided by the forces of history uncivilized people are seen to emerge out of anarchy and subject themselves to the authority of the state.

## Origin of the State: the Marxist Perspective

The Marxists view politics and state as a part of the superstructure which is founded on the substructure or the economic system of society. F. Engels gives a clear exposition of the Marxist theory of the origin of the state in his famous book *The Origin of the Family, Private Property and the State* (1884).

The origin of the state, for the Marxists, rests on historical materialism. They consider state as a product of society at a certain stage of development. They associate the origin of the state with the division of society into classes with conflicting economic interests which lead to struggle of classes. State emerges as an organization of the possessing class for its protection against the non-possessing class. The State is merely an instrument of exploitation. The dominant class uses it to maintain and perpetuate its class hegemony.

The state is neither a natural institution (Aristotle), nor a creature of contract (Hobbes, Locke, and Rousseau), nor a boon from God (theory of divine origin), nor is it the image and reality of reason (Hegel). Rather the state becomes necessary at a specific historical moment when the society becomes entangled in an insoluble contradiction with itself. A power seemingly standing above society in the form of state arises to keep antagonisms and class struggles within the bounds of order. This new entity is called state. It acts as a moderating influence on the fiercely raging conflict. Despite its role as a shock-absorber in the interest of the dominant class, the state fails to end the class struggle.

The Marxist believes that the state has originated only with the emergence of classes; it has not existed from all eternity. The primitive communal society has been a stateless society. It is with the cleavage of society into classes and owing to this cleavage, the state becomes necessary.

The state of antiquity is a slave-owning state: its purpose is to own the slaves. The latter-day development, the feudal state is the organ of nobility intended to hold down the peasants, serfs and herdsmen. The modern representative state is an instrument of exploitation of wage labour by capital. But if society becomes classless, due to development of socialistic mode of production, thus argue the Marxists, the state will inevitably fall and wither away automatically.

Gramsci examines the relationship between base (substructure) and superstructure. He concludes that state originates through the struggle of three types of social forces—(a) which provide leadership (b) against whom struggle is waged and (c) some auxiliaries or allied forces which lend active or passive consent to the leaders.

In short the state comes into being through domination and hegemony. The state suppresses some enemies, dominates antagonistic groups which it tends to liquidate, or to subjugate, perhaps even by armed force. But indeed it maintains its supremacy by means of intellectual and moral leadership. It gets the consent of people by creating false consciousness through its superior means of propaganda or ideological apparatuses at its command.

Since the state in modern times has founded 'hegemonic rule' through domination and intellectual and moral leadership, it is imperative that a revolution to be successful must break the hegemony and ideological basis of the state at the same time. Gramsci assigns this task to "organic intellectuals" and party organization.

The Marxist theory of the origin of the state is a revolutionary philosophy of change. It envisages the seizure of the bourgeois state by a socialist revolution. In the first phase it is a dictatorship under the leadership of the organized working class who will forcibly capture the state power and establish a 'dictatorship of the proletariat'.

According to Engels, the bourgeois state does not wither away, but is abolished by the proletariat in the course of the revolution. What withers away after this revolution is the proletarian state or semi-state but not before it has established a classless society by building a socialist economy, abolishing private property and creating a non-alienated social man and an exploitation-free social order.

## Function of the State: Liberal, Welfare and Socialist

The modern analysis of the nature and function of the state has been dominated by both the Liberal and the Marxist perspectives. The liberal perspective of the state has undergone a change from the 'let alone', non-interfering state, *i.e.,* negative concept of state to a positive, welfare and all-inclusive state. The seventeenth century liberalism advocates for negative state while the twentieth century liberalism supports and argues for positive and welfare state.

The neo-liberalism is once again seen to be questioning the welfare concept of the state. As against them the Marxist perspective counters every liberal notion of the state. It terms the state as an instrument of a dominant, exploitative class and calls for the establishment of a classless and stateless society through the proletarian revolution. However, after the Russian revolution, the state in place of withering away is seen to become stronger, resulting in statism. It has forced the Marxist scholars to reassess the true nature, role and functions of the state.

In this context, there are the following major perspectives:

1. State as an End in itself.
2. Liberal-Individualistic Perspective: The Negative Liberalism
3. Social Democratic Welfare Perspective: The Positive Liberalism
4. Socialist Perspective

### 1. State as an End in Itself

What does the state exist for? Is it a means to an end or is it an end in itself? What are its proper functions? These questions have been agitating political theorists since ancient times. In fact they are abiding issues of Political Theory and have evoked differing responses. The Greeks had an idealist notion of the state. They regarded it as an end in itself. For Aristotle state is prior to the individual and that it exists for promoting good life. For Plato the state is the supreme entity for which the individual must sacrifice every thing including his family life. The man who does not need the state is either a God or a beast. The individual has no right and existence apart from the state. To achieve good life, the state should control every aspect of an individual's life.

## 2. Liberal-Individualistic Perspective: The Negative Liberalism

The liberal views on the functions of the state have been changing in response to historic compulsions and class requirement of the rising bourgeoisie. The 18th and early 19th century has been an era of "classical economists" who advocate negative liberalism. Negative liberals like Adam Smith advocate the theory of laissez faire or the police state. They assume that production develops on the basis of market mechanism of demand and supply and that the economic system has a capacity for a natural equilibrium. The individual should be left alone by the state to develop his or her own personality in his or her own way. The state is a necessary evil and it can be assigned only negative functions. These functions include: To maintain law and order, to check violence, disruption, disorder, fraud etc. Besides it is to protect individuals against internal enemies and also from foreign aggression. It is also to protect them against each other, that is, from physical injury, slander and personal taint, from robbery or damage, false contracts or breach of contract and finally to protect them against preventable evils such as plague and malaria.

On the economic basis, negative liberalism advocates free and unhindered economic development without state interference. It assumes that economic system will develop through free competition and exchange in society.

On the political and moral basis, it views any increase in the sphere of state as an enemy of human liberty and bar to his self-development. It reduces the self-dependence initiative and drive of the individual and makes him a parasite on the state. This most surely retards his growth.

On the scientific basis, negative liberalism upholds Social Darwinism. It applies survival of the fittest doctrine to society: That those who have the capacity to survive must survive and that the state should not come to the rescue of the unfit.

## 3. The Social Democratic Welfare Perspective: The Positive Liberalism

In later half of the nineteenth and twentieth century, there occurs a perceptible shift in the liberal thinking. Negative Liberalism of earlier time changes to Positive Liberalism which advocates positive state with welfare functions. What contributes to this sudden shift in liberal world view? Titmun aptly delineates the factors: "The forces behind the process of historical development of the welfare state have been varied and complex. Fear of a social revolution, the need for a law abiding labour force, the struggle for power between political parties and pressure groups, a demand to remove some of the social costs of change—for example, industrial accidents from the backs of the workers, and the social conscience of the rich, all played a part". Many more factors such as the emergence of working class movements, enfranchisement of the masses, increasing crises of bourgeois economic systems etc. also have had their share. Mill, Green, Hobhouse, Tawney, Lindsay, Laski, Cole, Barker, Maclver, Bertrand Russel etc. stand out as the champions of the positive state and supporters of the welfare functions of the state.

Positive Liberalism is also known as the Theory of Revisionist or Reformist Liberalism. Likewise, the Theory of the Positive State is also called the 'Theory of Welfare State' and 'Theory of Industrial State'. Unlike the police state of the negative liberals, the positive state performs various social, economic, political, cultural and moral functions. The state is no longer regarded as a necessary evil, but seen as a vehicle of social welfare, helping the all-round development of the citizens. The state can create equilibrium by controlling crises of capitalist economy and appeasing the working classes.

According to Woodrow Wilson, the specific functions of the state may be divided into two categories : fundamental and ministrant. Professor Garner divides them into three categories : essential, natural but unnecessary, and neither natural nor necessary. The usual practice is to divide the functions into two categories—compulsory (essential) and optional (non-compulsory). Compulsory functions of the state include maintenance of law and order, enforcement of justice, defence, regulation of external affairs etc. The optional functions aim at the promotion of general welfare of the society, health, sanitation, medical relief, education and social security, regulation of trade and industry, construction of railways, roads and bridges and a hundred other functions.

Modern state today has become an 'industrial state'. It is penetrating into economic life as a major partner. The public sector is becoming the key sector, various big industries have been taken over by the state. The ideas of post-capitalist economy now hold the ground. By taxing the rich and helping the poor, the state is showing itself as the agent of silent social revolution.

### 4. Socialist Perspective

Socialist state stands for the extension of state activity to the maximum possible limit. It seeks to control all social and economic and cultural activity with a view to achieving the highest level of equality and social justice. The functions of the socialist state may include the following:

1. To establish the dictatorship of the proletariat; the abolition of all class distinctions; the abolition of all conditions of production on which they are based; the abolition of all relations of production which correspond to those conditions of production.
2. To establish planned economy and to organize production according to social requirements.
3. To secure industrial and agricultural development through scientific techniques.
4. To reorganize production on socialist lines.
5. To establish exploitation-free economic system based on social ownership of the means of production.
6. To establish socialist ethos through cultural revolution, education, mass line etc.

7. To set up communes and cooperative or model farming.
8. To provide welfare services to the working class including measures of social security *i.e.,* pension, insurance etc.
9. To establish a healthy exploitation-free social order.

A Socialist State is a transitional state. It must prepare the condition for its withering away after accomplishing the social revolution. According to Marx, "Between the capitalist and the communist society lies the period of the revolutionary transformation of the one into another". A socialist state, which is the revolutionary dictatorship of the proletariat must fulfill its historic destiny. Indeed it must wither away in a classless society.

# 5

# CITIZENSHIP

## The Concept of Citizenship

It is a perennial question in the history of Political Thought to define the ideal relationship between the state and individual, the rights of the individual against the state, liberties of the individuals inside the state and the duties of the individuals towards the state. On the basis of the rights and duties of the individuals enjoyed and discharged within the state, all the members of the political community *i.e.,* the state, are as citizens and non citizens, voters and aliens, citizens and residents etc.

The word citizen and citizenship has been derived from a Latin word 'civic' which means a resident of a city. Citizen, therefore, is one who lives in a city and citizenship is the status of the citizen, what is conferred on the person as a resident of the city. According to Heater, 'He who has no sense of civic bond with his fellows or of some responsibility for civic welfare is not a true citizen, whatever his legal status'. So, citizenship includes the status, a sense of loyalty, the discharge of certain duties and the enjoyment of rights not as an individual but in relation to the state as well.

Today, citizenship provides various opportunities to the individual. One may ask: What does possessing citizenship mean to an individual? What are the benefits one enjoys as a citizen? And in return, what are the responsibilities or duties a citizen has to do? In our country, what is the criteria for citizenship, and why do we think this is so?

Most people being legal citizens of one or another nation state, are entitled to certain privileges or rights. Being a citizen also imposes on them certain duties in terms of what the state expects from individuals under its jurisdiction. Thus, citizens while they fulfill certain obligations to their state, in return, they may expect protection of their vital interests. However, there are two main questions that complicate this simple equation:

1. Which rights are states obliged to guarantee their citizens and on what terms?

2. What happens to those citizens that do not, for one reason or another, have the protection of the country in which they are resident?

The idea of citizenship, when viewed in a historical perspective has various strands of meaning that are relevant even today :

* The origin of citizenship can be traced back to Ancient Greece, when "citizens" were those who had a legal right to participate in the affairs of the state. But by no means everyone was a citizen: slaves and women, in particular, were mere subjects. For those who did have the privileged status of being citizens, the idea of "civic virtue" or being a "good" citizen was an important component of citizenship. This tradition led to an emphasis on the duties that citizens were supposed to perform.
* The association of citizenship with national identity arose naturally from the fact that the legal status of a "citizen" was always tied to a nation state. Hence there was an inherent link between citizenship and patriotism.
* The liberal view of citizenship, which was developed in the nineteenth century, emphasized the importance of rights for all citizens. As the franchise began to be gradually extended, so justice and political rights became a reality for an increasing proportion of the population.
* In the twentieth century, the supporters of "social citizenship" went further, in recognizing that civil and political rights are only part of what citizens ought to be able to expect from the state. The rise of the welfare state in the last century owed a great deal to thinkers who argued that rights of citizens ought to cover their own living and working conditions, rather than just their participation in "high" politics.
* The concept of "multiple citizenship" has been in existence for a while. It allows that individuals may simultaneously be citizens of more than one state or organizing body. For example, with the development of the European Union, citizens of the member states increasingly possess some rights from and duties to the Union as a whole, in addition to their own nation state.
* A final strand in the concept of citizenship, but one that is gaining increasing importance, involves the idea of education. If citizenship in the traditional sense involves enjoying rights and also performing duties, then there is a sense in which citizens may be said to be not born, but created. Loyalty and responsibility, for example, are qualities that need to be learned and cultivated. So, if these are qualities that are essential to being a citizen in the full meaning of the term, then "real" citizens need to be educated–in the broadest sense of the word.

The notion of citizenship as it prevails in different nation states will include elements of each of the six concepts outlined above, may be in varied proportions. If some people emphasize the "duties" element, others give more importance to "rights" or "patriotism", or such other attributes associated with citizenship.

On the basis of the conditions of the state, exercise of sovereign power and the relationship between the individual rights towards the state authority of the state, different theories of citizenship have emerged in different times.

## Theories of Citizenship in Different Phases

On the basis of the conditions of the state, exercise of sovereign power and the relationship between the individual rights towards the state authority of the state, different theories of citizenship have emerged over the different phases of human history:

### I. The Greece Theory of Citizenship

The concept of citizenship was first developed by Aristotle in his book *Politics*, where he justifies the participation in the state activity as a precondition for proper development of individual personality. Aristotle suggests that citizen is a man, who enjoys the rights of sharing in the deliberative or judicial office. Citizens are all those who share in the civic life of ruling and being ruled in turn. Excluded from the category are those who are not 'capable of having a virtuous life'. So the concept of citizen does not include all the people but an exclusive group.

Citizenship contains three elements:

i. a citizen must perform certain functions,
ii. participate actively in the activities of the states, and
iii. the number of persons competent to share in this is limited.

So in Greece, as Aristotle perceives, citizenship is a citizen's right to be claimed and not a status to be conferred on anybody outside the established ranks of the class. It is a privilege and status inherited. All peasantry, women, slaves and foreigners and rural agriculturalists are excluded from the definition of the citizenship. The citizens only can participate in the realm of city state affairs. Only citizens can exercise the ownership of property and act as politicians, judges, and soldiers.

### II. The Roman Concept of Citizenship

The Roman citizenship is based on law, the sole criteria being the equality before law. In the concept of citizenship, religion and riches do not play any role. The Romans introduce the Double Concept of Citizenship *i.e.,* the man can be citizen of his own city as well as Rome. The basic difference between Greek citizenship and Roman citizenship is that the citizenship in the latter case (Roman) is extended to the plebeian—the underprivileged, aliens, traders and merchants. The Roman citizens are based on the enjoyment of the six privileges:

(a) service in the army,
(b) voting in the assembly,
(c) eligibility in the public office,

(d) legal rights of the aliens and appeal,
(e) inter marriage and
(f) trading with the other Roman citizens.

In the fourth century, the Romans are seen also extending its citizenship to the male members of the conquered territories. But gradually class status becomes more important than the rank of citizenship. The landowners and military class is treated with more respect than the poor. In fact the poor and slaves are denied the citizenship.

## III. Citizenship in the Medieval Times

The Medieval times, witnessed many conflicts between ecclesiastical authority *i.e.,* the Pope and the temporal authority *i.e.,* the King. On religious basis all are considered as equal, the creatures of the same spiritual power, God. But the class structures are based on the basis of birth which is hierarchical and rigid. The monarchy and slavery are based on the principles of birth and heredity. The king enjoys the power to rule as a representative of the God on this earth and the people hardly play any role to challenge, change, or influence the king. Though the citizens firmly believe in equality of religion, the political powers are enjoyed by a very few and are based on heredity which runs counter to democratic concept of citizenship and democracy.

## IV. Citizenship in the Modern Age

The Modern concept of citizenship has its own history. It can be traced way back to the signing of Magna Carta in the year (1215) in England and introduction of a bill of rights and representative from the government. The introduction of representative system of government in 1265, the King Simon De Mont Fort, consulted two citizens from each borough, the citizen from each county, and the close associates to devise the important events of the state. In this way the two houses *i.e.,* the House of Lord and the House of Commons are created. Subsequently the House of Commons becomes more powerful.

In these times political philosophers are seen to debate on the best form of government having a generous measure of virtues and goodness towards the fortunes of the state. The important two virtues of the citizen are as follows: (a) martial qualities to defend the state at the time of foreign attack and internal disorder and (b) patriotism in the citizen to ensure that the state does not become tyranny. So in this sense, the martial spirit and patriotism are emphasized as the two essential qualities of the citizenship.

Bodin emphasizes that the citizenship should be based on the principles of eligibility to public office and enjoyments of rights and privileges. For Bodin, the citizenship is based on the mutual obligation between the subject and the sovereign. The sovereign must provide protection and assistance to the subject and in return the subject offer trust and obedience to the state.

The citizenship can be acquired by birth, adoption, enfranchisement and not on the basis of the status. In his theory of citizenship Aristotle subjects the whole body of a citizenship to the single sovereign power inspite of many diversities in the people's faith, language, customs and traditions.

Citizens are distinguished from noncitizens on the basis of the degree of rights and privileges, enjoyed by the individuals by residing in a sovereign state and the obligation and duties tendered by the individuals with the state. The citizenship which is based on the absolute power of the state, the importance of the state as an exclusive association are supported by morality of the state and hence continuance of the state and citizenship. But, the philosophers who are behind the state as a class character, represent a particular dominant class seeking to overthrow the particular class by whatever means and extend citizenship rights and privileges to the members, who are otherwise deprived from political participation.

**V. Liberal Theory of Citizenship**

John Locke (1634-1704) advocates the limited power of the state and restricts its functions in a limited sphere of state activities. His emphasis is on the limited government to be based on the popular consent. He accepts the citizens right to overthrow the government if it fails to protect the rights and liberties of the individuals. The right to life, liberty and property are inalienable rights which he wants to be protected by the state. The state is a means and not an end in itself.

According to the utilitarian school of thought based on the Political Philosophy of Jeremy Bentham and J. S. Mill, the essence of citizenship lies with the individual's rights, liberty, participation in the government and ownership of property. Bentham and Mill argue in favour of democratic institutions. They justify the principle of greatest good of the greatest number, which to them, can be possible in a representative democracy. The utilitarian thinkers perceive that the trustee should allow the ruler to continue as long as the policies are beneficial to the whole community. The possibility of abuse of freedom in the hands of minority can not be ruled out in the utilitarian concept of citizenship.

J. S. Mill shares the socialist belief that the distribution of ownership of property and workers' participation within factory are very essential for citizenship. This is because those who are hardworking should enjoy the benefits of economic production and also political rights. As the participation in case of political life should be in the state, so participation in economic sense should extend to the industry. T.H. Green advocates that the essence of the citizenship is promotion of good life for all irrespective of social class; to foster the moral nature of man and to provide a basic minimum of social welfare. The purpose of the state towards the citizen is to promote and provide an environment for good life.

The twentieth century liberalism comes to equate the concept of citizenship with a state system which is based on the principle of welfare of the people, the values of equality, liberty and justice. The property rights which are confined to a section of people are now extended to all, including the women. The democratic principles including universal franchise that are accepted by the European states as well as other states result in the extension of true and fair citizenship to all irrespective of class, status, gender, faith and colour. The feminists, the critics of the male power of the state and citizenship, justify citizenship for women as women. The socialists advocates citizenship rights for the weakest and most backward sections of people in the society. Their plea is for an equally genuine citizenship for all.

### VI. Marxist Theory of Citizenship

While modern state expands its activities along with expansion of rights to all sections of people based on the principle of equality before law as well as equal opportunities for participating in the governmental activities, the Marxists believe that the principle of equal rights and privileges is not possible in an unequal society. Marxism, conscious about the individual citizenship, considers the rights and privileges contrary to the class interests of the people who hold the state machinery. According to Marx, the bourgeois state, artificially abolishes the distinction based on caste, class, status, education and occupation, when it proclaims that every member of the society is an equal participant but actually it allows private property, occupation and education and thus protects the unequal conditions generated by them.

Though the liberal democratic tradition is a first step when seen in the prism of the earlier stages of historical development, the relationship between the ruler and the ruled, the continuance of the class character based on the principle of private property cannot provide equal rights and liberties to the individuals. Likewise, the people who are exploited by the owners of the means of production can hardly enjoy the rights guaranteed by the liberal democratic state. The limitations of citizenship which arise because of the class division of society can be overcome only through a social revolution in which the class basis of inequality will be overthrown with the concept of bourgeois state. Lenin in 1924, abolishes both the state and citizenship and the sovereign people are identified as proletariat, peasants and soldiers. But, Stalin in 1936 restores both the state and citizenship. The new Soviet Constitution promises a number of rights to its citizens which include the right to vote, freedom of conscience, speech, assembly, inviolability of person and his home etc. These rights are also preconditioned by obedience to the socialistic law which mentions the labour discipline, honest performance of the political duties, strengthening socialistic property and developing socialization.

## Theories of Citizenship: T.H. Marshall and Anthony Giddens

The concept of citizenship means a permanent member of a political society who has certain rights to exercise and certain duties to perform. However, with the growth of democratic ideas, there has been a corresponding expansion of citizenship with its rights and duties. Citizenship today has come to include political, social, economic, cultural and educational rights. Citizenship now is no more confined to political rights but embraces also a set of social and economic rights. Its historical growth cannot be traced back to 'the emergence of democracy', but to 'the origin and development of capitalism'. Citizenship connotes not merely a formal observance of laws, but its eternal association with the society as a whole, including the state. The political theories of democratic government attribute to the concept of citizenship, its nature, rights and duties.

Aristotle's conception of citizenship and its practical difficulty in its applicability in the modern nation states, questions the very foundation of the same. There are two reasons: (i) Aristotle considers citizenship as the privileged status of the ruling group of the city-state, and hence he excludes mass of the people; (ii) Aristotle considers the effective participation in the deliberation and exercise of power as the prerequisite to the status of citizenship. Hence he excludes certain categories like slaves, women etc. from political participation, exercise of franchise or of system of representation.

The concept of citizenship, after having been in long oblivion, comes to the fore with the modern period of capitalism. The dynamics of its areas of operation has been expanded with established principles of democratic ideas and institutions. All citizens are equal before law and thus no person or group is legally privileged. But Marxists criticize this view and argue that despite legal membership of the state, legal equality may not help the disadvantaged people in a class-divided society to participate in the affairs of the state fully and completely. As Marx says: "The state in its own way abolishes the distinctions of birth, rank, education and occupation where it proclaims that every member of the people is an equal participant in popular sovereignty. Nevertheless, the state allows private property, education, and occupation to act and assert their particular nature in their way. Far from abolishing these factual distinctions, the state presupposes them in order to exist."

Yet in certain respects Karl Marx is not in complete opposition to the principles of modern citizenship. While describing its achievements as a big step forward, he insists that mere political emancipation in citizenship is quite inadequate in respect of total human emancipation, in which persons are freed from the determining power of private property and its associated institutions. Karl Marx's theory of citizenship is based on two fundamental questions :

(i) should social inequalities be made irrelevant for membership in the status of citizenship or
(ii) should these be abolished through social revolution?

Marx hopes that the growth of labour movements will ultimately expand the area of citizenship. In this connection there are two opposing views, one by Ossowski who says that as the movement for citizenship grows, it will lead to gradual reduction of social inequalities and the other is by Goldthorpe who says that advances in citizenship are likely to leave class structures intact.

Marshall's systematic and general understanding of citizenship is entirely conventional. According to Marshall (i) citizenship is a status attached to full membership of a community and that (ii) those who possess this status are equal with respect to the rights and duties associated with it. He says that different societies are likely to attach different rights and duties to the status of citizen, since there exist no universal principle of rights and duties of citizenship in general.

Marshall is credited with providing a synthesis of the historical evolution of modern conception of citizenship and rights in Britain. He divides the entire process of the historical evolution of the citizenship into three phases: civil, political and social.

The first phase, Marshall says, takes place in the eighteenth century. It leads to the consolidation of civil rights, such as 'liberty of the person, freedom of speech, thought and faith, the right to own property and to conclude valid contracts, and the right to justice'.

The second phase is seen to take place in the 19th century. It witnesses the consolidation of political rights such as participation in the exercise of political power either as a voter or an official.

The third phase takes place in the 20th century. It involves the creation of social rights expanding from the right to economic welfare and security to sharing in full social heritage and living the life of a civilized being according to the standards of the prevailing society.

Marshall does not regard these three phases of citizenship based on different rights as distinct from each other but interrelated with each other. The exercise of political rights is in consonance with the civil rights such as freedom of speech, a sufficient level of education etc. He sees the three phases as forming part of a dialectical process whereby rights as privileges of feudal system are changed into universal entitlement of all the members of the society. He approaches a near communitarian view as he shifts his view of citizenship from status to contract implying thereby that people possess human rights as persons pursuing their own lives in their own way.

The most important aspect of the theory of Marshalls's citizenship is the relationship between citizenship and social class. In his view, the development of the institutions of modern democracy is seen to coincide, as in England, with the rise of capitalism. Surveying the whole historical process involving class conflict between the capitalists and the workers, Marshall recounts that the passing of Reform Acts, emergence of the workers in trade-unions, the Chartist movement in England, establish the claim of the workers that they, as citizens, are entitled, in addition to political rights already won, to certain social rights as well. The inclusion of these social rights in citizenship rights means, for Marshall, war between citizenship and the capitalist class system. In conclusion he says that social citizenship has not destroyed class, nor social inequalities, but "imposed modifications on class has the result that changes are being made in the class system through the exercise of citizenship rights by the working class movement".

Marshall's theory of citizenship gives rise to more detractors than admirers. Ralph Dahrendorf, for instance, while commenting on Marshall's theory, refers to 'the gradual expansion of citizenship from the legal to the political and social sphere,' but the process is 'still unfinished', he adds. This is because new dimensions of citizenship may be discovered by political organizations and social groups.

Anthony Giddens, taking strong exception to Marshall's characterization of industrial rights affirms the significance of Marshall's analysis of citizenship for Contemporary Social and Political Theory. Giddens criticizes Marshall because the latter (Marshall) treats the development of citizenship as if it were something that unfolded in phases according to some inner logic within the modern world. Anthony Giddens argues that Marshall's understanding of citizenship in three stages is an oversimplification and neglect of the role of politics as well as the state. Marshall, says Giddens, understands the unfolding of citizenship rights from the eighteenth to the twentieth century as a process which is supported and buttressed by 'the beneficent hand of the state'. Giddens assests that, Marshall underestimates the way 'citizenship rights have been achieved in substantial degree only through struggle'. The industrial rights, *i.e.,* the right to form unions or to go on strike are not mere extensions of the civil rights, as Marshall makes out, but, have been achieved through struggle by the workers.

Giddens also attacks the evolutionary conception of the development of citizenship as advocated by Marshall. He states that the battle for civil and political rights are won through the hard way and that the battle continues into the future. Marshall's argument, as against Gidden's is that citizenship has been achieved through gradual process and through continuous struggle which is still going on. He cites the example of the British and other societies and the efforts of the unprivileged to improve their lot. In his view, the groups previously excluded have had to wage fierce struggles for having a better deal.

According to Giddens, more fundamentally each category of citizenship right should be understood as an area of contestation or conflict, each linked to a distinctive type of regulatory power or surveillance, where that surveillance is both necessary to the power of superordinate groups and an axis around which subordinate groups can seek to reclaim control over their lives.

Giddens is in disagreement with Marshall not only on the chronology of the three phases but also on categories of rights: (a) civil rights, (b) political rights, and (c) later social rights. Gidden's argument is that, both civil and political rights have developed together consolidating the capitalist class power, with political rights seen to be aiding and strengthening it. He sees citizenship, thus, rising from the shadow of democracy and, developing with the growth and expansion of state sovereignty. The different types of rights are the result of class struggle. Not only have they been the medium of the extension of citizenship rights, but they are also the basis of the creation of an insulated economy, polyarchy and the welfare state. The forging of state sovereignty may be seen as a critical impetus to the struggle for rights and to the remoulding of citizenship. The increase in state administrative power has also contributed to the creation of new aspirations and demands and to the development of institutions which are responsive to them.

## Citizens in the Modern State

A modern state expects of its citizens to be always vigilant to guard those conditions of life which are essential for the realization of their highest ideal. They must not silently accept whatever the government may put before them. Rather they should always ensure that their voice is properly heard and that things are done according to their own will.

But the criterion of what they demand is not their own selfish good, but the good of the community as a whole. This entails a sense of responsibility on the part of the citizens who after having an intelligent grasp of the trend of affairs of the nation must be prepared to give their unbiased and independent opinion on matters of urgent importance. In order to do so, every citizen must have sound education for which government must make arrangements. In short, a citizen must have freedom as well as preparedness to perform the obligations associated with the exercise of his rights as a citizen.

The population of a modern state consists of citizens and aliens or foreigners. The chief point of distinction between a citizen and an alien is that while the former owes his allegiance to the state, the latter owes his allegiance to another state. The citizen as alien may be living in the state temporarily or permanently but they do enjoy the rights of protection as citizens. They have the right to sue and be sued at all the law courts. If the government fails to use reasonable diligence to protect them from attacks in a riot, insurrection or civil war, they may take recourse to diplomatic interposition through their own government. But the tendency of modern legislation is to accord aliens the same civil rights as the citizens. But so far as political or public rights are concerned, an alien is not generally allowed to vote or to hold public office. Seemingly the status of an alien is like that of a citizen who does not enjoy franchise. But this is not true. A citizen, whether he is enfranchised or not, cannot be expelled from the state whereas an alien may be expelled on the ground of political expediency: Besides, the citizens are, and the aliens are not, liable to conscription into the military service.

## Principles Governing the Acquisition of Citizenship

There are two general principles governing the acquisition of citizenship of a state viz. *Jus Sangunis* and *Jus Soli* or *Jus loci*. The older principle adopted by the ancient Greeks, Romans, and Germans is known as the *Jus Sanguinis*. According to this principle the nationality of the child follows that of the parents or one of them. In feudal times, however, when idea of territorial sovereignty emerged, the nationality of a person was determined by the principle of *Jus Soli* or *Jus Loci*, that is, by the place of birth irrespective of citizenship of the parents.

Thus owing to the combination of these two principles in the United States and in England the children born abroad of citizens are treated as citizens and at the same time children born within these states even of aliens are also regarded as citizens. Owing to the divergence of practice adopted by different states conflicts can easily arise in regard to the determination of nationality of a person. This may apply more to a person having a double nationality. Such an anomalous position may be avoided by two means:

First, a state does not usually claim a person as citizen so long he remains outside its jurisdiction.

Secondly, many states allow such persons residing within their limits the right to choose their nationality on attaining their majority. As regards the comparative merits of these two principles are concerned, it may be said that the *Jus Soli* is illogical despite the fact that the place of birth is easily determinable. It is illogical in as much as it determines nationality by mere accident of the place of birth and does not take into consideration the political allegiance and cultural affinity of the parents of the child. In this respect *Jus Sanguinis* is more logical. But there are practical difficulties in the way of proving the parentage of a person.

## Modes of Acquiring Citizenship

Citizenship of a state may be acquired by one of the following ways :

(1) birth within a place subject to the jurisdiction of the state including an embassy in a foreign country or through inheritance from a citizen father;
(2) Direct grant or conferment of citizenship by the state;
(3) Indirect grant or recognition of citizenship through other modes, such as marriage, legitimation, adoption, purchase of real estate, long residence in the country, ways of entrance into the public service of a state and the acquiring of citizenship etc.

Apart from the process of acquiring of citizenship by birth there is the other mode of acquiring citizenship termed as naturalization. According to Professor Garner, naturalization in the wider sense includes the bestowal of citizenship on an alien in any manner whatever, whether through legal option of naturalization of the children, through the naturalization of the parent, the naturalization of a woman through marriage to a citizen, naturalization through the purchase of real estate, through service in the army or navy or the civil service, through the operation of the law of domicile, or through annexation of foreign territory, etc.

In its narrower sense, however, naturalization refers to the grant of citizenship by a court or an administrative officer on the fulfillment of certain prescribed conditions by the applicant.

The conditions require to be fulfilled before acquiring citizenship differ from state to state. But generally the following conditions are insisted on:

(i) A period of residence within the jurisdiction of the State.
(ii) the declaration of an intention to become citizen is required in almost all the states;

(iii) taking of an oath of allegiance at the time of admission into citizenship;

(iv) the applicant for naturalization must have "behaved as a person of good moral character";

(v) several states require security that the applicant and his family shall not become a public charge.

## Duties of Citizenship

The basis of duties of citizenship is the realization that as members of a community we share one another's life in social and economic affairs, as well as in moral and spiritual spheres. In a society so connected as ours, the action or even the thought of it, influences for good or evil the life of others in society. Consciousness of this idea enables a man to determine his life according to the conception of common good and as a good citizen. He begins to perform all his civic duties cheerfully, though some of them are imposed by law. But a good citizen realizes the highest freedom in discharging all the moral and legal duties of citizenship. For true freedom implies the existence for everyone the opportunity to contribute out of the richness of one's own experience to the furtherance of common good.

The state gives protection to the citizens and confers upon them various benefits. In return for these benefits the citizens owe to state certain services or duties. These duties or obligations no citizen can disregard without causing great injury to himself and to the state he lives in. The interest of a citizen is not something different from that of the state, because the well-being of the state means the well-being of the citizens. Suppose the state is threatened by a foreign enemy. It is the duty of the citizens to take up arms in defence of the independence of the state. If the citizens neglect to perform this imperative duty, the state will be conquered by the enemy. If the state loses its independence, the citizens will be deprived of all their civil and political rights and will become mere 'hewers of wood and drawers of water'.

Similarly, if the citizens fail to show 'eternal vigilance which is the price of liberty', they will become mere chattel in the hands of a despotic government. In the categories of the duties of the citizens, obedience to law comes first. For, law is the basis of order and progress in any community. Even if the conscience of a citizen tells him that a particular law is bad, he must not disobey it. Rather he should try to persuade his fellow citizens of the badness of the law and put the pressure of public opinion on the government to have it changed. It is difficult, if not impossible, to maintain peace and order in a state if every citizen takes law in his own hand. Most of the people are law-abiding by nature. If some are refractory or antisocial in their conduct, the government should force them to obedience to law by punishment.

Another important duty of the citizen is allegiance to the state. Allegiance means the wholehearted service of the citizen to the state. Allegiance implies (a) service in war, (b) support of the public officers in the performance of their duty and (c) performance of other public duties. Every citizen should support the police and the legally constituted authorities in the suppression of riots and disturbances. The public officers alone can hardly control the disturbing elements in society, if the general body of the citizens are apathetic in maintaining order. A hearty cooperation between the public and government is essential. For this the government will have to be responsive to the public opinion.

## Holding Public Offices: An Important Duty

The citizen should not be reluctant to discharge civic and state duties even if it involves a considerable personal sacrifice. Offices like those of jurors, commissioners of municipalities or of a local body have no pay attached to them. Yet there is no dearth of men to fill up these posts. This shows the sense of civic duty in the general body of citizens. In the modern democratic states, most of the citizens, both men and women, above a certain age, possess the franchise. Everyone cannot occupy public office, but everyone who is physically fit, can vote. It is highly important that the majority of voters should exercise their franchise. If a large percentage of people habitually abstain from the polling process, mafia-type political groups and wirepullers will find it easy to get their own nominees elected. Government rests on the will of the citizens. Unless the citizens express their will through their votes, they cannot complain if the government does not function to their satisfaction. Hence the duty to vote is not only a moral and political duty but it is also a necessary condition for the continuance of good government. Franchise should be seen not merely a right but also a duty.

The voter should vote for the very best candidate. He should not be influenced by any consideration of caste, creed, colour or selfish interests. Payment of taxes in time is another duty of a citizen. No government can maintain itself without money. Money must be secured in normal times through taxation. If the rich and powerful hide their income with the idea of evading payment of Income Tax, the government will also find it extremely difficult to maintain the standard of efficiency in civic matters and the burden of taxation may fall more heavily on the poor. Prompt payment of municipal rates should therefore be taken to be bounden duty of the citizens to get high level civic amenities provided by the municipal authorities.

## Hindrance to Good Citizenship

The excellence of a government depends on the capacities of its citizens—intelligence, self-control and conscience. Without these attributes no good citizenship is possible, nor good government. But the average citizen is much below the required standard. He is usually seen wanting in the one or the other of the qualifications. Three major obstacles that stand in the way of the proper discharge of the civic duties are : (1) indolence, (2) self-interest, and (3) party-spirit.

They are great obstacles in the way of the proper performance of civic duties. Duties which do not satisfy the individual self-interest of a man are seldom carefully attended to because in these affairs the spring of self-interest is absent. This is why public duties are sometimes neglected and not considered imperative. Also when a citizen finds that others about him can afford to do without performing their civic duties and that he is but a unit in a million, he too becomes indolent. Therefore, it is no wonder that even the best men are sometimes found unwilling to exercise their right of voting or to serve on municipalities, district boards and other self-governing institutions. Education and the press have done much, no doubt, to decrease indolence. Yet there are several causes which tend to increase it such as an indulgent spirit, due to vast size of the modern states, less dependence in huge communities and other interests competing with politics.

Indulgent spirit has been the chief cause of indolence. In ancient Greece, no breach of duty, either by commission or by omission, was tolerated but rather promptly punished. Hence a citizen has had to perform his duties carefully and on time. He can not turn away from them. Some time, in order to perform his duties he has to be stern and inflexible in his dealings with other citizens. Suppose if he finds a citizen unworthy of his office, the duty of a citizen would be to express his disapprobation of the citizen in office by words and deeds. He should instantly expose his faults. He should take prompt measures to eject or oust him from his office and to punish him. But in modern times, the whole outlook on the duties of a citizen has changed. Manners have grown gentler and passions less violent. This tends to make citizens unreasonably indulgent towards one another even for their laxity in the performance of important civic duties.

Since the Greek city-states were small, every citizen could take an active part in the administration of the state. Contrasted with them, the modern states have a tendency to expand and thus a citizen with a single vote is like a drop of water in an ocean: Yet it does not mean that his responsibility in the administration of the state becomes less onerous, since his share in the same is getting smaller. The fact is that this responsibility increases in proportion with the power that the state wields. The most difficult duty of a citizen is to fight bravely for his convictions even though in a minority. The task gets difficult in proportion to the vastness of the community. Also a citizen is expected to take interest in various departments of culture, viz., art, science, literature, sports, trade and commerce. But these may not be allowed to interfere with the discharge of the civic duties.

The indolence of the citizen towards civic duties may express itself in anyone or many more ways:

* In democratic countries, efficient administration depends, to a great extent, upon the proper exercise of the privilege of voting. The government rests on the will of the people.
* Unless the people express their will through their vote, they cannot complain if the government is not conducted according to their desires.
* Undeniably only people who have leisure, wealth, and brain should be in office to serve the state. But such men sometimes avoid taking part in

public life and even their civic duties. This can be attributed more to their thoughtlessness than to any conscious indifference to the call of duty on their part.

Every citizen is duty-bound to help the governments in putting down insurrections and warding off foreign invasions. Negligence in the performance of civic duty may be ascribed to the following causes :

(a) Want of time and opportunity after their hard study and struggle to earn their bread.
(b) Imperfect education which makes it impossible for them to form an independent opinion on any question of public interest.
(c) Allurement of self-interest which is a dominating passion with men. It is what impels them to abuses which affect the efficient administration of the state. Some of them are: buying of votes may be one such as may result in individual voters voting for unfit candidates.
(d) The tendency of voters often to elect their own men in order to avoid the burden of taxes and to shift them upon other persons, classes and areas.

## Citizenship and Democracy

In a democracy, the source of all authority *i.e.,* the legitimate basis of all power is the collective body of the people, the citizens of the polity. It is through popular sovereignty of the citizens that government by consent of the governed is obtained. A citizen is a full and equal member of a polity, especially in a democratic nation-state. In most democratic states there are established legal procedures by which people without a birthright to citizenship can become naturalized citizens.

Citizenship confers certain rights which are enforceable. Equality before the law is one such basic right of the citizen; other examples include political rights like voting and participating in public interest groups. There may be constitutional distinction between the rights of citizens and of inhabitants of the political community and of those who are and who are not citizens.

The people of a democratic country or nation-state may have various and overlapping identities. They may be based on such factors of society as religion, race, ethnicity, social class, and gender. However, the single identity as being possessed equally by all citizens of the polity, brooks no other civic identity. This core identity is held in common by all citizens. It is based on freely given commitment to certain civic principles and values of the democracy. In countries with widespread diversity in religious, racial, and ethnic identities, there exists a common and overarching civic identity. It is the bond that holds citizens together in a single democratic political order.

The citizens must, in order to have security for their rights, respect the rights of others. They must act to defend their own rights and the rights of others against those who would abuse them. They need to exercise their rights in order to make democracy work. The rights to vote, to speak freely on public issues, and to participate in voluntary organizations, for example, have significance in political and civic life only when citizens regularly and effectively use them.

Democratic nation-states are the only dependable agencies for enforcement of their citizens' rights and for the exercise of their citizens' responsibilities. In fact citizenship is a key to comprehend what democracy is and how it works, what citizenship is, how it is acquired or lost; what rights, responsibilities, and duties it entails; and how they are connected to the institutions in various political systems of particular nation-states, especially their own.

## Some Varieties of Citizenship

Citizenship is membership in a political community, originally in Greek parlance a city but now usually a state. It carries with it rights to political participation. A person who has such rights and membership is a citizen. Generally it is largely coterminous with nationality, however it is possible to have a nationality without being a citizen. One may be legally subject to a state and entitled to its protection without having rights of political participation in it. Conversely, it is also possible to have political rights without being a national of a state. For example, a citizen of a Commonwealth country residing in the United Kingdom is entitled to its full political rights.

Citizenship is also the political rights of an individual within a society. One may have a citizenship from one country and be a national of another country. Nationality, most often, derives from place of birth and, in some cases, ethnicity. Citizenship may also derive from a legal relationship with a state. Of course nationality can be lost, as in denaturalization, and gained as in naturalization.

### Supranational Citizenship

In recent years, some intergovernmental organizations have extended the concept of citizenship to the international level. It is applied to the totality of the citizens of their constituent countries combined.

The ultimate version of supranational citizenship would be some sort of global citizenship. Today the United Nations, though an international body, does not represent this concept directly. For it is seen acting more of an international forum than a structure intended to express individual rights and responsibilities.

### European Union (EU) Citizenship

The Maastricht Treaty introduces the concept of citizenship of the European Union and this citizenship flows from national citizenship. One holds the nationality of an EU member state and as a result becomes a "citizen of the Union", in addition. EU citizenship offers certain rights and privileges within the EU. In many areas EU citizens have the same or similar rights as native citizens in member states. Such rights granted to EU citizens include:

* freedom of movement and the right of residence within the territory of the Member States;
* right to vote and stand as a candidate at elections to the European Parliament and at municipal elections in the Member State of Residence;
* right to diplomatic and consular protection;
* right of petition to the European Parliament; and
* right to refer to the Ombudsman.

The right of residence connotes both the right of abode and the right to apply to work in any position including national civil services with the exception of sensitive positions such as defence or the highest political offices like President, Prime Minister etc.

EU member states also use a common passport design. Most people also use a common format for their driving licences in order to simplify their use within the whole EU.

**Commonwealth Citizenship**

The concept of "Commonwealth Citizenship" has been in vogue ever since the establishment of the Commonwealth of Nations. As with the EU, one holds Commonwealth citizenship only by his being a citizen of a Commonwealth member state. With this form of citizenship are attached certain privileges within some Commonwealth countries:

* Some such countries do not require tourist visas of citizens of other Commonwealth countries.
* In some Commonwealth countries resident citizens of other Commonwealth countries are entitled to political rights, *e.g.,* the right to vote in local and national elections and in some cases even the right to stand for election.
* In some instances the right to work in any position (including the civil service) is granted, except for certain specific positions (*e.g.,* defence, Governor-General or President, Prime Minister).

**Subnational Citizenship**

Citizenship most usually concerns membership of the nation state. But the term can also be used for membership at subnational level. Subnational entities may impose certain requirements, of residency or otherwise, in order to permit citizens to participate in the political life of that entity, or to enjoy what benefits are provided by the government of that entity. But in such cases, those eligible for this membership are also sometimes seen as "citizens" of the relevant state, province, or region. An example of this is Swiss citizenship; if one has a citizenship of an individual commune, thus of a canton and then automatically of the Confederation.

## Honorary Citizenship

Some countries extend "honorary citizenship" to those especially admirable or worthy of the distinction.

## New Citizenship in the Networked Information Economy

The "Emerging Networked Information Economy" today offers vast improvements over the traditionally dominating mass media that is assigned to foster and further public discourse. Dan Gillmor analyzes the impact of citizens at the edges of communication networks who participate in gathering and disseminating news. For him these new activities depict an evolving vision of politics in a networked world.

Undeniably the technological tools are seen shaping the emerging "modern citizen." These multimedia tools include the world wide web, e-mail (personal and lists), blogs, wikis, SMS, mobile connected cameras, internet broadcasting, and countless others. They have expanded the communication network from the mass media's hub-and-spoke model to a truly networked communication infrastructure.

One important aspect of the Programme on Education for Democratic Citizenship is that it is aimed at supporting various youth networks, partnerships, model initiatives, etc., in order to encourage young people to participate in civil society. As a key objective young people form an important part of the target population.

Citizenship is a multidimensional concept. It means membership in a specific nation-state having the formal rights and obligations that this membership entails. Citizenship can also be understood as a status and an identity. Nation-states can set and control the parameters of membership.

Citizenship and nationality are often used interchangeably, for example dual nationality, and dual citizenship. However, nationality signifies membership in a community on the basis of common cultural characteristics while citizenship refers to membership conferred by a state. Citizens of a nation-state may include those who see themselves as part of a single nation based on a common culture or ethnicity, but more often they also include some groups who are seen as outside of national culture and incapable of belonging.

## The Growth of Multiple Citizenship

Today, holding citizenship in more than one country is becoming more common. People may have dual citizenship by operation of different laws rather than by choice. For example, a child born in a foreign country to US citizen parents may be both a US citizen and a citizen of the country of birth.

Historically, most countries have sought to discourage dual citizenship. They aim to achieve this by requiring newcomers to renounce their country-of-origin's citizenship in order to naturalize, and origin countries take away citizenship if immigrants become naturalized citizens of other states. However, such policies are not always enforced.

The increase in mobility, the ability of children to acquire the citizenship of not only their father but their mother, the development of new norms and human rights standards, and changing policies—these all in their own way have contributed to the growth of dual and sometimes multiple citizenship.

"Immigrant dual citizenship" permits immigrants to maintain their origin citizenship while becoming a citizen of the they-opt-to-settle country. These policies are beneficial to the original sending states. The growing importance of remittances and investment from nationals living abroad is a case in point.

Although many countries have had liberalized policies related to dual citizenship, since the September 11 terrorist attacks, some have questioned this policy, especially in cases where a dual citizen has been involved in suspect activity.

In some countries, Germany in particular, dual citizenship has been subject to a great deal of political debate because some see it as weakening of citizenship and/ or loyalty to Germany. Others argue that immigrant dual citizenship facilitates integration in the receiving community by encouraging immigrants to naturalize.

## The Growth of Quasi-Citizenship

Immigrants today are more likely to be members of two states, either as origin citizens and as settled migrants. They are also known as quasi-citizens or denizens of another, or as citizens of both. The rights of quasi-citizens may include long-term or permanent security of residence status; protection from deportation; the right to work and seek employment; voting in local elections; and entitlements to some social benefits. In the United States, legal permanent residents, or green card holders, are quasi-citizens who can live and work permanently anywhere in the country; they can become naturalized citizens once they are eligible. In Europe, the growth of quasi-citizenship is linked partly to restrictive naturalization policies and the growing importance of international human rights standards to which many European countries are signatories.

Internationally protected civil, political, economic, and social rights may not lessen the importance of national citizenship rights. In fact they do serve as an alternative source of some rights and decouple rights from the national context. However, many states do not adhere to them. Individuals face constraints in successfully claiming these rights.

## Supranational Rights

Supranational rights have developed over the past century in British Commonwealth and Europe. British Commonwealth Citizenship is an example of a supranational membership or citizenship system that predates modern regional and political associations such as the EU.

EU citizenship embodies the idea of a common citizenship across all EU Member States. This has a potential that may serve as the basis for a European identity. EU citizenship transforms the notion and practices associated with state sovereignty. A key principle underlying citizenship is freedom of movement, the most widely known such right is of EU citizenship. It restrains the ability of states to exclude foreigners, thereby weakening national sovereignty.

Although some have hailed EU citizenship as a new, post-national form of membership, it remains subordinate to national citizenship. It is linked to the citizenship of a Member State, and Member States still control who can receive their citizenship.

## The Broadening of Citizenship in a Globalized World

With the rise of globalization, the concept of citizenship as a form of membership and identity in one nation-state has changed. The increase in the number of countries allowing dual citizenship and noncitizen rights has made the acquisition of citizenship less pressing.

In addition, migrants' transnational behaviour has made national citizenship less relevant. As against this, the rise of nativism, which in part is the result of globalization and concerns about the risks of immigration linked to terrorism, have reinvigorated debates about national membership and loyalty to one state.

The inhabitants of a democratic country or nation-state may have various and overlapping identities. They may be having their basis in such factors of society as religion, race, ethnicity, social class, and gender. However, the single identity that all citizens of the polity, regardless of differences, possess equally is civic identity. This civic identity is held in common by all citizens. It is based on freely given commitment to certain civic principles and values of the democracy. In countries marked by widespread diversity in religious, racial, and ethnic identities, a common and overarching civic identity has to become the binding force to hold citizens together in a single democratic political order.

# 6

# CIVIL SOCIETY

### The Meaning and Definition

The concept of civil society is a product of the contemporary democratic government. Despite deep philosophical roots, it appears randomly in the works of political philosophers and historians. The concept is very often related with the state and society where the former is influenced by the latter. David Held defines civil society as made up of areas of social life, the domestic world, the economic sphere, cultural activities, and political interaction. They are organized by private and voluntary arrangements between the individuals and groups outside the direct control of the state. Christopher Cand Land states that, civil society is that diverse interest groups and social organizations that are strong enough to provide some autonomy and protection to individuals from the authoritarian and hegemonic tendencies of the state. In this sense he undermines the importance of the market and liberal statutes in preference to independent social life. Jean Cohen defines the civil society as the society in which people are involved in social and political interactions free of state controls, regulations. It entails participation in community groups, voluntary associations, religious groups etc. In this sense the division between the civil society and the state reflects a private and public device. Civil society consists of the institutions which are private, that is they are independent of government and organized by the individuals for their private ends.

Obviously thus, civil society is composed of institutions like trade unions, human right groups, political parties, religious organizations, environmental protection groups, interest groups and pressure groups. The concept of civil society is very well related with the concepts and problems of mass movement and citizenship. Almond and Lipset emphasize the role played by a civil society to make the democracy strong. The object is sought to be achieved by also supplementing the role of political parties in stimulating political participation and increasing citizens political efficiency and skill.

Group associations and individual's activities are the hallmark of the civil society. Almond observes that they help individuals to formulate their interests, put forth their interests before the government, provide information and participate in the political activities.

The meanings attached to "civil society" in the West have been so various. David Held offers a sociological definition when he says that "civil society retains a distinctive character to the extent that it is made up of areas of social life—the domestic world, the economic sphere, cultural activities and political interaction—which are organized by private or voluntary arrangements between individuals and groups outside the direct control of the state." Some may add that, to amount to a civil society, such political interaction cannot be fragmented and excessively particularistic. Rather it has to be in the domain of "the public sphere."

According to a normative political definition, civil society or the commonwealth is 'an assemblage (of men) associated by a common acknowledgment of right and by a community of interests'. This concept of civility is a common ground shared by the state with the rest of society. It has been traditionally grounded in philosophy and it has emerged out of some concept of universal, rational human nature.

In more recent times, however, especially as the philosophical derivation comes under fire, this idea of civility has been used in a more simple empirical or anthropological sense. Civility refers to the political culture very much needed by the normative modern society.

The civil society in modern parlance is often viewed as combining the structure of the modern national state, economic modernization, great interconnectedness with the other societies. It is illustrated by the global economy free enterprise. John Dunn calls it, "the modern constitutional representative democratic republic."

## Genesis and Development

The origin of the concept of civil society goes back to seventeenth century when Roman philosopher Cicero equates it with the living conditions of civilized political community and as inclusive of cities, the legal code, civility and urbanity, the refinement of the civil life and commercial arts. It is defined as opposed to lawlessness. It is a society based on a life governed by rule of law, constitutionalism etc.

Anthony Black observes that the concept civil society has originated from Latin word *Civilie Societas* which means living with the help of civil laws, the refinement of "civil life" and the "commercial arts".

For John Locke civil society is equivalent to political society. Locke perceives the civil society as contrasted with paternal authority and the state of nature. The implication is that the money economy, ready exchange in something like a free market, technological development affording comfort and convenience to civilized and intelligent persons and a law-abiding political power that entails a satisfactory and progressive state of human affairs.

## Factors Contributing Emergence of Civil Society

The following are the factors as a result of which the civil society comes into being:

(a) democratization, (b) reforms of political structures, (c) institutional rebalancing, (d) economic liberalization, and (e) globalization.

(a) **Democratization:** The spread of democratization in recent years have been stupendous. It has changed the political and institutional environment in which civil society organizations operate. In some cases civil society is the locus of active opposition to authoritarian governments. It provides a critical breeding ground for political parties. In some others civil society is marginalized through state repression or withdrawal from active engagement in politics.

But civil society represents an advanced state of human development. It may constitute the locus in which civic values and norms of democratic engagement are nurtured. At the same time greater political freedom can be exploited by self-interested groups to advance their narrow, self-interested agendas. This may exacerbate political conflict and thus undermine governance.

(b) **Reforms of Political Structures:** Democratization entails the reform of existing political structures or the creation of new democratic structures. This involves constitutional redesign, the devolution of power to local government, and formal arrangements to widen public access to policy making. These are the ways to provide space for civil society organizations, engage in new activities, strengthen their interaction with politicians and public officials, and involve larger number of people in active politics and government affairs.

(c) **Institutional 'Rebalancing':** Challenges to the fiscal capacity of states, and doubts about their institutional efficacy and political character, have led to efforts to 'rebalance' systems of social welfare provisions in favour of market and civil society organizations. This has sometimes meant that civic organizations have taken on responsibilities for providing social goods and public services to their own constituencies and wider communities. This has warranted a rethink of their organizational structures, financial base and relations with government.

(d) **Economic Liberalization:** Economic liberalization has brought with it a number of contradictory consequences for civil society. In some contexts it has weakened predatory state structures. It has also limited the scope for rent-seeking behavior by political and bureaucratic elites. It has made some groups as better-placed than others to exploit the opportunities created by liberalization for advancing their own economic agendas. This has enabled some organizations representing societal interests to wield considerable influence over decision-making. The removal of safety-nets and reduction in government welfare spending has given rise to a proliferation of self-help groups and development associations whose mandate is to provide relief and services to people marginalized or impoverished by market reforms.

(e) **Globalization:** The process of globalization has exercised an ambiguous impact on civil society organizations. While like other domestic agencies such as the state and private business, they have seen their autonomy compromised by invasive pressures of global markets, globalization. It is particularly manifest in terms of freer flows of information across national boundaries. This has fostered the spread of 'transnational communities' and an incipient global civil society.

## 1. From Natural Society to Civil Society

John Locke, (1632-1704) one of the contractualists believes in the natural rights which are inalienable and prior to state. In his view the protection of natural rights results in all individuals to go for a civil society which not only is recognized by the state but the same shall protect it.

Locke advocates that in the state of nature there is no authority to make laws, to properly execute them and penalize the violators. The civil society is created by a contract between the people who surrender their three natural powers to the community on the condition that, these three natural rights–life, liberty and property–shall be protected. Locke finds no difference between civil society and political society. For him, civil society is the legitimate political order. The individuals as citizens are empowered by the right to check the state and the state is constricted to possess all material resources to control and influence all aspects of social life and it should be guided by certain moral principles.

German philosopher George William Friedrich Hegel (1770-1831), states that civil society is not formed by contract but it is in the sphere of contract *i.e.,* free association among individuals. Civil society is not the complete entity but one aspect of the political order, another aspect of which is the state.

## 2. Civil Society as Commercial Society and Civilization

The concept of civil society as a commercial society and civilization is developed by eighteenth century thinkers such as Hutcheson, Adam Ferguson and Adam Smith. With the rise of capitalism the focus shifts to production and commercial activity. The money-making becomes a rational exercise leading to a new type of commercial society based on the relations between unrestricted commercial activity and the jurisdiction of a limited state. With it emerges the idea of civil society. The theorists of civil society are seen to argue that the commercial society is a higher form of society. It is a new and a higher form of civilization since it cultivates the arts and sciences. It brings within reach of its members, a life of fullness and choices, driven by uninterrupted production of goods, and services. In addition, it inaugurate a society of civility entailing social order, pacification and restraint. It is a society based on gentle manners and inhabited by men of peaceful disposition. This civil society still is coterminous with the state but it has been raised to a 'civilized society'. It applies to countries of the level of development such as Britain and France.

The theorists of commercial society also maintain that the former is not held together simply by the relations of utility, rational self-interest and the needs of the society. It also points to a realm of personal human bonds, free interpersonal connections, private friendly ties, affection and sentiments. According to Adam Smith commercial society creates a realm of needs and markets. It expands into a sphere of non- instrumental human relations governed by natural sympathy, and the moral affection and social duties.

Commercial society as a higher form of human association cannotes a social, economic and moral order: The practical achievements of this society are an unintended outcome of human actions and not an outcome of utility. Its various social practices and institutions — whether they be family, marriage or property, and government—have not their base in utility alone but also in the sentiments and values which animate them.

Commercial society is composed of integrated individuals knitted into larger societies and connected to more inclusive groups. Non-impersonal market and private social relations come to be founded on more mature basis. As a result, civil society comes to be coterminous with a specific type of state having characteristics of the rule of law, limited government, laissez faire, freedom of contract, market and commercial activities. Even though conflicts do not altogether cease in such a society it comes to represent the growth of higher civilization where society is seen to be polished, civilized and an antithesis of the primitive, barbaric society.

## Hegel on Family, Civil Society and State

After the theorists of the commercial society and civilization, it is Hegel who is central figure in shaping a state-centred concept of the civil society. Instead of the diad of civil society and the state, Hegel introduces a triad of the family, the civil society, and the state. Hegel terms family as the private domain; both civil society and the state as the public domain. Also applying his dialectics *i.e.,* the triad, he terms family as thesis, civil society as antithesis and state as the synthesis. Civil society is to him, one moment in the progressive realization of ethical life realizable in fullness only through the state.

According to Hegel the earliest form of social organization is the family. It is what the Spirit creates on the way to its fulfillment to freedom. Family not only serves the sensual needs of man, but also satisfies his simple wants. In family each partner thinks of others, be it wife or children. The family embodies the rational idea of mutual love and trust. Thus the family, the thesis, is the starting point for Hegel to begin his analysis of the civil society and the state. But despite its civilizing and liberating influence on the individual, its small size and one sided narrow outlook makes it an inadequate agency to satisfy the material and spiritual needs of man who leads purely private life in the family. However, man remains a prisoner of natural impulses so long as he is caught in sensate desires. Hence he cannot be free in the true sense of the term.

Hegel finds antithesis of the family in the civil society. Compared with family civil society is deemed more suitable for large scale impersonal functions of economic and social life needed by the state. So far as the civil society is the social, economic and ethical arrangements of modern industrial capitalist society it is seen to be separate from the state. In this respect it differs both from the family and the state. It is the realm of instrumental relations between isolated individuals and an arena governed by utility and indeed a realm devoid of any moral qualities. The civil society requires skills to develop a trust but it is not the same trust as is in the family. It is bedevilled by competitive interests which are partial, deeply entrenched and having vast resources under their control.

Civil society is, according to Hegel, the state of human development so far reached by advanced people. But unlike family and primitive society, civil society is self-seeking, avaricious, and lacking in warmth and moral cohesion. The civil society is an economic and social order moving according to its own independent principles. It free from the ethical demands of law and political association. This tends to bring all incipient conflicts of civil society to the surface threatening the precarious balance of various competing interests and factors.

Hegel considers civil society as a negative institution which belongs to the realm of mechanical necessity. Being the product of individual's irrational desires it is ruled by ethically anarchical impulses and passions. In such a realm no universal interest or ideal of freedom can be realized. This necessitates another level of sociability and a distinct moral order over and above the family and civil society. It is indicative of the overriding nature of some common interest, represented by the idea of the state and the bureaucratic universal class. The thesis (the family) and the antithesis (the civil society) merge into the state (the synthesis). The synthesis *i.e.*, the state comes to have the universality of the civil society driven by competition and consumer wants and the individuality of the family exuding the warmth, love and trust of small communities and governed by primordial loyalties. It (the state) preserves what is best in the family and the civil society and gives them a unity and harmony.

## Karl Marx and Gramsci on Civil Society

Karl Marx takes his concept of civil society from Hegel and makes it the foundation of his (Marxist) theory of history, society and state. While accepting the Heglian distinction between the state and the civil society, Marx rejects the idea that the state is an all-inclusive political community. The state, as subservient to the conflicting forces of civil society, means 'the economic sphere of production and exchange' in the capitalist society. Since means of production and economic relations are the foundation of Marx's civil society, it follows that civil society belongs to the infrastructure or the 'base'. As against this the state or the political order is the superstructure. The civil society being the realm of economic relations, is the decisive element.

According to Marx, all true history therefore is the history of civil society. Marx sees the emergence of civil society as reflective of the post-feudal separation of the sphere of the state from the sphere of the private production. This is borne out by his statement that 'civil society as such only develops with the bourgeoisie'

Marx calls civil society 'a profane being', basically a terrible lie, with no human element. It is nothing but the animalization and dehumanization of man. It is 'the primary source of conflicts' expressed in the form of general competition, egoism and privatization.

For Marx the resolution of the conflict between the civil society and the state will be achieved through a proletarian revolution and the establishment of a classless, stateless community of free cooperative producers. From the false and uncivil society of the individual of the bourgeois society, Marx presents the possibility of genuine humanity, the new human society or 'the socialized humanity'.

Combining Hegel and Marx, Gramsci identifies civil society neither with the 'state of nature' nor with the industrial society but with the factor of 'hegemony inclusive of both *i.e.,* the political and cultural leadership.' Reflecting on the question why capitalism survives when there are objective conditions for its transition to communism, Gramsci sees the answer in the superstructure which he divides into two components : First, 'civil society, that is, the ensemble of organisms commonly called 'private' , and the other 'political society' or the state. These two elements determine the function of hegemony which, according to Gramsci, the dominant group exercises throughout the society by coercive as well as ideological means.

Civil society, for Gramsci, belongs to the superstructural sphere and includes all the material relationships as well as ideological and cultural relations. They comprise not only the whole commercial and industrial life but also the spiritual and intellectual life including institutions such as church, political parties, trade unions, universities, the press, the publishing houses, voluntary associations of all kinds. They are instrumental in disseminating the ideology of the dominant class. This is their way to ensure the cultural and spiritual supremacy over the subordinate classes who consent to their own subordination. The state uses the coercive power only when the ideological factors do not avail.

Comparing civil society with the 'second line of defence' in the army, Gramsci by using a metaphor from the army, says that civil society is "like the trench system of modern warfare. In the war it would sometimes happen that the field artillery attack seems to have destroyed the enemy's entire defence system whereas it has only destroyed the outer parameter; and at the moment of their advance and attack, the assailants would find themselves confronted by the line of defence which was still effective. The same thing happens in politics". Viewed in this light the civil society in the form of trenches forms a second line of defence of capitalism against the revolution.

According to Gramsci, the civil society does provide the industrial workers a chance to gain 'hegemony' and prepare the way for revolutionary struggle. But where the social order rests on the consent of the governed and ideological integration, the strategy of revolution cannot be an imitation of what happened in countries like Russia or China.

Marx and Gramsci differ on the question of the origin and purpose of civil society. While Marx's civil society refers to the infrastructure, the totality of material conditions and relations or the base, Gramsci considers civil society as a part of the superstructure since it embodies ideological and cultural hegemony.

**Liberal Individualistic Perspective of Civil Society**

Within the liberal tradition, a shift is noticed away from the total notion of civil society to the individual citizen in the nineteenth century. For example, Alexis de Tocqueville develops a society-centred notion of civil society. He, while maintaining a distinction between the civil society and the state, introduces a third term *i.e.,* the associations within the civil society. According to De Tockeville while political society and the state are institutions about matters of government and power, civil society involves the private relationship between the citizens and their nonpolitical associations. In the context of American democracy, Tockeville writes that it is not the conflict and disorder generated by the particular interests in the civil society but rather the growth of a new type of state despotism which is the real danger to democracy. He insists on active participation of the people in the egalitarian institutions and civil associations, as well as in the relevant political organizations. Without such political participation there is no way to maintain the democratic character of the political culture as well as social and political institutions. In this connection he highlights the role of the voluntary associations. He sees in them the means of contributing to the effectiveness and stability of democratic system of governance. He also sees in pluralistic and self-organizing civil society independent of the state as a fundamental condition of democracy.

In the liberal tradition, apart from civil society there are a vast array of intermediate bodies which are seen to lie between the state and the individual. In these bodies citizens are seen to freely associate with each other on issues of common concern and act politically to realize the shared interests. These associations can be 'churches, trade unions, neighbourhood associations, cultural associations, clubs' and the like. Civil society in this sense, may be seen a realm of free choice, personal freedom and individual responsibility. Unlike the state which operates through the coercive authority, civil society allows the individuals to exercise free choice and create an order of their choice. Viewed thus, a healthy civil society is an essential adjunct of liberal democracy. Now all liberal opinion is centred on the question how to minimize the scope of public authority and maximize private space.

Another powerful advocate of civil society is Hennah Arendt. She argues that free associations which lie between the state and the individual can prove to be vital bulwark against totalitarianism. Through participation in these grassroot and small face-to-face associations, the citizens are enabled to act along with their fellowbeings for the common good. A civil society can thrive only through plurality of associations. It is what pluralism means. Thus opportunities to participate in the associations of the civil society rescue the individual from privation. They instill in him the virtue of public spiritedness and sense of cooperation. This is how civil society performs its educational function.

Habermas too sees civil society as crucial to the successful implementation of public policy. According to Habermas when previously voiceless individuals associate, they can articulate the needs which have hitherto eluded even the policy makers. Public policy, even the best one, is foredoomed for the lack of participation. Thus to remove the gap between policy formulations and policy implementations partnership between the state and civil society is a necessary condition.

Diamond delineates at length how the civil society helps in the consolidating of liberal democracy through performance of the following functions:

1. Civil society limits and controls the state power. It compliments and improves the state by enhancing its democratic legitimacy and effectiveness;
2. civil society stimulates political participation and promotes democratic skills among the masses;
3. civil society helps promote democratic political culture, norms and values informing it;
4. civil society may structure multiple channels beyond political parties to articulate, aggregate and represent different interests, as well as myriad pressures;
5. civil society generates and balances a wide range of crosscutting interests thereby reducing political polarity;
6. civil society recruits and trains political leaders, policy makers and publicists;
7. civil society carries out such functions as election monitoring, political campaigning and disseminating information;
8. civil society helps to achieve economic reforms in new democracies. It does so by disseminating information and mobilizing demand for such reforms;
9. civil society offers services and develops techniques of conflict mediation and resolution, and
10. civil society strengthens community initiative. thereby reducing burden on the state.

In short, civil society is seen to act as a (i) zone of contestation *i.e.,* a force to bring down authoritarianism, and (ii) as a protector *i.e.,* a method and framework to safeguard the stability of democracy.

## Revival of Civil Society – Contribution of East European Intellectuals and Neo-Marxists

The theories of civil society in Eastern Europe after the fall of the communist, regimes have come to equate civil society with conditions of freedom, pluralism and participation on the one hand and a commitment to preserve some limited amount of social independence and give it an institutional expression, on the other. The enterprise entails rebuilding of associations including political parties, movements, unions, business associations, publishing houses, churches and cultural associations and the like, with a view to reviving the national, ethnic and religious identities which have remained dormant under the communist rule.

The Western liberal theorists of civil society proceed to suggest more and more new reformulations. For example, the scheme with which Cohen and Arato seek to replace the traditional state and civil society dualism is by a tripartite framework of civil society: Civil society in this framework is equally distinguished from both the political society and the economic society. Their quest is for universal and pure definition of civil society. This may involve creating institutions of civil society, the public sphere and new social movements unspoiled by the influence of political power and money conflicts. Habermas visualizes an emerging public sphere between the realm of public authority (*i.e.,* the state) and the private realm (the family). It consists of private individuals who assemble here to debate among themselves about the regulation of the civil society on the one hand and the conduct of the state on the other.

Civil society also encompasses the institutions of sociability. They are seen to express themselves in the social movements through the communicative action and strategy of self-mobilization of voluntary associations outside the realm of state and economy. Viewed in this light civil society can provide corrective to the aberrations of the private and public sphere, state and economy and repair the wrong of excessive disruptions and bureaucratization as well as ensure probity at all levels of the participation and decision making.

### Civil Society: The Contemporary Perspective

Today, civil society has become the dominant note in the contemporary debates which tend to view it in opposition to the state. However, the critics of civil society have underlined certain risks to the overall health of the society. These risks concern one's identity as a member of a particular group of the civil society and may colour his thinking and approach to the common good. Yet public policy needs may not correspond with social interests since there is no guarantee that participation in civil society will ensure an increased development or inculcation of character among the members so that they are guided by common interests. The risk is even much greater in a divided and fractured civil society lest it should further contribute to segmented nationality and partisan response.

Will Kymilica talks of the various risks that many civil society associations may face, most pernicious of them being the trait of disruption which militates against the values of liberal democracy. Since many associations are built around subservience and authority instead of equality and freedom of individual, these associations promote virtues which directly run counter to the liberal values. Moreover, some associations of the civil society may embody illiberal norms which may be used to restrict the membership in illiberal and unacceptable ways. Such imposition of unjust norms among its members is antithetical to the values of liberal democracy. In this context the point at issue is whether such associations of the civil society may be allowed to continue any further or how to restore them back to their true state of health where organized interests may aid good governance instead of creating insurmountable obstacles.

## Civil Society and Good Governance

The contribution of civil society to good governance is enormous. It is essentially concerned with the means by which organized interests seek to influence and engage with state institutions. In doing so, they help strengthen state legitimacy. They also build relations of trust between public officials and ordinary citizens.

While it is true that not all civic organizations engage in activities designed to promote better governance, however there are some who actively conspire to undermine good governance. They seek to do so by aggressively pursuing self-interested goals or by fomenting violence against the state or other organized groups. Yet there are others who consciously seek to evade or disengage themselves from formal state structures through various forms of collective action in the informal economy.

The contribution of civil society to good governance may be summarized under four heads:

(a) public policy and decision making;
(b) enhancing state performance;
(c) transparency and information; and
(d) social justice and the rule of law.

The role of civil society organizations in mobilizing particular constituencies to participate more fully in politics and public affairs is well acknowledged. It is commonly agreed that wealthy and socially dominant groups are better able to organize themselves. They can do so because they have superior resources and social status. This enables them to exert considerable influence over public policy. In addition, they can form and support intermediary organizations to represent and articulate their interests in an effective manner.

Poor and socially disadvantaged groups usually exert little influence on public policy: marginal peasants, sharecroppers, landless labourers, artisans, informal sector workers, urban slum dwellers, disabled people and certain categories of women usually exercise much less influence over public policy and resource allocations. As a matter of fact higher rates of political participation often result from institutional innovations such as democratic decentralization. They are designed to promote local involvement in decision-making. But the relevance of these innovations will only be visible if grassroots organizations and social movements are able to organize the poor to articulate their demands at local and higher levels.

Civil organizations are said to contribute to better governance. They can do so by improving transparency and increasing the availability of information about the making and implementation of government policy. Major activities from within civil society are designed to promote these goals that include the discovery, publication and dissemination of information about items of legislation as well as legal provisions. Further they may do so by highlighting public expenditure allocations, the implementation of policy and programs, and special enquiries. The process is hastened by ensuring that such information is directly published and circulated by groups within civil society, or distributed through new or existing media outlets.

These groups within civil society may also seek to mobilize citizens to pressure governments into implementing existing legislation and by taking action to indict public officials who are involved in malfeasance. Efforts to enhance transparency in government may contribute to poverty reduction. This can be secured by helping citizens monitor the delivery of development resources and in the process stem the appropriation of resources by bureaucrats and local elites. This suggests a more activist role for civil society. It will entail civic actors becoming proactive to back up information and dissemination activities with mobilization and public advocacy work.

Civil society may contribute significantly towards the quality and effectiveness of public services and expenditures which are integral to good governance. They may do so by working directly with government in shaping, financing and delivering public services in a variety of ways. These may take the form of public-private partnerships, civil society organizations in this collaborative relationship can work closely with state institutions to design and provide health and educational services. They can achieve better state performance by mobilizing funds from among client groups and other sources. They can do so by providing services directly, and by monitoring quality and coverage. State institutions can acquire greater legitimacy and improve their performance by developing responsive working relationships with civil society. The process can be hastened by drawing on reservoirs of social capital built up in local communities.

Admittedly effective state-society partnerships arise in the context of a particular set of institutional and political conditions. They may be context-specific and not easily replicable. These conditions and the types of groups can form such partnerships in such circumstances as are conducive to fostering synergy.

### Civil Society and Democracy

The link of civil society and democracy goes back to the early liberal writers like De Tocqueville. The conceptual development in the twentieth century can be ascribed to the works of Gabriel Almond and Sidney Verba. They identify the role of civil society in a democratic order as vital. They argue that the essence of civil society provides better awareness, more informed citizenship and better voting choices. Besides it ensures a better participation in politics and holds government to account better as a result. Robert Putinam stresses that the non-governmental organizations in civil society are very vital for democracy. They build the social capital, trust and shared values. They help transfer social capital into the political sphere, hold society together, and help understand the relationship of society and various interests within it.

## Civil Society and Globalization

There are two contradictory views about the civil society and globalization. The one line of critics argue that the globalization is antithetical to civil society. They see it acting beyond boundaries and across different territories. The others see globalization as a social phenomenon. They see it bringing with it classical liberal values. They envisage that this will inevitably lead to a larger role for civil society at the expense of politically derived state institutions.

Among the examples of civil society institutions we may list the following:

* Non-governmental organizations (NGOs)
* Private voluntary organizations (PVOs)
* People's organizations
* Community based organizations
* Civic groups
* Civic clubs
* Charities
* Social and sports clubs
* Cooperatives
* Trade unions
* Gender, cultural and religious groups
* Policy institutions
* Consensus organizations
* Religious organizations
* Environmental groups

The above institutions, comprehensive enough though, do not exhaust their continually expanding scope and area of activities.

## Strengthening Global Civil Society

The idea of global civil society has its roots in Europe. While many organizations may continue to be western dominated, it is not true to say that it is the sole preserve of Europeans or Westerners. Today, civil society exists in all regions of the world. But for obvious reasons it tends to be stronger in more democratic and liberal states than in authoritarian and illiberal ones.

More prominent are global civil society movements that are working to promote gender equality, human rights or democracy. However, rather than imposing a set of western values, or being perceived to do so, progressive global civil society organizations should aim to work in solidarity with local partners in defence of universal principles and standards. This has sometimes been described as 'bringing the global home'. This may help local civil society groups to hold their national governments to account for the agreements they have made in international forums, for example on issues such as women's rights or environmental standards.

Global civil society has been traditionally most visible in its mass demonstrations aimed at global institutions like the World Trade Organization (WTO), the International Monetary Fund (IMF) and the World Bank. In 1999 in Seattle, for example, coordinated protests from a wide range of organizations and movements involved around 50,000 people in over 500 protest groups – with similar protests in cities in more than 20 countries. These protests hastened the collapse of the Seattle trade meeting. In addition, the annual gatherings of the World Social Forums (also known as the Porto Alegre Forums) have provided a space to criticize the actions of the International Financial Institutions and other global institutions on issues like trade.

Global civil society actors and movements have also put new issues onto the international agenda. They have played a key role in providing a more competitive pool of policy ideas, as also provide new research and information to mobilize public opinion around an issue. Some campaigns have succeeded in identifying issues previously ignored by states. For example, in relation to environmental standards, including tackling climate change, it is unlikely that the international agreements signed up to in last 20 years would exist without the advocacy, campaigning and intellectual input of NGOs and others. There are many examples of where the efforts of global civil society have brought about changes in national and international policy. The Jubilee 2000 campaign is an obvious example of successful global civil society activism. Drawing on an international movement of organizations, based in Europe, Africa, Asia and Latin America, it put pressure on politicians in developed countries to reduce the debt burden borne by some of the world's poorest countries. These efforts played a significant role in securing debt relief concessions from G8 countries, including an expanded Heavily Indebted Poor Countries (HIPC) initiative and bilateral commitments to write off debt.

Global civil society makes a range of other contributions to global policy discussions. They can be used to counter 'global hypocrisy'. Global civil society networks can play a role in holding governments and international institutions to account for the commitments they make and for the inconsistencies of their actions and policies.

Global civil society can also be an important source of support (both moral and practical) to people living under authoritarian regimes where local civil society is repressed. Indeed, the rise of global civil society is often associated with the fall of authoritarian states in Eastern and Central Europe in 1989 and with the rise of democracy movements across Latin America in the 1970s and 1980s. However in general it is important to acknowledge that governments, global organizations and the private sector are much more powerful and influential than civil society groups. But it would not be correct to assume that global civil society can be an alternative to national governments or global institutions, or can it fully be a substitute for the formal procedures that legitimatize global intergovernmental institutions and global decision-making.

Another point to recognize is that global civil society organizations, almost by definition, ignore the trade-offs between political priorities. Global civil society actors rarely face the difficult task of balancing competing demands, which is the business of political parties and governments. Global civil society while it can make an important contribution to politics and policymaking, it should not be seen as a replacement for functioning political parties and systems.

One of the potential strengths of global civil society is the role it can play in bringing the voices of marginalized people into global debates about public policy, particularly people from the global south. But it can only do this effectively if global civil society organizations allow the voices of the global south to be properly heard.

Global civil society organizations and movements have made important contributions to some aspects of global policymaking and the working of global institutions, particularly on issues of human rights, development and the environment. But their expertise is still underused, and the processes for consulting global civil society, by global institutions, are still inadequate.

In the context of global civil society, it is important to 'connect the global with the local'. This may call for locally designed strategies for globally agreed goals like the Millennium Development Goals and emphasize the importance of engaging with local and national civil societies.

# 7

# IDENTITY

## What is Identity

Identity as a concept is of very recent origin. Its roots lie in the current upsurge in demands for recognition of cultural, religious, ethnic, racial or national identities. The assertion of identity on the part of people can, on the positive note be regarded as "liberation movements". They can be viewed as strategies devised by certain groups to challenge oppression and injustice. By proclaiming that they are different, they are infact seeking to rediscover the roots of their culture. In so doing they wish to further cement their group solidarity and aspire to political self-determination. Through various necessary and legitimate attempts they seek to escape from their state of subjugation and enjoy a certain measure of dignity.

But the negative aspect of their claims of identity manifests in their involvement in militant action for recognition. This tends to make such groups more deeply entrenched in their narrow sectarian attitudes. It makes the cultural compartments into which they are divided even much more watertight. The assertion of identity then starts to turn into self-absorption and isolation. This can be a prelude to any time sliding into intolerance of others. Fired by negative ideas of ethnic "cleansing" and xenophobia, racism and violence, such militant assertiveness can work havoc.

Human societies and their cultures at large have been responsive to change. Isolated societies unaffected by historical events are exceptions. However, such societies have seldom prospered.

So the fact of being different from others is at the heart of a group's identity, though every group may contain individuals who share many points of resemblance with people in other groups. According to the cultural aspect on which emphasis is placed (religion, culinary habits, dress, language etc.), groups shift frontiers and overlap. As a result the limits become more blurred, and distinctions between one's own and others' identity become hazy. In fact they may be seen to be a matter of degree or of place in the same continuum.

## Characteristics of Identity

The problems of identity are related with the following three things :

(i) what men do for living,
(ii) what group, community or region they come from, and
(iii) what commitment and relations they have with other groups.

In short, identity has three characteristics: competence, community and commitment.

First, identity is competence which is usually expressed in a job, role, vocation or a profession. Competence is established when ability is matched by social recognition. Assertion of competence is not possible unless we have others who are persuaded to accept it.

Second, identity is how people see themselves as natives of a particular region; or subscribe to a certain ideology or a particular religion to which they seek to conform; or belong to a particular ethnic community etc. This is what is meant by the community element of identity.

Identity is based on two factors: (a) Racial ethnicity and (b) National generality. For example a person can be a Tamilian Hindu (ethnic) and an Indian (national).

Third characteristics of identity, refers to commitment which one may have to others—whether through marriage, partnership, familial responsibility, team loyalty or other forms of mutuality. These three indicators of identity are quite distinct but consistently applicable to individuals, groups, classes, races and cultures.

## Identity in Political Context

In political context, identity has much to do with self-identification of individuals, groups, associations and classes:

First, as members able to distinguish themselves from others on the basis of competence, community or commitment.

Second, competence to denote their distinctive character in words, gestures or practices. This provides a rationale and reassurance of existing as they should exist *i.e.,* a distinct entity and their sense of belongingness to it. For example, the emergence of the national identity. The Indians during the British rule had a growing sense that they are Indians who belong to this land, with a natural feeling of living together, as sharers of common interest, common history and common destiny. This is what contributed to a growing sense of national identity among them. The search for identity has been at the back of different nationalities and ethnic groups during the twentieth century.

## Nature of Identity

The term identity describes a wide range of political struggles concerning legal, political and constitutional recognition and accommodation of the identity of individuals, groups, immigrants, refugees; ethnic minorities, cultural and religious minorities, nationalities within the nation-states, indigenous peoples, non-European cultures and religions against the Western imperialism etc.

Identity refers to the various forms of activism, politics, theorizing and other similar activities. Identity involves members of a social group who have shared experience of oppression. It involves groups that engage in identity politics and include those that are organized around ethnicity, nationality, race, religion, gender, environment, disability etc. Without sharing identity of a particular oppressed group, it is not possible to understand the specific form of oppression. As a result it may not be possible to find adequate solution to the problems that members of the group face. Identity politics, oppressed groups and struggles for self-determination have strong correlation.

Every civilization is an ensemble of identities that inhere certain progressive values so crucial for their survival. Every culture elicits and rewards the kind of competencies needed for survival. Besides it negates all such competencies as are destructive of and damaging to group solidarity. The injustice and unfreedom which are distinctive markers of identity politics can be overcome through hard bargaining and negotiation, reciprocal recognition and accommodation. There are cases when an alien identity is imposed on the natives or aborigines through a process of subjection, as some writers believe, was done by the *Aryans* over the *Dravidians*, or through a process of assimilation as in America in case of native Indians or through marginalization as in case of shudras or scheduled castes and tribes in India. Invariably the colonizers term them as 'lower', 'less developed', 'inferior race' etc. Anything that demeans and disrespects the identity of various groups through recourse to racism, linguistic and cultural domination, imposition of dominant culture, assimilation or marginalization is unjust and gives rise to movements of assertion of identities with redoubled force.

The present identity movements also base themselves on socioeconomic, cultural and religious factors in relation to groups, races, classes, immigrants, refugees, the victims of poverty, unemployment etc.

In short, the word 'identity', identity politics thus signifies 'the quality or condition of being the same; the absolute or essential sameness, oneness . . . individuality, personality . . . The condition of being identified in feeling, interest, etc.' The term perhaps derives from the discipline of psychoanalysis where the problem of 'identity' has long been the focus of many discussions and debates.

**Range and Dimensions of Politics**

Viewed thus, identity politics concerns the struggles of the oppressed groups against the exploitation, domination and inequalities. Some struggles such as against casteist oppression have histories which predate the emergence of the concept of identity. Ever since Fanon interprets decolonization as a struggle both against the identity imposed by imperialism and an identity imposed by the dominant national elite after independence, these struggles have come to be termed as struggles for identity.

These identity related struggles have the following three characteristics:

**Firstly,** heterogeneity and diversity. Identity politics does not concern separate and internally uniform minorities, cultures or nations each seeking its separate recognition, but including even those articulated demands that are competing and having overlapping allegiance. They may pertain to struggles for assertion of identity based on indigenousness, nationality, culture, region, religion, ethnicity, language, or gender. A minority or a language group demanding recognition from the larger political entity may be faced with several other minority groups voicing similar demands for protection and recognition.

The identity related demands may be crossed by ethnic, national, linguistic, cultural, religious differences among people belonging to various groups. Judged in this light, diversity or the multiplicity of overlapping identities and their corresponding allegiances and loyalties constitute important characteristics of identity.

**Secondly,** the demand of identity or recognition may be articulated by a particular group of people who may rally to defend and promote this identity related differences, hoping that this identification can be sustained for generations. This characteristic concerns priority granted to one identity, the way it is articulated, the form of recognition and accommodation it seeks to achieve. Despite this there may always remain a scope of reinterpretation and recognition by the bearers of that identity over time. For legal and political recognition, there may be ongoing tripartite negotiations: (a) among the groups struggling for recognition, (b) between them and the groups to whom the demands are made, and (c) whose identity comes into question as a result of struggle whether they like it or not.

**Thirdly,** the concept of identity involves both theoretical identity and practical identity, *i.e.,* a form of both self-awareness and self-formation in relations to and with others. It lets a particular group find the life worth living which others recognize and respect. In this sense practical identity is always relational implying the mode of conduct while living in the world with others. Such practical identity is acquired, sustained and renegotiated through a dialogue with those who share it and those who do not. When in respect of identity diverse citizens in a society live in mutuality, adjustment and cooperation.It is under some form of mutual recognition and accommodation, the question of identity remains dormant.

## Identity Formation and Demands of Identity Related Differences

Every civilization is based upon differences of race, religion, caste, colour, gender etc. Politics is an act of domination and submission. It is the process of identity formation and its defence therefore have a flip side. The manifold discriminations. It includes the myriad modes of oppressions and varieties of chauvinisms and sectarianisms practiced by the dominant groups, elites or classes. These have been identified as the principal causes of identity formation.

The anticolonial struggles against the imperialist powers during the first half of 20th century and the democratic politics based upon freedom—civil and social—

spurred the different nationalities, races, groups and classes to fight for the recognition of their identities. The national liberation movements or the group movements based on specific issues such as the cause of woman, minorities and dalits etc. may add momentum to identity struggles.

The purpose of identity politics is to (i) condemn the imposed identity, and (ii) to justify the recognition of an identity related difference. While suppressed nations and indigenous people demand the right to self-determination, women want equality with men, and suppressed language groups put up their demand for freedom from the dominance of certain language groups. This multilayered demand for identity leads many experts to reconceive national identity along the lines of diversity and public negotiations.

This articulation of identity related difference centre around three types of demands. They are: (i) Cultural Diversity, (ii) Multicultural Citizenship and (iii) Multinational Constitutional Associations.

The first type of demand which relates to cultural diversity calls for mutual recognition and respect for identity related differences in the cultural field. Such a demand has as its aim, to overcome racism, ethnocentrism, linguistic, and cultural stereotypes. It aims to inculcate and foster awareness and respect for diversity in all areas of life and society to let all members interact with each other in a spirit of mutuality and esteem.

The second type of demand which involves multi-cultural and multi-ethnic citizenship relates to right of participation in public, private and voluntary institutions. It seeks to recognize and accommodate rather than exclude the diverse identities of citizens. Several gender-based movements, as well those involving linguistic, cultural, ethnic and religious groups or minorities participate in the same institutions as the dominant groups. They very much like to protect at the same time their identity related differences. They have preference for schooling in their minority language and culture. They prefer using their language in the political and legal institutions and raising demands for reform. They are always working towards restructuring of the representative institutions to seek fair representation of their identity-related diversities and differences. Also they may observe their distinctive religious or cultural practices in public without any let or hindrance. They may seek constitutional safeguards for religious freedom. Multicultural policies in England as well as in India, the policies pertaining to Muslims and other minorities in India, USA, UK, France, Germany etc. are a few examples of multi-culturalism.

The third type of demand concerns the suppressed nationalities within the multinational societies. In it these groups and the indigenous people want recognition of their identity as 'nation' or as 'people' with the right for internal self-determination. In addition, they want to have their own autonomous political, legal institutions in some areas as per the international law. They consider it as a necessary safeguard to protect their identity and thereby letting them live their life in accordance with it. They are all the time haunted by a sense of insecurity lest their identity—related difference should be assimilated by the majority. This type of identity politics has given rise to innovations in nation-building and federalization of multinational political associations. While some earlier suppressed nationalities do enjoy some regional autonomy, others too have shared sovereignty. Still others of varied multiculturalisms, flexible federations etc., despite the complexity of demand, have to convince their own people through public dialogue that they are not a mere province, region or a minority but a distinct 'nation' or 'people'. Besides they have also to convince and persuade the majority society to enter into negotiations with concerned parties in the dispute for effecting the necessary changes in the constitution. Even as this multinational and multicultural diversity merit recognition and accommodation but it has to be accomplished in a form that does not infringe too deeply or undermine the identity and integrity of the nation as such.

## Who Decides about Identity

Who should decide which identities are unjust and which are not, remains an important problem in any discourse on identity. Associated with it is the question as to what procedure may be followed to review decisions regarding recognition of identity where such demand merits reconsideration. Most writers agree that the identities worthy of recognition must be worked out by the members of the affected groups themselves. It may be done through the exercise of well-reasoned negotiations and agreements. In the contemporary democratic regimes, it is commonly assumed that claims that merit approval must have the backing of all those affected in their capacity as participants in the practical discourse and ongoing negotiations. The principle behind this reasoning is that 'what touches all must be agreed by all'. In this context democratic practices and processes, and the connected techniques of listening, consultation, negotiations, referendum and dispute resolutions can help matters in arriving at solutions satisfying to all parties in the dispute.

As a matter of fact the demand for identity must come from people as a whole and not merely elite. Where they find that identity has been unjustly imposed on them they must come together to support a demand for the recognition of another identity. They are expected to very much gain mutual recognition, respect and support of others who do not share that identity and may not feel affected by such unjust imposition of identity.

Until an identity is recognized and affirmed by others in the same fashion the demand will fall short of its wider acceptability. Therefore, before the demand for recognition of an identity is put forward we must need ensure that this demand has not only supports those for whom it is made but also that it does not silence or suppress other identities or identity–related differences. Those that are going to be affected by this recognition must be allowed to put forward alternative proposals and others be given the opportunity to raise their doubts, defend the status quo or present counter proposals. This means giving full play to the democratic negotiations in settling questions of identity and identity-related differences through new experiments in federalization of multilingual and multinational associations.

Thus assumption behind identity politics is that people having varied racial, religious, cultural, gender and linguistic identities can arrive at overlapping agreements on forms of mutual recognition and accommodation especially in cases of shared identities. The search for identity involves the democratic freedom of diverse groups and the right of people to modify the norms of public recognition of their political associations to accommodate the demands of identity-related difference and dynamics of identity politics. As long as there are suppressed nationalities, marginalized and oppressed groups, some people or groups discriminated against on the basis of race, colour, gender, class or caste, the struggle for identity will continue to generate public response for recognition and accommodation of new identities.

**Policy Approaches on Identity**

Identity can be a force for self-recognition and self-dignity. Its negative side-effects must be avoided at all costs. How can contradictory aspects of identity may be reconciled remains the moot issue with administrators and policy makers.

The first line of approach relates to the *mobility of identity*. If any identity, whether it be cultural, ethnic or national, is to function properly it has to overlook or disregard the fact that all such configurations are arbitrary and can be drawn in many other possible ways.

In view of the arbitrary nature of identity each one has several identities at the same time. This realization has its own special uses. So when people realize that all identities are arbitrary and that they can switch from one to another to suit the circumstances, they can often respond in a more effective and imaginative way to pressures exerted on them from outside or inside the group. This realization also prevents people from becoming self-absorbed and withdraw into a single identity. Hence it becomes easier for them to engage in dialogue and establish cross-group bonds of solidarity regardless of their cultural, racial, ethnic or national origins.

Another angle to look upon identity may consist in *reinstating the present and contemporary history*. At a time when the "end of history" is being predicted "there are futures that operate in silence and are almost imperceptible". Even in hopeless situations there are hidden possibilities, They are being constantly and unexpectedly created by cobbling together of new ways of acting and thinking, as well as fresh and original combinations of elements, and counter-cultures.

What is happening in many cases today is the regeneration of the social fabric through new principles of solidarity and new forms of social participation. They include self-managed micro-organizations, grassroot economic organizations, religious communities, neighbourhood associations, young people's and women's movements, environmental groups and so on. In the sphere of economy too, informal-sector activities are springing up all over the place. They embody a mixture of resourcefulness and ingenuity. They are based on ideas of production and consumption in many ways different from those of the capitalist economy.

All these examples may have their counterparts in the most marginalized sectors of the industrialized countries—prisons, teenage gangs and also grassroots organizations. They actually testify to the emergence of a new third way showing up under appalling conditions, nevertheless holding out hope for the future.

## Identity: Not Static but Dynamic

Identities thus formulated in these terms no less deserve attention. Far from being based on unchanging and exclusive membership rules, like those of blood ties, parentage or mythical origin, many of these identities are *open-ended*. In them there is a continual inflow and outflow of members. This prevents them from taking on a self-perpetuating existence of their own. This is more true, for example, of identities based on places of residence, like neighbourhood associations, or those based on membership rules that are not handed down from one generation to the next. As a matter of fact they are defined by individuals themselves through the institutions they create.

Citizenship is another form of identity. It can be defined in the course of struggles directly related to current issues. A number of these identities may also have the attribute of being tied to the present and being short-lived. It may not last longer than a particular plan or militant action. It prevents them from turning into hard and fast identities.

Such identities, with their continually changing memberships and limited life-spans have an intrinsic merit. They give rise to communities which even as they are relatively vulnerable and unstable, they may possess the strength to maintain an enquiring and tolerant relationship with other such groupings or identities. At the same time they need to counter the unhealthy selfabsorption that is still so prevalent in the world of ours.

Identity issues have assumed a critical position in contemporary politics. These issues have in fact impacted on the women's question as well. Within the space of the past decade and a half, the seeming coherence of the woman category has come to be debated within the movement itself.

In contrast to the longer history of the term 'identity', 'identity politics' has a more recent origin. Within India, and remarkably the world over as well, the concept of 'identity politics' has acquired currency mainly in the late '80s and the early '90s in the context of assertions of a range of identities. Specifically these are identities that seek to naturalize certain cultural characteristics.

Valentine Moghadam points to this global dimension of identity politics and the range of issues covered by it: "During the 1980s, discourses and movements centering on issues of identity are seen to erupt around the world with considerable force. Questions of cultural, religious, national, linguistic, and sexual identity command centre stage. They relegate questions of *economic justice*, at least temporarily, to the background . . . The phenomenon of identity formation is not unique to a specific geographic area".

## Politics of Identity in India

The question of the identity of India has been at the top of the agenda at debates on culture, politics and Indian nationalism. On the one hand there is an upper-caste *Sanskritic* Hindu identity, and on the other hand, there are voices from below, from bottom of the social pyramid viz. from tribals, dalits, religious, linguistic and ethnic groups. They are seen voicing demands for an elbowroom and acceptance of their specific cultural identity in the Indian national commonwealth.

The Indian Nation is described as multi-cultural civilizational state. The Indian Constitution is a product of the multi-ethnic challenges and contending visions. India's cultural, religious and ethnic plurality have had a bearing on India's society and polity. It is these which have gone to shape the various institutions in the course of the Indian freedom struggle. It is these conflicting visions and perspectives too that have gone into making of the secular form of the modern state.

India is a subcontinent with a vast population of the most diverse types and levels of culture. Almost all known racial groups have migrated to India at different times in the past. They have come with their own language, religion and culture. With plenty of space available, these migrating cultural and racial groups have been able to pass on their racial experiences and unique features of their cultures in a spirit of adjustment and reconciliation. Without much opposition they are further able to penetrate into the interior. Thus, the various cultural groups instead of seeking to destroy each other, continue to live on in a spirit of amity and mutual adjustments. They are thus able to consolidate themselves into the main components of the present-day population. The caste system also considerably has helped to keep the diverse racial, social and cultural groups apart. It has effectively prevented them from mixing with one another.

Undeniably variety and diversity permeate the whole subcontinent. It is true of every state and district, every town and village. Indian civilization is the outcome of a confluence of various cultural, religious, linguistic, and ethnic traditions. Over the years of mutual fecundation, synthesis and challenge, Indian civilization has come to be characterized by diversity of culture, religion, language, race and caste groups. According to Rajni Kothari, "In the absence of a centralized political authority it was 'the Indian civilizational enterprise' which over the centuries achieved a remarkable degree of cohesion and held together different subsystems in a continental-size society". Viewed thus, the unifying force of Indian civilization is the mutual acceptance of multi-culturality and linguistic diversity rather than a political ideology of regimentation.

In the colonial era, predominantly two major strands on the reconstruction of identity are seen to emerge from the upper caste Hindus. One is seen attempting to reconstruct Indian society on the basis of Western ideas of the Age of Enlightenment and Liberalism, and the other wanting the reconstruction to take place on the basis of ancient Hindu traditions. These two visions of India have developed their own ideology, leadership and organization in the course of freedom struggle in India. A third view is what has been voiced by oppressed and marginalized people of India. These three visions of modern India shaped the nature of Indian polity at the time of India's independence. It has defined the character of the Indian nation. Again it is this which has impacted the framing of Constitution. These perspectives have also been influential in the current political debates today.

The theorists of Hindu identity defined race as a population with a common origin and with one culture. Therefore, any endevour to maintain racial unity in a nation necessitated the assimilation, and inextricable fusion, of foreign populations into the mother race. In other words, it was emphasized that they should merge fully into an original national race not only economically and politically but also religiously, culturally and linguistically. It was reiterated that secularism was not their path for national integration, but that it should come through Hinduization. That the best solution to the problems of minorities lay in one word—assimilation. That they should be "wholly subordinated to the Hindu nation, claiming nothing, deserving no privileges, far less any preferential treatment – not even citizen's rights". It gave an inkling of the cultural changes which Indian Muslims were expected to undergo in order to become acceptable nationals of the Indian (Hindu) state of the future and these would include the following:

First, they need to accept the Ramayana and Mahabharata as their epics in preference to the Arabic and Persian classics.

Second, they should regard Rana Pratap, Shivaji, as well as Hindu gods like Rama and Krishna as their heroes, and condemn certain Muslim historical figures as foreign invaders or traitors.

With the emergence of Militant Hindu Nationalism the concern for social reform was given a back seat. The upper caste Hindus identified "Nation" and "National Culture" as basically Hindu. It was assumed to be derived from Vedic times. It was fundamentally a creation of the Aryan people. They employed high-caste religious symbols in their mass mobilization campaigns. They also made use of the "Aryan Theory of Race" in interpreting cultural traditions.

The alternative vision of prominent Non-Aryan or Non-Brahmanic leaders within India was born as a reaction against this dominant Indian national culture which was essentially an upper caste phenomena. The prominent figures of this larger Non-Aryan and Anti-Brahmin vision of Indian Nationalism were Jotiba Phule, E.V. Ramaswami 'Periyar', Babasaheb Ambedkar, Narayanswami Guru in Kerala, and Acchutanand in Utter Pradesh. They attacked the dominant Indian National identity. They viewed it as conspiracy to establish the hegemony of the North India over the South India. Hence movements like Self Respect Movement and Dravid Identity Movement rose from the South as a challenge to the Hindu Aryan Identity with its roots in the Indo-gangetic plain in the North where Vedas were written.

**Dalit Identity: The Vision of Jotirao Phule (1826-1890)**

Among the leaders of the identity movement that rose from the South, Jotirao Phule

(1826-1890) stands out as the tallest figure who proclaimed the new dispensation for the common man, the downtrodden, and the Indian woman. He wanted to reconstruct the new social order on the basis of social equality, justice and reason.

The "Aryan Theory of Race" was central to any discussion on caste and society in Phule's time. European Orientalists underlined an ethnic Kinship between Europeans and the ancient Vedic peoples on the basis of this theory. The renewed interest of European scholars in ancient Aryan society and their high praise to the glorious achievements of the Aryans proved a great morale booster to the high caste Indians. They interpreted Indian civilization as the continuation of the ancient Aryan civilization. They saw in Varnashram Dharma and the caste system as a great civilizing and unifying force among people of diverse racial and cultural backgrounds who had made India their home in distant past.

Jotirao Phule argued that the low castes, whom he sometimes called "Sudras and Ati-Sudras" were in fact the original inhabitants of the country. It were the conquering Aryans who enslaved and exploited them. Their innovative caste-based Hinduism and Hindu social organization known as Varna Vayavastha were but means of deceiving the masses so as to legitimize their power.

Jotirao Phule saw in the ancient history of India the struggle between Brahmins and Non-Brahmins. Hence, he made a conscious attempt to bring together the major peasant castes. These were, the Kumbis or Cultivators, the Malis or 'Gardeners' or Cultivators and Dhangars or Shepherds along with the large untouchable castes of Mahars and Mangs. They all formed 'a Common Front' against the centuries-old phenomena of Brahmin domination. Launching a frontal attack on Brahminism, Jotirao realized that the seeds of Brahmins' powers, supremacy and privileges lay in their scriptures and Puranas. These works and the caste system, he asserted, were created to exploit the lower classes.

Jotirao Phule laid the blame on Hindu priestcraft and the caste system for the miserable lot of the Sudras, Ati-Sudras (untouchables) and women. He started a movement to achieve a casteless society. For this he founded the Satya Shodhak Samaj on 24 September 1873. The Samaj opened the first school for girls and untouchables. It initiated a movement for widow remarriages, and marriages without Brahmin priests. According to Phule the source of exploitation of the Sudras and Ati-sudras (untouchables) lay in the cultural and ethnic factors rather than economic or political ones.

**Dalit Identity: Periyar's (1879-1973) Self-Respect Movement**

E.V. Ramaswamy Naicker, known as 'Periyar' (Great Sage), was born in 1879 in Erode of a respectable middle class family. He married at the age of 13, but after six years he became a sannyasi. He traveled as a religious mendicant over the whole of India. In his visits to pilgrim centres, he gained an intimate knowledge of the evils of popular Hinduism. He also came to realize the exploitations of the masses by Brahmin priests.

For Periyar, casteism and Hinduism were one and the same. Therefore with caste disappearing Hinduism too will go out. Basing his plea on racial consciousness he launched a 'Dravidian Movement', to defend the rights of the Dravidians against Aryan domination. He blamed the Aryans for introducing an unjust and oppressive social system in the country.

Periyar was quick enough to realize the implication of the ideology of the Indian elite. The Aryan and Sanskritic culture which formed as the basis of "Indian Nationality", in fact gave preeminence to the culture of the North Indian upper castes. By doing so they mistook this fraction of Indian culture for the whole.

In 1925, Periyar organized the "Self-Respect Movement", designed as Dravidian Uplift movement. It's aim was to expose Brahmin tyranny and the deceptive methods they used to control all spheres of Hindu life. He attacked Hindu religion as a tool of Brahmin domination. He termed it as an opiate by which the Brahmins had dulled and subdued the masses. "A Hindu according to the present concept may be a Dravidian, but a Dravidian in the real sense of the term cannot and shall not be a Hindu". Ravana, a Dravidian hero represented as a demon in the North, was a Dravidian of "excellent character". In his Preface to *The Ramayana : A True Reading,* Periyar states that "the veneration of the story any longer in Tamil Nad is injurious and ignominious to the self-respect of the community and of the country". Periyar, thus resurrected the Dravidian Identity as against the Aryan which was being viewed as one with Indian Identity.

**Dalit Identity: Dr. B.R. Ambedkar (1891-1956)**

Dr. Bhimrao Ramji Ambedkar (1891-1956) was very much inspired by Mahatma Jotiba Phule's example and it made an indelible impression on Ambedkar's mind. He was determined to complete the work begun by Jotiba and this became his life's mission. A born revolutionary Dr. Ambedkar led the fight against untouchability, Hinduism, and the Brahmin caste. The fight against casteism and untouchability became central to his agenda.

Dr. Ambedkar wanted society to be based on the principles of liberty, equality and fraternity. He was convinced that if caste was to be destroyed then its religious foundation, *i.e.*, the Vedas and Shastras, must also be destroyed. Faith in these scriptures was no more than a legalized class ethic favouring the Brahmins. Ambedkar was convinced that a breach in the system will not be possible unless the dynamite was applied to the Vedas and Shastras which denied any part to reason, or any part to morality. Besides the Religion of the Smritis also needed to be destroyed.

Thus Phule/Periyar/Ambedkar tradition was a serious attempt at defining an alternative identity for the Indian people. It was to be based on non-Aryan and low caste perspectives. It entailed total rejection of the oppressiveness of the dominant Hindu castes. In addition it was to be a refutation of claiming that the Aryan tradition was the mainstream national tradition. In Ambedkar's view the issue was not basically racial but cultural. It was indeed a matter of group identity.

## CONCLUSION

The above survey of identity in India is a pointer that there did not exist one all-encompassing Mainstream Tradition but several visions of Indian Identity. A continuous dialogue and interaction among these visions have been a fact of Indian history and civilization. Historically its role has been crucial to the formation of the modern Indian state and identity in India over the ages.

In Indian context differences are as important as integrating factors. The concern for equal citizenship and equal rights is no doubt important but no less important is ethnic, linguistic, cultural and religious pluralism in India. This pluralism needs be nurtured along with assured recognition and protection for all nondiscriminatory state policies. It would also involve articulation of a secular and inclusive nationalism. In it every citizen is to be provided equal opportunity and equal liberty, regardless of religious affiliation or social status. The state itself is to stay above all groups, showing no preference for any particular religion. The equidistance to all religions is the quintessence of secularism. The constitution of India tries to ensure it through many of its provisions.

In sum, India is a multi-cultural, multi-religious country. Its unity derives from its diversity. On the issue of the nature of Indian Nationhood there has been an extensive debate during the freedom struggle. The discussions in the Constituent Assembly point to contending visions of India. Based on India's perennial philosophy and the continuous dialogue an inclusive Secular Constitution took shape. The vision enshrined in the Indian Constitution and the legacy of the freedom struggle can guide us in our present situation. The foremost concern is that Indian Nationalism and for that matter the Indian State should give dignity to all Indians. They should make them wanted and respected citizens. Apart from some affluent sections Indian society is inhabited by Dalits, Tribals, Backward Castes and other marginalized and suppressed communities who are deserving of special treatment. All-out efforts are needed to bring them at par with those belonging to the upper and middle caste Hindus. These groups are in search of a nation inspired by egalitarian values and social justice. They also like their counterparts, the privileged and affluent among the high castes, are entitled to economic opportunities and participation in political decision-making.

# 8

# RIGHTS

## Meaning and Definition

The concept of a "right" is derived from the Latin, *jus* (jus) or *justus* (justus) meaning "just" and "justice." The concept of right has been given different meanings throughout history. St. Thomas Aquinas treats the concept of *jus* as meaning "law," "justice," or "what is owed to others." William of Ockham (A.D. 1280-1349), the Franciscan philosopher, is credited with having been the first writer to use *jus* in the modern sense of a right as constituting a claim. In the 17th and 18th centuries, the concepts of "natural rights," "human rights," and "option rights" become predominant. They influence Thomas Jefferson's *Declaration of Independence*, Thomas Paine's *The Rights of Man*, and the *U.S. Bill of Rights*. Rights in this sense mean the liberty to pursue one's own conception of the good. In the 19th century during the Industrial Revolution, the notion of rights as an "interest" or as "welfare rights" is introduced. The concept of rights as "interests" emphasizes the importance of well-being. It entails claims to those good needed for one's well-being as opposed to merely the liberty to engage in one's own pursuits.

Rights are the essential conditions of a society given to the citizens for the development of his individual personality. The state, in particular the modern state does not believe in the concentration of all powers in its own hands. It allows its citizens certain rights against itself, against other individuals to seek their best self. The individuals by enjoying certain rights not only participate in the political powers of the state but also rectify the authoritarian tendency of the state.

When persons have capacities and opportunities to particular actions they are supposed to possess rights. In fact status provides capacity, capacity provides power, and power ultimately the rights. Both the aliens and the citizens possess civil and social rights but the aliens do not possess any political rights. Bentham and Hobbes define rights as claims recognized by the state. These rights are maintained by the orders of the state based on the interpretation of the judiciary. According to Laski, Rights are those conditions of social life without which no man can seek in general to be himself at his best.

## Features of Rights

The following are the salient features of rights upon which the various theories of rights are based:

(a) The rights are powers vested in the individual to protect his best self.
(b) Society is the precondition of origin of rights and no right is against, beyond or before the society.
(c) Rights promote social welfare and no right can be antisocial, or against the society.
(d) Rights are granted by the society but maintained and secured by the state.
(e) Rights and duties are correlative. The very basis of the state and sovereignty exists with the obligation and obedience to the state. So the duties towards the state enable the state to protect and promote the rights. In this way the duties of individual towards the state come first, then come the duties of the state towards the individual.
(f) The rights and duties are dynamic and not static. They change with the changing political structure, the form of government and kind of governance.
(g) The rights are based on the fulfillment of other conditions which are deemed essential for enjoyment of the same. In the absence of economic equality the rights are not enjoyed by all equally.
(h) The socio political and religious discrimination based on class, caste, religion, language and gender create impediments for the true exercise of the rights.

## Nature of Rights

Rights by their very nature flow from the general system of 'right' which is the basis of the state and its laws. Right is the Grand Norm and all rights are its creature. They embody its essence, the common consciousness of the common good. Right as distinct from wrong, has its basis in ethics-normative order regulating all verities. Hence rights have no existence apart from the notion of right. All law is based on the notion of right. Rights in the legal sense too have it their basis in the notion of right. So does the basis of the legal system. This is the immediate ground whereon stands the concept of rights embodying the notion of right. It is also the ultimate ground that identifies the conditions of achieving the ends which inspire and determine the whole system of rights. Rights help in realizing the highest possible development of the personality of the individual and are indeed the demands of the individual from the society.

The source of rights is the individual himself. Rights flow from the individual's own moral personality, his human essence, the inviolability of his moral and his social nature. The rights are thus natural and human. There are no rights which are not secured and enforced by the state. In this sense, the source of rights lies outside man. It is something more than one's own personal nature. The fact is that the state is the immediate source of all rights, eventhough in a sense they (rights) are derived from individual personality. They are the quality and condition of man's highest development. Thus Rights by their very nature are secured and guaranteed by the force of law.

Rights are essentially about human relationship in the society. Therefore their enjoyment involves conforming to certain fundamental canons of social welfare. There are no absolute and unlimited rights. Indeed all rights are governed by the social interest. They impose certain social moral restraints on every individual. While enjoying rights, an awareness of the similar rights of others is a must. Rights and duties are co-relative. They are the obverse and subverse of the same coin. Only in a world of duties rights become significant.

Rights are not selfish claims but given equally to all individuals in the society. They are distinct from privileges, prerogatives and immunities. They belong to all men irrespective of birth, caste, creed, economic status, religion etc.

Rights are dynamic with a tendency to grow with the socioeconomic development and new demands of individuals and groups for identity and recognition. It is the state that through its law confers rights. Right to work, right to strike, right to leisure etc. are such rights as are recognized in socialist and welfare state.

Rights are mostly limited in time and space. They are real only in the context of a particular human society. Also the content of some rights may differ from age to age, country to country. Of course, some rights may still be there having universal application.

## Hohfeld's Concept of Right

Hohfeld distinguishes right from liberty, and power from immunity. These concepts are often used interchangeably in nontechnical discourse, though philosophically they are different. By examining the relationships between these concepts, Hohfeld hopes to explain the legal interests that have evolved in the real world of civil society. He does so to answer the question whether citizens of a state have any right to access any of the possible forms of social security.

The legal opposite of liability is immunity. In some countries, government departments exercising sovereign powers cannot be sued in tort and likewise the President or the Prime Minister cannot be personally liable in respect of any contract made or assurance given for purposes of the state. These are examples of immunities.

The word 'right' is often used to describe liberty, power, or immunity. Indeed, Hohfeld describes liberty as an *a priori* condition of the rule of law. It comes into existence long before any Bill of Rights. It offers an individual power to the extent that it is not restricted by any law. Essentially, Hohfeld believes that anyone who tries to encroach on the liberty of a citizen must be required to demonstrate his clear right to do so.

Robert Nozick (1938–2003) offers a model of a "minimal state". He describes it as libertarianism. Nozick argues that no state is ever justified in offering anything more than the most minimal of state functions. Whatever might exist by way of rights exists only in the negative sense of those actions not yet prohibited. He denies the possibility that any citizen can have rights that require others to offer him or her services at the state's expense. He tests whether exchanges between individuals are legitimate by an entitlement theory.

The entitlement theory of Nozick has three components: Transfer, Acquisition and Rectification. He explains these three principles as follows:

* The *Transfer Principle* holds that goods or services "freely acquired from others who acquired them in a just way are justly acquired"
* The *Acquisition Principle* states that people are entitled to retain all holdings acquired in a just way.
* The *Rectification Principle* requires that any violation of the first two principles be repaired by returning holdings to their rightful owners as a "one time" redistribution, a reference to the Rawlsian Difference Principle.

Nozick, therefore, believes that there are no positive civil rights except only rights to property and the right of autonomy. For him, a just society does as much as possible to protect everyone's independence and freedom to take any action for the benefit of one's self. This is akin to the Jeffersonian position *i.e.,* right to the pursuit of happiness is the freedom to engage in any action so long as it does not infringe upon that same right exercised by others.

Critics of the minimal state-model argue that a state which provides no services to citizens is inadequate. John Rawls (1921–2002) develops a model of a different form of just society which relies on the "liberty principle" and the "difference principle". The former principle *i.e.*, "the liberty principle" in substantive terms means that citizens require minimal civil and legal rights to protect themselves. The latter one, *i.e.,* the "difference principle" suggests that every citizen would want to live in a society where improving the condition of the poorest becomes the first priority.

For Rawls, a right is an "entitlement or justified claim on others". It comprises both negative and positive obligations. It refers to both of them, that others must not harm anyone (negative obligation), and surrender a proportion of their earnings through taxation for the benefit of low-income earners (positive obligation). This enunciation blurs the relationship between rights and duties as proposed by Hohfeld. For example if a citizen has the right to free medical care, then others, through the agency of the government will be obligated to provide that service.

Critics of Rawls' approach to right doubt if the Difference Principle accords with a state seeking to consistently apply the capitalist model. Rawl's ideas however have influenced the implementation of social market economies within a capitalist system in European countries like Germany.

The difference between Rawls and Nozick is that Rawls thinks that a state should always provide the basic fundamentals of physical existence, whereas Nozick gives no guarantee save that an individual always has the freedom to pursue his or her own ends.

In Nozick's model, every citizen is free to offer employment and/or to offer their labour. Any interference with these freedoms will diminish autonomy. In capitalist countries, this philosophy resonates powerfully with citizens who oppose any restriction on their right to use, for their own benefit, what they consider "justly acquired" wealth .

For Rawls, the "Liberty Principle" means that no one person should be any less "equal" than any other. Therefore, it will be appropriate to restrict liberty and impose duties to promote social justice. This model works best in countries where the principle of wealth distribution is accepted by the majority. Hence, particular notions of what may constitute fairness or justice will always drive public calls for coercive antidiscrimination laws to fill in the gap where the naming and shaming of "offenders" is not an effective deterrent.

## Theories of Rights

There are various theories of rights, depending upon the basis of the state, its origin, continuance and relationship between the state authority and individual rights. These theories are as follows:

1. Theory of Natural Rights
2. Theory of Legal Rights
3. Historical Theory of Rights
4. Moral Theory of Rights
5. Social Welfare Theory of Rights
6. Recent Developments in Liberal-Individualistic Theory of Rights
7. Marxist Views on Rights

### 1. Theory of Natural Rights

The believers of the social contract theory of the origin of the state argue that certain rights are inalienable, *i.e.,* prior to the state. These rights are: right to life, liberty and property. The people in order to protect their rights go for social contract among each other. They create the state to protect their rights. Hobbes and Locke, the early pioneers of natural theory of rights, view these rights as the gift of the nature and claims of the individual. To Hobbes natural rights means the liberty of each man to oppress the weak through the concept of self-preservation. In that sense he advocates only one natural right *i.e.,* the right to life whereas Locke admits that there are three fundamental natural rights *i.e.,* right to life, liberty and property.

Rousseau in his book *The Social Contract* (1762) glorifies the concept of natural rights. Rousseau and Hobbes argue in favour of surrender of natural rights for civil rights. The concept of natural rights which is based on the law of the nature, prior to the origin of the state is criticized on the following grounds:

1. The natural rights are non-juristic and there is no sanction behind them.

2. The existence of rights prior to the society is hypothetical. Before the state and in the state of nature these rights cannot be called natural. For, these are based on the physical force, self-interest and domination of the strong over the weak.
3. The rights before the society, *i.e.,* the inalienable rights are also not valid. The theory supported by Greek political traditions is that no right exists before the society and the state. Aristotle's statement that 'no man can live without the society; and if it be so he is either a beast or god', also testify that, no right exists beyond society.

## 2. Theory of Legal Rights

The advocates of legal theory of rights are Bentham, Hegel and Austin. They hold that the rights are granted by the state and no right, as the theory of natural rights believes, exists before the state. Hobbes recognizes only one fundamental right of the individual *i.e.,* the Right to self-preservation. He admits that this right can be better preserved by the state than the individual. Hence, he insists that all rights are in the state and the individual is permitted to do only that which is not restrained by the state.

The basic features of legal theory of rights are as follows:

(a) the state is the fundamental source of law and no right exists prior, beyond, or against the state,
(b) the state also enforces the enjoyment of rights, and
(c) concept of rights also changes with the changes of law.

The legal theory of rights holds that the state is the protector and promoter of rights. By enforcement of law it can take away any right. This rule has also been subjected to various criticisms. While the supporters of this theory do not find any difference between the state and society, but in actuality, they very much exist.

## 3. Historical Theory of Rights

The pioneer of the historical theory of rights is Edmund Burke (1729-1797). He advocates that the rights which every individual enjoys today is not the result of a particular point of time but are a product of the historical evolution. The historical theory of rights is not only opposed to the theory of natural rights but also the legal theory of rights. It lays emphasis upon the state's role in recognizing the rights which have evolved since long. Edmund Burke criticizes the French Revolution (1789) because it is based on the bloodshed for liberty, equality and fraternity. He accepts the glorious revolution of Britain (1689) based on *Magna Carta* (1215) and *Petition of Rights* (1628).

The historical theory of rights attaches special importance to historical facts, customs and traditional setups. It is related with the time, place and people of a particular geographical location. Conditioned by these the right is not the outcome of reason and rationalism. The individual therefore has but little role in shaping and changing them.

The greatest defect and drawback of the historical theory of rights is that it fails to distinguish the right customs and traditions from the wrong ones. The success of the historical theory of rights lies in providing the necessary correctives to the concept of *sati*, child marriage, polygamy, slavery and racial discrimination. This is because they are contradictory to justice, laws and values of democracy and not that they are conservative and reactionary.

### 4. Moral Theory of Rights

The advocates of moral theory of rights are Hegel, Kant, Rousseau, Green and Bosanquet. To them rights are associated with morality, the conscience, the ethical values and common good. These rights are the external conditions by which the individual can attain his moral freedom. Green observes that rights are the powers necessary for the fulfillment of man's vocation as a moral being. The commonness of the individuals, the common purpose, the values based on the community and society as well as the common consciousness of the common good contribute enough for the fabric or moral foundation of the principle of moral theory of rights. The moral theorists relate the individual rights with social rights. They associate individual good with social good. Accordingly this seldom results in the welfare theory of rights. This has a limited application because of the common code of conduct, morality and ethics.

### 5. Social Welfare Theory of Rights

Roscoe Pound and Chafee are the most prominent advocates of the social welfare theory of rights. They believe that, all the rights whether based on natural theory or historical theory should be based on the principle of social welfare of the people and the social conditions. The supporters of social welfare theory argue that the rights should be socially useful and determined by the social conditions.

This theory is criticized by Marxists and other theorists on the ground that no uniform factor can determine the universally valid social welfare. Bentham's formula of 'greatest good of the greatest number', in reality, creates an anomalous condition. As a result, either a few or organized few determine the essence of social welfare by possession of the state power.

The social welfare theory of rights is also criticized on the basis of its interpretation, *i.e.*, who, when and wherein will decide the welfare of the society. If the answer to this question is the state, then this theory like the legal theory of rights is found deficient. This is because its basis is the capitalist state which is the representative of the owners of the production.

### 6. Recent Developments in Liberal-Individualistic Theory of Rights

The influence of John Rawls and Robert Nozick has been crucial on the liberal-individualistic theory of rights. They are the dominant voices of the liberal tradition.

They have also influenced other contemporary writers like Dworkin, Galstone, Ackerman, Barry and the like, to propound their own theories of rights.

Rawls and Nozick represent two dominant socioeconomic perspectives. Nozick symbolizes the classical-liberal view of free market. He is a votary of free trade capitalism and minimal state, whereas Rawls represents the Keynesian tradition of liberal egalitarianism. Rawls' appeal lies for those who believe in the desirability, efficiency and future of capitalist market. If the latter does not function well and it generates serious inequalities, then he is keen to find efficient ways to address those inadequacies. He wishes to achieve this without altering the essential nature of the system.

As against Rawls, Nozick sees the theory of rights as derived from the principle of natural right of 'self-ownership'. It means treating people as they are *i.e.,* an end in themselves. According to Nozick, "The individuals have rights and there are no things, person or groups may do to them. (without violating their rights)." Society must respect these rights considering individuals as ends and not as means. Rights affirm the separate existence of man. Taken seriously, it means that the individuals in no way are the resources of some other persons.

Respect for rights means respecting people's claim to be equal. A libertarian society by respecting the individual respects his rights. It lets us realize our ends, aided by the voluntary cooperation of other individuals possessing the same dignity. With regards to the substance of rights, Nozick believes in right to acquire and hold property and freedom of contract. Property right, he upholds, excludes welfare rights of the individual and their protection by the state.

For Nozick, an individual is an owner of himself and his talent. He is free to use his powers as he wishes. Every individual has an exclusive domain. It must not be breached without his consent. All political institutions are coercive by definition. They must command the unanimous assent of the governed. They must be brought into existence purely by voluntary transaction. The state has no legitimate powers beyond the function of protection, justice and defence. Rights are prior 'to the civil law' from which the latter is derived.

John Rawl in his theory of Justice, uses the words 'rights' and 'justice' interchangeably. To him, rights must be embedded in justice and belong to all disinterested political individuals beyond the veil of ignorance. But they have no natural rights except what they unanimously choose in their original position. The rights which people accept in their original position include an equal right to the most extensive liberty. This right must be compatible with a similar liberty for others. The arrangement of social and economic inequalities have to be done in such a way that they (i) benefit the greatest to the least advantaged, and (ii) attach to positions and offices open to all under conditions of fair equality of opportunity.

Basic liberties, to Rawls, connote the standard civil and political rights such as right to vote, to run for offices, due process of law, free speech etc. which are recognized by the liberal democracies. Also the rights should guarantee a fair share of economic resources. Rawls thus in the *second category* gives certain egalitarian rights to citizens. He urges that the social and economic inequalities should be so regulated that those with least material goods such as income, wealth, education etc. will get a larger share. Rawls conceives of a market economy in which material inequalities serve as incentives. They tend to increase the overall stock of goods available for distribution. He wants the tax system to be proportionately used to redistribute goods to the worst off. To bring this about he is convinced that the people's rights to social goods should not be dependent upon their natural endowments.. The talented do not deserve any greater income but when they receive more income it must be ensured that it benefits the less well off also.

Both Rawls and Nozick reject the Utilitarian Theory of Rights. Both believe that individual is an end in himself. However for Nozick, the most important right is the right over oneself *i.e.,* the right to self-ownership. For Rawls, it is the right to a certain share of society's resources. Nozick accepts the plea that the goods produced by the talented should be used to improve the well-being of the disadvantaged since 'If I own myself then I own my talent as well and what is produced of that talent'. Hence Nozick considers any redistributive taxation as wrong. As against Nozick, Rawls' position is that the right over the talent does not necessarily include the right to unequal rewards from those talents. The very fact that talent is unequally distributed by nature, the state has a duty to guarantee that the untalented have a right over the naturally advantaged.

Ronald Dworkin in his book *Taking Rights Seriously* ( 1978), tries to build a new theory of politics based on the primacy of moral rights. Dworkin identifies only two moral rights of the citizens which are to be treated as natural or inalienable: (i) the right of the citizen to be treated equally, and (ii) right to have respect for human dignity.

Dworkin's theory, far from being based upon history or philosophy or tradition, is based on a speculative claim based upon reason. His theory differs from those by other liberal writers in that he holds that there can be no general right to liberty. He says that 'the idea of a right to liberty is a misconceived notion. It does disservice to Political Thought.' Yet he concedes that some specific liberties are important because they are based upon right to equality. To Dworkin, citizens, "have distinct rights to certain liberties like the liberty of free expression and of free choice in personal and sexual relations, but they do not have a right to free use of property".

Dworkin's theory is distinct from other variants of liberal theory in extreme individualism. In the context of the right to freedom of speech and expression, Dworkin considers it wrong for a law to ban speakers in a demonstration by taking public safety as the basis for such measure. For such a law restricts the individual right of the demonstrators to speak. Equality and human dignity, he values most. He justifies the right of the blacks to get admission in the colleges with lower qualifications than the white.

Thus, it is the emergence of a new type of liberalism from 1960s onwards that has given rise to a number of theories of individual rights. But the question is: whether a coherent theory of fundamental rights is possible? For Birch, these new theories are lacking in a view of human nature, as well as a view of society and a view of functions of the state. As Peter Jones observes, 'while fundamental disagreements sill persist among philosophers over the conceptual question of what a right is, a progress in recent years registered in this direction has been towards an unfolding of diversity rather than progress towards a single truth'.

### 7. Marxist Views on Rights

For the liberal thinkers, the existence of the rights of man has been a common creed. That every human being is morally entitled to a certain mode of treatment at the hands of his fellow men and the state. Whether the basis of rights is in nature, law of the state, history or social welfare—may be a matter of dispute—but there can be no dispute on the question if all individuals possess certain rights. But as against the liberal views, Marxism does not propound any precise theory of rights. Since the Marxist critique has been associated with property, its chief concern consists in a radical criticism of the capitalist society. Independently Marxism does not have any theory of state and citizen nor a theory concerning the relationship between state and individual.

Marx yet does not disapprove every affirmative theory of rights, though he exposes the hollowness of the bourgeois structure of rights. The fact is that the later Marxists following his lead have done very little to develop a Marxist theory of rights in an affirmative sense. Hence in case of Marxism we are confronted with non-availability of an authentic theory of rights. Although there are substantial rights incorporated in the constitutions of China, erstwhile USSR and other communist countries but in practical terms the realization of these rights have remained a dream.

### Marx's Critique of the Bourgeois Concepts of Rights

In his early writings, Marx offers a critique of the character of rights granted by the bourgeois state which makes him conclude that economic inequalities lead to political inequalities. As a result, in such a state the workers even though in a majority will never become a part of the government and their rights will remain hollow. In an essay on *The Jewish Question (1843)*, Marx discusses at length the inclusion of the human rights in the American and French constitutions. He writes that these human rights are partly political rights which they can exercise only in the community along with other men. Their content is formed by participation in the common essence, the political essence, the essence of the state. They fall under the category of 'political freedoms' and 'civil liberties.' Contrasted with them, Marx underlines that there are certain other human rights termed as 'rights of man'. They are quite distinct from the 'rights of the citizen'. Among them the prominent are freedom of conscience or freedom to choose religion.

In the bourgeois society, the 'rights of man' are differentiated from the 'rights of the citizen'. Since Man as man is a member of the civil society, this, according to Marx, provides the rationale behind man and his rights as human rights. This can be explained on the basis of the relationship of the political state to the civil society, and the nature of political emancipation.

For Marx the rights of man are rights what one has as a member of the civil society. They are not the rights of an egoistic man. Such a man is the one separated from other men and the community. He cites the example of the most radical constitution of 1793 which declares the rights of man as equality, liberty, security and property. The liberty it refers to consists of 'a power that belongs to man to do anything that does not infringe the rights of someone else, or power to do anything that does not harm others'.

This right to freedom, Marx argues, is of an isolated man withdrawn unto 'himself' and is based not upon the 'union of man with man but on the separation of man from man'. It is rights of this separation and the rights of the limited individual who is limited to himself. Similarly, the right to property, according to the constitution of 1793, consists of the right of the citizen to enjoy and dispose of at will their goods and revenues, the fruits of their work and industry. This freedom, writes Marx, to enjoy and dispose of their possessions arbitrarily without regard to other men and independent of society is nothing but the 'right of selfishness'. Liberty and property which form the basis of civil society, see in other men not the realization but the limitation of their own freedom. On the right of equality, Marx writes, equality in its nonpolitical sense means a counterpart of liberty. It means that each man shall without discrimination be treated as a self-sufficient unit. The law will be the same for all, whether it protects or punishes, Similarly security means the protection afforded by the society to each of its members for the conservation of his own person, rights and property, Security is the highest concept of civil society. It is very much related to the concept of police and other coercive apparatuses of the state. In fact the whole society is there merely to guarantee to each of its members the preservation of his person, rights and property. It is this concept of security which does not allow civil society to raise itself above that egoism. Indeed security is more an assurance of that egoism rather than its negation.

Thus, none of the above so called rights, Marx notes, go beyond the egoistic man. Their entire focus remains not on man as in the civil society but man as individual withdrawn behind the private interests and whims and separate from the community. Society does not appear as embodying the rights of man as a species-being or species-life itself, but as a framework exterior to individual, and a limitation to their original self-sufficiency. The only bond that binds them together is natural necessity. It includes needs and private interests, the conservation of their property and egoistic persons. Marx points to a paradox that liberalism which originally stands for freeing and tearing down all barriers between different sections of people should justify the egoistic man and see him as separate from the society and his fellowmen. It reduces the sphere in which man behaves as a communal being to a partial being. As a result, now it is not man as a citizen but man as a bourgeois man that is seen to be a true man.

Again, it is a liberal boast that the modern state is not based upon society of privileges but it is a society in which privileges have been abolished and dissolved. Since man has been set free from the privileges, he is no longer bound to other men even by the semblance of common ties. It is this which has produced the universal struggle of man against man and individual against individual. Indeed, the individual considers his own freedom and his movement in particular, his alienated life elements like property, religion, industry etc. no longer curbed or fettered by a common tie or by any other man. In reality, this is the perfection of slavery and his inhumanity. Rights here take the form of privileges.

Marx's criticism of the bourgeois concept of rights, have been summarized as follows:

(i) In the absence of appropriate institutional changes the human rights remain abstract and formal. For example, right to life means right to the means of subsistence on which life depends.Property as a social relation, for Marx, is not merely a form of power over things but also a power over men. Therefore, an ownership which legally means the right to exclude others from the use of things owned, carries with it real power over the lives of those who must work in order to live.

(ii) While equality before law is a necessary condition for social justice, but by itself equality is not sufficient, particularly where economic disparities are substantial. There even the equality before law is also not of much avail because the law cannot and does not protect or punish equally. Even the commitment to equality of rights in a class-divided society does not mean much unless it is accompanied by continuous social reconstruction. It is because every right, as Marx puts it, is in general a right of inequality in its content. It does not mean a denial of the validity of the principle however, equally right.

(iii) In a bourgeois society, says Marx, every right is affected by the conditions of its operation, whether it is the right to a fair trial, or to an adequate education or to freedom of speech or press. As a matter of fact rights are never higher than the economic structure but are conditioned by it.

(iv) In the struggle for social and economic democracy involving economically classless society compliance with the form of political democracy is deemed unnecessary. Rights in a bourgeois society are formal and lacking in substance. They are therefore, of inconsequential importance. Hence if they interfere with the concrete social progress towards communism, *i.e.,* a classless, stateless exploitation-free social order, they can and should be ignored or violated.

## The Concept of Human Rights

Human rights have been defined as 'basic moral guarantees that people in all countries and cultures possess simply because they are people. Calling these guarantees "rights" suggests that they attach to particular individuals who can invoke them. They are of high priority. Compliance with them is mandatory rather than discretionary.

Human rights are frequently held to be universal. It means all people have and should enjoy them. They are independent in that they exist and are available as standards of justification and criticism whether or not they are recognized and implemented by the legal system or officials of a country.

The moral doctrine of human rights aims at identifying the fundamental prerequisites for each human being for leading a minimally good life, such as rights against torture and rights to health care. This aspiration has been enshrined in various declarations and legal conventions starting with *The Universal Declaration of Human Rights* (*1948*) and perpetuated by, most importantly, *The European Convention on Human Rights* (*1954*) and *The International Covenant on Civil and Economic Rights* (*1966*). Together these three documents form the centerpiece of a moral doctrine concerning human rights. Many consider them capable of providing the contemporary geopolitical order amounting to *An International Bill of Rights*.

What human rights do primarily aim to identify is the basis for determining the shape, content, and scope of fundamental, public moral norms. Even though the practical efficacy of promoting and protecting human rights is significantly aided by individual nation-states legally recognizing the human rights doctrine, yet, the ultimate validity of human rights is characteristically seen to be not conditional upon such recognition.

The moral justification of human rights is seen to precede considerations of strict national sovereignty. An underlying aspiration of the doctrine of human rights is to provide a set of legitimate criteria to which all nation-states should adhere. Appeals to national sovereignty should not provide a legitimate means for nation-states to permanently opt out of their fundamental human rights-based commitments.

Thus, the doctrine of human rights is ideally placed to provide individuals with a powerful means for morally auditing the legitimacy of those contemporary national and international forms of political and economic authority which confront us and which claim jurisdiction over us.

The doctrine of human rights rests upon a particularly fundamental philosophical claim: that there exists a rationally identifiable moral order. It is an order whose legitimacy precedes social and historical conditions. It applies to all human beings everywhere and at all times. On this view, moral beliefs and concepts are capable of being objectively validated as fundamentally and universally true.

Human rights rest upon moral universalism. They are based on the belief in the existence of a truly universal moral community comprising all human beings. Moral universalism posits the existence of rationally identifiable trans-cultural and trans-historical moral truths.

## Human Rights: A Few Landmarks

Human rights may generally be defined as those rights which are inherent in our nature and they make our life as human beings livable. They constitute the essential condition of man's dignified existence. They enable us to develop and use our human faculties, talents, intelligence for fulfillment of our spiritual and other needs. They offer safeguards to the inherent dignity and worth of each human being.

Human rights lie at the roots of all organizations aiming at human development. The entire UN Charter bristles with it. The Preamble of the UN Charter expresses resolve "to affirm faith in Fundamental Human Rights, in the dignity and worth of the Human Person, in the equal rights of men and women and the nations, large and small".

In its various articles (Articles 13, 55, 62, 68 and 76) the Charter insists on the promotion of universal respect for the Human Rights. The Charter does not contain any Bill of Rights.

The Economic and Social Commission set up in 1946, after two and a half years of labour under the chairmanship of Roosevelt drafted Universal Declaration of Human Rights which was to serve as a common standard of achievement for all people and all nations. The Declaration was approved by the General Assembly on December 10, 1948. The Declaration consists of a Preamble and thirty articles.

The Universal Declaration of Human Rights is the first proclamation of the International Bill of Human Rights. It is followed by International Covenant on Economic, Cultural and Social Rights by the General Assembly (1966), the International Covenant on Political Rights (1966), and the Optional Protocol (1966) to the latter Covenant. Both come into force in 1976.

The International Covenant of Economic Social and Cultural Rights lays down the principle that all people have the right of self-determination. It means, that they have the right freely to determine their politics, status and freely to pursue their economic, social and cultural development. The Human Rights which the Covenant seeks to promote and protect include the right to work, the free choice of jobs, favourable conditions of work, equal pay for equal work, safe and healthy working conditions, and rest and leisure. The Covenant also recognizes the right to form and join trade unions, the right to strike and the right to social security, including social insurance. It also enjoins that protection and assistance are to be provided for the family, and special protection accorded to mothers and children. The Covenant states that an adequate standard of living is also everyone's right. This includes adequate food, clothing and housing. It thus recognizes the fundamental right of everyone to be free from hunger. It also provides everyone the right to seek the highest attainable standard of physical and mental health and education.

The International Covenant on Civil and Political Rights and the Optional, Protocol to that Covenant guarantee to everyone the right to life: no one would be deprived of his/her life arbitrarily; the death penalty, where it has not been abolished, may be imposed only for the most serious crimes in accordance with the law; no one shall be subject to torture or to cruel, inhuman or degrading treatment or punishment; no one shall be held in slavery; no one shall be subject to arbitrary arrest/detention.

The Covenant also guarantees that all persons deprived of their liberty should be treated with humanity. No one shall be imprisoned merely on the ground of inability to fulfil a contractual obligation.

The Covenant provides for liberty of movement. It includes the right to leave a country and freedom to choose a residence. It places limitations upon the expulsion of aliens lawfully in the territory of a State party to the Covenant. It provides for the equality of all persons before the courts and guarantees in criminal and civil procedures.

The Covenant prohibits retroactive criminal legislation and guarantees the right of everyone to recognition as a person before the law. It also prohibits arbitrary or unlawful interference with an individual's privacy, family, home or correspondence.

In addition, the Covenant recognizes the right to freedom of thought, conscience and religion and to freedom of expression—including the right to seek, receive or impart information. The Covenant provides for the prohibition by law of any propaganda for war or any advocacy of national, racial or religious hatred that constitutes an incitement of discrimination, hostility or violence. It also recognizes the right of peaceful assembly and the right to freedom of association.

The Covenant also recognizes the right of men and women of marriageable age to marry and to found a family, and the principle of equality of rights and responsibilities of spouses as to marriage, during marriage and at its dissolution.

The Covenant also guarantees the right of every child, without discrimination, to necessary measures of protection on the part of his family, society and the State, as is the child's right to acquire a nationality. It also recognizes the right of every citizen to take part in the conduct of public affairs, to vote and to be elected, and to have access, on general terms of equality, to public services in his country.

According to the Covenant all persons are equal before the law. They are entitled to equal protection of the law. It guarantees measures for the protection of such ethnic, religious or linguistic minorities as may exist in States which are parties to the Covenant. Finally the Covenant obliges each country which is a party to it to ensure that if someone's right be violated, he or she will be given an effective remedy within that country.

## Suspension and Limitations of Human Rights

The Universal Declaration of Human Rights affirms that the exercise of a person's rights and freedoms may be limited. It provides that the limitations must be determined by law. These limitations should be only for the purpose of securing due recognition of the rights of others and of meeting the just requirements of morality, public order and the general welfare in a democratic society. Rights may not be exercised contrary to the purposes and principles of the United Nations.

The Covenant on Economic, Social and Cultural Rights states that the rights listed therein may be limited by law. But the limitation shall hold only in so far as is compatible with the nature of the rights, and solely to promote the general welfare in a democratic society.

The Civil and Political Covenant contains no general provision applicable to all the Covenant's rights authorizing restrictions on their exercise. Yet there are several articles in the Covenant which provide that the rights being dealt with shall not be subject to any restrictions, the only exception being those provided by law and those which are necessary to protect national security.

The Covenant on Civil and Political Rights allows a State to limit or suspend the enjoyment of certain rights in cases of officially declared public emergencies posing to threaten the life of the nation. Such limitations or suspensions are permitted only "to the extent strictly required by the exigencies of the situation". They should never involve discrimination solely on the ground of race, colour, sex, language, religion or social origin. These limitations or suspensions must also be reported to the United Nations, though certain rights, however, may never be suspended or limited even in emergency situations. These include the rights to life, freedom from torture, freedom from enslavement or servitude, protection from imprisonment for debt, freedom from retroactive penal laws, the right to recognition as a person before the law, and freedom of thought, conscience and religion.

In fine, the United Nations and the other international organizations are thus pledged to promote universal respect for observance of Human Rights and Fundamental Freedoms for all without distinction of race, sex, language or religion. From Civil and Political rights termed First Generation Human Rights has mankind progressed to Second Generation Rights such as Economic, Social and Cultural Rights, as also Civil and Political Rights. Now the stage is set for the Third Generation of Human Rights namely the Right to Development which, according to Justice P.N. Bhagwati, involves effective access to tangible and intangible resources. It is to achieve their basic needs of productive and equitably paid work; sufficient nutrition, health care and hygienes; shelter, energy resources, clean water and air; the necessary intangible resources, especially education and information. These resources are necessary to enable them better to utilize resources, and to participate freely in the process of development structures of production and government to assure the fair and equitable allocation to the people of the above resources and facilities and services. The aim of all these is to organize themselves to participate, monitor, evaluate and review development programmes and processes, and to hold accountable those responsible for their implementation.

Human Rights merit to be extended equally to all persons regardless of any distinction of religion, race or nation. They are to be subscribed and enforced by all the states, regardless of their ideologies. They are essential moral conditions which ought to be guaranteed to citizens of any social and political order.

The significance of Human Rights may briefly be summed up as under:

1. They embody rights as are essential for the development of human personality.
2. They, even though not binding on the members-states, provide a yardstick to measure the progress of the states.
3. They serve a very useful purpose in struggle of emancipation and empowerment.
4. They find an unmistakable place on the Constitutions of new Nations and regional agreements.
5. Even when they are not vested with any legal force, they are potent instrument in defending and preserving human dignity and humane values of civilization.
6. They are in the nature of norms permeating every system and give life and order to it. They are mankind's most cherished ideals which ought to be achieved. For this institutions which can make them operative must be devised.
7. They may not be applied with equal fervour by all. Yet their importance can not be minimized. On a close scrutiny human rights do not sound democratic in the sense that they some times conflict with the policies determined by a democratically constituted authority. But their true utility consists in that they offer a meta-political moral framework for politics and social interaction among the states and the citizens. They provide standard for a just treatment to the individuals and the groups. Moreover, they help evaluate the activities and achievements of numerous governments.
8. They are the locomotives of development, orderly progress and universal brotherhood. They are rallying points for movements of social justice, political liberation and cultural diversity. By mobilizing world public opinion they take to task the erring States and subject them to sanctions and censure if they are found to be the violators of the Human Rights.

## CONCLUSION

We live in a period of civilization when human rights have received recognition through universal instruments and in some countries through national constitutions. It is claimed that man, right from the moment he is born, becomes endowed with certain universally acclaimed human rights: However, the paradox of contemporary times is that everywhere such rights are ignored and violated with impunity. Human beings without rights are on the increase, and what we witness everywhere is a tale of blood and tears, cruelty and torture. Man's inhumanity is seen to take many forms. Social divisiveness and political instability are rife. The preponderance of different institutional frameworks and social systems along with inadequate resources make it impossible to comply with the requirements of UN Declaration. It is argued that human rights laid down by UN are too vague to make it possible to establish what constitutes a rights violation. Or alternatively they require to be interpreted by reference to the particular value or tradition of each particular society to give substance to them.

The rights defined primarily in terms of civil liberties and political rights are seen to exist in the liberal democratic system. People by and large enjoy these rights and liberties, at least in substantial terms. This is what the socialist countries criticize, especially the nature of human rights from the beginning of their introduction. In addition, in the underdeveloped countries, social and political dislocations caused by the process of nation-building tend to reduce governments' observance of human rights as defined by UN Declaration.

The development of liberal democratic institutions usually is seen to occur in societies with high levels of communications, urbanization and per capita income. Thus a certain minimum level of socio–economic development is necessary for liberal democratic values and institutions to take hold in a country. The socio-political structures of underdeveloped societies are usually too fragile and inflexible to maintain the level of human rights. As a result millions of people are being deprived of basic and minimum human rights.

The different theories of rights evolved in the different points of human history have their respective merits and demerits as well. No single theory of rights can justify the true rationalization of the meaning, utility and essence of rights.

In fine, human rights are indispensable to the understanding of the contemporary man : how human beings should be treated, by one another and by national and international political bodies. Human rights are best thought of as potential moral guarantees for each human being to lead a minimally good life. In various societies the extent to which this aspiration has not been realized represents a gross failure of the emerging global civil society in contemporary world to institute a morally compelling order based upon human rights.

# 9

# LIBERTY

The word liberty is derived from the Latin word *liber* which means 'free'. The disagreement among the people about the concept and its nature is more than any other concept. Sometimes liberty is defined as the absence of oppressive or discriminatory restraint upon the existence of those social conditions which are necessary guarantee of individual happiness. Sometimes liberty connotes availability of positive social conditions for the fulfillment and development of human personality.

## Positive and Negative Liberty

On the basis of presence of obstacles, barriers and hindrances and absence of the same, the liberty can be negative as well as positive. Negative liberty is the possibility of acting or the fact of acting in such a way as to take control of one's life and realize one's fundamental purposes. While negative liberty is usually attributed to individual agents, positive liberty is sometimes attributed to collectivities, or to individuals considered primarily as members of given collectivities.

Here it is useful to think of the difference between the two concepts of liberty in terms of the difference between factors, external and internal, to the agent. While negative freedom is primarily interested in the degree to which individuals or groups suffer interference from external bodies, positive freedom is more attentive to the internal factors that affect the degree to which individuals or groups act autonomously. Given this difference, one may think that a political philosopher need concentrate exclusively on negative freedom. It is because a concern with positive freedom is more relevant to psychology or individual morality than to political and social institutions.

In its political form, positive freedom has often been thought of as necessarily achieved through a collectivity. Rousseau's theory of freedom can be seen as an example in this sense. According to this theory, individual freedom is achieved through participation in the process whereby one's community exercises collective control over its own affairs in accordance with the 'general will'.

## The Paradox of Positive Liberty

Many liberals, including Issiah Berlin, have emphasized that the positive concept of liberty carries with it a danger of authoritarianism. It is worthwhile to appraise the fate of a permanent and oppressed minority. So far as the members of this minority participate in a democratic process characterized by majority rule, they may be said to be free. The rationale given is that they are members of a society exercising self-control over its own affairs. But in so far as they are oppressed, they are also surely unfree. Moreover, it is not necessary to see a society as democratic in order to see it as self-controlled. One may instead adopt an organic conception of society, according to which the collectivity is to be thought of as a living organism. The underlying assumption behind this organism is that it will only act rationally. It will only be in control of itself, when its various parts are brought into line with some rational plan devised by its wise governors In this case, even the majority may be oppressed in the name of liberty.

In so far as the concept of negative freedom concentrates on the external sphere in which individuals interact, it seems to provide a better guarantee against the dangers of paternalism and authoritarianism as perceived by Berlin. To promote negative freedom is to promote the existence of a sphere of action within which the individual is sovereign. Within this sphere they can pursue their own projects subject only to the constraint that they respect the spheres of others.

Other theorists of freedom have remained closer to the negative conception of freedom, even though they have attempted to go beyond it. They hold that freedom is not merely the enjoyment of a sphere of noninterference but the enjoyment of certain conditions in which such noninterference is guaranteed. These conditions may include the presence of a democratic constitution and a series of safeguards against a government wielding power arbitrarily and against the interests of the governed. As Berlin admits, on the negative view of freedom man is free even if he lives in a dictatorship just as long as the dictator happens, on a whim, not to interfere with him. There is no necessary connection between negative freedom and any particular form of government.

Liberty thus has both a negative and a positive aspect. Negative liberty as the absence of restraint is a concept closely associated with the philosophy of individualism.

Renaissance gives rise to the multidimensional demand of liberty:

Firstly this demand of liberty is against the church and Papacy. It is a demand for religious liberty.

Secondly, it is against the feudal economic order. It is a demand for economic liberty of free contract and free market.

Thirdly it is against despotic monarchies. It is a demand for political liberty. It assumes that the individual, as a free agent with free will, is endowed with natural liberty from birth itself.

But this negative liberty in practice becomes a principle of anarchy rather than a body of claims read in the context of social process. It is the liberty of the possessive individual, the man of property. It has no meaning for the propertyless. The laissez faire doctrine of liberty fails to take account of the fact that differences between men are too great under such conditions to make self-realization possible for more than a few.

During the 19th century, the doctrine of negative liberty is attacked by Utopian Socialists, Marxists and Positive Liberals etc. They all vehemently protest against the exploitation of the workers which is the bane of the laissez faire society. This clamour of protest gives rise to a novel view of positive liberty having relation with equality, rights and justice. The theory enjoins that liberty in this sense means not the absence of restraint, but it is a social requirement of social man. Liberty in this sense is an aid to the development of man as a social being.

Liberty is not an abstract claim, but it is related to right, justice and equality. Liberty also is no antithesis of law. For, the state creates the positive conditions for the realization of liberty. The state limits by law such liberties of a few individuals as obstruct social welfare. Thus the doctrine of positive liberty supports the positive state with welfare functions.

Putting the two aspects of liberty together, liberty in a state ensures:

(a) the maximum of freedom consistent with social solidarity.
(b) Equal freedom to all.
(c) Similar opportunities to everyone for an all-round development of their physical, mental and moral faculties.

Marxism rejects the concept of negative liberty. It does not consider absence of restraint as liberty. Nor does it recognize the liberal freedoms described as fundamental rights as of emancipative import for man, especially in a class-divided society. It defines freedom in terms of human essence and purpose of man and his living life to the fullest extent. Liberty connotes the economic ability to satisfy the needs of the body, an effective opportunity to cultivate the mind, develop one's personality and assert one's individuality.

But true freedom is inconceivable without a free society. No society can free itself unless its each individual is free. In a society based on private property and class distinctions there can be neither equality nor freedom. Thus freedom from exploitation as well as dehumanizing effects of a capitalist social system are the preconditions of liberty under communism. In order to do away with alienation, private property must be abolished. This necessitates the socialists to take over the state, set up the dictatorship of the proletariat with a view to accomplishing communist revolution. Marxism thus advocates a revolutionary praxis to realize the goal of liberty.

## Forms of Liberty

On the basis of the nature, objectives and its relation to the various aspects of human life, liberty can be seen essentially classified into three forms:

1. Civil Liberty
2. Political Liberty
3. Economic Liberty

### 1. Civil Liberty

Civil Liberty refers to liberties available to a man in society:

1. There is right to life, It is the most fundamental of all rights. It is indeed the foundation on which the superstructure of other rights is built up. That is why all the Constitutions recognize this as a fundamental right. The assumption is that man and his life is basic to nature. Without man the world has no meaning. Therefore, man's life is sacrosanct. Thus liberty ensures not only the right to life, the protection of life, no harm to life by others and even by himself. The capitalistic society also strives to protect the right to life, both externally and internally, and violation of the same results in severe punishment.
2. Laski speaks of private liberty, which means the opportunity to exercise freedom of choice in those areas of life where the results of one's efforts mainly affect him in that isolation by which, atleast ultimately, he is always surrounded. The right to follow one's religion belongs to private liberty. There should neither be any penalty nor any advantage in following one's particular religion.
3. There is the right to privacy. This right is special to the individual. It is the right to be left alone. It means protection from governmental authority or any private individual to intrude into privacy of one's home, correspondence, or thoughts. Individual has a right to protect where he lives, what he thinks and communicates, even his free time from unauthorized intrusions.
4. Civil liberty also entails freedom of speech and expression. A democratic form of government and way of life ensures the right to public opinion, the right to self expression, the right to speech, the right to thought and occupation if they do not conflict with the public morality, common good, public health. It also includes the right to criticize the government, freedom of press, opposion of the government and its plans, programmes and policies through peaceful means.
5. Right to civil liberties, means the right to form association. In modern pluralist society, the individual can develop his personality and pursue and contribute to the common good through associations only.
6. There is the right to assemble peacefully and without arms.
7. There is the freedom of movement as well as many more civil liberties

which are provided to the citizens in various countries. They depend upon the political conditions prevailing there and the nature and form of political regime.

According to the political scientist Blackstone, civil liberty touches the three aspects of one's life: personal security, especially of movement, personal property, or the free use, enjoyment, and disposal of all acquisitions.

However, there is still one more important type of civil liberty *i.e.,* the right to equality. Here equality does not mean complete equality but equality of opportunity, equality before law, equality of treatment etc. Even in a democratic society aiming at an egalitarian society, equality may only mean elimination of man-made discriminations in which the suffering man has any role to play. These are based on colour, caste, creed, religion, belief, sex and other factors. According to Barker, "Civil liberty consists in three differently expressed articles: physical freedom from injury or threat to the life, health and the movement of the body; intellectual freedom for the expression of thought and belief; and practical freedom for the play of will and the exercise of choice in the general field of contractual actions and relations with other persons." All persons living in the state, irrespective of whether they are the citizens or aliens, are entitled to these civil liberties.

### 2. Political Liberty

Political liberty is available to an individual in his capacity as a citizen of the state. Blackstone considers political liberty as a negative liberty entailing the power of curbing government. His view assumes, that government is something external to man. But this is not true. As Barker puts it, 'Government is not external; it is in us, or springs from us.' Laski rightly points out, 'Political liberty means the power to be active in affairs of state:" The universal adult franchise and such other political rights stem from this assumption. The political liberty is exercised by the citizen through the right to vote, right to contest in the election, right to be elected, right to participate in the democratic processes subject to fulfillment of the provisions of the Constitution.

Political liberty also connotes the right to political dissent through peaceful means. It also signifies limits on powers of the government. The government has to be responsible to the people who are sovereign and are the very source of governmental authority. Laski lays special emphasis on two conditions which he considers essential for the political liberty to become real :

First is education *i.e.,* a citizen must be educated to the point where he can express what he wants in a way that is intelligible to others. He finds an education system to be defective which trains the children of the rich in habits of authority and the children of the poor in habits of submission. He doubts if such a division of attitude can ever produce political freedom because 'a class trained to govern will exert its power' (as it is conscious of it), while the other class will 'not fulfil its wants because it does not know how to formulate its demands.' For, to laski, "It is only when men have learned that they themselves make and work institutions that they can learn to adjust them to their needs."

The second condition refers to the free flow of information and news. Laski asserts, "A people without reliable news is, sooner or later, a people without the basis of freedom." Therefore, he pleads for the mass media, press, radio and television to be free and a source of impartial and reliable news.

**3. Economic Liberty**

The above discussed two liberties shall not be realized by the individual citizens if they are not accompanied by economic liberty. A hungry man knows no law, in a sense that neither he can exercise his liberty in actuality nor under obedience to the state. Therefore, individual must be free from poverty and hunger. With this end, the minimum economic requirements of food, clothing and shelter must be available to all. So does right to work and a decent wage.

In almost all modern liberal democracies, the government ensures a minimum wage for both the skilled, semiskilled as well as unskilled workers to maintain a fair standard of life by satisfying the basic needs like food, clothing, shelter etc. However this does not mean abolition of property.

Property certainly shall continue to exist but in a highly regulated form. Economic liberty also does not assume equality of income but it definitely stands for the elimination of wide economic disparities. It is believed that a state with wide economic disparities in effect becomes two States: of the rich and the poor. In such a State stability and democracy will never acquire permanence.

Laski advocates democracy in industry for purposes of economic liberty. It would be wrong to treat the worker like a commodity that can be bought and sold in the market like steel, coal, tools and furniture etc. The worker should have a respectable place in the industry and he must not live at the mercy of capitalist.

The worker should have a role not only to set up the standards but also measures of their application to judge his contribution. He must not work under fear, of being thrown out of job and the resultant starvation. Laski rightly says: "A system built upon fear is always fatal to the release of the creative faculties and it is, therefore, incompatible with liberty." In this context he urges the worker's participation in the management of industry as the best bet.

The nature of the three forms of liberties and their primary objectives can also be in conflict with each other. The enjoyment of civil liberty like the right to free expression, thought, faith, personal life, privacy etc. many times are in mutual conflict in a democratic state and so does enjoyment of political liberty by the same individual and with others. That means the civil liberty of one citizen can conflict with his political liberty.

Similarly, the workers' demand for more wages is restrictive of the employers' freedom of contract and so is the reservation of seats in legislative assemblies and jobs restrictive of others' liberties.

While in some cases political liberty may have to rescue economic liberty especially where there may be conflict of interest between the employer and the employee. In some other cases political liberty may be required to be curtailed for economic liberty.

Barker rightly points out liberty is a complex notion. It at once unites men in allegiance and divides them by its division. To bring out a harmony and reconciliation in all forms of liberty of one citizen and many, the concept of justice—law as regulative mechanism—very often acts as a guide, reference, and interpretative yard sticks.

## Safeguards of Liberty

Liberty is the prerequisite and condition for any civilized existence. Without liberty, the individual finds hardly any opportunity to develop his inborn potentiality or seek his individual best self. Therefore liberty is sacrosanct which deserves to be protected at any cost. It is feared that the government together with social and individual attitudes are some of the factors which may encroach upon and limit liberty. Hence how to protect liberty from various encroachments and what safeguards to be provided to ward off dangers to it?

Some of the safeguards of liberty are as follows:

(i) **Rule of Law:** The early liberals viewed state as a necessary evil. It is because the state restrains and every restraint constitutes a limitation upon liberty. Anarchists dismiss state as an unnecessary evil and consider all laws to be bad. For them a free people and a free society can only exist when all the laws are abolished. But these are only negative views and not deserving of general approval. Liberty cannot be a licence to do anything one likes to do. If liberty becomes synonymous with licence, then in the society there will be the law of jungle where brute physical force, deceit and fraud will rule the roost. In such a situation, instead of liberty, there will be only chaos and confusion.

(ii) **Democracy:** Democracy is the only system that can guarantee a free and fair opportunity to the individual to develop his personality. Lincoln's famous definition that democracy is 'a government by the people, of the people and for the people', remains still the standard. In a democracy it is the people's, welfare which is supreme because people arc sovereign. As against this, the dictatorship or a monarchy gives freedom only to the servile and submissive. Oligarchy also gives freedom only to a particular section of the people. It is only in a democracy that the entire population enjoys the high principles of liberty through safeguards like rule of law, application of law, interpretation of the law, by the organs of the government. Viewed thus, democracy is still found to be the best from of government the world has ever achieved.

**(iii) Independent Judiciary:** The independence of judiciary is a must for the protection of liberty. The judges must be free from the executive control and enjoy independent constitutional status. This is absolutely necessary to protect individual's liberty from any encroachment or invasion either from other individuals or from the government. For this the judges have to be fearless and impartial in dispensing justice. Only persons of high integrity should be appointed to judicial offices. Their tenure, their mode of removal, their terms of office, their salaries and perks etc. should be protected under adequate constitutional provisions. That is why all the democratic Constitutions lay down a cumbersome procedure for their removal. For example, in India judges of Supreme Court and High Courts can be removed only on grounds of proven misbehaviour or incapacity by a special majority of both the Houses of the Parliament. This is equally true of constitutional safeguards provided to the judges in USA and other countries. As J. Kent rightly says, "To give the judges the courage and the firmness to do their duty fearlessly, they ought to be confident of the security of their salaries and station."

The impartial, independent integrated and hierarchical system of judiciary in any democratic setup is highly essential for safeguarding the individual citizen's liberty for the development of their potentiality, personality as well.

**(iv) A Bill of Rights:** A detailed and written Bill of Rights is essential for the safeguard of liberty. It also helps citizens to understand their rights. It also defines and imposes specific limitations on governmental authority. The Indian Constitution provides a detailed list of Fundamental Rights of the citizens and enjoins a special procedure to effect any modifications in them.

**(v) A Democratic Social Order:** Democracy is a system of governance and a way of life. It means an attitude of tolerance, mutuality and adjustment together with a fellow feeling for each other. It implies respecting every man's dignity. A caste-or class-divided society prohibits the development of such necessary conditions for the enjoyment of liberty. For liberty to become tangible and real, there should not be any discrimination on the basis of race, colour, caste, class, creed, religion or sex etc. Similarly, liberty cannot be enjoyed in a society where widespread economic disparities prevail. The availability of minimum economic requirements of food, clothing and shelter to every person in the society is another necessary condition for the enjoyment of liberty.

**(vi) Vigilance:** The eternal vigilance is the price of liberty. In order to be free, men must be ready to pay price for it. The people should protect their liberties. They should vigilantly watch and carefully scrutinize the programmes and actions of government. They should raise their voice of protest whenever they feel their rights and their liberties being threatened. The existence of such an informed and vigilant people will deter a government from any undue interference in their life and liberty.

Liberty may be deemed as the essence of a man's democratic living. Both the Liberals and the Marxists emphasize the importance of liberty in a man's life. While the Liberals tend to limit it to the individual's political life, the Marxists seek to extend it to the entire universe which include individual, society, nature, all life itself. Liberty, according to both, is the tangible realization of human essence and an important ideal worth cherishing. It has the enriching quality of life as also the strengthening of democratic polity.

## Liberty and Pluralism

The contemporary British political philosopher, Isiah Berlin tries to identify a connecting link between pluralism and liberalism. He sees it on the centrality of choice in case of both. Berlin argues that the conflicts between values and ways of life that are the matter of pluralism require people to make choices. These choices are of utmost importance. For they involve the most basic and essential questions of human life—what one is to be and do?

Berlin's liberalism strikes a balance between conservatism and democratic society. It is inclusive of a conservative or pragmatic appreciation of the importance of maintaining a balance between different values. It also includes at the same time a social-democratic appreciation of the need to restrict liberty. For him, this is necessary to promote equality and justice and thus to protect the weak against victimization by the strong. Nevertheless Berlin remains a liberal throughout. He maintains that preserving a certain minimum of individual liberty is a primary political priority. He justifies this by an appeal to an empiricist version of a natural law argument. He writes of the existence of 'natural rights' based on the way human beings are constituted, mentally or physically. He points to attempt to alter or limit human life in certain ways. One of it entails blocking the desires, goals, aspirations inherent in us as human beings. He draws attention to an important fact that to deprive human beings of certain basic rights is to dehumanize them.

According to Berlin, liberty should not be the only goal pursued by society. It should not always trump other values but rather allow ethical pluralism to lend it a special importance. He favours letting people to be free in order to allow for the recognition and pursuit of all genuine human values. Society, he asserts, should therefore make it a priority to provide the liberty necessary for million 'experiments in living' and for the perpetuation of social and personal variety.

### John Stuart Mill *"On Liberty"*

Mill defines civil liberty as the limit that must be set on society's power over each individual. He undertakes a historical review of the concept of liberty. He begins with ancient Greece and Rome and then proceeds over to England. In the past ages, liberty is said to mean primarily protection from tyranny. Over time, the meaning of liberty has changed along with the role of rulers who come to be seen as servants of the people rather than masters. This evolution brings with it a new problem. It gives rise to the tyranny of the majority, in which a democratic majority forces its will on the minority. This state of affairs can exercise a tyrannical power even outside the political realm, when forces such as public opinion stifle individuality and rebellion. Here, society itself becomes the tyrant by seeking to inflict its will and values on others.

Next, Mill observes that liberty can be divided into three types, each of which must be recognized and respected by any free society:

First, the liberty of thought and opinion.

Second, the liberty of tastes and pursuits, or the freedom to plan our own lives.

Third, the liberty to join other like-minded individuals for a common purpose that does not hurt anyone.

Each of these freedoms negates a society's propensity to compel compliance.

Mill in his "*On Liberty*" examines the question, whether one or more persons should be able to curtail another person's freedom to express a divergent opinion. In Mill's view any such activity is illegitimate, no matter how beyond the pale of or at a tangent, that individual's viewpoint may be. We must not silence any opinion, because such censorship is simply morally wrong. Mill asserts that a viewpoint's popularity does not necessarily make it correct. This justifies why we must allow freedom of opinion. He holds dissent as vital, since it helps to preserve truth. For truth, he does realize, can easily become hidden in sources of prejudice and dead dogma. Dissent, to Mill, is the freedom of the individual to hold and articulate unpopular views.

Mill discusses whether holders of unpopular views should be allowed to act on them without being made social outcasts or face a legal penalty. Actions, for Mill, cannot be as free as ideas or viewpoints. He wants that the law must limit all actions whose implementation can harm others or be an outright nuisance. He states that human beings are fallible. Therefore they need to experiment with different ways of living. However, individual liberty must always be allowed free expression in order to achieve social and personal progress.

Mill's concern is to examine whether there are instances when society can legitimately limit individual liberty. Mill rejects the concept of the social contract, in which people agree to be a part of society. He recognizes that society can offer certain forms of protection while asking for certain forms of obligations. However, he does suggest that because society offers protection, people are obliged to behave in a certain way. Each member of society must defend and protect society and all its members from harm. In brief, society must be given power to curtail behavior that harms others, but no more.

Summarizing his views Mill advances twofold argument:

First, individuals are not accountable to society for behavior and in particular actions that affect only them.

Second, a person is answerable for any type of behaviour or action that harms others. In such cases it is the responsibility of society to punish and curtail such behavior and action.

However, Mill maintains that there are some types of actions that certainly harm others but bring a larger benefit to society. An example of it is when one person succeeds in business more than his rival.

The key concept in Mill's "*On Liberty*" is that liberty is essential to ensure subsequent progress, both of the individual and society, particularly when society becomes more important than the state. This state of affairs may obtain in a representative democracy. In such a system the opposition between the rulers and the ruled disappears. The rulers only come to represent the interests of the ruled. Such a democracy tends to make the liberty of the individual possible. But it does not guarantee it. When society becomes free of the constraints of government, it begins to entrench the interests of a select and powerful few. This brings threats to individual liberty in a new way. Mill's problem is to envision society progressing in such a way as to prevent the repression of the individual by the ever more powerful and confident majority. Social progress can only take place if limits are placed on individual liberty, but the freeing of the individual from such limits also becomes necessary.

For Mill, the only important thing is the happiness of the individual. Such happiness may only be attained in a civilized society. Here people may be free to engage in their own interests working with all their skills and capabilities, developed and honed by them through a good system of education. Mill's emphasis is on the fundamental value of individuality. He considers it most essential for personal development, both for the individual and society and for their future progress. For Mill a civilized person is the one who acts on what he or she understands and who does everything in his or her power to understand.

Mill's model is relevant to all people. It is not just meant for the specially gifted, or for advocates of individual initiative over social control. He asserts that things that individuals do are better done than those done by governments. Moreover, individual action advances the mental education of that individual. This is something that government action cannot ever do. In his view, government action always poses a threat to liberty and must be carefully watched.

Even in cases in which the government can do the job better, it is best to have the individuals manage things themselves so that they may learn and expect to take responsibility. This is not directly a matter of liberty, but it encourages habits of mind, of independence and responsibility that are required for a free people. Furthermore, it permits many experiments of various kinds of welfare. The government can act as a repository for the information and techniques.

### The Positive Use of Liberty

Liberty has a close associations with little and big causes that contribute to the mitigation of the economic privation of the masses. Broadly speaking, wealth is concentrated in every country in the hands of a few persons. They are the ones who own and control the instrument of production. They hire the services of workers to produce goods which they sell at a profit. This leads to unequal distribution of wealth which produces grave social consequences. The young children of the working class cannot get good education. Consequently the earning capacity of the former (the capitalist) becomes much greater than that of the latter (the worker). It is this which perpetuates the inequality between the different classes. On account of the unequal distribution of wealth the productive resources of the community are employed to satisfy the less urgent needs of the richer class. This is the process that results in the neglect of the production of goods and services which could have satisfied the more urgent needs of the poor.

All lovers of liberty today agree that men and women are truly free only when their bodies are free from want and their minds from external control. Freedom of speech, of writing, and of association should therefore be used in a positive way. Its chief purpose lies in securing a rational system of distribution and a rational system of education with protection against the insidious propaganda of the interested parties. The economic system can be modified by peaceful means if the general body of citizens use their liberty with courage, determination and rationality.

### Limits of Liberty

The state exists to promote certain ends. These include development of personality, the right of every individual to conceive what good life is, and the right to pursue it as he conceives it. Liberty is absolutely essential for the development of individual and society. But these ends can be realized only by living in an organized society or the state as it exists where men of diverse character, inclination and aptitude live. The majority of individuals are virtuous, honest and law-abiding. Only there are a few who have antisocial tendencies. If the function of the state is to make possible the pursuit of the good life for its members, it has also to put curbs on such evil tendencies. In fact certain uniformity of conduct has to be maintained. For this checks and curbs have to be placed in the interest of the welfare of all on these antisocial tendencies.

But force of society is to be applied only when there is commission of some obvert act by any citizen. Mere expression of an opinion or criticism of the government should not be considered enough for punishment. In this context Mill declares that 'the sole end for which mankind are warranted, individually or collectively, in interfering with the liberty of action of any of their number is self-protection.' The state exists to promote the interests of all. If it is found that a person or a group of persons is pursuing a course of action which is detrimental to the interests of many, the state should interfere with the liberty of action of those evil-minded antisocial persons. In the sphere of conduct the state should maintain a minimum of decent behaviour on the part of all so that a few are prevented from preying on the many. In the economic sphere the blind results of many of the economic actions which are voluntarily undertaken for gain by the few need to be checked. This may involve social control of economic forces. It is also necessary that the freedom of contract or of association be restrained when such freedom interferes with the economic security and protection of the majority of people.

An individual can have no rights against the state. But important still is to draw a line of distinction between the state as a whole and the persons who exercise the authority of the state. If a particular class of men exercise that authority for the sake of promoting their own selfish interests, citizens should take courage in both hands and fight to safeguard their liberty against the state. But in an ideal state founded on and, representing the interest of all, no right which is detrimental to the state can be claimed. The individual's right to freedom of person is fully protected, but in times of emergency, such as war or threatened revolution, suspected persons may be kept under restraint. Right to life is of paramount importance, but the state can inflict capital punishment on a dangerous criminal. Similarly, the right of enjoyment of property is guaranteed to the individual, but property may be attached or confiscated either as a punishment or for reasons of state's safety.

Further the citizen may make contract or form association, but if this is done for illegal or immoral purposes or to endanger the safety of the state, these are liable to be made invalid by the state.

### Decline of Liberty in the Modern State

Liberty has declined in some states and disappeared from others. Under Nazism and Fascism, French revolution and Russian revolution the dissenting voices were put down with an iron hand. Even those who had committed no crime except that of holding views on political questions other than those held by the political authorities in their state, the rulers in these states arrogating to themselves a power over men's minds unprecedented in history inflicted the worst torture and misery on the people. The tyranny they exercised was far more oppressive than the rule of any Czar, Sultan or Emperor. They dismissed freedom of thought as useless. They prohibited all freedom of association. They imposed severe restrictions upon freedom of movement as well. Even in a country like England the cause of liberty came under eclipse. As C.E.M. Joad puts it, "There have been more prosecutions in England for the expression of opinions disliked by the Government during the fifteen years that have elapsed since the war than in the half century before 1914."

Various circumstances conspired to bring about the decline of liberty everywhere in the world. As the development of science made the world increasingly a single economic unit, economic actions taken by some nations and peoples produced results upon people unknown to and even unmagined by those who have taken an action. The blindness of economic action and the growing size and complexity of the modern state have had the effect of frustrating and even benumbing the political consciousness of the individual. He no longer feels that his opinions, desires and purposes matter in the context of the larger society or they are of any importance. As he finds himself politically negligible or a nonentity, he becomes either apathetic or indifferent to politics. His sense of despair and frustration drives him to work for a revolution with the purpose of bringing a forcible change in the system which has squeezed him out. Neither sort of frame of mind is conducive to the maintenance of liberty, peace and well-being of the individual and the state.

Another reason for the decline or eclipse, of liberty is the complexity of administrative organization as well as the shrinkage of distance brought about by the wireless, the telephone and the aeroplane. The vastness of organizational structures and advances in communications have rendered the devolution of governmental functions wasteful and unnecessary. Centralization of government authority has become the order of the day. It is seen taking away the incentive of citizens to serve upon the local bodies. Those in command are becoming impatient of local differences. Such a system tends to forget the citizen and pays scant attention to the development of his personality.

Moreover, during the last century crises after crises have arisen in the different states of the world. In a period of crisis unity of purpose and unity of command are most necessary. Since criticism impairs unity and sows distrust, the voice of opposition to government is suppressed. Such an atmosphere is not congenial for liberty to flourish.

Cheap newspapers, the cinema, the radio, the TV and other electronic media are making it possible to dominate the minds of the people from outside. These appliances are used by governments to instill positive opinions into the minds of their citizens thereby making them cease to think for themselves. The grave consequences of this phenomenon are forcefully stated by Dr. Inge in the following words: "A completely mechanized society would be a servile state in which all spiritual and intellectual life would be strangled. The consummation of this type of polity may be studied in the beehive or the ants nest."

## Marx's Concept of Freedom

Throughout history, the class struggle which is going on has always taken the form of struggle for freedom. This has been a struggle for specific freedoms which people either fight to retain or see the possibility of winning. Such freedoms have been traditionally of two types: negative and positive *i.e.,* 'freedom from' and 'freedom to'. People seek to free themselves from the rule of monarchy, aristocracy, the injustice as have resulted by the traditional forms of authoritarian and regimented governments. Striven for freedom from fear and favour to establish a democratic participatory democratic social order where the life of each and all are protected in the name of personal liberty and majoritarian rule. The political freedom every citizen enjoys today has a long historical evolution entailing emancipation from the monarchical, authoritarian state. The human history has experienced the struggle for independence from the foreign rule, the authoritarian internal rule, the domination of the traditional dominant group or class or caste of people to form a rational democratic form of government based on self rule and majority participatory principles of governance.

But, for Marx, freedom means absence of man's domination by inhuman external forces. It is a state of freedom from the material dependence *i.e.,* absence from domination of money power. It is freedom from the social division of labour. It is freedom from the state understood as an instrument of a class. It is freedom from religion as false consciousness. It is freedom from labour as an objectified activity imposed upon man by economic necessity, *i.e.,* scarcity. Positively speaking, freedom means that man is free not from something but for something. It implies participation, autonomy, creativity, development and self-determination. It means all-round development of man. Man is, by nature, the creator of his own life as well as the circumstances in which he lives. For Marx, "man is a social being able to change circumstances by changing himself" The economic liberty is the precondition of political and other forms of liberty which can be achieved only by ceaseless class struggle culminating into stateless society, classless society. There is emphasis on the material conditions of man's life. In being the substructure it can enable him other forms of libetry including the political liberty.

## 1. Freedom as End of Alienation

The concept of alienation, according to Karl Marx, is the logical outcome of the capitalistic society where the means of production, mode of production, productive relations and objective of production serve the interests of the people who hold the government machinery because they own the means of production. The labour, the mass of people are alienated in the process of capitalistic production for the following reasons : (a) loss of personal feeling of identity; (b) separation of labour from labourer, the man who is forced to sell the labour for a market price to maintain himself; and (c) commodifications of labour and the product which no longer belongs to him (labourer) but the purchaser of the labour.

Referring to the effects of alienation on the worker and the capitalist, Karl Marx notes, alienated labour deprives man of his species life. Other human beings become alien to him. Communal existence becomes impossible to him and life merely a system of conflicting egoisms. Property which arises from alienated labour, becomes, in turn, a source of alienation. The process which has its effect on the worker, has its effect on the capitalist too. It deprives him the capitalist of his personality in a different way. As the worker is reduced to an animal condition, the capitalist is reduced to a symbol of money power. He becomes a personification of this power. All his human qualities are just transformed into an aspect of it. In such a situation, where labour becomes a servitude, a forced labour, there can be no freedom. To quote Karl Marx, "An alienated man is an enslaved man, enduring torment in his productivity".

True freedom can be achieved only by doing away with alienation. In such condition the true essence of labour shall be integrated with the existence and in long the run the existence shall be subservient to the essence of one's life. The abolition of private property in the means of production and the division of labour is an essential condition to realize this goal. But the final step towards true freedom where all forms of alienation have ceased to exist shall come about only through a revolutionary transformation of society from a capitalist mode to a socialist communist one.

**2. Freedom as End of Exploitation**

Like early Liberalism, Marxism too believes that freedom means absence of restraint. But regarding the quality of restraints that the latter (Marxism) wants to throw off and which the former (Liberalism) is quite content to accept, there is a fundamental disagreement. Marxism wants to shed, apart from the restraints of law and the state, such others restraints as long hours of work; arduous, dull and unrewarding job; lack of good food and living conditions and above all, constraint of finding work in which one can put his heart and soul. Again constraints imposed by lack of education also needs be broken. Liberalism, on the contrary, believes that if it were possible to control the power of rulers to dictate to the citizens, freedom will not be for off. But it will be at best political freedom. As long as the working class has to live under the constraints of productive relations and the imposition of economic slavery, Marxism believes, the individual can not enjoy a freedom which he has never enjoyed *i.e.,* freedom from exploitation of labour.

The essence of freedom consists in making oneself the master of all the means of production. This has to be attained in order to use them in accordance with a social plan. This will help usher in a society that would put an end to the former's subjection of men to their own means of production. This will mean giving 'each individual the opportunity to development and exercise of all his faculties—physical and mental, In actual fact, the realm of freedom actually begins only where labour which is determined by necessity and mundane considerations, ceases. Thus in the very nature of things this realm of freedom lies beyond the sphere of actual material production. Freedom as a goal is, so do Marxists believe, worth striving for and this can be realized only on the basis of social ownership of the means of production. The necessary condition for this is something which can only be realized by social action. It would entail the fullest development of social production on the basis of social ownership of the means of production and planning. In its developed state, it can overcome the crippling effects of division of labour. It can abolish all exploitation of man by man. It can also reduce to the minimum the hours of necessary labour for each individual and the individual energy expended on them. Marx envisions that not by controlling the ruler, curtailing the political authority and ensuring individual liberty shall the concept of proper freedom be actualized. But instead it shall be realized by introduction of the institution of socialism, by (a) social action, (b) social production, (c) social ownership and (d) social planning.

### 3. Freedom as Recognition of Necessity

Man cannot achieve freedom until he makes himself free by his control and use of material conditions for his own purpose. For the achievement of freedom depends on understanding and mastering the necessities of material existence. As Engles states, 'Freedom is the recognition of necessity'. It means necessities exist in nature and society in the shape of objective laws such as the law of gravity, law of mode of production, law of private property, law regarding the development of society etc. Until we know the laws of nature, existing and acting independently of and outside our mind, we are made the slave of blind necessity. But once we come to know these laws we become masters of nature. Viewed in this light, freedom is based on the knowledge of necessity or objective laws and in the possibility of making them work towards definite objects.

Apart from nature, man's freedom is also restricted by his dependence on social forces which dominate him under certain historical conditions as what prevails under capitalism. In a society divided into classes, the social relations are seen to stand opposed to people and dominating them. In this context, freedom lies in understanding the laws of capitalist development, destroying class antagonism and freeing people from social oppression. In the course of building socialism/ communism, the conditions of life which hitherto have been dominating people as alien elemental forces come under man's control. 'A leap from the realm of necessity into the realm of freedom takes place'. This is how the march towards freedom where necessity ends, begins.

### 4. Freedom: The Collectivist Dimension

Marxist concept of freedom is more collectivistic in nature and can be properly understood by identifying itself with class, nation and mankind than a group of people or class of people who dominate over others. The freedom of each is integrated with the freedom of all and the freedom of all is linked with complete abolition of capitalist mode of production and control over means of production.

Thus the right to liberty, Marx says, has to be deduced from the association of man with man rather than from the separation of man from man. It has to be deduced from a life in the political community where man sees himself a communal being rather than coming from civil society seeing himself as a private individual. Since man is a social being, and his human essence is his communal essence, he may become a social being only in and through the community. This community is based on common sentiments, interests, intentions, ideas and values. Here classes have been abolished and it (the community) has become cooperative in spirit. Here power has been transformed into authority. It is a community which rests upon mutual aid, assistance and solidarity. It is based upon self-government and self-management'.

Man's entry into the realm of freedom can come through the instrumentality of revolution. As Karl Marx says, "Both for the production on a mass scale of this communist consciousness and for the success of the cause itself, the alteration of men on a mass scale is necessary, an alteration which can only take place in a practical movement, a revolution". Marx continues to explain that the revolution is necessary because the ruling class cannot be overthrown in any other way. At the same time revolution has a historic role. It is that the class overthrowing it can succeed in getting itself rid of all the muck of ages and become fitted to found society anew. Thus to become emancipated, man has first to be changed and reeducated through a revolution. In short revolution is the key to both the classless society and the transformation of man.

Furthermore, freedom, to Karl Marx, is associated with humanism and different from the liberal version of it on the following grounds :

(a) Marxist freedom is based on free society rather than the open society as preached by the liberal tradition,
(b) Marx conceives of freedom which is not only the absence of restraint but also the absence of the dehumanizing factors related with the capitalist society such as alienation, exploitation, domination etc.
(c) It is based on the principle of freedom of all which can be possible only in a communist society where there is a complete harmony and concrete freedom; and
(d) This is opposed to liberal concept of majority freedom because it divides the society into rank, class, gender, and social position based on the ownership of means of production.

**Problem of Freedom in Socialist States**

The Marxist concept of freedom may be philosophically fascinating but as a political concept in practice, it is lacking in popular acceptability. Selucky blames Lenin for his failure to understand properly Marx's famous passage in the third volume of *Das Capital* about the realm of freedom as well as Engles' clarification of it in *Anti-Duhring* concerning the 'kingdom of necessity' and the 'kingdom of freedom'. The Marxist analysis of freedom in broader philosophical sense that presupposes the end of the state as an organization superimposed upon the society may be true only for this kind of freedom, and not for freedom in the political sense. Therefore, as Selucky explains, when Lenin repeats Engles' dictum that while the state exists there can be no freedom and 'when there is freedom, there will be no state'. Lenin simply means that politically the freedom is antithetical to the existence and continuance of the state and the political freedom of choice in a given circumstance.

However, Lenin uses the doctrine of Dictatorship of the Proletariat and the concept of the party as the vanguard of the proletariat after the revolution, to justify one party rule and the absence of democracy in the party itself. Soviet union soon turns into an autocratic regime which was later perfected by Stalin.

Rosa Luxemburg protests against the suppression of freedom in the name of the theory of revolution, prohibition of rival workers, parties, the suppression of freedom of press etc. Under Stalin, democracy and freedom of choice give way completely. The dictatorship of the proletariat gives way to dictatorship of the party and the dictatorship of the party ends in dictatorship of one man, the leader or Stalin himself. This is the transition in actual practice from the identity of interests of the people and the party and the leader.

In 1936 when USSR Constitution was promulgated, it guaranteed democratic freedoms to all Soviet citizens and also included a comprehensive list of rights. However, in practice, all these rights and liberties were subordinated to the monopoly of the communist party as the vanguard of the people. It is the party which was invested with the monopoly of leadership. The problem of dissidence and labour camps suppressed the right to choose their rulers in the Soviet Socialist States.

From 1970s onwards the problem of freedom became the subject of fierce debate in all socialist countries. Critical voices were heard from Neo-Marxists like Kolakowaski, Selucky, Stojanovic as well as from dissidents like Solzehnitsyn, Roy Medevedev and the like. They attacked the orthodox doctrine of party and state. They based their argument chiefly on Marx's early works. For example, Medevedev wonders, even after sixty years of the revolution, when all the enemies of the revolution have been annihilated, there should have been no relaxation in the political system. In this context, he demands the establishment of political parties apart from the communist party, freedom of speech and expression, freedom of press, democratization of the party structure etc. He highlights these as the basic conditions for protecting freedom. Again, the protest movements from many East European countries explode the myth that the State and the Communist Party are one and the latter represents the will and interests of the community as a whole. The collapse of USSR and the rejection of communist rule by the East European countries in 1989 confirm that the state sponsored freedom does not go well with the freedom of the individual.

## CONCLUSION

The balance of the real individual freedom and the community freedom lies with the integration of economic freedom with political freedom and the responsibility of the state to ensure the common standards of living to every body to exercise the freedoms given by the law, guaranteed by the law of the land, protected, implemented by the political organs of government. The liberal democratic freedom as it is today also seems to us imaginary and unrealistic because of the dichotomy of plenty and poverty. While the liberal freedom becomes the freedom to accumulate private property, Marxism precludes other more valuable freedoms like freedom of thought and expression, freedom to dissent etc. In practice, by not recognizing liberal freedoms as freedoms, Marxism legalizes their wholesale suppression and denial, and this all is done in the name of freedom.

# 10

# EQUALITY

## What is Equality

Liberty and equality are inseparable, one being the correlative of the other. Equality does not mean that all men are equal in all respects. Obviously they are not. Nature delights in diversity. Men differ in physical strength and mental equipment. Hence equality does not deny the natural differences among people. Yet equality connotes that every individual should have equality of opportunity to develop his faculties.

There are conventional inequalities, to borrow Rousseau's dictum, which are the creation of society. These can be removed by human deliberation and social planning. For example, in this category fall inequalities based on money which overshadow all natural and physical defects.

Equality also does not mean identical treatment to all. But it means only proportional equality among equals and inequality among unequals. However the basis of this treatment should be rational and just. Here the issue of equality becomes valuational involving subjective choice penetrating, so to speak, the sphere of ideology.

Equality is one of the many concepts like rights, liberty, justice etc. It is of pivotal importance in a world weighed down by many differences and discriminations based on race, colour, religion, gender, caste etc. Every modern constitution has some notion of human equality enshrined as fundamental law.

In Political Theory no concept has been more debated in regard to its nature and feasibility than this concept of equality. However, to define equality is indeed to achieve it in practice. The concept of equality can be understood not in its abstract sense but in tangible terms. It can be understood only in a relatively concrete context. Equality is neither identity of treatment nor of reward but it is differing in wants, capacities and needs. For example, 'because of the nature of their work a mathematician cannot be equated with bricklayer'. Inequalities are gifts of nature. They are inescapable facts of life. They have to be accepted in the society. Treating unequals equally can lead to as much injustice as from treating equals unequally.

Equality like liberty has also its negative and positive aspects. Equality, throughout the ages has been a great force for change, dismantling privileges—

feudal, social, economic etc.. Hence equality in the negative sense implies the end of such privileges.

In its positive sense equality entails 'the availability of opportunity' to provide equal chance to everyone develop his personality. According to Laski equality means:

(i) Absence of special privileges. The will of one is equal to the will of any other. It implies equality of rights.
(ii) Adequate opportunities are laid open to all. But it is the training offered to the citizens that makes all the difference. What ultimately counts in society is the power to utilize knowledge. Disparities of education result, above all, in disparities in the ability to use that power. Opportunity should be given to everyone to let him realize his potential and the implications of his personality.
(iii) All must have access to social benefits. No one should be restricted on any ground. The inequalities by birth or because of parent and hereditary causes are unreasonable handicaps.
(iv) Absence of economic and social exploitation.

Writing in the same vein, Barker defines "the principle of equality to mean, whatever conditions are guaranteed to me in the form of rights shall also and in the same measure be guaranteed to others and that whatever rights are given to others shall also be given to me."

The right to equality proper, for Raphael, connotes "a right to the equal satisfaction of basic human-needs, including the needs to develop and use capacities which are specifically human". To Bryan Turner, equality means the following four elements:

1. Fundamental equality of persons.
2. Equality of opportunity.
3. Equality of condition *i.e.,* making the conditions of life equal for relevant social groups.
4. Equality of outcome or result.

The first kind of equality is common to various cultural, religious and moral traditions. It is typically expressed in statements like 'all are equal in the eyes of God' or the equality of 'men as men', or in terms like 'human nature', 'human dignity' 'personality', 'soul' etc. it denotes all these concepts that they all treat men as fundamentally equal.

The second kind of equality means that all men should have equal access to important social institutions. They should be open to all on the basis of achievement and talent.

Thirdly, to have equality of opportunity in any significant content, the guarantee of equality of condition is the prerequisite. It means all competitors in the race should start from the same point with identical handicaps.

Lastly, the most radical notion of equality is the equality of outcome or results. This entails transforming inequalities at the beginning into social equalities at conclusion. Social programmes of progressive discrimination or social affirmation in favour of disadvantaged individuals and groups such as scheduled caste, scheduled tribes, women, children, handicapped etc. are meant to compensate them for significant inequality of condition This is to bring about a meaningful equality of opportunity to secure equality of results.

### The Concept of Equality–Historical Analysis

Both Rousseau and Marx trace the origin of inequalities in the rise of private property. In the primitive society, writes Rousseau, there was a complete equality and there existed no discrimination on any ground. Man for his survival was dependent upon the nature which provided for him in plenty. But with the rise of private property, the society came to be divided into haves and have nots. This is how inequality entered into the human society. From this Marx was led to conclude that without the eradication of private property equality in the true sense can not be achieved.

However there have been theorists like Plato and Aristotle who accepted and promoted inequality as a basis of their ideal states. Aristotle even justified the institution of slavery. In the Greek city-states the slaves had no political or social rights. Generally the slaves were not even treated as human beings fit enough to be citizens but as chattels or as a form of property.

Alongside the proponents of inequality there were the Stoics and other philosophers in the Greek political tradition who supported the idea of equality among men. Stoics were fired by the spirit of humanism and were opposed to slavery. They stood for universal brotherhood and citizenship. The Roman juristic concept *Jus Jentium* was indeed an advance towards the conception of equality of people. However, the Romans did practise inequality vis-a-vis non-Romans.

The medieval feudal order was out and out inegalitarian and the whole system rested on inequality. The society was divided into three groups comprising the clergy, the nobles and the common people. Only the first two groups enjoyed the rights, while the third was supposed to be unequal. Even though the Christian vision embodied the idea of universal brotherhood, it clearly proclaimed that the idea of equality was to be realized in heaven and not in this world.

In modern times the bourgeoisie employ the concept of equality in their struggle against the theory of divine right of kings. Hobbes asserts that 'men are equal' and Locke notes that to understand political power as a right, and derive it from its original, we must consider a state also of equality, wherein all the power and jurisdiction is reciprocal, no one having more than others.

Rousseau distinguishes between two kinds of inequality—natural inequality and conventional inequality. He views natural inequality like intellectual and physical strength, age, health, beauty etc. as the creation of nature and are therefore unalterable. However, as against natural inequality conventional inequality involving cases like discrimination based on caste, creed, colour, sex, property etc. as man-made and hence alterable.

The liberal tradition confronted a paradox. On the one hand it raised the slogan of equality and on the other it practised inequality. While they demolished the absolutist powers of the king in order to achieve democracy, they gave rise at the same time to a negative state whose chief objective was to maintain law and order with a view to protecting the interests of property-owners.

The ideology of Marxism arose to oppose this trend and to emancipate the proletariat from thraldom of the capitalist. Marxism was a powerful movement having a great impact on the individualist liberal tradition. It brought about modification in the functions of the liberal state. It made it a positive state performing welfare functions. But it was still far away from the ideals of equality. For it failed to raise the lot of the multitude who lived below the poverty line and did not have the minimum basis to human survival.

## Dimensions of Equality

Equality has thus many dimensions—economic, political, social and legal. Equality does not necessarily involve flat equality of income, but all citizens having the inherent right to work on fair remuneration. It also means removal of economic exploitation of man by man or of one class by another or of one people by another. In its ultimate form, equality means common ownership of the means of production and distribution.

Political equality postulates that all citizens, barring criminals and imbeciles, should have an equal share in the government of their country. On the one hand, it entails universal adult franchise and on the other, denial of political rights on ground of wealth, race or sex. For it was held that such denial violates political equality.

Social equality means absence of oppression and discrimination between man and man, group or group, on grounds of birth, race, caste, colour, creed etc. In this light, untouchability and caste system are denials of social equality.

Finally, legal equality means the equality of all before law.

Equality is thus a multidimensional concept. Its pervasiveness is felt in different fields of social life. Accordingly, the different dimensions of equality are as follows:

1. Legal Equality
2. Political Equality
3. Economic Equality
4. Social Equality

## 1. Legal Equality

Classical liberalism, in its fight against feudal and religious privileges, finds in equal distribution of opportunities and the equal allocation of basic rights of life, liberty, property as the most potent weapons. It assumes that if legal privileges are abolished and legal rights are protected, all obstacles to the pursuit of happiness will disappear. Its cardinal principles are said to be rule of law and equality of law. Rule of law means that the law is sovereign. No person, no matter how great he is or thinks he is, can declare himself above law. For that will be tantamount to arbitrary rule.

Equality before law means that law guarantees freedom and equality to each citizen. Its twin aspects are equality before law and equal protection of law. Equality before law means 'equal subjection of all classes to the ordinary law of the land administered by the ordinary law courts'. It means that amongst equals the law should be equal. It should be equally administered. That 'like should be treated alike'. In short the law must not make any distinction between rich and poor, feudal lord or peasant, capitalist or worker, since in the eyes of law everyone is equal.

In other words, equality before law entails equality of rights and duties in law. It implies equal protection of life and limb of everyone under the law. It also means equal penalties on everyone who may violate them.

However, law creates classes with special rights and duties such as landlord versus tenant, police verses people, member of parliament versus judges etc. Therefore in such circumstances, differences in rights are bound to be there.

Equal protection of law signifies equality before law. But this does not mean absolute equality. While the law does not make any distinction between the rank and file, equal protection of law means that on grounds of reasonable circumstances, certain discriminations or exceptions can be made. In other words, it means that the law, in certain special circumstances can make rational discriminations. It implies equal laws for equals and unequal laws for unequals. For example, the Indian Constitution, while it does not recognize any distinction based upon birth, caste, creed or religion, it does accept certain rational discriminations like reservation of posts for scheduled castes and tribes. Such discrimination based upon backwardness are considered rational discrimination. Law thus protects the people by unequal rather than equal application. Commenting on legal equality, J.R. Lucas observes that equality before law does not mean that the law will treat all alike, but rather it ensures that law will be within the everybody's reach. In other words, neither anyone will be small enough to be unable to take the shelter of law nor anyone will be big enough to be not accountable to law. Viewed thus, all can ask for the help of courts and are bound to obey its orders. The decisions of courts will be impartial.

However, without equal opportunities to get justice legal equality becomes meaningless. In the liberal societies, justice is both costly and time-consuming. Even though people may possess equal rights but they do not have an equal power to vindicate those rights, especially when it involves that some are more able to live it than others. Thus despite the rule of law, in actual operation of the courts, inequality is a fact of life. Yet indeed it is seen steadily diminishing due to the several reforms being carried out in various spheres of life.

**2. Political Equality**

Political equality means 'right to participate in the political process.' Political equality usually goes with democratic institutions such as suffrage, representation and majority rule. Early Liberals did not make political rights as basic rights to be given to all. According to them, only wealth should replace birth as the criterion for franchise. It implies extension of franchise given to the propertied class. It was indeed in a way an egalitarian demand directed against the privileged nobility. According to Lipson, "Humanity as a general rule has lived under regimes of inequality and privilege. The bases of inequality in political matters have been knowledge (Plato), religion and God (monarchy), birth (aristocracy), money (Plutocracy), colour (South Africa), race (Hitler), elite (Pareto, Michels, Mosca) etc. The demand for political equality, against all these, is 'one-man-one-vote'." This, in Lipson's view, is the basic principle of political equality which has now found wide acceptance. The principle entails the right to vote, the right to stand for elections, to hold public office and to exercise these rights without any distinction on the basis of caste, colour, sex, religion, language etc.

Laski also interprets political equality to mean rules of democratic governance. It may entail modifying its liberal meaning from the ability and skill to influence others. Or it implies an individual exercise in controlling, managing and arranging things according to his will. Or it may refer to the will of the party to which he may belong. Viewed in this light we cannot say that everyone is politically equal. In modern times, functioning of the government has become very complex. The real political power has come to vest in bureaucracy, police and army. People have virtually little control over these coercive agencies of the state.

According to the elite theory of democracy the participation of the people in political affairs is a myth. Again, despite all our talk of political equality, the fact is that the chief executive or party boss of this or that party can never be said to be politically equal. Political equality and political power seldom go together. Many constraints are put upon the common man not to let his voice be heard. Among the multiplicity of factors the prominent ones being different abilities or the power to assert oneself. Above all, it is uneven distribution of wealth and property. However, political equality understood as equality in law, in actual practice diminishes the right of governance.

### 3. Economic Equality

The twentieth century gave rise to a renewed interest in the economic aspect of equality, along with the means to secure it. The liberal system and the socialist system presented two models to achieve the content of equality. With it also came an increased awareness that equality of opportunity cannot be achieved by the 'majestic equality of the law'. For equality of opportunity does not imply merely the equal allotment of certain rights but also the satisfaction of certain basic needs. Tawney considers "Equality of opportunity not simply a matter of legal equality, its existence depending not merely on the absence of disabilities but the presence of abilities. Each member obtains in the community, not whatever his birth or occupation, or social position warrants, but, equal chances of using to the full his natural endowments of physique, of character and of intelligence."

For early liberals economic equality meant equality of choosing one's trade or profession irrespective of his caste, creed or economic status. Everyone was equal in regard to the contractual obligations. Economic equality also implied equalization of wealth and income. But, all these meanings failed to convey the precise connotation of the term, economic equality. As Rousseau puts it, 'By equality, we should understand not that the degree of power and riches be absolutely identical for everybody, 'but that no citizen be wealthy enough to buy another and none poor enough to be forced to sell himself'. In another sense economic equality means bringing the poor to the general starting line. It is to compensate them for those initial disadvantages by resorting to social legislation and social services. This may involve social measures like minimum wages, tax exemption, unemployment benefits, free public schooling, scholarships etc.

Laski views economic equality basically a problem in proportion involving things without which life is meaningless. He wants them to be made accessible to all without distinction in degree or kind. All men must eat and drink and obtain shelter. Thus equality, to Laski involves, up to the margin of sufficiency and identity of response to primary needs. It implies the equal 'satisfaction of basic needs as a precondition for equality of opportunity'.

According to Laski, any reduction of extreme economic equality has two aspects:

(i) it is a matter of status, and

(ii) it is a matter of property and income.

The matter of status raises the issue whether the state should seek to turn the industrial production into something like a 'partnership of equals' and should introduce a system under which the directing and managing elements stand on an equal footing.

With regard to property and income the issue is what methods the state should seek to correct inequality in their distribution. The liberal state through its policy of mixed economy, methods of differential taxation, regulation and raising the wages by methods of social expenditure, and other welfare services have been making corrections in the wide disparities of wealth. The state taxes the rich to provide welfare to the poor. While liberal sociologist like Dahrendorf, Raymond Aron, Lipset feel that through the extension of welfare services to all strata of society and redistribution of income and wealth through progressive taxation, the state can be enabled to lessen economic disparity and assure satisfaction of basic needs of all. Galbraith has gone to the extent of declaring that economic inequality has ceased to be an issue in men's minds in the Western democracies.

### 4. Social Equality

Social equality refers to equality of opportunity for every individual for the development of his personality. It involves abolition of all kinds of discriminations based upon race, colour, caste, creed, religion, language, sex, education etc. Social equality is very much linked to the issue—how the state and its laws should help promote equality of different castes, classes and races. That the state should ensure emancipation of women, equality in property and voting rights and also equality of right of admission to educational institutions.

Similarly equality of race and colour means that the class whose cause it champions is not inferior to any, be it the Negroes, blacks, Jews or the Scheduled Castes etc. It implies that no race is superior to others and that there is gender equality, that physical and psychological difference between men and women in general do not make the latter (women) inferior to men in intelligence, business capacity, soundness of judgment etc. Social equality does not admit any discrimination between the sexes in respect of voting right, entry to profession, educational opportunity, level of remuneration etc. 'Equal pay for equal work' also implies the same things that men and women should be paid equally if they work equally well.

Social equality also connotes openness of educational institutions on an equal basis to facilitate social mobility. There is ample evidence that in this field extreme inequalities prevail. In most liberal countries, education has been organized around social classes and educational opportunities associated with wealth and position. Different kinds of schools serving different social strata of society such as the elite, middle class, lower middle class and the poor masses is a common sight. In the prestigious schools and colleges where children of the affluent receive their education, they are encouraged to look upon themselves as belonging to the ruling classes, whether in the field of politics, administration or business.

Social equality means imparting same education to one and all, regardless of status, property, wealth or other similar considerations. The measures to promote equality of educational opportunity and the removal of all inequalities in the field of education should proceed together to let the society become unstratified or the school system totally undifferentiated.

## Potentialities and Limitations of Equality

The problem of equality in the liberal societies has continued to evoke differing responses from social scientists due to the complex relationship between politics and economics. While people in most liberal societies seem to be more equal socially than they have been before the advent of the welfare state in the twentieth century, basic inequalities in terms of power, prestige and wealth are very much evident today. Despite all liberal professions of public principles of impartiality and open government, there persists inequality in the economic sphere associated with capitalism. In fact, massive inequalities in the distribution of wealth, both through inheritance and personal achievements in the occupational field, are the natural outcome of the liberal-capitalist society. The industrial society under capitalism is economically unequal while politically as democracy, it is open, free and equal especially at the level of opportunity. Even though as a welfare state, the welfare and redistribution of resources do get the attention of the government, but at the same time, the requirements of free capitalist economy impose their own imperatives.

The socialist state has also not been able to solve this dilemma. However, there are American political sociologists like Talcott Parson, Kingsley David, E.M. Wilburt and the like who regard inequality as a necessary condition of all social organizations. Rather than racking their minds on the issue of the origin of inequality and social classes, they have been at pains to demonstrate that social differentiation and stratification have been indispensable to the very existence of the social structure. They have been attempting to demonstrate that each society has functional norms which promote the kind of inequality which they desire. Viewed thus, the debate over equality has been an unending one and every new resolution proves to be just the beginning for a new one. This is indeed the way of progress.

## Relation between Liberty and Equality

The concept of equality does not mean that all men are equal in mental and physical powers. The newly born babes differ amongst themselves in weight and strength. As they grow older, their inequality in the qualities of head and heart become very much evident. Such inequality may be partly due to the difference in the strength and vigour of their parents and partly to the environment in which they are brought up. But Nature seems to take delight in diversity in unity. A case in point is of two brothers who, born of the same parents and reared up exactly in the same way, do not attain the same level of physical and intellectual powers. Democracy cannot realize equality in the sense of total parity. But it can assure to every citizen equality of opportunity whereby he is enabled to develop his or her potential capacities. It can give an equal right of access to the culture of the community as well as an equal right to training in all educational institutions.

Equality also means that every one should have the equal facility to express what he thinks in words or in writing. No particular class, sect or party should monopolize such a facility. Equal opportunity should be available to everybody to combine and form associations, whether to raise wages or to oppose the government or to improve the existing conditions. Above all, equality means that everybody is equal before the law and that no one is above it. Democracy thus postulates social, economic, legal and political equality.

Some writers think that equality is incompatible with liberty. Lord Acton, for example, has observed that 'the passion of equality makes vain the hope of freedom'. This may be true if liberty is interpreted to mean freedom to exercise one's powers and opportunities in any way one may like to do. But this will be an unlicensed freedom. Such freedom is extremely harmful to the general well-being of the community. Democracy, therefore, imposes legal restraints on such actions of an individual as may prove detrimental to the interests of others. In a modern state no capitalist employer is allowed to do whatever he likes with his employees. Every government imposes a heavier burden of taxation on the rich with a view to securing a rough sort of economic equality. Similarly, there are some checks on the liberty of the rich and powerful to seize political power. The equality of voting power of all adult citizens is one such check.

In fact, true liberty is far from being incompatible with real equality, rather it is complementary to the other. Liberty without some measure of equality is hollow and equality without political liberty is meaningless. As Professor R. H. Tawney rightly notes that if liberty means the continuous power of complimentary expansion in the human spirit, it is rarely present save in a society of equals. Where there are rich and poor, educated and uneducated, we find always masters and servants. He continues to explain that gross economic inequality is the deadliest enemy of liberty. The richer classes try to keep all the advantages to themselves through their power of purse.

Equality without liberty may also mean the reduction of the vast mass of population to the uniform level of servitude. If the people are denied the right to vote, the right of liberty to express their thoughts, equality will mean only a common subjection to the power of one or a few individuals.

Conversely, liberty promotes equality and equality fosters liberty. History has shown that when a particular class is enfranchised, better opportunities for education and development of personality for its members are also provided by the ruling class.

Equality before the law also helps to bring about political liberty which, in turn, prepares a higher order of citizenry, so essential in a democracy. It paves the way for social and economic equality of the individual in society and polity.

The relation between liberty and equality has thus engaged the attention of proponents of liberalism right from the beginning. Their concern has been to know, whether liberty and equality are opposed to each other or whether they are complimentary to each other? In all modern constitutions both liberty and equality find a place in the list of fundamental rights, though in actual practice they do not enjoy the same importance. Liberty is accorded a much higher place in English liberal tradition than what it has in the French tradition. In fact the latter has always sought to secure recognition of the principle of equality. While early Negative Liberalism preferred liberty to equality and held preservation of liberty in the sense of 'absence of restraints' as the principle function of the state, the Positive Liberalism viewed equality as something good and basic to liberty. It considered both the attainment of liberty and equality as essentially complimentary to each other.

## Liberty and Equality: Whether Opposed to Each Other?

Classical liberalism believes that liberty is natural and so is inequality. So by nature liberty and equality are opposed to each other. Early liberal thinkers like Locke, Adam Smith, Bentham, James Mill, are inclined to favour minimum of restrictions on the liberty of the individual. They give premium to the idea of free market and open competition among the egoistic rational individuals. They view the outcome of economic competition, though unequal, as basically benevolent and progressive. This is a sort of legitimization of inequality which goes well with the doctrine of individualism.

From the political point of view early liberalism sees a necessary contradiction between liberty and equality. It holds that liberty is associated with the individual and equality with social intervention. Hence any move to equalize conditions and to remove existing privileges involves massive social and political intervention which is likely to adversely interfere with the individual and his private exercise of freedom. All such programmes of social equalization entail interference with the democratic rights of the individual. Hence early liberalism sees it inappropriate for the state or some other body to interfere in the life and liberty of the private citizens.

In the twentieth century, this classical liberal theory get several forceful supporters such as Bagehot, Stephen, Hayek, Milton Friedman, Mosca, Michels Pareto etc. They consider the financial and social inequalities as something given. In their view any political programme promotive of social equality of conditions or equality of outcome would require massive social and political regulation by the state culminating in totalitarian and authoritarian regime. As Hayek writes: "From the fact that people are very different, it follows that if we treat them equally, the result must be inequality in their actual position and the only way to place them in an equal position would be to treat them differently". The equality before law which freedom requires leads to material inequality. The desire of making people more alike in their conditions cannot be accepted in a free society and is a justification for further discriminatory coercion. In the same vein Keith Joseph states: "The pursuit of equality has in practice led to inequality and tyranny is not a mere accident". From the above it follows that any deliberate move on the part of the state to create significant equality would add to political despotism subordinating individual talent and achievements.

Radical equality of persons and outcome which requires a totalitarian system of regulation fails to provide sufficient guarantee to actualization of equality. Neither through total regulation nor through absolute regimentation with which authoritarian regimes seek to inform institutions of production and exchange that the prevailing inequalities can be removed. Some degree of inequality of outcome instead appears inevitable despite all social and political attempts to eradicate such inequalities.

The elite theorists argue that people are politically unequal. To save democracy and liberty from mobocracy, they think it essential that only elites (i.e., individuals and groups who are superior and hence unequal) should participate in the political process. For them inequality and not equality is the basis of liberty.

They view liberty and equality as incompatible and equality as desirable only before law. They would like to limit political equality to right to vote and election of elites. They feel that social and economic equality, to the extent it increases the powers of state, is a tangible threat to liberty.

## Liberty and Equality: Whether Complementary to Each Other ?

As the early Liberals argue that equality and liberty are mutually exclusive and conflicting, there is an implicit assumption in their view that there exists an inevitable conflict between personal interest and social requirements. As against them Positive Liberals see liberty and equality as complimentary to each other. They assign the state a crucial positive role of correcting the social and economic imbalances through legislation and regulations. The theory of positive liberalism has had such eminent supporters like Rousseau, Maitland, T.H. Green, Hobhouse, Lindsay, R.H. Tawney, Barker, Laski etc. The Positive Liberals see the individual as a social being and feel that his or her personal desires and purposes can be satisfied in the context of a social relationship of cooperation and in a social environment. They interpret liberty as 'equality of opportunity'. To them this means free and uninterrupted availability of opportunity to everyone so as to realize the implications of his personality. That such opportunity can not be provided unless deliberate social restraints are placed upon the individual freedom. As Tawney clarifies, the liberty of the weak depends upon the restraint of the strong and that of the poor upon the restraint of the rich. Everyman should have this liberty and no more to do unto others as he would want they should to do him. In other words, opportunities we need to make available to all so that they can be their best selves. It is liberty which makes equality real and the object of common pursuit.

The satisfaction of economic needs is the prerequisite of liberty. A society of economically unequals is one where gross inequalities prevail. Liberty in such a society becomes privilege of the few. According to Laski, "An interest in liberty begins when men have ceased to be overwhelmed by the problem of sheer existence; it is when they have a chance of leisure, economic sufficiency and leisure for thought; these are the primary conditions of the free man". The chief objective of equality is to put an end to all inequalities of wealth and power. Tawney supports the view that a "large measure of equality far from inimical to liberty, is essential to it. A society which permits gross inequalities cannot secure political or civil liberty. Where there are rich and poor, educated and uneducated, we find masters and servants". Inequality of wealth results in the division of society between rich and poor. In such a divided society the rich use their wealth to capture power and thus to promote their selfish ends. The same is the case with social inequality which inhibits people from enjoying liberty. Likewise equality in justice is a primary condition to attain civil freedom. But the poor owing to their inability to employ skillful lawyers are unable to get justice.

The positive liberals disregard state regulation in the economic and social spheres denying that it will lead to authoritarianism. Infact they take the view, as Hobhouse does, that the state has been driven by the manifest teachings of experience that liberty without equality is a name of 'noble sound and squalid results'. The welfare legislation, far from being an infringement of the two distinct ideals of liberty and equality, is in fact a necessary means of their fulfillment. A tangible proof of it is that the social legislation concerning unemployment, health insurance, old age pension, free education, increase in the general amenities etc., have gone well with governments to reduce the inequalities in the society. Though a fuller equalization is yet to be reached, liberty and equality complement and supplement each other. There is no equality without liberty and no liberty without equality. As Deane puts it: "Liberty and equality are not in conflict or even separate but are different facets of the same ideal. Indeed since they are identical, there can be no problem of law or to what extent they are, or can be related; this is surely the nearest, if not the most satisfactory solution ever devised for a perennial problem of Political Philosophy". Gans writes in the same vein, "there is no inherent conflict between liberty and equality. The society we must create should provide enough equality to permit everyone the liberty to control his or her own life as much as possible without inflicting undue inequality".

However, if out of liberty and equality a choice has to be made even Positive Liberalism may prefer liberty to equality. Barker writes to clarify that whatever claims are to be made in the name of equality, they cannot be viewed in isolation, for the principle of equality stands by the principles of liberty and fraternity. But still there are reasons for thinking that liberty matters even much more than equality because it is more closely connected with the supreme value of personality and the spontaneous development of its capacities. Liberty is a greater value because "the cause of liberty unites men together in something which each and all can possess, while the cause of equality, exclusively pressed, may make them sink into jealousy or myriad forms of invidious difference and produce division rather than unity". Barker goes on to add that "Equality, if pressed to the point of uniformity, would defeat its own purpose; the subject will become the master and the world is turned topsy turvy". However the better alternative is the reconciliation of both liberty and equality since the aim of both is the cultivation and development of the individual's personality.

## Marxist Notion of Equality

The Marxist-Leninists define equality as 'abolition of classes and equal social status for all'. Equality, to them, means identical conditions of people in the society. But at the same time it also involves having different contexts in different historical epochs and among different classes. In the liberal society, equality is seen as equality before law. This is in spite of the fact that the exploitation of man by man, economic and political inequality and the actual absence of rights for the working people as such remain intact in the society. Although liberal theory proceeds from the right of every man to own private property, it tends to ignore the main thing *i.e.,* relations to the means of production. Marxist humanism is convinced that whether it is economic equality *i.e.,* in the sphere of production, distribution and consumption of material wealth; or it is political equality *i.e.,* classes, national or international relations; or it is cultural equality, *i.e.,* in the sphere of production, distribution and consumption of cultural values; —they all are impossible of realization without the abolition of private ownership in the means production and liquidation of exploiting classes. According to Engles, "the demand for equality has either been the spontaneous reaction against the crying social inequalities, against the contracts between rich and poor, feudal lords and the serfs, slaves and masters, the surfeited and the starving; or the demand has arisen as a reaction against the bourgeois demand for equality and serves as an agitational means in order to stir up the working class against the capitalists. In both cases, the demand is for the abolition of classes." In the same vein, Lenin writes that only the abolition of classes will achieve social equality and help promote the all round development of human personality.

According to Marxists-Leninists equality means:

(i) abolition of the private ownership of the means of production;
(ii) end of human exploitation,
(iii) elimination of classes, and
(iv) eradication of all political and cultural discrimination against the proletariat.

Marx does not think that it is ever possible to establish equality between men in the sense of equality of physical and mental capacities. In his view, the aim is not leveling but an enhancement and differentiation of personal needs. It is only by collectivizing the means of production and by material incentives that the productive forces can be developed to a point where every human need is finally satisfied in a fair measure.

However even during the phase of the Dictatorship of the Prolctariat, Lenin makes it clear that the socialist system retains some elements of social inequalities owing, among other things, to the inadequate development of material production, the survival of substantial distribution between mental and physical labour and between town and country. Political inequality also continues to operate to the detriment of the former class of exploiters for whom there would neither be democracy nor rights. This is because classes as such would not be entirely abolished. Although classes still exist but they are now harmonious and they tend to draw closer. Prior to the formation of classless society all citizens have the same political rights; all enjoy electoral franchise and eligibility for getting elected to the various political offices.

However, the system of government remains centralized and authoritarian and the whole apparatus continues to be controlled by the politbureau of the communist party. This group virtually controls the means of production and distribution of national resources. It formulates all policies and manipulates public opinion. It exercises strict control over press, radio, television etc. This prevents the masses from knowing the prevailing inequalities and its implications.

In contrast, in the Western liberal societies, equality is constitutionally guaranteed as a political and legal principle. Here an individual's attitude towards its acceptance or its opposition is tolerated as an expression of dissent or ideological opinion. Behind all this there lies an assumption that toleration of the most diverse opinion is essential to the political principle of equality. An ideal society shall not be realized unless equality becomes all-pervasive and informing every sphere of activity. It is opposed to every form of repression and resistant to authoritarian identities.

## Equality and Justice

Justice is derived from *Jus* implying bond or tie. Justice is a social system in which men are bound together in affections and duties. However, justice like liberty is also a very complicated concept. Plato defines justice as doing one's duty and noninterference in other's. He divides people on the basis of reason, spirit and appetite, as the rulers, soldiers and the producing classes. Justice, to Plato, is concerned with the observance of duties related to one's station of life. However such a view of justice does not conform to the spirit of modernity. As Barker writes, "The end of any legal association or state is to assemble and establish the external conditions required by every citizen for the development of his capacities; and this end is the justice." For Robert Tucker the idea of justice connotes "a rightful balance in a situation where two or more parties or principles are in conflict." In view of Benn and Peters, "Justice is to act justly treating all men alike except where there are relevant differences between them." To Merriam, "Justice consists in a system of understandings and procedures through which each is accorded what is agreed upon as fair." Again as Rees puts it, 'justice requires that if two persons are equal they should have equal shares; if they are unequal they should have unequal shares in proportion to their inequality." This view has much in common with the concept of distributive justice based on proportionate equality. However, Marxists believe that private property is an evil and until it is eliminated, no truly just society can be achieved.

Thus justice is a relative concept. It has different meanings for persons of different backgrounds. A truly just society is one which provides opportunities to the individuals to develop their faculties. Viewed in this light, equality and justice are intimately related. Only in a society of equals real justice may be possible. But the idea of complete equality is a myth. It is neither feasible nor desirable. In a society of unequals, justice connoting equality would mean the following propositions:

1. Absence of special privileges and equality of opportunities.
2. Equality before law and equal protection of law.
3. Provision for political, social and economic rights.
4. Fulfillment of minimum basic needs of man *i.e.,* food, shelter and clothing.
5. Negation of wide economic disparities.
6. Absence of discrimination in terms of descent, race, colour, sex, property, caste, creed, religion etc.
7. Restraint on the rich for protection of the weak. Special consideration in politics and economy is to be given to socially and economically backward individuals and classes.
8. A balanced view of industry and economy and a just reconciliation of the interests of labour and capital.
9. Equality is to be pursued as the immediate goal to be realized even when complete equality is an impossible ideal.

In fine equality and justice together contribute to a harmonious development in the society and they together satisfy the ideals of modern polity.

# 11

# PROPERTY

According to McPherson, "The concept of property which now prevails in western societies is largely an invention of the seventeenth and eighteenth centuries, and is fully appropriated only to an autonomous capitalist market society." In feudalism there is a limited right to property—only a right to revenue. Land which is an immovable property can not be sold by the feudal lord. But with capitalism comes an unlimited right to property and property is seen as wealth or capital. In the world of capitalist market society, the idea of common property virtually drops out of sight. Instead private property—an exclusive, alienable, 'absolute' individual or corporate right in things—gets wide currency. Liberal thinkers like Locke consider the right to property as natural; it is pre-social and pre-political.

## Meaning of Property

The idea of property is an offshoot of the development of capitalism and commodity production which go together. Property in the common usage means 'private ownership'. Property confers upon the individual the right to use and dispose of what he owns in the most absolute manner. When we talk of property we mean private property. In this sense property is defined as a right *i.e.,* an enforceable claim of an individual—natural or artificial—to use some benefit of something (like land, capital, labour power and other commodities) or to some revenue from the position he holds in political society, and the right to exclude others from that benefit.

Richard T. Ely views property as 'an exclusive right to control an economic good'. Public property, for him, means 'the exclusive right of a political unit –city, state, nation etc.– to control an economic good'. The essence of property is the relation among men arising out of their relations to things over which their might extends and it implies the right 'to exclude others.'

Property may also mean a set of rights and obligations which define the relations among individuals or groups in respect of their control over material things or even persons treated as things.

Property as an institution, according to Macpherson, is "man-made device which establishes certain relations between people". Its maintenance as a system requires the consent of people and positive support of the leading class in the society. It is founded on the belief that the institution serves some useful purpose or fulfils some need.

## Development and Growth

The concept of private property is a modern concept. Its systematic development is associated with the particular set of economic conditions which are seen to hasten the arrival and consolidation of capitalism.

In the early human society which is mainly food-gathering pastoral society, everything is owned by the tribe jointly. But as the tribe settles down at one place, it comes to possess land and with it comes some dwelling units as well. However, the system of communal ownership of all the properties yet prevails. Gradually the hutment in which a family is staying by general acceptance comes to belong to that family. Private property in the form of consumable products like foodstuff also exist side by side. But as the production techniques develop and wants of people become more complex, new arrangements become necessary to cope with the changing requirements of the society. This results in the extension of private property from consumable to productive goods.

Development of private property is marked by rise of domestic and foreign trade and accumulation of wealth, sharpening of class divisions between rich and poor, and the ever growing enslavement and impoverishment of the masses. The resultant unjust order necessitates the demand for limitations on private property.

In Greek city states, the evils of private property are well understood. That is why Plato deprives the rulers from having private property. In his ideal state the rulers have no motive for economic exploitation. Plato enunciates the concept of communism of property and wives. Later on, this concept is attacked by his disciple, Aristotle. He does so on the basis of incentive argument that communal property is not looked after as carefully as private property. Besides conflicts are bound to take place, when men, unequal by nature in skill and industry are not differentiated by varying opportunities of work and enjoyment. That is why Aristotle emphasizes the need of private property for the development of individual personality. Yet he is well aware of danger of economic disparities and how they may contribute to revolution. He does not advocate abolition of property, but wants only its more enlightened and liberal use. He also justifies the inhuman system of slavery, which constitutes the basis of socioeconomic progress of his times.

The Roman Empire favoured the right of private property almost without any limit. It also guaranteed freedom of contract. This significantly added to the growing poverty of the general masses.

The medieval society, highly dominated by the Church, witnessed sharp division in terms of social classes and groups. Though the Church sometimes condemned those economic ideas as of increasing exploitation and inequality but it failed to prevent the organization of society on the basis of a solid economic system which rested on private property and thriving trade.

## Liberal Theories of Property

The liberal concept of property is a peculiar capitalist concept which is in consonance with the demands of competitive capitalist market society taking shape at the end of seventeenth and early eighteenth century. The foundation of this concept is laid initially by John Locke but soon the theory gets such powerful supporters as Adam Smith, Bentham, James Mill, J.S. Mill, Blackstone, Hegel etc. Capitalism matures under pressure of criticism by socialists from the later half of nineteenth century onwards. As a result the concept of property begins to change in direction of social responsibility. This finds expression in writings of Hobhouse, R.H. Tawney, Harold Laski, Rawls etc. In contemporary Western societies, according to Macpherson, property can be increasingly seen once again as a right to revenue and for most people this must now be a right to earn an income. Thus, under liberalism, two themes of property shoot into prominence which can be distinguished as (i) Property as an absolute right, and (ii) Property as a limited social right.

## Property as an Absolute Right

According to Macpherson, the essence of early liberal theory of property is that (i) it is an individual right, (ii) it is an enforceable claim by the state, and (iii) it is a right and not a thing. For Aylmer also 'the early idea of property is associated with absolute ownership'.

John Locke, the leading light of liberalism defends private property with two related questions: (i) why private property at all and, (ii) how those who have acquired private property can justify their privileged position? The main thrust of his justification of property points to the fact that property ownership is necessary if men are to have the wherewithal to lead good life.

Locke's natural individual right to property which is prior to government is central to his theory of civil society and government. Government has been constituted, in his view, to protect the right to property. Even if the government is dissolved or abolished, the right is retained by each individual.

Locke's defence of private property is based on grounds of individual efforts and initiative. He by making labour as basis of property and source of value, heralds the rise of new political economy and a new class to power.

Adam Smith tests various forms of property on touchstone of how much they contribute to efficient market. Even Bentham who does not approve the theory of natural rights and replaces it with utility, justifies property as a reward of one's labour. Its justification lies in security of enjoyment of fruit of one's labour, and its value as an incentive to labour and utility.

J.S. Mill sees in each portion of wealth a corresponding portion of happiness and writes; "The institution of property when limited to its essential elements, consisted in the recognition in each person, of a right to the exclusive disposal of what he or she have produced by their own exertion, or received whether by gift or by fair agreement, without force or fraud, from those who produced it. The foundation of whole is the right of producers to what they themselves have produced". Similarly for Green, the rationale of property lies in the fact that "everyone who will conform to the positive conditions of possessing it *viz.* labour, and the negative condition *viz.* respect for it as possessed by others should, so far as social arrangements can make him so, be a possessor of property himself, and of such property as will atleast enable him to develop a sense of responsibility, as distinct from mere property in the immediate necessities of life."

From the above discussion of the early liberal theory of property the following characteristics emerge:

1. Property is identified with private property. It is a right of the individual to exclude others from certain benefits. Locke defends this right as natural whereas Bentham defends it on the basis of utility.
2. Property is a right to material things rather than a right to revenue. It is an exclusive, inalienable, absolute and unlimited right to acquire, accumulate, keep or dispose of property. Property in this context can be equated with the right to ownership.
3. Property is a prerequisite of liberty. That no man is fully free unless he owns right to property in something. For property helps him develop his personality. Property helps him overcome his dependence on the will of others. Property is in itself a good thing. It is a legitimate aspiration for human striving and incentive for higher attainments.
4. Property is associated with orderly, peaceful relations among individuals. It is promotive of good life and autonomy of the individual, and above all Justice, efficiency and consumer's sovereignty.
5. Property is associated with individual effort and initiative as well as human labour. By making labour the source of value, liberal theory of property paves the way for the rise of a new class to power. The derivate of property in things from the property in one's labour makes property an exclusive right.
6. The chief function of the state is to protect property. For Locke, protection of property is the basis of the social contract. But the state while providing legal protection to property must not be seen to interfere with the free decisions of the individuals.
7. Liberalism justifies a kind of property contributive of a competitive capitalist market society. A man's own labour, his capital and land, is made such a private exclusive property as to be marketable.
8. Rights, needs, labouring capacity etc., are all associated with property. The programme of liberalism can be summed up in a single word 'property', that is, the means of production. All other demands of liberalism are derivate of this basic demand.

## Property as a Socially Limited Right

The early liberals are seen to justify the right to property on the ground that the latter provides a sense of security, opportunity to develop one's personality, meaningful freedom, indeed all the wherewith of a good life. In advocating this they give no thought to the condition of those who do not possess any property or the right to it. However, they do at times highlight the havoc that the unlimited right to property can cause to the lot of the dispossessed. When the classical liberals defend property as a sacred right, they have in mind only one or two types of property etc., land or tools used by the owners in production. Personal possessions fall in the category of the necessities or amenities of civilized existence. This kind of property, far from being a burden upon society, is a condition of its health and efficiency. It is indeed a condition precedent of its continued existence. However, as capitalism matures, the content of property also undergoes many changes:

**First,** a divorce of ownership and work occurs. Ownership becomes passive. For those owners of property, it becomes an instrument for the acquisition of material thing or a means of gain or the exercise of power. It is no longer a means of work and enjoyment.

**Second,** property consists not of personal acquisitions such as household goods and furniture etc., nor of the owner's stock-in-trade but property as rights of various kinds on things such as land, industrial machinery and plants, mines and mineral wealth, ground rents, profits, interests, shares in industrial undertakings, dividends, financial houses, business corporations, cartels, monopolies and other types of unearned incomes. Thus in reality, the greater part of property is held not for use for work or enjoyment but for acquisition's sake, for exploitation, domination, power and subjugation.

The utopian socialists have been the first to draw attention to the evil consequences of such property. Of course, it is Marx and Engles who take lead in subjecting the institution of property as propounded by classical liberals to critical analysis. While the socialists' demand have been confined to a more equitable distribution of property, Marx and Engles see in property the root cause of class division and class struggle in the society. They call for its abolition. Even the liberal writers realize that property as an absolute individual right has resulted in the extreme concentration of wealth in a few hands and massive exploitation of the working class. This accounts for transformation of negative liberalism into positive liberalism by advocating property from an absolute individual right to a socially limited right.

Many liberals at the end of the 19th century and the beginning of 20th century scrutinize the right to property and they find it not commensurate with the changed nature of capitalism. They seek answers to some fundamental questions like: Whether the right to property is unlimited? On what grounds can the state resist or through what taxation and other means interfere with this right? What is the ultimate justification of such a right? Is it a freedom to be enjoyed by a few at the expense of others?

There are liberals like Hobson, Hobhouse, Barker, Tawney, Laski etc., who plead for a limited right to property. Hobson views the classical doctrine of property as "impropriety". Hobhouse point out that before we may recognize the specific right of unlimited property we must admit a general right of property by putting due emphasis on social service and reward.

Similarly Barker writes, that the sanctity which Locke attributes to property and what is further defended by laissez faire is a right which needs be qualified and made relative to a variety of other rights. He further adds that the right of acquisition of property claimed as a condition of development of the capacity of one's personality is to be reconciled to the right of others to acquire it.

R.H. Tawney, writing in a similar vein, makes a fervent plea for the abolition of those types of private property in return for which no performance of a function may be needed.

However, the best exposition of a limited right to property is made by Professor Harold Laski.

## Marxist Theory of Property

Marxism views private property not as an individual right or a relationship between man and things, but associates it with the relations of bourgeois production. Marxism also distinguishes between personal and private property and interprets property as private property. It find its essence in its relationship with the social and economic system of society. Marxism is not against all property, but is opposed only to its exploiting variety, that is private property which carries with it relations of oppression and subjugation in all spheres of production.

Marxism rejects the view that property is a natural institution or as what Locke points out as pre-social and pre-political. Marxism also rejects the notion that property has existed since times immemorial. It maintains that in primitive society man lives on common property on the basis of communal sharing of land and goods. It is with property that socioeconomic and political inequality is born. It is due to property that society gets divided into classes and class struggle begins. In a class-divided society, rights, liberty, equality and justice remain impossible ideals and democracy becomes just a sham. Economic exploitation becomes horrible. Cut-throat competition gets sharpened and monopolies originate and thrive.

Unemployment, economic crisis like depression, recession, inflation, fall in production, trade cycles etc. are intimately connected with capitalist economy based on private property. Man gets alienated from his real self, his labour and its product. He gets dehumanized because of private property. Driven to sell his labour, the worker sinks to the level of a commodity. He becomes, indeed, the most wretched creature, a commodity of commodities. In a society based on private property, money becomes the common denominator of all values. Property becomes the criterion of honesty, goodness, beauty, power etc. and this distorts all human relations.

Marxism envisages the end of alienation only as the result of the abolition of private property. Since the totality of alienated social relations and social processes are property driven, thus by abolishing private property, Marxism claims, communism will put an end to the alienation of man owing to oppressive production forces and relations of production. It will bring about the genuine acquisition of human essence by man and for man. The essence of socialist property is that it belongs to the whole of society and is not exploitative. Its object is to generate collectivity in production, uniformity in consumption and equitable, if not equal distribution of the benefits of socioeconomic system.

Karl Marx is also well aware of the positive effects of private property. He considers it responsible for development and progress in human society. However the net effect of this development has not been healthy because the property divides the society into two classes—the property owners and those who do not possess property, in other words, haves and have-nots. These two classes struggle as their interest in terms of property clash with each other. In this struggle, the state is always on the side of property-owners. They, through their control over the state, further their interests. The property owners not only control the state apparatus but they also control other institutions like religion, ethics, family etc. through their ideology. Thus the history of mankind is a history of domination of the property owners over the propertyless or the have-nots.

Marx differentiates two kinds of property: The first is consumable items or personal property which is meant for consumption such as food stuff, house, utensils, car etc. Marx has no objection to their possession by the individuals. Second is the producible or private property which includes land, rent, profit, cash in banks etc. It is a property which is used for making more and more property. And thus it is this which is the cause of all the evils in society and therefore he pleads that it must be abolished.

Marx considers property as responsible for the creation of state. As Engels says, "The state did not exist from all eternity. There have been societies without it, that had no idea of any state or public power. At a certain stage of economic development which was of necessity accompanied by a division of society into classes, the state became the inevitable result of this division. This stage of economic development was that of the beginning of private property whose protection gave rise to the state. Property creates classes and class conflict, and the class conflict creates the state. The highest purpose of the state is the protection of private property." Marx and Engels declare in the *Communist Manifesto* that the theory of communism may be summed up in a single sentence—the abolition of private property.

Marxists are also critical of modern democratic society. They hold that political power is exercised and controlled by the people for their own benefits. That the liberal state is just like any other state designed to protect and promote the private property and oppress the working class.

Marxian critique of capitalism can be better understood in terms of theory of alienation.

## Marx's Concept of Alienation

Property, for Karl Marx, is a form of failed appropriation. We acquire only the external nonhuman aspect of things, and fail to acquire their richer substance.

Marx finds man's alienation in capitalist society in four ways:

(i) from nature
(ii) from his product,
(iii) from his species being and
(iv) from himself.

In other words man's alienation can be viewed and understood from four different perspectives:

(i) in relation of worker to the product of his labour
(ii) in relation to the activity of production and its impact on the worker
(iii) in relation to himself and
(iv) in the context of his social life to other men.

## Man's Alienation —The Result of Private Property

It is private ownership of the means of production that leads to man's alienation from his labour. Marx says : "The more the worker produces, the less he has to consume; the more value he creates, the more valueless, the more unworthy he becomes; the better formed his produce, the more deformed the worker; the more civilized his object, the more barbarous becomes the worker; the more powerful labour becomes, the more powerless becomes the worker; the more ingenious becomes the worker and more he becomes nature's servant." The worker thus himself becomes a commodity like labour and more the commodities he creates the more cheaper becomes his labour. Whatever he creates he has no control over it as it is independent of him.

His work becomes his enemy, as an alien power confronting him. Thus the capital, according to Marx, is the cause for man's alienation. The worker does not enjoy the work or the creation he makes. The worker, therefore, only feels himself outside his work and in his work feels outside himself. His labour is therefore not voluntary, but coerced, it is forced labour. All the human values also come to be dominated by the consideration of private property. Money, thus, becomes the basis of honesty, gentleness, beauty, powers, and wisdom. One is judged by his ability to amass more and more property. In this respect the capitalist is no way better than the worker. He also becomes a machine to produce more and more money. Thus, according to Marx, alienation is not limited to worker alone but the capitalist as well. He also becomes a victim of the same kind of alienation. Capitalism is thus doubly condemned, from the worker as well as capitalist's point of view. For none of them controls its operations and enjoys its product.

Marx concludes that property is the cause of all political, economic and social evils. He sees the only remedy in the overthrow of the capitalist system and the regulation of property under Socialism and Communism. The overthrow of capitalism will be followed by the establishment of socialist democracy or dictatorship of the proletariat where the institution of private property has been done away with. People will be rewarded according to their efforts and 'each will get according to his needs.' In communism, man will really be a freeman, an unalienated man, a total man. In communism, there will be no private property, no classes, no class exploitation, no class conflicts and hence no government or state.

However, even during the times of Marx and Engels and also later, there develops a different brand or shade of socialism which does not share many of their views including views on private property. The list includes evolutionary socialists, the Fabians, the Guild Socialists and the Democratic Socialists who do not want the abolition of property. Rather they share the liberal idea of property. They justify its existence and consider it necessary for the development of individual's personality. However, what they really favour is the regulation of property, so that it is not used for exploitation but for common good.

## Laski's Views on Property

In his book entitled *A Grammar of Politics*, Laski discusses the concept of property under the following heads:

1. The present system of property
2. Moral basis of property
3. Property and effort
4. Property and theory of industrial organization
5. Property and the new social order.

### 1. The Present System of Property

To Laski, the possession of property means security, protection from the fear of starvation. One may not accept the work he does not desire. He can take leisure, indulge in artistic things, can avoid the grim routine, become an explorer. He can protect his children against the dread of want.

However, the problem is that men of property who own property dominate the political system. Those devoid of property live no meaningful lives. This is despite ownership of property has no relation with the performance of duties or the possession of virtue. Property controls capital, which in turn, involves the power to direct the lives of those who depend upon the application of capital in the production process. Again, regime of private property makes the state very largely dominated by the owners of private property where the propertyless do not have substantial rights.

In this way property perpetuates division between rich and poor. It severs the poor from the conditions which make possible and effective their citizenship and their lives livable.

In the present system of property, Laski writes, production is carried on wastefully and without adequate plan. The distribution is never related to the needs or social urgency. Things are produced not so much for use but to acquire more profit. Profit, competition, adulteration, corruption become the hallmark of production.

Laski refutes the justifications of property given by classical liberalism. As he explains it is not correct to hold that man needs property because it provides an incentive to labour. The truth is that the power to acquire property may defeat more incentives than it creates.

The ethical justification that property is the reward of individual's efforts is also not tenable because in a capitalist society, it has become the reward only for that particular kind of ability which consists in the capacity to make profit. It is not correct to emphasize that property is the nurse of virtues essential to society such as love is to the family. For, virtues like generosity, inventiveness, energy, are not seen in the majority as satisfying the impulses essential to social well-being.

Laski considers even the historical argument not tenable. He finds as misleading that the progressive societies are those built upon the regime of private property because private property is not something unchanging.

Thus Laski concludes that there is little rationale in the present basis of property as an individual right. For all property depends upon the sustenance of society and its rights are socially created and they are relative to social needs. Hence he pleads that we need to reconsider if property is to be made a right.

### 2. Moral Basis of Property

After rejecting the classical doctrine of property, Laski offers a new basis why property is needed in the society. He argues that as a member of society, man should have the right to control things in order to be his best self. He has a right to such a claim so that he may be able to satisfy his primary material wants—hunger, thirst, demand for shelter etc. These needs are the basis for the realization of an individuals personality and these minimum claims are universal.

Thus, to Laski, this right of property is relative to the duties performed in the society. No man has a moral right to property except as a return for functions performed. No man has a right to live because another has earned what suffices for the formen's maintenance. That alone is moral which is the result of one's personal efforts. Those whose property is the result of other men's efforts are parasitic upon the society. They have legal rights but because those legal rights are not born of their personal efforts, 'they lack the moral penumbra which entitles them to respect'.

Laski's total rejection of the hereditary wealth is because it produces a class which is free from legal obligation to labour. However, inheritance to him is always justified as the provision of an income for widowhood and the children. In short, property is entitled to exist where it results from personal efforts. It is rational when it is the outcome of functions.

### 3. Theory of Reward

Laski asks if property is the result of functions, then what needs be ascertained is how much income one should receive for his labour. Here Laski puts forward four theories of reward, the first three he rejects and upholds the fourth one.

The first theory is regarding the general communist theory of equality of income to all. Laski's plea in not accepting this theory is that 'when effort is demanded of all, there seems no justice in an equal reward for unequal effort. Nor does it seem just to reward equally where needs are unequal.'

The second theory postulates that the reward should be fixed on the basis of free contract and the principles of demand and supply. But Laski rejects this theory too on the ground that where parties to the contract (workers and capitalist) are not in a position of equal bargaining power, freedom of contract is meaningless. It is also lacking in moral worth because it leaves one third of the average industrial community on the verge of starvation. It means in their case 'poor health, undeveloped intelligence, miserable homes and work which can find no source of human interest.'

Laski also rejects the third theory which connotes that each individual may contribute to society according to his powers and be rewarded by society according to his needs. This principle does not hold water because it is not clear by what criteria can we judge the needs of a person.

As against these three theories, Laski puts forth his own theory based on the principle that the reward must satisfy the two conditions: First, it should enable the individual "to reach out towards his best self, and second it should preserve and develop the necessary functions in the society."

Allthrough Laski's concern is how to reconcile the interests of the individual and the community. He asserts that the needs of the citizens must be met in the degree of their importance but without impairing the general productive fabric. No person is entitled to secure remuneration except on the condition of performing work which is recognized by the society as useful.

Moreover Laski favours in fixing the just principle of remuneration, apart from the wage that covers the cost of one's effort. He urges that wages must be paid in a manner that each socially necessary occupation is able to attract a sufficiency of talent to run them adequately.

Laski's theory of reward also entails that all alike are entitled to find the wherewithal to full life. However, beyond those means and amenties differences must be reconciled keeping in mind the common good of the society.

### 4. Property and Industrial Organization

The right of property, according to Laski, also involves a theory of industrial organization. Since property in industry means 'capital to be hired,' therefore a discussion of its rights is indeed the discussion of the powers which should belong to those who loan it on hire. Working on the theory that no man is entitled to wealth he has not earned, Laski says, no man should have capital to hire which is not the result of his personal effort. In his scheme of things hereditary business enterprise has no place. Industry must be made a profession *i.e.,* it must be inspired by the principle of public purpose.

In order to professionalize industry Laski recommends three types of changes:

(i) The owner of wealth should be changed into a person to whom a fixed dividend is paid for the use of his wealth. He must cease to be the controller of the business in which the property he owns is invested;
(ii) the control of the industry should be handed over to the working class; and
(iii) social element of the industrial equation must be improved.

This can be achieved, according to Laski, by socializing those elements meant for the common welfare either through nationalization or through other means. Other suggestions include: introduction of standard hours of work and rates of pay in all the socialized or private industries; and insistence upon qualifications and publicity. By taking such measures, he thinks that the ill effects of property on the working class can be avoided as well as the overall industrial capacity can also be improved.

### 5. Need for a New Order

Thus referring to views on total rejection of the system of private property as propounded by classical liberalism, Laski sounds a note of caution: "No effort is more suspect in our time than the criticism of the existing right of property. It is wrong because it is subversive. It is futile because it is utopian, erroneous because it is counter to external laws of human nature."

However, to Laski, the existing right of property represents a moment in historic time; it is not something permanent and inviolate. Property is a social fact which is prone to change like every social fact.

Laski considers the present system as inadequate because it inhibits the exercise of those qualities which would enable them to live a full life. Morally, the system is inadequate and deficient because it confers rights upon those who have done nothing to earn them thereby depriving the rest of the community to live an ample life. It is economically inadequate because it fails to distribute the wealth it creates. Besides it is unable to provide the necessary conditions of health and security to those who live in want. Hence, the system is in constant danger of collapsing as it has lost the allegiance of the vast majority.

To Laski, there is nothing wrong with the notion of private property so long as it derives from personal effort and organized in such a way as to involve an addition to the common welfare. Neither must it be so large in amount that its owner exercises power by its sheer magnitude nor must it be so small that its possessor cannot be himself at his best. The more equal its distribution, the more likely is the citizens' contribution towards social good.

## Twentieth Century Changes in the Notion of Property

The twentieth century liberal notion of property while it rejects property as an absolute individual right, it believes in a regulated economy with regulated private property. This equally applies to the advanced capitalist countries, where the society as a whole operates through the instruments of welfare. The welfare state too is a regulated state and is very much concerned with the allocation of property. Through its policies of progressive taxation, police powers and compulsory acquisition of property for public purposes after giving due compensation, the present day welfare state has created new forms of property management and distributed them widely. According to Macperson, "When the allocation of natural resources, capital and labour was being done by the market, property as an exclusive inalienable individual or corporate right in things was necessary. But in the twentieth century, when the role of allocation of resources has been taken over by the state, 'property as an exclusive individual right in things has become less necessary'. This does not, however, mean that this kind of property is less desired by individuals or corporations; it only means that as this kind of property is less necessary to the work of allocation, it is difficult to defend it as an essence of property."

The welfare state today has taken a number of measures to provide amenities to remove 'economic hardships' such as old age pension, unemployment compensation, medical care, retirement funds, welfare benefits, employment opportunities etc. Due to welfare measures taken by the state, incomes have risen above the level of subsistence. Work is no longer compelled by stark need. This is in spite of the fact that the state today also provides such things as family allowances and various free and subsidized services. Thus, in a sense, almost everyone has some property in such rights. However, most people still have to work for most of their income. In the advanced capitalist societies, salary earners are increasingly coming to see property as the right to a job or right to be employed. Since this may involve a right to access to the means of labour which they do not own, they have come to espouse what has been earlier done by socialist and radicals in the nineteenth century. Today, it is becoming very much a part of the thinking of non-socialist organized labour movements who view the worker's main property as his right to a job.

Property today is seen as a right to access to some of the existent means of labour, no matter by whom are they owned. This amounts to a considerable transformation of the concept of property. For example, Rawls omits private property from the basic rights of men. He sees a market socialist economy as well as a capitalist economy as compatible with liberalism.

## CONCLUSION

Thus property in the present context, connotes a right. It amounts to the recognition of property as "right not to be excluded from the society's whole material output and from the access to the accumulated means of labour." This is an advance to the liberal doctrine as it develops from Locke to Bentham. Property now is no longer seen to be an exclusive, inalienable individual right over things. It is not a right to unlimited accumulation of property to the extent of treating private property as an end. It does not imply equating property with personality, freedom and human essence or orderly and peaceful relations among the individuals. As against this the new liberal version classical liberalism has been underlining the benefits of private property and the political conditions of its maintenance. This essential liberal theory of property is based upon three essential principles:

(i) Property as right to material means of life,
(ii) Property as a right to a free life, and
(iii) Property as a right to the fruits of one's labour.

In the latter half of 19th century, the classical liberal notion of property comes under criticism by the socialists and radicals. Also the maturity of the capitalist economy itself brings about certain changes in the notion of property. In the twentieth century, with the emergence of welfare state, many amenities and social services which have been hitherto purchased by the propertied class with their property becoming accessible to the propertyless through the state. The role of the state in the allocation and regulation of property is emphasized. The State becomes an agency to get the money through taxation and other compulsory means from the rich and distribute it in the form of social services to the poor and the downtrodden including the working class. Today, the salary and wage earners see their right to job as property. Thus in today's context, property has become not an individual right to exclude others but more as a right not to be excluded from the material resources as well as from an access to the means of labour. In this way the rights to the means of life, liberty and labour today can be better secured by the guarantee of access to the means of labour on equal terms rather than by treating property as a mere private individual right.

# 12

# JUSTICE

## The Concept of Justice

The word "justice" has myriad connotations: To a man of law, justice may mean the judgment pronounced by a judge; to a man of religion, it may mean a set of morals and values which we ought to follow; to a poor man it may mean abolition of poverty. Again to a Cephalus, justice may mean keeping one's word; to a Polemarchus, it may mean helping a friend and harming the enemy; to a Thrasymachus, justice may mean the will of the stronger to be imposed on the weaker; and to a Glaucon, it may mean the protection of the weak. The list is not exhaustive and only contains a few noted examples. The fact is that the meaning of the word 'justice' depends on our view of society. It may vary according to men's perception as to where do they find themselves in the society. A worker's justice would include, among other things, adequate wages; a subaltern's, absence of outrages committed on him; and a feminist's, abolition of male repression.

## Etymology and Development

The concept of justice has developed over the ages. Its etymology and meaning have varied with inhabitants of different states.

Justice is derived from the Latin word *jus*. It also includes *justus* and *justitia*, and is also connected with the word *jungere.* So originally the Latin word, Justice with differing shades, means what Professor Barker says "primarily a joining or fitting, a bond or a tie, gliding into a sense of binding or obliging." Defining the word *jus,* Professor Barker remarks that in its original form, it means something "what is fitting and therefore, also binding".

Reflecting on the etymological meaning, Barker sees the word *jus* to convey "the idea of valid custom to which any citizen can appeal, and which is recognized and can be enforced by a human authority." Thus while largely drawing from the original Latin word, Barker gives justice a legal connotation. So, he says, the word *jus* in its developed form means, body of binding or obliging rules which the courts recognize as binding, and not only recognize but also enforce. However justice, as he puts it, is not merely a relationship between man and man (as about law and as in courts), but is a relationship between value and value. So the function of justice in this sense may be said to be that of adjusting, joining or fitting the different political values. Viewed thus, justice is the reconciler and the synthesizer of political values: justice is their union in an adjusted and integrated whole.

The word 'justice' has been given different meanings in different times. For the Sophists of ancient Greece, justice means the interest of the stronger. It means, the social group which is militarily stronger and economically richer is to impose its will on the other groups. As against these, Plato gives preeminence to the moral and ethical element in justice. For him justice is said to mean performing one's duties with all abilities and capacities towards the social whole. For Aristotle justice means equal share to the equals and unequal to the unequals, distributing power and position proportionately to the worth or contribution of the individual.

The Romans are known for their contribution to law in the Western Political Thought. They use *jus* (justice) to denote the body of laws and the courts which enforce them. By it they mean to include laws emanating from customs, legislative declarations and judicial pronouncements.

During the medieval period, Christianity and the institution of the Church have been dominant. It is then that the idea of justice comes to be related to the idea of the rule of right, the idea of morality, the idea of righteousness, the idea of justness. Significantly there is to be seen four categories of law in the hierarchical form in the writings of St. Thomas Acquinas.

For Acquinas, there is the *lex aeterna*, the eternal law, the supreme and the one that exists in God; the *lex divina*, the divine law which is below the eternal law and one that exists in the scriptures; the *lex naturalis*, the natural law which is at number three below the eternal law and the divine law. The one that exists in the reason implanted in man by God and below the natural law, is the *lex humana*, the human law. It expresses itself in accordance with all the higher types of law and is made and imposed by human authority.

Justice, during the medieval period, mostly means a body of ethical rules emanating from the scriptures. They reflect man's sense of morality and those made by man conforming to the principles of eternal, divine and natural law.

The natural rights theorists of the early modern period view justice as the rule of reason. They see it as a bridge between the medieval religious notion of justice and the ethical notion of justice as developed by a modern rationalist being. Locke upholds this concept of justice. Moreover, law also means the expression and embodiment of justice. This is the meaning given to the word 'justice' by theorists during the most part of the eighteenth-nineteenth centuries. They declare law to mean the declared will of the state and as the most obvious dimension of justice.

With the advent of democracy and democratic institutions and processes, justice comes to mean an equal participation of all the sections of society in political and public affairs. In liberal parlance justice becomes another word for legal and political equality. It includes in it, the rule of law, equality before law, equal protection of law, one person one vote etc.

Again, with the development of industry and industrialization, economic dimension of justice comes to be advanced and emphasized by socialists, syndicalists and anarchists of various hues. Justice comes to refer to the establishment of a just social order in which there is no economic exploitation and political enslavement. They are joined by the Marxists who develop their own idea of socioeconomic justice which not only comprises just laws, but also a just society.

Social justice too, which is a recent phenomenon, is associated with an egalitarian order of society based on the social ownership of means of production, if possible and without private property, if necessary.

Thus Justice, in the Marxist sense, means distribution of productive load 'according to each one's capacity, and of its benefit according to their needs.' In the contemporary liberal and libertarian usage, Justice has now come to mean sufficiency for all and thereafter competition for greater benefits.

## Dimensions of Justice

The concept of justice has been changing over the ages according to the socio-economic and political requirements of society. If it is dispensed by the state through its law, it also refers to the political, economic and social aspects of the political system. Justice has various dimensions, the most popular being:

1. Legal Justice,
2. Political Justice,
3. Economic Justice, and
4. Social Justice.

### 1. Legal Justice

Legal justice is seen to be associated with the legal system, civil and criminal laws, judicial process and institutions of the society. In legal terminology, the system of law has come to mean the system of justice. It refers to how the laws are made by the legislature, how they are executed, and how the obedience to laws is secured.

Broadly speaking, legal justice has two interconnected components:

(i) just laws, and
(ii) just administration of laws.

By just laws is meant the substantive element of the laws. That is, the laws made by the legislature should be reasonable. They should be in consonance with the prevailing social and moral values and norms of the society. In the liberal democratic societies, the aim of law is not only to protect the individual from violence, assault, assassination, libel or slander, false imprisonment, or adultery but also to guarantee the fundamental rights, civil liberties, and equality before law and protection of property. Thus any laws, customs, traditions or conventions which violate these basic principles are deemed as unjust.

The laws should not only be just, but no less important is that they be administered in a just manner. With a view to ensuring security to the life and property of the individual there is need to remedy if there exists any defect or delay in the administration of justice or any partiality or ambiguity in the interpretation of laws. The true test of the excellence of a government lies in the efficiency of its judicial system. For there is nothing that more nearly secures the welfare and security of the average citizen than his sense that 'he can rely on the certain and prompt administration of justice'. Those who administer justice in the courts, the way they perform their functions, the mode of their appointment, the terms and conditions of their services—they all are central to just administration of justice.

Aristotle is credited with making a distinction between 'the government of law' and 'the government of men'. This has come to be a part of the great liberal tradition.

Just administration of laws include:

(a) Rule of Law,

(b) Impartiality of the judges, and

(c) Independence of judiciary.

### *(a) Rule of Law*

According to Dicey, justice consists in equal subjection of all classes to the ordinary law of the land; the principle of equality in the eyes of the law; that every body irrespective of caste or creed, wealth or position is equal in the eyes of the Jaw and has to obey it. Justice is thus termed as the impartiality of law.

Secondly, none shall be detained or wrongfully arrested unless his guilt has been established in a duly constituted court of law and in accordance with a duly constituted procedure. This doctrine seeks to secure the fundamental freedom of the individual through law. The basic requirement is that differences in treatment must be justified by a reference to relevant differences of attribute or condition i.e., differences recognized by the rules. Differences in treatment must be proportionate. That is, given the grounds of distinction, one can still challenge the degree of discrimination.

### *(b) Impartiality of the Judges*

Legal justice is associated with certain special expectations: Since we have to live in a society in which we have to be subject to rules not of our own choosing, we have to submit our disputes before the courts and commit to abide by their decisions. We are entitled to have an assurance that justice is being done; that the decisions of the courts conform to the principles of just laws; that the judges do not decide cases in the light of personal considerations like fear for their job or hope of reward. In other words, we need to be assured of the impartiality of the judges. For they have a duty not only to do justice but also to make their decisions strictly conform to the law. For the law is not simply a guide for the judge, but it is also a basis for prediction.

### *(c) Independence of Judiciary*

Independence of judiciary has a deep relation with impartiality of judicial decisions. The judiciary is seen as the watchdog of the constitution and protector of the rights of the people. For this the executive or the legislature should not be permitted to have control over the judiciary. Otherwise there are fair chances of manipulation of justice in favour of one or the other. The manner in which judges are appointed, the terms of service under which they work, should all be settled and secure so that they feel free to act in an independent manner. Also justice should be swift and sure, and very much within reach of the poor. In other words justice must not be costly and the judicial process should be simple, direct and inexpensive.

## 2. Political Justice

The political component of justice is the gift of liberal democracy. It involves the availability of equal political rights to all citizens and their association with the decision-making process at the political level. Liberalism redefines the relationship between the individual and the state in terms of concepts of rights, liberty and equality. Political justice consists in the equal dispensation of political rights. These rights include universal adult franchise, right to contest elections, and hold public offices. They also include right of association, freedom of movement, freedom of speech, thought and expression, and right to criticize the government. Political justice also entails the belief that political power is based on the consent of the governed. It is a trust reposed by the people in the government. It considers the holders of power responsible to the people. It sees people as the ultimate source of power, the final arbiters, the rulers. The other dimension of political justice refers to more and more people gaining entry in the decision-making process at the political level. It implies the democratization of the political process as well as decentralization of political power. It involves participation of individuals and groups in the decision-making process, respect of public opinion, and a broad consensus among the people regarding fundamental political issue(s).

## 3. Social Justice

Social justice connotes the reconciliation of the individual with the social interest. It is intended to promote the idea of social good. Social justice means that everyone has equal opportunities for the development of his personality, without any discrimination on grounds of race, colour, caste, sex etc. It sees every kind of discrimination as illegitimate since it deprives individuals and groups of people from certain benefits that are generally acknowledged to be common rights. In other words, the aim of social justice is to correct the arbitrary and uneven distribution of talent and natural abilities on the basis of the principle of equality of opportunities. It is to level up uneven distribution of wealth and income, secure the protection of minority rights and abolition of untouchability, apartheid, poverty, ignorance and illiteracy. The purpose of social justice is the interest of the community as a whole which can be better ensured by the development of the underprivileged. Social justice implies the predominance of the interests of the community and restricting the rights of individuals, interests. Social justice also denotes the notion of reform and social change. It involves reformative justice, a restructured social order and redistributed rights to promote the sense of equity, fairness and justice. The modern welfare state provides for social equality, social security, unemployment allowance, old age pension. These welfare measures were unheard of in classical liberalism. But they have become today a part and parcel of the twentieth century idea of social justice.

### 4. Economic Justice

The economic dimension of justice has been the basic element of the socialist movement. Marx and his followers found the capitalist system a symbol of economic exploitation and injustice. They called for a revolutionary transformation of society with a view to attaining economic justice. As against them, the evolutionary socialists and Fabian socialists demanded drastic economic reforms. The votaries of social welfare liberalism of the twentieth century associated economic justice with the satisfaction of the basic economic needs of society. Their chief concern was to provide food, clothing, shelter, and employment to every able-bodied citizen. Positive liberalism of later years, thus, holds that for a hungry and an unemployed man freedom is just an empty word if it fails to secure economic justice. And economic justice also comes to imply equal pay for equal work, provision of social security like old age pension, gratuity, provident fund, and equitable tax regime to keep the income/wealth differences within reasonable limits. Economic justice also comes to mean the building up of a national economy in order to meet the essential needs of the society and to secure benefits of increased production and wealth to the masses.

In the modern-day liberal democratic societies the purpose of economic justice is primarily redistribute justice. This view has received support from the neo-liberals like Laski, MacIver, Barker, Hobhouse in the first half of the twentieth century and by John Rawls, Chapman, Plattner in recent times. Their plea is that the state through its intervention in the economy should protect the interest of the weaker sections of society. In the process it should further the cause of justice and liberalism. However, they are well aware that the policy of redistribution should receive due attention. But at the same time, we need understand economic equality which is the basis of economic justice and is a cherished value. It cannot be had at the cost of efficiency and fast-track growth. Society must also need to use material rewards as incentives to production.

## The Concept of Justice: An Overview

Justice has been conceived historically in two separate ways: as a supramundane eternal idea which is independent of man, and as a temporal man-made social ideal.

The two meanings illustrate the difference between contemplation and action, philosophical reflection and practical conduct. In between the two there is a space termed as a middle ground in which theory and practice of justice are intermingled.

According to the first view, an idea or tradition of justice is conceived to exist apart from man. It is seen to stem from a higher source. Man seeks to know its nature and draw inspiration from it in his actions.

According to another view justice is completely dependent upon man in its inception and practice.

There is also an intermediate ground in which we find each of the preceding two conceptions in various intermingled forms. The fact is that each of these conceptions or positions may be discerned in the writings of ancient and modern thinkers. But it is in the middle ground where the tradition of justice appears currently in the form of man's faiths, ethical beliefs, and social institutions.

## Development of the Concept of Justice

Plato's theory and definition of justice is found in his conception of the division of the ideal state into three classes: They consist of a small body of rulers in whom wisdom is found, who have attained a knowledge of absolute justice. The guardians (military or auxiliaries) are those in whom courage flows naturally. Lastly, the artisans or governed (slaves are excluded). Justice is the unifying and harmonizing principle that keeps all three in equilibrium. The state of justice occurs when each individual functions properly and in harmony with the others. Plato wants it to be realized in compliance with each one's proper function according to his class. And he does this without interfering with the other two classes. For injustice consists of intermeddling and a refusal to give another his due. Justice is thus the only way to achieve the ideal state on earth, "for the gods have a care of anyone whose desire is to become just and to be like God." Plato's "counsel is that we hold fast ever to the heavenly way and follow after justice and virtue always . . ."

The idea of justice, according to the Platonic tradition, is generally to be considered as being an immutable, eternally valid, and universal idea. It is the highest or supreme one. It is now sought to be understood and applied by man as natural justice obtained through pure reason. The idea thereby offers a formula or standard to determine the acceptance or rejection of positive rules set by legislation to govern man's conduct and actions. The natural justice is also the basis for the natural rights theory.

Aristotle does not disagree with Plato completely. As he states that ". . . rules of justice vary is not absolutely true, but only with qualifications". He divides political justice into two parts, "one natural, the other conventional". In this way Aristotle supports a concept of natural justice. So does Edmund Burke who later holds that human laws "may alter the mode and application, but have no power over the substance of original justice".

Some critics have denounced all this as a metaphysical play upon words. They argue that not only is the idea of justice unknown, but as reason, and the catalyst itself, it must be defined and understood. Thus, they urge, there can never be a concretization of justice as a standard for man to approximate or to apply in a given situation to determine conduct, or guilt, or punishment. Hobbes, for example, denies that there can be any standard of justice apart from utility or expediency, whereas Grotius maintains that there is an essential morality as well as a natural justice governing men and nations, despite their varying customs. Hobbes's view leads him to justify the state and support the imposition of justice by it. He thus provides a base for other man-made law proposals from which we can logically infer the irrelevance of morality or even justice in the enforcement of the laws.

A parallel criticism has been urged by Epicurus who sees no sign of justice or morality in the universe. He therefore rejects any theological basis for conduct. He regards perception and feeling as sole criteria for ethics. In Epicurus there is thus no fear of gods or death. Man is the aim of all action. Intellectual pleasure and freedom from pain are good in so for as they produce peace of mind, and the converse is evil. It is therefore the purpose of law to secure man against injustice. It means that the wise abstain from unjust conduct and the others are deterred so that justice results in this negative fashion.

Another form of criticism concentrates upon the human factor. All men differ in every significant aspect of time, place, etc. Therefore each one has a different mentality and reason. Thus whatever is defined as natural law and applies to a given situation, is really no reflection of the universal idea. It is only man's personal and distorted effort. This criticism is illustrated by Sir Frederick Pollock's statement that "Natural justice has no means of choosing one practical solution out of two or more equally plausible ones. Therefore "Positive law, whether enacted or customary, must come to our aid". This criticism is illustrated also by the disagreement among the Justices of the Supreme Court of the United States over the definition and application of "due process of law." As to this constitutional term, as early as 1898, a majority of the Justices subscribed to the view that "there are certain immutable principles of justice which inhere in the very idea of free government," Therefore due process language implies "a conformity with natural and inherent principles of justice. . . ." Strong minorities later opposed this contention in matter of the application of the concept "to the Court, with no guide but the Court's own."

Plato's "doctrine of ideas" is severely "criticized" by Aristotle in his Metaphysics. Despute the fact that Aristotle does not devote the time or space to justice that Plato does, he makes known his views in several places. For example, in his *Politics* he writes that "all men cling to justice of some kind". In the Nicomachean *Ethics* he concludes that "there is more than one kind of justice". For example, this involves "the rightly framed law". It "is complete virtue, but not absolutely, but in relation to our neighbor". Aristotle thus believes that man as a political and social animal, "alone has any sense of just and unjust". Aristotle is keen to reconcile justice with the conflicts he observes about it. In his *Politics* he states that 'justice is the bond of men in states". In the *Rhetoric* he gives it some content by saying that justice "is a virtue which assigns to each man his due in conformity with the law." In contrast injustice is a vice whereby man "claims what belongs to others, in opposition to the law".

In the *Ethics* Aristotle initially divides "the just into the lawful and the equal or fair". These are, respectively, his universal or general, *i.e.,* legislative, and judge-made decisions in individual cases. The legislative type of justice requires obedience to the law. Therefore it comprehends a civic virtue. Judicial decisions are distinguished from morality. They are divided into distributive and corrective. Distributive justice is "the distribution of honour, wealth, and the other divisible assets of the community . . . and that which supplies a corrective principle in private transactions." This corrective principle is still further subdivided into "those acts and relations which are voluntary and those which are involuntary". As examples of it he refers respectively to commercial dealings, and then to personal crimes or torts upon which one involuntarily is made a participant.

Aristotle's main concern is with the particular and corrective or remedial type of justice. Here the judge's task is to redress and not to punish. Aristotle further regards justice *(dike)* as embracing many if not all the other virtues. It includes a relation to persons as well as to things. It involves a just distribution of the latter. It is a fair meting out of punishment. In his *Ethics* Aristotle rejects the "simple" Pythagorean formula for justice as equal reciprocity. In his view since this does not apply to either distributive or retributive justice, he tentatively suggests a third kind of exchange or commercial justice.

There are three types of persons whom Aristotle describes as acting justly. They are namely: (a) the legislator or statesman who rewards; (b) the judge who decides; and (c) the farmer or entrepreneur who exchanges goods and services. It is this last one in whom he does not include a moral virtue. It is therefore only an economic type of justice, *i.e.,* entitled to a just price. In his *Politics* Aristotle argues that equals, should be treated alike, but un-equals proportionally to their relevant differences, and all with impartiality, whereby justice now would be understood and served. As Muller puts it, "Plato and Aristotle would a millennium later state the logic of Hammurabi's code by arguing that justice consists not in giving equal rights to men naturally unequal, but in giving every man his due".

Almost all thinkers throughout the whole history of philosophy, down to our own century, have agreed with Aristotle's definition. However, Aristotle points out that the problem of what constitutes equals and what constitutes un-equals cannot be solved easily. There may be those who are superior in wealth, they tend to feel they are superior in everything. He sees no problem in assigning some, *e.g.,* slaves, to an inferior position, so long as they are given their due within this group. Anatole France's caustic version of Aristotle is that "Justice is made to give everyone his due; to the rich his richness, to the poor his poverty." Aristotle's solution is that equality must be judged on the basis of goodness shown by noble actions. Anything short of such virtue is only a part of justice.

Plato and Aristotle therefore agree in several respects: For example, they both regard ethics and morals as basic to a philosophy of law which is subsumed under a theory of justice. They provide their ideas and applications of the nature of justice which do not coincide with each other. Aristotle ties at least one form of justice to man. Plato's "realization" of justice in his *Laws* depends on the police power of the state, whereas Aristotle sees it in various types of law including the one relating to man and justice. It is Aristotle's tying of justice to diverse human situations which may be termed as the most distinguishing feature of his disagreement with Plato's central idea of justice as harmony.

Aristotle's four illustrative types of voluntary acts therefore disclose that only in the last type, where man acts by a deliberate choice, render the act and doer unjust. In his *Rhetoric,* Aristotle further links justice to the human condition. He says that "equity is justice that goes beyond the written law". It is left by the legislators to permit a margin of fairness to soften the rigours of the statutes. He therefore provides judges with a degree of discretion. This may be Aristotle's greatest practical contribution to "justice." The English and American common law too divide justice into law and equity, as do all nations in one fashion or another. However legal positivists such as Kelsen nevertheless object to any extra legal criteria. Kelsen rejects any effort to include such a conception of justice in the field of law.

After the Greeks, we must consider three historically important versions of justice in the Hebraic, the Roman, and the Thomistic teachings. The latter two are seen exercising a more direct and broader impact on theorizing about justice by latter day philosophy.

## Justice as Strict Observance

Religion, morals, righteous conduct, and strict application to duty go into the Hebrew concept of justice. So long as man obeys the Commandments he will receive justice through divine deliverance. This "give and take" type of justice may be compared with that of the "reciprocity" or "equality" of the Pythagoreans. However, it is to be distinguished from the pagan notion whereby the gods will dispense with justice as a matter of favouritism, not of right.

The Stoic philosophy, however, is the main inspiration in the further development of Roman jurisprudence. It (the latter) becomes oriented to the world rather than to the gods. Rome's great expansion into a world power, with a consequent *"Pax Romana,"* requires a *jus gentium i.e.,* "law of nations". It is to be founded upon the concept of a universal and uniform idea of justice. It is to be equally accessible to all through reason. The term justice is, for Rome, given legal content first by Ulpian and later by Justinian where in it is seen repeated almost verbatim.

Later Aquinas defines justice as "the set fixed and constant purpose which gives to every man his due." Aquinas formulates the natural law from man's enjoyment "of a certain share in the divine reason." But this share can be limited to such law itself and therefore need not partake of justice. There is also an uncompromising position taken by Aquinas with respect to "divine" reason which is made the touchstone for all his conclusions. His formulation of the idea of justice follows both a Platonic and Aristotelian tradition.

Like Aristotle, Aquinas proposes the secularization of the idea. Aquinas advances his view that the state, for one, can independently so dispense justice even though ultimately there is the divine idea. It is in Grotius that this tentative ideological severance is given rationality. It acquires a significant independence from God with a resulting dependence solely upon nature or man. Grotius argues that first he agrees with Aristotle that man is naturally a social creature. So he utilizes the social contract doctrine necessarily requiring some minimum form of law and justice. He clings to this idea that even if God did not exist—though surely He exists. Second, this minimum is a resultant of man's reason. *Ergo*, this universal or natural law "is unchangeable even in the sense that it cannot be changed by God.... He cannot cause that which is intrinsically evil be not evil" or, conversely, tamper with the intrinsic concept of justice.

In the seventeenth century Hobbes's man is see to war in a "state of nature" in which notions of justice and injustice has no place. But his third law of nature requires the performance of covenants, for in this "consists the Fountain and Original of Justice.... And for the definition of Injustice, is no other than the not performance of Covenant. And whatsoever is not Unjust, is Just".

## Characteristics of Justice

The following are the characteristics of justice:

1. The foremost is the principle that the like be treated alike. It means equality, impartiality, to each his due. Other versions of the idea refer to: harmony ethics, morality; justice righteousness, equity, fairness; reason, divine, religion; reciprocity, contract, eye-for-eye; utility, pleasure, pain;
2. Justice may also imply custom of a group, tribe, *polis* as also man, his interests and needs, especially of order; or Leibniz's mature definition of justice is *caritas sapient i.e.,* the charity of the wise man; or the idea of justice can also be understood by means of historically concrete illustrations and in the bases used for making judicial decisions, or in the political treatment of minorities which is allegedly the mark of a civilized society.
3. Justice may also be understood in a negative aspect. It can be seen as in diplomatic practice or in international claims or procedures which use the phrase "denial of justice" to indicate a departure from some sort of international standard. This negative approach, however, is better disclosed

where treatment based upon color, national origin, etc., is labeled as unjust. That injustice flows from certain facts.

4. There are, of course, other variations of this negative terminology. This sense of injustice in effect creates a series of negative criteria. They, by contrast, reveal the positive content of the idea of justice more clearly.

## Principles of Distributive Justice

Principles of distributive justice are normative principles designed to allocate goods in limited supply relative to demand. The principles vary in numerous dimensions. They vary in what goods are subject to distribution (income, wealth, opportunities, etc.) on the nature of the subjects of the distribution (natural persons, groups of persons, reference classes, etc.); and on what basis the goods should be distributed (equality, according to individual characteristics, according to free market transactions, etc.).

### 1. Strict Egalitarianism

One of the simplest principles of distributive justice is that of strict or radical equality. The principle says that every person should have the same level of material goods and services. The principle is most commonly justified on grounds that people owe equal respect and that equality in material goods and services is the best way to give effect to this ideal.

Even with this simple principle some of the difficult specification problems of distributive principles arise. The two main problems are the construction of appropriate indices for measurement (the index problem); and the other is about specification of time frames. Because there are numerous proposed solutions to these problems, the 'principle of strict equality' is not a single principle but a name for a group of closely related principles. This range of possible specifications occurs with all the common principles of distributive justice.

Money is an index for the value of material goods and services. Nevertheless, using money as index for the value of material goods and services is the most practical response so far suggested to the index problem and is widely used in the specification and implementation of distributive principles.

The second main specification problem involves time frames. One version of the principle of strict equality requires that all people should have the same wealth at some initial point, after which people are free to use their wealth in whatever way they choose. Principles specifying initial distributions after which the pattern need not be preserved are commonly called 'starting-gate' principles.

The most common form of 'strict equality principle' specifies that *income* (measured in terms of money) should be equal in *each* time-frame, though even this may lead to significant disparities in wealth if variations in savings are permitted. Hence, 'strict equality principle' is commonly conjoined with some society-wide specification of just saving behavior.

## 2. The Difference Principle

The wealth of an economy is not a fixed amount from one period to the next. More wealth can be produced and indeed this has been the experience of industrialized countries over the last few centuries. The most common way of producing more wealth is to have a system where those who are more productive earn greater incomes. This partly inspires the formulation of the Difference Principle.

The most widely discussed theory of distributive justice in the past three decades has been that proposed by John Rawls in *A Theory of Justice,* (Rawls 1971), and *Political Liberalism,* (Rawls 1993). Rawls proposes the following two principles of justice:

1. Each person has an equal claim to a fully adequate scheme of equal basic rights and liberties, which scheme is compatible with the same scheme for all; and in this scheme the equal political liberties, and only those liberties, are to be guaranteed their fair value.
2. Social and economic inequalities are to satisfy two conditions: (a) They are to be attached to positions and offices open to all under conditions of fair equality of opportunity; and (b), they are to be of the greatest benefit to the least advantaged members of society.

Under Rawls' proposed system, Principle (1) has priority over Principle (2). In addition to (2b) it is possible to think of Principles (1) and (2a) as principles of distributive justice: (1) to govern the distribution of liberties, and (2a) the distribution of opportunities. Looking at the principles of justice in this way makes all principles of justice, as principles of distributive justice (even principles of retributive justice will be included on the basis that they distribute negative goods).

The main moral motivation for the Difference Principle is similar to that for strict equality: equal respect for persons. Indeed the Difference Principle materially collapses to a form of strict equality under empirical conditions where differences in income have no effect on the work incentive of people. The overwhelming opinion though is that in the foreseeable future the possibility of earning greater income will bring forth greater productive effort. This will increase the total wealth of the economy and, under the Difference Principle, the wealth of the least advantaged as well. Opinion is divided on the size of the inequalities which would, as a matter of empirical fact, be allowed by the Difference Principle. Opinion also differs on how much better off the least advantaged would be under the Difference Principle than under a strict equality principle.

Rawls' principle however gives fairly clear guidance on what type of arguments will count as justification for inequality. Rawls is not opposed to the principle of strict equality *per se.* His concern is about the *absolute* position of the least advantaged group rather than their *relative* position. If a system of strict equality maximizes the absolute position of the least advantaged in society, then the Difference Principle advocates strict equality. If it is possible to raise the absolute position of the least advantaged further by having some inequalities of income and wealth, then the Difference Principle prescribes inequality up to that point where the absolute position of the least advantaged can no longer be raised.

Advocates of strict equality argue that inequalities permitted by the Difference Principle are unacceptable even if they do benefit the least advantaged. The problem for these advocates is to explain in a satisfactory way why the relative position of the least advantaged is more important than their absolute position, and hence why society should be prevented from materially benefiting the least advantaged when this is possible.

The utilitarian objection to the Difference Principle is that it does not maximize utility. In *A Theory of Justice,* Rawls uses Utilitarianism as the main theory for comparison with his own, and hence he responds at length to this utilitarian objection and argues for his own theory in preference to utilitarianism.

Libertarians object that the Difference Principle involves unacceptable infringements on liberty. For instance, the Difference Principle may require redistributive taxation to the poor, and Libertarians commonly object that such taxation involves the immoral taking of just holdings.

The Difference Principle is criticized as a primary distributive principle on grounds that it mostly ignores claims that people deserve certain economic benefits in the light of their actions. Advocates of Desert Based Principles argue that some may deserve a higher level of material goods because of their hard work or contributions even if their unequal rewards do not also function to improve the position of the least advantaged. They also argue that the explanations of how people come to be in more or less advantaged positions is relevant to their fairness, yet the Difference Principle wrongly ignores these explanations.

Like Desert Theorists, advocates of Resource-Based Principles criticize the Difference Principle on grounds that it is not 'ambition-sensitive' enough, *i.e.,* it is not sensitive to the consequences of people's choices. They also argue that it is not adequately 'endowment-sensitive': it does not compensate people for natural inequalities (like handicaps or ill-health) over which people have no control.

### 3. Resource-Based Principles

Resource-based principles (also called Resource Egalitarianism) prescribe equality of resources. Interestingly, resource-based principles do not normally prescribe a patterned outcome—The idea being that the outcomes are determined by people's free use of their resources. Resource Theorists claim that the Difference Principle is insufficiently 'ambition-sensitive'. Provided people have equal resources they should live with the consequences of their choices. They argue, for instance, that people who choose to work hard to earn more income should not be required to subsidize those choosing more leisure and hence less income.

A related complaint of the Resource Theorists is that the Difference Principle is not sufficiently 'endowment-sensitive.' While part of Rawls' motivation for the Difference Principle is that people have unequal endowments, Resource Theorists explicitly emphasize this feature of their theory though they differ on which endowments are relevant to questions of distributive justice. They agree that, ideally, social circumstances over which people have no control should not adversely affect life prospects or earning capacities. Some Resource Theorists further argue that, for the same sorts of reasons, unequal natural endowments should attract compensation. For instance, people born with handicaps, ill-health, or low levels of natural talents have not brought these circumstances upon themselves and hence, should not be disadvantaged in their life prospects.

The most prominent Resource-based Theory, developed by Ronald Dworkin, proposes that people begin with equal resources but end up with unequal economic benefits as a result of their own choices. What constitutes a just material distribution is to be determined by the result of a thought experiment designed to model fair distribution. Suppose that everyone is given the same purchasing power and each uses that purchasing power to bid, in a fair auction, for resources best suited to their life plans. They are then permitted to use those resources as they see fit. Although people may end up with different economic benefits, none of them is given less consideration than another in the sense that if they wanted somebody else's resource bundle they could have bid for it instead.

## 4. Welfare-based Principles

Welfare-based principles are motivated by the idea that what is of primary moral importance is the level of welfare of people. Advocates of welfare-based principles view the concerns of other theories—equality, the least advantaged, resources, desert-claims, or liberty as derivative concerns. Resources, equality, desert-claims, or liberty are only valuable in so far as they increase welfare. Of course all distributive questions should be settled according to which distribution maximizes welfare. Distribution, according to some welfare function, is most commonly advocated by economists, who normally state the explicit functional form.

## 5. Utility-based Principles

Historically, Utilitarians have used the term 'utility' rather than 'welfare.' Utility has been defined variously as pleasure, happiness, or preference-satisfaction. So, for instance, the principle for distributing economic benefits for Preference Utilitarians is to distribute them so as to maximize preference-satisfaction.

However, Utilitarianism has been criticized on many counts: The first is that it fails to take the distinctness of persons seriously. Maximization of preference-satisfaction is often taken as prudent in the case of individuals. It is suggests that people take on greater burdens, suffering or sacrifice at certain periods of their lives so that their lives are overall better. The complaint against Utilitarianism is that it takes this principle, commonly described as prudent for individuals, and uses it on an entity, society, unlike individuals in important ways.

A related criticism of Utilitarianism involves the way it treats individual preferences or interests referring to the holdings of others. For instance, some people may have a preference that some minority racial group should have less material benefits. Under Utilitarian theories, in their classical form, this preference or interest counts like any other in determining the best distribution. Hence, if racial preferences are widespread and are not outweighed by the minorities' contrary preferences, Utilitarianism will recommend an inegalitarian distribution based on race.

Utilitarians have responded to these criticisms in a number of ways. Utilitarians may apply their theory to the preferences themselves. They argue that utility is best promoted in the long run when people's preferences are shaped in ways that are harmonious with one another, suggesting that racist preferences should be discouraged.

Most formulations of Utilitarianism require interpersonal comparisons of utility. This means, for instance, that we must be able to compare the utility one person gains from eating an apple with what another gains from eating an apple. Furthermore, Utilitarianism requires that differences in utility be measured and summed for widely disparate goods (so, for instance, the amount of utility a particular person gains from playing football is measured and compared with the amount of utility another gains from eating a gourmet meal).

Critics have argued that such interpersonal utility comparisons are impossible, even in theory, due to one or both of the following:

(1) It is not possible to combine all the diverse goods into a single index of 'utility' which can be measured for an individual;
(2) Even if you could do the necessary weighing and combining of the goods to construct such an index for an individual, there is no conceptually adequate way of calibrating such a measure between individuals.

There is an explanation for why Utilitarians are faced with greater difficulties in implementation. Other distributive principles can rule out relatively quickly some practical policies if they are seen to clearly violate the guiding principle, but Utilitarians must examine, in great detail, all the policies on offer. For each policy, they must determine the distribution of goods and services yielded by the policy and at least three other factors: the identity of each person in the distribution (if individuals utility functions differ); the utility of each person from the goods and services distributed to them; and the utility of each person from the policy itself. The size of the information requirements makes this task impossible.

### 6. Desert-Based Principles

Another complaint against welfarism is that it ignores, and in fact cannot even make sense of claims that people deserve certain economic benefits in light of their actions. The complaint is often motivated by concern that various forms of welfarism treat people as mere containers for well-being, rather than purposeful beings, responsible for their actions and creative in their environments.

The different desert-based principles of distribution differ primarily according to what they identify as the basis for deserving. Most contemporary proposals for desert-bases fit into one of three broad categories:

1. Contribution: People should be rewarded for their work activity according to the value of their contribution to the social product.
2. Effort: People should be rewarded according to the effort they expend in their work activity.
3. Compensation: People should be rewarded according to the costs they incur in their work activity.

Aristotle argues that virtue should be a basis for distributing rewards, but most contemporary principles owe a larger debt to John Locke. For, Locke argues people deserve to have those items produced by their toil and industry, the products (or the value thereof) being a fitting reward for their effort. His underlying idea is to guarantee to individuals fruits of their own labour and abstinence.

According to the contemporary Desert Theorists, people freely apply their abilities and talents, in varying degrees, to socially productive work. People come to deserve varying levels of income by providing goods and services desired by others. Distributive systems are just insofar as they distribute incomes according to the different levels earned or deserved by the individuals in the society for their productive labours, efforts, or contributions.

Contemporary Desert-Principles all share the value of raising the standard of living collectively. Under each principle, only activity directed at raising the social product will serve as a basis for deserving income.

The main moral objection to desert-based principles is that they make economic benefits depend on factors over which people have little control. John Rawls has made one of the most widely discussed arguments to this effect. The problem is most pronounced in the case of productivity-based principles. A person's productivity seems clearly to be influenced by many factors over which the person has little control.

### 7. Libertarian Principles

Most contemporary versions of the principles allow some role for the market as a means of achieving the desired distributive pattern. Difference Principles use it as a means of helping the least advantaged; Utilitarian Principles commonly use it as a means of achieving the distributive pattern maximizing utility; Desert-Based Principles rely on it to distribute goods according to desert, etc.

In contrast, advocates of Libertarian Distributive Principles rarely see the market as a means to some desired pattern. It is because the principle(s) they advocate do not ostensibly propose a 'pattern' at all, but instead describe the sorts of acquisitions or exchanges which are themselves just. The market will be just, not as a means to some pattern, but insofar as the exchanges permitted in the market satisfy the conditions of just exchange described by the principles. For Libertarians, just outcomes are those arrived at by the separate just actions of individuals; a particular distributive pattern is not required for justice. Robert Nozick has advanced this version of Libertarianism, and he is its most well known contemporary advocate.

Nozick proposes a 3-part "Entitlement Theory" according to which, if the world were wholly just, the following inductive definition would exhaustively cover the subject of justice in holdings:

(a) A person who acquires a holding in accordance with the principle of justice in acquisition is entitled to that holding.
(b) A person who acquires a holding in accordance with the principle of justice in transfer, from someone else is entitled to the holding.
(c) No one is entitled to a holding except by (repeated) applications of (a) and (b).

The complete principle of distributive justice would say simply that a distribution is just if everyone is entitled to the holdings they possess under the distribution.

The statement of the Entitlement Theory includes reference to the principles of justice in acquisition and transfer. The principle is meant to govern the gaining of exclusive property rights over the material world. For the justification of these rights, Nozick takes his inspiration from John Locke's idea that everyone 'owns' themselves their talents and, by mixing one's labors with the world, self-ownership can generate ownership of some part of the material world. However, of Locke's mixing metaphor, Nozick legitimately asks: "...why isn't mixing what I own with what I don't own a way of losing what I own rather than a way of gaining what I don't? If I own a can of tomato juice and spill it in the sea so its molecules... mingle evenly throughout the sea, do I thereby come to own the sea, or have I foolishly dissipated my tomato juice?" Nozick concludes that what is significant about mixing our labor with the material world is that in doing so, we tend to increase the value of it, so that self-ownership can lead to ownership of the external world in such cases.

The obvious objection to this claim is that it is not clear why the people who need acquire some part of the material world should be able to exclude others from it (and, for instance, be the land owners while the later ones become the wage labourers). In response to this objection, Nozick puts a qualification on just acquisition, called the *Lockean Proviso,* whereby an exclusive acquisition of the external world is just, if, after the acquisition, there is 'enough and as good left in common for others'. One of the main challenges for Libertarians has been to formulate a morally plausible interpretation of this *proviso*. According to Nozick's interpretation, an acquisition is just if and only if the position of others after the acquisition is no worse than their position was when the acquisition was unowned or 'held in common'.

For Nozick's critics, his *proviso* is unacceptably weak. This is because it fails to consider the position others may have achieved under alternative distributions and thereby it instantiates the morally dubious criterion of whoever is first gets the exclusive spoils.

Will Kymlicka has given a summary of the steps in Nozick's self-ownership argument:

1. People own themselves what is unowned.
2. The world is initially unowned.
3. You can acquire absolute rights over a disproportionate share of the world, if you do not worsen the condition of others.
4. It is relatively easy to acquire absolute rights over a disproportionate share of the world.
5. Therefore once private property has been appropriated, a free market in capital and labor is morally required.

Libertarians inspired by Nozick usually advocate a system in which there are exclusive property rights, with the role of the government restricted to the protection of these property rights. The property rights commonly rule out taxation for purposes other than raising the funds necessary to protect property rights. The strongest critique of any attempt to institute such a system of legally protected property rights comes, from Nozick's theory itself. There seems no obvious reason to give strong legal protection to property rights which have arisen through violations of the just principles of acquisition and transfer. But putting this critique to one side for a moment, what other arguments are made in favor of exclusionary property rights?

Nozick argues that because people own themselves their talents, hence they own whatever they can produce with these talents. Moreover, it is possible in a free market to sell the products exercising one's talents. Any taxation of the income from such selling, according to Nozick, 'institute[s] (partial) ownership by others of people and their actions and labour'.

People, according to this argument, have these exclusive rights of ownership. Taxation then, simply involves violating these rights and allowing some people to own (partially) other people.

Moreover, it is argued, any system not legally recognizing these rights violates Kant's maxim to treat people always as ends in themselves and never merely as a means.

The two main difficulties with this argument have been:

1. To show that self-ownership is only compatible with having such strong exclusive property rights; and
2. that a system of exclusive property rights is the best system for treating people with respect, as ends in themselves.

**8. Feminist Principles**

There is no one feminist conception of distributive justice; theorists who name themselves feminists defend various positions across the political spectrum. Hence, feminists offer distinctive versions of all the theories considered so far as well as others. One way of thinking about what unifies many feminist theorists is an interest in what difference, if any, the practical experience of gender makes to the subject matter or study of justice; how different feminists answer this question that distinguishes them from each other and from those alternative distributive principles which most inspire their thinking.

John Stuart Mill in *The Subjection of Women* (1869) gives one of the clearest early feminist critiques of the political and distributive structures of the emerging liberal democracies. His writings provide the starting point for many contemporary liberal feminists. Mill argues that the principles associated with the developing liberalism of his time require equal political status for women. The principles Mill explicitly mentions include a rejection of the aristocracy of birth, equal opportunity in education and in the marketplace, equal rights to hold property, a rejection of the man as the legal head of the household, and equal rights to political participation.

Feminists who follow Mill believe that a proper recognition of the position of women in society requires that women be given equal and the same rights as men have. For, these rights would primarily protect their liberty and their status as equal persons under the law. Thus, government regulation should not prevent women from competing on equal terms with men in educational, professional, marketplace and political institutions.

From the point of view of other feminisms, the liberal feminist position is a conservative one. It requires the proper inclusion for women of the rights, protections, and opportunities previously secured for men, rather than a fundamental change to the traditional liberal position. The problem for women, on this view, is not liberalism but the failure of society and the state to properly instantiate liberal principles.

One phrase or motto around which a whole range of feminists have rallied, however, marks a significant break with Mill's liberalism: 'the personal is political.' Feminists have offered a variety of interpretations of this motto, many of which take the form of a critique of liberal theories. Mill's contribution is crucial in developing the liberal doctrine of limiting the state's intervention in the private lives of citizens. Many contemporary feminists have argued that the resulting liberal theories of justice have fundamentally been incapable of accommodating the injustices that have their origins in this 'protected' private sphere. This particular feminist critique has also been a primary source of inspiration for the broader multicultural critique of liberalism.

The feminist critics recognize that liberalism correctly identifies the government as one potential source of oppression against individuals, and therefore recommends powerful political protections of individual liberty. They argue, however, that liberal theories of distributive justice are unable to address the oppression which surfaces in the so-called private sphere of government noninterference.

While the political effects of personal freedom pose a serious challenge to contemporary liberal theories of distributive justice, the feminist critiques are somewhat puzzling because, as Jean Hampton puts it, many feminists appear to complain in the name of liberal values. In other words, their claims about the fundamental flaws of liberalism at the same time leave in fact the various ideals of liberty and equality which inspire the liberal theories of justice. Moreover, the task of defining feasible pathways for modifying the structure of liberal democracies without undermining their virtues and protections has proved more difficult than the meeting out the criticisms of liberalism. Indeed, despite a legitimate feminist worry about the effects of so-called government neutrality on women's material status, the relative neutrality of liberal democracies compared to non-liberal societies has been one of the significant contributing factors both to the flourishing of feminist theory and to the many significant practical gains women in liberal democracies have made relative to women in other parts of the world.

### 9. Marxist Principle of Justice

Justice is not a static but a dynamic and multidimensional concept. This singlemost fact has contributed to different theories associated with morality, equality, liberty, property, law, welfare etc. However, the Marxist concept of justice is totally different from the classical and liberal notions of it. Marxist theory of justice does not allow any place to justice in analyzing the capitalist mode of production. The theory is more of a critique of the liberal theories of justice rather than an independent theory of socialistic/communist justice. Moreover, a number of contradictions it has pointed out in the liberal theories of justice have been resolved by the egalitarian theory of justice and the theory of distributive justice as explained by John Rawls.

There are two variants of Marxist theory of justice today: First objects to the very idea of justice. It argues that the need for a theory of justice can arise where society is conflict-ridden and theory is needed to mediate. Since in communism all conflicts cease, hence in a communist society, there will be no need of any theory of justice. Communism is beyond Justice.

Then, there is the other theory of justice which shares the liberal emphasis on justice. Appraising justice in the context of private ownership of the means of production, the theory firmly believes that justice can be achieved only in a classless and stateless society. In so far as private property is exploitative and alienating, justice requires socializing the means of production and establishing a communist society.

#### Communism and Liberalism

According to the liberal theory of Rawls, justice is the first principle of social institutions and a standard of other values. The Marxian theory objects to the very idea that liberalism is based on the principles of justice. It draws on Marx who attacks the very idea of justice as 'equal rights' or 'fair distribution' since such terms obscure the underlying capitalist exploitation. For example, as Marx puts it, since some people have greater natural talent, 'the equal right becomes an unequal right for unequal labour'. Consequently, the right to equality becomes in fact a right to inequality.

Similarly, Marx attacks the notion of 'just distribution' as it concentrates too much on distribution rather than on which is much more crucial *i.e.* production or distribution. Even if the income is redistributed from those who own means of production to those who do not, there will still be classes and exploitation. As a result, injustice in one form or another will continue. Instead we therefore need to concentrate on the distribution of the ownership of the means of production. It is because when this is accomplished, the question of fair or just distribution will automatically become obsolete. Without this happening any attempt to rectify 'injustice' on the distributive front has to assume some sort of equilibrium between the irreconcilable class conflict in the capitalist society. Moreover, if justice helps to resolve conflicts, it also tends to create conflicts and thus reduce the natural sociability of man. Hence, to Marxists, justice is a necessary evil. In the present societies, it is a barrier to the emergence of a higher form of community *i.e.,* the communist society. The better course is if people act spontaneously out of love for each other, rather than out of calculation, viewing themselves and others as but bearer(s) of just entitlements.

The above objections advanced by the Marxists explain some obvious limitations in the way of developing any Marxian conception of justice. The core of Marxist critique of bourgeois justice is that it objects to the very idea of a juridical community. It argues that the question of justice arises only when we are in the circumstances which create the kind of conflicts that can only be solved by the principles of justice. These conflicting circumstances are usually of two factors *viz.* conflicting goals and limited material resources. If either the conflicts between the goals or the scarcity of resources can be eliminated, then there will be no need for a theory of juridical equality.

The moot question before Marxism is how to overcome conflicting circumstances and create a kind of community where there is identity of interests and where the need for justice is felt no more. The other question is how to eliminate scarcity, to which the Marxist answer is that it can be accomplished through the creation of a communist society based on the principle of 'from each according to his capacity to each according to his need'.

### Marxists on the Question of Justice/Injustice

At this stage it is pertinent to ask, what is the communist justice? Since Marxism subjects the early liberal as well as the egalitarian liberal views on justice to scathing criticism , it is natural for us to assume that the communist justice should be more equalizing than the liberal versions. Marxism emphasizes not only the need to equalize resources but also the amount of private property : Hence to be settled first is the extent to which resources are to be equalized and how the equalization of the private property can be achieved. In this context, Marxism favours the abolition of private property. It is a fundamental postulate of Marxism that 'there is no moral right to the private ownership and control of productive resources'. It is because private ownership of the means of production gives rise to wage labour relationship which is unjust, inherently exploitative and alienating. It is only a socialist society which takes command after the proletarian revolution can, by equalizing resources in the modern industry, create the basis of a just society.

Marxism sees the root cause of injustice in exploitation. In modern industrial society, this exploitation is of the worker by the capitalist. The basic flaw of liberal state consists in that it legalizes exploitation by allowing buying and selling of labour. The Marxist argument runs like this, as cohen states, labourer is the only person who creates the product which has value. Since the capitalist receives some of the value of the product, therefore, the labourer receives less value than the value of what he creates. Hence labour is exploited by the capitalist. Besides, the worker is forced to work for the capitalist because the former does not in general own any productive assets. He has thus no choice but to earn a living by working for the propertied class. Hence he has to enter into wage-relationships which are inherently exploitative.

Another writer John Roemer expands the theory of exploitation to include disenfranchised women, the unemployed, the wage-workers. In his view because of unequal access to the means of production they all suffer from injustice. As a result, the capitalists benefit from it (this unequal access to the means of production). The exploitation of the worker by the capitalist is just one form, but the worse form of exploitation is for women, unemployed or those who lead their existence from crime, begging etc. Moreover, it is untrue that the capitalists acquire their property through conscious savings or through their hard work or better talent. Marx clarifies that it is through conquest, enslavement, robbery, murder, force, that they are able to accumulate the greatest part of their property. This unjust initial acquisition of wealth and property gives a lie to the argument that capitalist class is entitled to excessive profits for their having taken risk in investing their capital in industry or other entrepreneurial ventures. Marxists lament that the working class faces much more risks of ill-health, occupational diseases, unemployment, low wages, etc.and they find its cause in private property. They are convinced that until the property is abolished there cannot be any hope of justice for the working class.

## Justice and Alienation

Marx views private property and the mode of production based upon private property as inhibitive factors in the development of man's most important capacities. By its very nature private property is exploitative. Even those who benefit from its exploitative character are alienated from their essential human powers. Therefore Marx's theory of justice urges that the resources should be so distributed that it should encourage the 'realization of distinctively human potentialities and excellence'. Besides it should well discourage such ways of life as are lacking in these excellences. Marx explains them as 'our capacity for freely creative cooperative production'. Any production system that stunts this capacity tends to alienate us from our true 'species nature'. To overcome such a condition Marx proposes abolishing of wage labour and socializing the means of production. He is convinced that this will ensure for each person an effective say in how his work life is to be organized. In addition, it will also enable him to organize production so as to increase its intrinsic satisfaction rather than increasing profit of the capitalist. While capitalism reduces life's activity to a means of securing a decent living, socialism restores work to its rightful place, as an end in itself, as 'life's prime want'. Also socialism has this as its goal that the labour should assume his rightful place in the production process. Justice in the true sense can be achieved only in a society where private property has been abolished and the means of production socialized.

## CONCLUSION

Marxists analyze the question of justice and injustice in the context of capitalism, exploitation based on private property and monopolistic control of means of production in hands of the capitalists. The struggle against this capitalist injustice takes the form of struggle between two hostile classes viz. capitalist and proletariat. Only the working class armed with revolutionary ideology has the power to challenge the edifice of capitalist injustice. Marxist Theory of Justice provides the justification for class struggle which will end in the overthrow of capitalism and the establishment of the dictatorship of the proletariat.

However, this Marxist view of centrality of working class to revolutionary politics is not tenable in the context of our contemporary times. We are today witnessing several contemporary struggles for justice. Most of them are associated with groups which are not oppressed by wage relationship. They include movements centred on racial groups, immigrants, disabled, minorities, women liberation etc. It is increasingly being realized that the exploited working class and the needy groups in dire need of justice are not always the same. Kymlicka observes that justice is much more than rectifying the wrongs in the society. Justice not only resolves the conflicts but more than that it also expresses the respect which is due to individuals as an end in themselves. In a just society the members of the community are equal. This equality is the outcome of rights and entitlements which an individual can rightfully claim. However, these rights are not to be exercised at the expense of others. Justice means that each member must feel concern for the other members of the community. Thus a community of equals cannot be created by abandoning the notions of fairness, rights and duties. They are essential components of every tenable theory of justice.

# 13

# DEMOCRACY

## Meaning and Definition

Literally, democracy means 'rule of the people'. It is derived from the Greek word *demos*, meaning the people. To the Greeks, democracy meant government by the many as opposed to monarchy *i.e.,* government by one; or Aristocracy *i.e.,* government by the few. Dicey defines democracy as "one in which the governing body is a comparatively large fraction of the total population." Seeley calls democracy a "government in which everyone has a share." Lord Bryce regards democracy as "a form of government in which the ruling power is largely vested not in only one individual, in a particular class or classes but in the members of the community as a whole". Thus democracy is a form of government in which the people as a whole have a direct or indirect share.

In its broad meaning, democracy as a form of government, is distinguishable from democracy as a social ideal. As a social ideal, democracy is normative and postulates the equality of all men. It is a polity formed by the spirit of ideal democratic man, democratic morality and democratic ethos. It is democratic polity and society as well as democratic economic system. In short, democracy is both an ideal and a political system. Indeed it is associated with socioeconomic, political and moral ideals.

As a form of government, democracy connotes adult franchise, periodic free elections, independent judiciary, representative and responsible executive, strong public opinion, free press, at least two political parties, plural sharing of power, popular participation in decision-making, limited and constitutional government, guaranteed fundamental rights etc.

Man is both political and rational being. He is capable of rational decision and moral choice. Democracy assumes the self-governing capacity of the people. It also assumes that every man is the best judge of his own interest. He must, therefore, be given a say in the business of government. The aim of democracy is to secure the 'greatest good of the greatest number'. The larger the number of people who share political power, the easier will it be to achieve this end. Hence Universal Adult Franchise is the prerequisite of democracy.

Democracy is the government by popular consent. Legitimate basis of political power is consent of the people. The basis of consent is majority opinion. People's participation in the business of government is necessary for the development of human capacities. Only representative and responsible government which takes into account responsive public opinion can be called democratic. Democracy assumes the common consciousness of the common good. It means, there is a specific common good which everyone knows and which can be realized only in a democracy.

Democracy has meant different things to different writers in different times. Some commonly accepted meanings are given below:

(i) A system of government in which power is vested in the people, who rule either directly or through freely elected representatives.

(ii) Democracy is a form of government in which members and the various groups have approximately equal political power. This is the opposite of dictatorship, in which most political power is in hands of a small subset of the members.

(iii) Democracy is also used to describe a set of social patterns that are commonly associated with democracy. These patterns include various political rights and civil liberties, such as freedom of speech and freedom of movement. A democracy in which these patterns occur is sometimes termed specifically as a liberal democracy.

Abraham Lincon gives pithy definition of democracy as "government of the people, by the people, and for the people." It is with this definition in mind that the succeeding generations of people, in the West as well as the East, have grown up.

Some modern writers define democracy as a system involving effective competition between political parties for positions of power. For Schumpeter, the phrase "government by the people" needs be substituted by "government approved by the people". He argues that in small and primitive communities with a simple social structure in which there is not much to disagree on, it is conceivable that all individuals who form the people as defined by the constitution actually participate in all the duties of legislation and administration. In all other cases, he asserts, it is inevitable that elected representatives should govern the people. He defines "democracy as the democratic method": It is that institutional arrangement for arriving at political decisions in which individuals acquire the power to decide by means of a competitive struggle for people's vote.

The extent to which people can organize themselves into small communities, where direct or almost direct interaction is possible, there will be no need for "representative democracy" to decide on matters of common concern.

Schumpeter's four prerequisites for the satisfaction of the conditions for the success of the democratic system are:

1. The human material of politics—the people who man the party machines,

are elected to serve in parliament, rise to cabinet office—should be sufficiently of high quality.

2. The effective range of political decision should not be extended too far.
3. Government must be able to command . . . the services of a well-trained bureaucracy of good standing and tradition, endowed with a strong sense of duty and a no less strong *esprit de corps*.
4. Electorates and parliaments must be on high intellectual and moral level.

## Democracy: A Brief History

The history of democracy is made complex by the use of varied concepts and definitions. They range from the very broad-based institutions in which adult universal suffrage is used to elect representatives, to very informal assemblies in which the people voice their opinions and leaders act upon those feelings.

Athenian democracy is the earliest well-documented democratic system. The word democracy was coined in Ancient Greece in the 5th century BC. It appears that voting rights were gradually expanded from a small group of landed aristocracy to eventually all eligible males who had completed mandatory military training, usually at the age of 20. Women, slaves, and metics were excluded from this citizenship. This fact leads us to estimate that around one tenth or less of the population of Athens was eligible to vote. However, all Athenian citizens were free to vote on creation of laws. A segment could even vote on when to go to war. All citizens had freedom to speak in the Assembly. This type of government is known as a form of direct democracy. Athens also had representative leaders. But most of them were selected by allotment rather than elected. Athenian democracy was effectively ended by the city's defeat by the Macedonians who abolished it in 323 B.C.

The seeds of representative democracy were seen to sprout in the Roman Republic. During the middle ages, there were various shades of democracies. They varied from very inclusive oligarchies to attempts at full democracy. And, democratic principles or elements have also been claimed for societies of the early Indian republics (*c*. 500 B.C.E.).

The Parliament of England has been the first major step towards a fully democratic system during the Middle Ages. It has its roots in the restrictions on the power of kings written into Magna Carta. The first elected parliament was De Montfort's Parliament in England in 1265. This Parliament was initially elected by only a few percent of the population. The system had acquired certain problematic features such as rotten boroughs. The power to call parliament was at the pleasure of the monarch and it was usually when he or she needed funds. After the Glorious Revolution of 1688, England became a constitutional monarchy. With it started regular sittings of parliament, although they were still subject to the monarch. During this time the two party system of the Whigs and Tories also developed. Parliament then gradually gained more decision-making and legislative powers. The process of parliament's empowerment continued until the reign of Queen Victoria, at which time the monarch essentially became a figurehead.

The United States can be seen as the first liberal democracy. It has a relatively wide franchise although it was initially limited by property and gender restrictions, and the existence of slavery. The United States Constitution protected rights and liberties.

A few years later, Revolutionary France adopted the Declaration of the Rights of Man and of the Citizen. It proved short-lived. The National Convention was elected by all males.

Notably liberal democracies were few and often short-lived before the late nineteenth century. Various nations and territories have claimed themselves to be the first democracies with universal suffrage.

## Twentieth Century Waves of Democracy

Twentieth century transitions to liberal democracy have come in successive "waves of democracy". This has variously resulted from wars, revolutions, decolonization and economic circumstances. World War I and the dissolution of the Ottoman and Austro-Hungarian empires resulted in the creation of new nation-states in Europe. Most of them were nominally democratic. The rise of fascist movements, and fascist regimes in Italy and in Nazi Germany, limited the extent of democracy in the 1930s. It gave the impression of an "Age of Dictators". However, the status of most colonies remained unaffected.

In the decades following World War II, most western democratic nations had a predominantly free-market economy. They developed a welfare state. They reflected a general consensus among their electorates and political parties. In the 1950s and 1960s, economic growth was high in both the western and communist countries. In the later period, it declined in the state-controlled economies. By 1960, the vast majority of nation-states could be described as nominal democracies. The majority of the world's populations then lived in nations that experienced sham elections, and other forms of dubious practices.

A subsequent wave of democratization brings substantial gains toward true liberal democracy for many nations. Several of the military dictatorships in South America become democratic in the late 1970s and early 1980s. This is followed by nations in East and South Asia by the mid- to late 1980s. Economic malaise in the 1980s, along with resentment of communist oppression, contributes to the collapse of the Soviet Union. This leads to end of Cold War, and the democratization and liberalization of the former Soviet bloc countries. The most successful of new democracies are those geographically and culturally closest to western Europe. They are now members or candidate members of the European Union. The democratic trend also spreads to some nations in Africa in the 1990s, most prominently in South Africa.

The number of liberal democracies currently stands at an all-time high. Their number has been growing for some time. As a result liberal democratic nation-states are becoming the universal standard form of human society. Francis Fukayama's "End of History" theory points to this trend.

### The Democratic State: The Search for Criteria

There has been a continuous philosophical debate concerning the applicability and legitimacy of criteria in defining democracy. The most important postulates are given below:

1. That there is a *demos*, a group which makes political decisions by some form of collective procedure. Nonmembers of the *demos* do not participate. In modern democracies the *demos* is the adult portion of the nation, and adult citizenship is usually equivalent to membership.
2. That there is a territory where the people's decisions apply, and where the *demos* is resident. In modern democracies, the territory is the nation-state. Since this corresponds in theory with the homeland of the nation, the *demos* and the reach of the democratic process here neatly coincide. Colonies of democracies are not considered democratic by themselves. In their case *demos* and territory do not coincide.
3. That there is a decision-making procedure. It is either direct, in instances such as a referendum. Or it is indirect, in instances such as the election of a parliament.
4. That the procedure is regarded as legitimate by the *demos*. It implies that its outcome will be accepted. Political legitimacy is the willingness of the population to accept decisions of the state, its government and courts even if they go against personal choices or interests.
5. That the procedure is effective in the minimal sense. It can be used to change the government. It assumes there is sufficient support for that change. Showcase elections, prearranged to reelect the existing regime, are not democratic.
6. That, in respect of nation-states, the state must be sovereign: democratic elections are pointless if an outside authority can overrule the result.

Proponents of democracy make a number of defences concerning 'tyranny of the majority':

1. That the presence of a constitution in many democratic countries acts as a safeguard. Generally, changes in these constitutions require the agreement of a supermajority of the elected representatives. Or they may require a judge and jury to agree that evidentiary and procedural standards have been fulfilled by the state, or two different votes by the representatives separated by an election have been met. Or sometimes, a referendum may become necessary to decide the issue. These requirements are often combined.
2. That the separation of powers into legislative branch, executive branch, judicial branch also makes it more difficult for a small majority to impose

their will. Yet a majority can still legitimately coerce a minority which is still ethically questionable, but such a minority would be very small. As a practical matter, it will be harder to get a larger proportion of the people to agree to such actions.

3. That majorities and minorities can take a markedly different position on different issues. People often agree with the majority view on some issues and agree with a minority view on other issues. One's view may also change. Thus, the members of a majority may limit oppression of a minority since they may well in the future themselves be in a minority.
4. That, despite the risks, majority rule is preferable to other systems. It means that the tyranny of the majority is in any case an improvement on a tyranny of a minority. Empirical evidence strongly shows that more democracy leads to less internal violence and genocide. This is sometimes formulated as Rummel's Law, which states that the less democratic freedom a people have, the more likely their rulers are to tyrannize over and murder them.

## Merits of Democracy

Not withstanding the severe attacks to which democracy as a form of government has been subjected, it remains the best form of government. Among democracy's numerous merits the most prominent are as follows:

1. That democracy is based on the principle of equality. It rejects the elitist or aristocratic dictum that, "some are born to rule and others to obey." Democracy does not countenance special privileges for certain classes. By espousing that all men are equal, democracy upholds the dignity of common man. Democracy rejects all distinctions of caste, creed, colour, wealth or sex which violate man's natural rights. By placing the supreme power of the state in the hands of the people as a whole, democracy guarantees equality of political and other socioeconomic rights to all.
2. Democracy is primarily government by discussion, dissent and consent. In it freedom of thought and association are assured. People enjoy the freedom to debate and criticize policies and acts of the government. They can use all peaceful and legitimate means to change the system of government if it does not reflect their wishes. The value of democratic government is that it provides the means through which the wishes of the people can be known and before enough damage is done it may be possible to take remedial action. This way the conduct of the state may be brought into conformity with people's wishes. Democracy, thus, upholds the principle of liberty and popular will. Where people govern themselves, they cannot be coerced into slavish submission. Liberty, equality and fraternity are the watchwords of democracy.
3. The strength of democracy lies as much in its theoretical excellence as in its practical utility. J.S. Mill considers democracy as the best form of

government because the rights and interests of the individual can best be safeguarded only when he is able to stand up for them himself. Besides, in a democracy the general prosperity attains a higher degree. Moreover it is more widely diffused in proportion to the amount and variety of personal energies enlisted in promoting it. The ideal of 'the greatest good of the greatest number', can best be realized under democratic government. It is rightly said that "the best school of democracy is democracy itself."

4. The democratic experience has the greatest educational value for the masses. It has very elevating and broadening influence on them. It develops their true potential, their intellectual and moral qualities. Self-rule and participation in public affairs makes them self-reliant thereby making them rise above self-interest. The citizens look upon themselves as part of bigger whole. In doing so they contribute their energies towards common welfare. Democratic experience inculcates and develops a sense of responsibility among the citizens. It motivates and helps them to be their best self. In short, democracy is a training school for achieving active and healthy citizenship.
5. Of all the forms of government, democracy may be least liable to revolutions. It has virtue of correcting itself in face of public criticism. The government, on feeling the pulse of the people, can avoid actions which are likely to arouse popular resentment, and precipitate a revolution. Democracy promotes among the people love of the country and government. When they come to feel that government is their own creation, they are likely to give their willing allegiance to it.

## Attacks on Democracy

Democracy has been attacked on the following grounds:

1. Democracy is the cult of incompetence. Plato sees government as the privilege of experts. In hands of common people democracy turns into rule of ignorance and irresponsible masses. Sir Henry Maine views democracy as "government by the ignorant and unintellectuals." Lecky describes it as "government by the poorest, the most ignorant and the most incapable, who are necessarily the most numerous."
2. Democracy lays emphasis on quantity or numbers rather than quality. It places the supreme power in hands of the people. In practice it comes to mean the rule of the majority that consists mostly of uneducated or half-educated people. Carlyle remarks that there are nine fools in the world for every wise man. Since people are moved by their emotions rather than by their reason, the demagogues and vote-catching slogans can easily say and beguile them. The greatest danger to democracy, therefore, is that it descends into mob-rule. In a Greek allegorical painting, democracy is represented as 'a drunken cleon' (a mob-leader in ancient Athens) surrounded by a yelling mob.

3. Democracy does not give proper consideration to worth and special fitness. A learned man's vote has no more importance than the vote of an ignoramus. The fact is that the problems of modern governments are beyond an average citizen or even his representatives. For the representatives cannot but reflect the qualities of their electors. Mill and Montesquieu realize that democracy, being the most difficult form of government, can succeed only where people possess a high degree of virtue and intelligence.
4. In modern times, as against the classical theory of democracy, several theories such as the Elitist Theory (Pareto, Mosca, Michels, Burnham etc.) and the Pluralistic Theory (Dahl, Presthus, Hunter etc) have emerged. One common underlying assumption behind all these theories is that mass democracies are not possible. That masses cannot be considered fit for open participation in the business of the government. They are usually found lacking in dealing with the complicated and tedious political processes. Both theories—the elitist and pluralist—are based on denial of practicability of 'governing democracies'. They argue that only 'governed democracies' are possible. 'Polyarchy' (Dahl and Sartori) and the concept of 'Plural Competing Elites' remain the highest approximation to which a democracy in practice can attain.
5. According to Marx, democracy is possible only in a communist society which will be a classless and stateless society. Only in such a society can man have freedom, equality, fraternity, justice and the unity between self and society. In this society there will be freedom, peace and mutual cooperation among the people and absence of alienation and exploitation in any form. It will be a society based on the principle, 'free development of each is the condition for the free development of all.'

## Anarchists Critique of Democratic State

Anarchists oppose the concept of the state, including the democratic one, as inherently corrupt and coercive. Many social anarchists tend to support a non-hierarchical and non-coercive system of direct democracy within free associations and many expect society to operate by consensus.

Some Individualist anarchists are vocal opponents of all or some forms of democracy. Benjamin Tucker writes, "Rule is evil, and it is none the better for being majority rule....What is the ballot? It is neither more nor less than a paper representative of the bayonet, the billy and the bullet. It is a labor saving device for ascertaining on which side force lies and bowing to the inevitable. The voice of the majority saves bloodshed, but it is no less the arbitrament of force than is the decree of the most absolute of despots backed by the most powerful of armies."

Pierre-Joseph Proudhon says, "Democracy is nothing but the tyranny of majorities, the most abominable tyranny of all, for it is not based on the authority of a religion, not upon the nobility of a race, not on the merits of talents and of riches. It merely rests upon numbers and hides behind the name of the people."

According to Robert Graham, "In *General Idea of the Revolution* Proudhon ostensibly rejects both unanimous and majoritarian direct democracy. Read more closely, however, his criticisms can be confined to national forms of direct democracy designed to replace representative government but which will effectively perform the same political functions." Graham continues to argue, that for Proudhon a "person is only obligated to do that which he has freely undertaken to do" and therefore, the "only form of direct democracy compatible with this conception of obligation is one in which it is recognized that a minority which has refused to consent to a majority decision has assumed no obligation to abide by it. Majority decisions are not binding on the minority. Any agreement to the contrary would itself be invalid because it would require the minority to forfeit its autonomy and substantive freedom."

Central to Proudhon's notion of contract is the idea of self-assumed obligation. Hence, Proudhon opposes Rousseau's social contract on the plea: "What really is the social contract? An agreement of the citizen with the government? No, that would mean but the continuation of [Rousseau's] idea...The social contract is an agreement of man with man...by which man and man declare themselves essentially producers, and abdicate all pretension to govern each other."

### Liberal democracy: Definition and criteria

In common usage, democracy is often understood to be the same as liberal democracy. Liberal democracy is, strictly speaking, a form of representative democracy. But in it the political power of the government is moderated by a constitution. A system where the rights and freedoms of individuals and minorities are protected by a constitution is called constitutional liberalism. The constitution therefore places constraints on the extent to which the will of the majority can be exercised. An illiberal democracy is a democracy where these rights and freedoms are not respected. However some liberal democracies have emergency powers. They can make them temporarily less liberal, if applied by the executive, parliament, or via referenda.

The term "liberal" in "liberal democracy" does not imply that the government must follow the political ideology of liberalism. While undeniably the initial framework for modern liberal democracy was created by liberals of the late 18th and early 19th centuries, since then, many non-liberals too have given their support to liberal democracy. In fact they all have contributed to its growth.

The defining criteria of liberal democracy may be summarized as follows:

1. A liberal democracy includes the presence of a middle class, and a broad and flourishing civil society. These are often seen as preconditions for liberal democracy.
2. Further liberalization and democratization is almost always associated with support for a market economy. In western liberal democracies they do seem inseparable. Many free-market proponents believe that the emergence of capitalism predates the emergence of democracy. They see a historical sequence at work: market economy is not only a precondition, but will

ultimately ensure the transition to democracy. No Marxist socialist holds that capitalism and democracy are at best unrelated and at worst contradictory.

3. The most liberal criteria now used to define "democracy", is political pluralism: the presence of multiple and distinct political parties; a political process that is competitive, like an economic market.
4. The liberal-democratic constitution is the overriding criteria which defines the democratic character of the state. The purpose of a constitution is often seen to set a limit on the authority of the government.
5. The other criteria of liberal democratic system is the separation of powers, an independent judiciary, and a system of checks and balances between its branches of government. European constitutional liberalism emphasizes the rule of law.
6. Liberal democracy is also defined by universal suffrage. It grants all citizens the right to vote regardless of race, gender or property ownership. However, the universality is relative. Many countries have been regarded as democratic even though they are seen to have practised various forms of exclusion. These exclusions may be from suffrage, or demanding additional qualifications except for being a citizen, like a registration procedure to be allowed to vote. Voting rights are limited to those who are above a certain age, typically 18. In any case, decisions taken through elections are taken not by all citizens, but rather by those who have to choose to participate by voting.
7. The most often quoted criteria for liberal democracy take the form of specific rights and freedoms. They are originally considered essential for the functioning of a liberal democracy. But they have acquired such prominence in its definition, that many people now think themselves to ba a democracy. The reason is that no state wants to admit it is 'unfree'.

Judged in the above light the criteria of liberal democracy may include the following:

* Right to life and security of person.
* Freedom from slavery.
* Freedom of movement.
* Equality before the law and due process under the rule of law.
* Freedom of speech.
* Freedom of the press and access to alternative information sources.
* Freedom of association and assembly .
* Freedom of education.
* Freedom of religion.
* An independent judiciary.
* The right to own property, and to buy and sell the same. Generally this right is often seen as a liberal freedom though this is a very hotly contested issue.

## Social Democracy

Social democracy is derived from socialist and communist system. The route taken by it is progressive, gradualist and constitutional. Many social democratic parties in the world are evolutions of revolutionary parties. They, for ideological or pragmatic reasons, come to embrace a strategy of gradual change through existing institutions. Or they come to adopt a policy of working for liberal reforms prior to more profound social change, or sudden revolutionary change. It may involve progressivism. This explains why today most of the parties that call themselves social democratic do not advocate the abolition of capitalism. Instead they want that it should be heavily regulated.

In general, the hallmarks of social democracy are:

* market regulation.
* social security, also known as welfare state.
* subsidized or government-owned public school and public health services.
* progressive taxation.

Furthermore, for ideological affinity or other reasons, most social democrats are also associated with environmentalism, multiculturalism, and secularism.

## Theories of Democracy

Democracy means rule by the people. This definition has raised more questions than it has helped to answer or resolve. Sharp disagreement has existed on what constitutes 'people' and what is meant by 'rule'. Also there has been no unanimity about the scope and extent of their (people's) participation or what conditions might be conducive to participation or how much control they (people) should exercise over law and order, and how much on economy and the public policies? Innumerable questions have been raised by various thinkers over the ages provoking diverse answers to the above questions. Some thinkers believe that people should directly participate in the decision-making, whereas there are others who think, they can also participate through their representatives. Still others think that people can choose their own rulers and want them to be accountable to them. This divergence of views on what democracy means has given rise to the different theories of democracy. The most prominent of these can be listed as follows:

1. Classical-Liberal Theory of Democracy.
2. Elitist Theory of Democracy.
3. Pluralist Theory of Democracy.
4. Participatory Democracy.
5. Marxist Theory of Democracy or Peoples' Democracy.

### 1. Classical Liberal Theory of Democracy

Liberalism is commitment to a set of methods. It aims at greater freedom of individuals. The term 'liberalism' as a system of thought and practice is the product of centuries of development. It refers to attitudes and responses widely shared among individuals. It has always meant freeing the individuals from the outdated restraints of old established institutions. Liberalism connotes:

(i) valuing of a free expression of individual personality;
(ii) a belief in men's ability to make that expression valuable to themselves and the society; and
(iii) the upholding of those institutions and policies that protect and foster both free expression and confidence in that freedom.

Liberalism, in both classical and its more contemporary, or "revisionist" forms, is essentially a modern phenomenon. In its thought and practice it focuses on two primary themes: First theme is the dislike of arbitrary authority which it wants to replace by other forms of social practice. Second theme is the free expression of individual personality. It implies a more equal distribution of liberty, the abolition of monopolies, the destruction of aristocratic privileges. The two crucial objectives of liberalism are noninterference and enfranchisement.

With the rise of liberalism in England and Europe democratic ideas have now come to be seen as imperatives of the governance of a society. These ideas just a decade before have freed themselves from absolute power of the kings and orthodoxy of beliefs and religious traditions. The ideas of liberty, equality, rights, secularism and justice become the clarion of liberalism. Democracy becomes a means of translating them into reality. Yet the liberal democracy is deemed as liberal first and democratic afterwards. According to Macpherson, before democracy comes in the Western world, there comes a society and politics of choice. It is also a society and politics of competition, as well as a society and politics of market. As the liberal state is democratized, in the process, the democracy is also liberalized.

Though the traces of classical-liberal democratic ideas are found in the writings of Thomas Moore, Winstanely and English Puritans as well as those of Levellers, it is the social contract theory which indeed lays the foundation of democracy. For, behind any contract there is an assumption that all are equal. Thomas Hobbes and John Locke elaborate the democratic principle *i.e.,* the people create the government through a social contract. However it is John Locke who advocates that government must be run by the people and aim solely at their good. The crux of Locke's argument may be summed up as follows:

(i) All political power finally inheres in the people.
(ii) The legitimate power of the government is a limited one. The government should not violate certain inalienable rights of the people. Otherwise this will result in dissolution of the contract between the government and the people.
(iii) Since individual rights are a part of man's nature a government ought to be dedicated to the needs of the individual and not vice versa.

Adam Smith complements Locke's ideas about politics. In the realm of economics he advocates freedom to produce, buy and sell the produce and support free and open competition and free economic exchange.

Montesquieu elaborates the theory of separation of powers having a great democratic significance and appeal. His theory influences the making of the American Constitution. Jefferson, Madison and Hamilton give institutional shape to the ideas of their predecessors in context of making of the American Constitution.

Among the latter day liberals Jeremy Bentham prepares the ground for democracy. He justifies democracy on utilitarian grounds. Bentham argues that individuals require protection from the governors as well as from each other. He wants an assurance that those who govern must pursue policies that are in consonance with the interests of the individuals. The governments must follow the wishes and interests of the community in matters of law and policy. This calls for a system of choosing and authorizing governments to make and enforce the laws needed by the society.

Bentham finds the solution in representative democracy, constitutional government, regular elections, secret ballot, competition between parties and leaders, majority rule etc. He sees democratic franchise as essential to achieve the goal of the greatest happiness of the greatest number. To act as a check upon the government, he suggests, the governors must be made frequently removable by the majority decision. However, his views on democratic franchise have been consistent. Broadly speaking, liberal democracy with universal franchise and constitutional government is seen as the best protector of individual rights and laissez-faire capitalist economy.

Bentham considers democracy as a means of protecting the citizens from the oppression of the rulers. He upholds the moral worth of democracy because it can ensure the improvement and development of mankind as a whole. J.S. Mill conceives democracy as a prime mechanism of moral self-development and the highest good. However, he considers participation in the elections as an essential means of human development. Yet he does not favour universal franchise or the principle of one-man-one-vote. His fear is that the working class being in majority, the principle of one-man-one-vote if it is introduced, may not lead to legislation in the interest of one particular class at the expense of other classes. In his *Representative Government* (1861) Mill argues for plural votes for some along with exclusion of others. Among people to be excluded from voting he includes specially those receiving poor relief, and who are bankrupts, illiterates, and who are not paying taxes etc. Mill concludes that a representative democracy, its scope and powers are tightly restricted by the principle of liberty and laissez-faire in economic relations, which are the best guarantee of a free community.

The above ideas of classical-liberal democracy find powerful support in the writings of T.H. Green, Hobhouse, Lindsay, Barker, Laski, MacIver, John Dewey and W. Wilson. The evolution of the party system in the twentieth century, lends further strength to the classical-liberal theory. Mill's fear regarding the seeming contradiction between universal franchise and the class interest turns out to be unfounded. Franchise comes to be extended to all adult population. The democratic party system is seen as the antidote to the ills of class government. Maclver sees in the party system an effective way of reducing differences of opinion to relatively simple alternatives. Similarly, John Dewey finds in democracy the best method to organize the disparate scattered mobile and manifold public, waiting for aggression and articulation of their demands.

Thus a Classical Liberal Theory of Democracy is an outcome of an evolutionary process. Its ideas and philosophy can be traced back to the Greek times though it emerges as a theory with individualism as its philosophical basis during and after the seventeenth century. It follows the establishment of a limited liberal democratic state with representative institutions. The essentials of liberal democracy can be reduced to the following four stipulations:

(i) An ideal of equal individual rights to self-development;
(ii) equality before law;
(iii) basic civil liberties; and
(iv) popular sovereignty with an equal political voice for all citizens.

Viewed in this light, the salient features of the Classical Liberal Theory of Democracy are as follows:

(i) To establish a government in which people can actively participate in the political process and public affairs.
(ii) To establish a "participatory government", aiming at defending and promoting the interests of man.
(iii) To strive for the development and welfare of man and the creation of an ideal society.

Liberal democracy is in fact a way of life. It aims at the all-round development of human personality. Along with liberty, equality and rights, it provides the necessary conditions for the development of a moral individual. It provides an atmosphere conducive for the development of man's personality, his capacities and abilities. Participation in the management of public affairs are a means to ensure intellectual, emotional and moral education of all citizens. Liberal democracy promotive of the greatest good must combine both the ideas of political liberty and socioeconomic equality.

The institutional expression of liberal democracy involves the existence of a democratic government in which the rulers are responsible to the ruled. It rests on the principle of public accountability and respect for the autonomy of the individuals. Its chief components are: public opinion, enjoyment of universal adult suffrage and a representative government. In it the people are the ultimate source of power. It ensures them the enjoyment of individual rights and freedoms. They enable the citizens to develop their personality fostering in them the fitness to govern. Democracy also believes in the rule of law and independence of judiciary.

Liberal democracy is based on tolerance, consensus and compromise. The majority should not be prompted by sectional interests. In no case they should disregard the interest of the minorities. Discussion and debate should help reduce tensions between different groups and resolve conflicts.

The liberal theory of democracy presupposes the existence of rational and active citizen. It seeks to realize a generally recognized common good through collective initiative, discussion and decision on policy questions concerning public affairs. The main principles of liberal democracy are – majority rule, government by discussion, recognition of minority rights and constitutional government.

The success of the Classical Liberalism in England owed much to the synergy of three Liberal Traditions—Constitutionalism, Economic Liberalism and Utilitarianism. In the process of its development both Classical Liberalism and the Traditions, get progressively modified. Social environment, social reforms, democratic processes and popular participation are given prominence.

Ever since the two world wars, Liberalism has been on the decline. It is due to scant support it has received from developing nations struggling for independence and material prosperity. The cold war also can be cited as a significant cause to weaken thc Liberalist Tradition. However the final challenge to liberty and constitutionalism has come chiefly from the communists.

As a result, the liberal-democratic society and state have undergone a significant change since the original theory is propounded. The change in the state has been in the ways the governments are chosen and authorized through democratic franchise. Despite perceptible changes in the society and economy, however liberal democracy even today is seen as democracy of a capitalist market society and this is so in spite of the rise of welfare state.

**Assumptions of Classical Liberal Democracy**

The Classical Liberal Theory of Democracy has the following assumptions:

- The theory assumes that every individual is the best judge of himself. He is aware of the common interest of the society. This is despite 'common good' or 'common interest' may mean different things to different persons. Individuals are often swayed by other considerations while exercising their franchise to elect their representatives. They are at times guided and motivated by parochial interests.
- The theory believes in the concept of 'political equality'. But this is not often realized that many a time it is elite in most democracies that enjoy political power disproportionate to their number. They always control the decision-making mechanisms and thus influence the goals of democracy.
- The theory claims that democracy reflects the will of the people. The basis of legitimacy of a democratic government lies in the fact that it is formed by the will of the people. But judged in empirical terms the claim is not always well- founded. Very often people are not in a position to exercise their 'free choice' due to poverty, illiteracy or ignorance as well as allurement of gain or fear of intimidation. The exercise of franchise is also seen to be influenced by money-power, muscle-power and parochialism.

- The theory assumes that the legitimacy of the democratic government is based on public opinion. But this assumption is also not correct. In many democracies, a large majority of people have a little chance of voicing their demands and their interests. Having massive resources and the propaganda machinery at their disposal, the governments and their various agencies are able to create or tilt 'public opinion' in their favour.
- The theory lays emphasis on the mode of discussion, debate and consultations to create a true democratic society capable of fulfilling aspirations of the people. Behind it lies an assumption that the people have a right to change a government which does not fulfill their aspirations. Such an assumption runs counter to the need of the stability of the political system.
- The theory does not give adequate importance to the economic dimension. The assurance of equal opportunity to all the people for participating in political process is seldom realized in actual practice. Even the so-called free election is really meant mostly for those who have a monopoly over resources—financial or otherwise. The emphasis laid by classical liberals on capitalist economy, often comes to mean preventing state intervention in the economic pursuits of the rich and privileged class.

The Classical Liberal Theory of Democracy continues to enjoy popularity till the beginning of the twentieth century. While the Early Classical Liberal Theory is seen to reflect needs of the newly emerging middle class, the New Liberal Theory of Democracy in its variant as the Elitist Theory, emerges as a political doctrine, highly critical both of modern democracy and modern socialism.

### Characteristics of Classical Liberal Theory of Democracy

The characteristics of Classical Liberal Theory of Democracy may be summarized as follows:

1. It enshrines supremacy of the people.
2. Individual is the basic unit of democratic model; he is rational, ethical, active and self-interested. The theory lays emphasis on individual freedom.
3. Participation in political life is most essential to protect individual interest and create an informed, committed and developed citizenry.
4. Participation is deemed a virtue because it widens the horizon of the individual and extends his knowledge. It makes his sympathies less parochial. It develops his practical sense and intelligence. It serves as a means of intellectual, emotional and moral education. It leads towards the full development of the capacities of the individual.
5. In institutional terms the theory advocates representative government with elected leadership, regular elections, secret ballot, constitutional state, independent judiciary, individual rights and civil liberties such as freedom of thought, discussion, publication etc.

6. The theory demarcates clearly between elected representatives and the bureaucracy. In terms of the benefit of popular control and efficiency it can best be had only by recognizing the distinctiveness of their functions and scope of activities.
7. Economically speaking the basis on which the theory is built is economic inequality, though its aim is political equality. It believes in competitive market economy, private property and control over the means of production and laissez faire economy. According to Macpherson, it aims at maximizing the liberty of citizens, securing their property and ensuring the working of the capitalist economy. Liberal democracy neither destroys nor weakens the state. Rather it strengthens both the state and the capitalist society.

**Critique of the classical Liberal Theory of Democracy**

The Classical Liberal Theory has been criticized on many counts. The main grounds of criticism are the following:

1. The theory is found inadequate to meet the needs of highly industrialized and technological states which emerges after the first world war.
2. The theory rests on a view of man as rational, active, informed and ready to take active part in the political process. However there are writers like Lord Bryce, Graham Wallas and several empirical writers who hold that man is not as rational, disinterested, informed or active as it is assumed to be. Also the theory either ignores, or underplays or simply condemns the role of organized groups, leaders or emotions in political affairs which in practice are quite important.
3. The theory believes that 'the people' hold a definite and rational opinion about every individual question which is not borne out in practice. However, it fails to provide any satisfying definition of terms like 'people' or 'rule' which are obviously central to a conception of government as the rule of the people. So is the assumption behind it that public opinion is the basis of government which as the facts reveal is another 'democratic myth'.
4. The theory further assumes that there exists a 'common good', (such as human self-development). But as Schumpeter points out there is no such thing as a uniquely determined common good on which all people can agree. So common good is bound to mean different things to different people.
5. The theory overlooks factors like the role of democratic leadership, mass psychology, group coercion and the influence of controllers of concentrated economic power. Walker sees classical liberal democracy as unrealistic because it employs concepts of the nature of man and the operation of society which are utopian.
6. In view of the prevalence of party system, democracy turns out to be essentially a competition among the elites rather than the masses. These elites become the driving force in running the system and to this end they formulate policies and issues which shape the destiny of the people.

7. The theory takes simplistic view of the complex procedures underlying decision-making processes. It is unable to provide any satisfying solution to the problems caused by simultaneous affirmation of majority rule and minority right. Since the process is quite complex and technical it is beyond the understanding of an average man who is too much engrossed in his own activities.
8. While the early liberals overlook the class character of liberal democracy and its exploitative consequences upon the working-class, the neoliberals like Lindsay, Barker, Maciver, Dewey appreciate democracy with its regulatory and welfare functions as the best way of achieving a good society.

**2. The Elitist Theory of Democracy**

The chief contribution of the Classical Theory of Democracy is that it emphasizes the idea of political equality and individual participation in affairs of government. But this theory comes to be challenged in the twentieth century by a number of thinkers mainly on empirical ground. They ask, how valid is it that the individuals participate in the day-to-day politics directly; and how feasible it is that the ordinary citizens bear the strain of playing a public role? They voice their fear: should liberty become casualty if the masses unaided by an externally imposed discipline seek to bring a variety of impulses in the province of politics? They also voice their fear if self-government is really possible? The answers to these questions give rise to various models of democracy from the Classical Liberal Model to Peoples' Theory of Democracy.

The elite theory, for all practical purposes, was developed to serve the interests of the bourgeois class. Its intent was to rationalize the existing political order wherein the power structure was dominated by the elites. The principal assumption of the elitist theory is that in every society there is a minority which effectively rules over the majority. Thus, the term elite refers to members of a top stratum in every sphere of life who hold higher status in the community.

The term 'elite' has been defined variously by different theorists. Vilfredo Pareto defines it as "people in a society who possess, in marked degree, qualities of intelligence, character, skill and capacity of whatever kind".

Parry Gariant defines elite as "small minorities who appear to play an exceptionally influential part in political and social affairs".

Suzanne Keller defines elite as "those minorities which are set apart from the rest of the society by their pre-eminence in one or more of these various distributions".

C. Wright Mills defines elite as "composed of men who have the most of what there is to have money, power and prestige who are able to realize their will, even if others resist it, whose positions enable them to transcend the ordinary environments of ordinary people and who are in positions to make decisions having major consequences."

T.B. Bottomore notes that the minority which rules over the majority consists of those who occupy posts of political command. He applies the term 'elite' to functional, mainly occupational groups which have high status in society.

According to H.D. Lasswell, "Political elite comprises the power holders of body politic. The power holders include the leadership and the social formations from which leaders typically come, and to which accountability is maintained during a given period".

Elite are also defined as those minorities which are set apart from the rest of the society owing to their preeminence in one or more spheres of distribution of various privileges and benefits.

Vilfredo Pareto (1848-1923) and Gaetano Mosca (1858-1941), the two Italian sociologists are the first to develop the theory of elite. They proclaim that in every sphere of social life there is an elite: this is the sense in which Pareto uses the term. Pareto classifies elite into two categories, namely, 'social elite' and the 'governing elite', though he also refers to several elites in each sphere of activity. These are, for example, military elite, political elite, business elite and academic elite.

Pareto divides society into lower stratum and higher stratum. The lower stratum constitutes the non-elite, whereas the higher stratum constitutes elite. Furthermore, the elite is subdivided into governing elite and non-governing elite.

Pareto's main interest consists in defining the nature of the governing elite. In a democracy, top leaders of political parties are the governing elite. Their power is based partly on force and partly on consent. The non-governing elite, on the other hand, are those who are at the top of nonpolitical structures.

For Pareto, in every society there are two types of individuals—foxes and lions. People get their rulers from these categories of lions and foxes in accordance with their own sentiments and preferences.

Pareto propounds the theory of "Circulation of Elite". It implies that with every change in the society, new men of money and power come to replace the old ones. There are two broad sets of factors that explain the downfall and replacement of elites. They are: 'structural' factors and 'socio-psychological' factors. The dominant minority is constantly being changed along with structural changes in the society.

The elite displacement can either take place independently irrespective of its character and motivation or due to the change in the attitudes or abilities of the elite. While moving from one group to another an individual generally brings with him certain inclinations, sentiments, attitudes and values which are peculiar to him and what he has acquired in the group from which he comes.

Joseph Schumpeter observes, "the democratic method is that institutional arrangement for arriving at political decisions in which individuals acquire the power to decide by means of a competitive struggle for the people's vote". His views on democracy have been widely endorsed by pluralist writers.

Some scholars see glaring differences between the notion of elites and the idea of democracy:

First the insistence in the elite theories upon the inequality of individual endowment runs counter to the fundamental postulate of democratic theory, which emphasizes an underlying equality of individuals.

Secondly, the notion of a governing minority also runs counter to the democratic theory of majority rule. However this contradiction between elitism and democracy is not absolute and real as it seems on the face of it. A political democracy presupposes an open competition for positions of authority and power. In the ultimate analysis, the rulers are accountable to those who elect them. Even as the actual shaping of policy is in the hands of elites, but this does not mean that the society is not democratic. For it is sufficient for democracy that the individual citizens, "though prevented from taking a direct part in government all the time, have at least the possibility of making their aspirations felt at certain intervals".

Finally, the conception of democracy as elite rule comes to be legitimized in the twentieth century due to the rise of Fascist or Marxist one-party regimes. They offer, by contrast, a certain degree of credibility to the identification of democracy with a multiparty and representative system. The concept of equality underlying democracy is perceived by the protagonists of elitist theories as "equality of opportunity". Viewed from this perspective democratic society presents an atmosphere conducive to open competition of elites in economic, political, cultural spheres. It also creates opportunities that the elites are recruited from different strata of society on the basis of their achievements and merits. Besides the electorate can choose between the notion of elites and democracy especially because of certain development which necessitate energetic role of leaders. The plurality of elites in a democratic country facilitates many checks and balances, preventive of the abuse of power.

The Elitist Theory of Democracy does not accept some assumptions of the Classical Liberal Theory of Democracy which include :

(i) That in it the people govern themselves,

(ii) the belief that the ultimate power resides in the people. Instead it is elites who possess and exercise ultimate power and take all major decisions, and

(iii) that the liberal democracy is "government by the people" and the existence of political equality in a democratic society runs counter to the ground reality.

The main features of the elitist theory of democracy may be enumerated as follows:

1. In every system, a small minority or a group of individuals are seen to exercise their influence that is disproportionate to their number. They occupy key positions of power and control the decision-making process and are called the elite. They are the products of social circumstances and the social conditions which facilitate their rise.
2. Elite are drawn from the different sections of the people. They are the ones who occupy the high offices. The elite get dominant position due to several factors such as certain social or religious factors – hereditary and personal

traits. They wield power and influence because they possess some superior qualities such as administrative acumen, intellectual ability, military power or moral authority. The elite are able to maintain power due to these qualities. Power by nature is cumulative and the elite's access to power makes them acquire more power and thus maintain their dominance. Additionally they use various devices to win and manipulate mass support.

3. In any social system there emerge various categories of elites who include social elite, political elite, military elite, economic elite, etc.
4. The elitist thinking is a negation of the Marxian theory. In effect, the Elitist Theory is intended to refute Marx's Theory of Social Classes. The elitist theorists hold that the Marxist conception of ruling classes is erroneous. This is demonstrated by the continual circulation of elite. This change of elite tends to prevent the formation of a stable or a closed ruling class in modern industrial societies.
5. The elite theorists argue that a classless society is impossible, since, in every society, there is, and must be a minority, which actually rules. This view runs counter to the Marxian emphasis that economics rather than politics is the determining force in history and it is the economic bond that holds societies together.
6. The elite theorists reject the thesis of classless society on the plea that there will always be a ruling class dominating others in the society. They also refute the Marxist notion that conflict between elites and masses is inevitable. As against this they hold that conflicting classes can live in peace and cooperation.
7. The elite theorists also dismiss the view that revolution would bring about radical transformation in the society by overthrowing one ruling class from power by another.

The Elite Theory projects two different views concerning the nature of elite in a democracy : First is the oligarchic view which is expressed by Pareto and Mosca. The second view is held by Dahl and others and is called the pluralist view as it speaks of the plurality of different elite within a society. Pluralism supports the idea of a continuous competition and adjustment between different elites in the society.

The Elite Theory has been criticized on following counts:

1. The Elite Theory negates the principle of equality and thus it is antidemocratic in nature. It is lacking in faith in the masses. Instead it pins its hopes on elites. This is against the thrust of modernity. Today all modern democracies lay emphasis on mass participation and power-sharing by the people in the decision-making process. This is what the elite theorists negate.
2. The principal concern of the elite theorists is the maintenance of the stability of the system. In this respect they are highly conservative in their thinking and approach. They argue that popular participation including recourse to

agitational methods in defence of democratic rights, gives rise to imbalances in the system 'overloading' it rather than increasing its democratic content.

### 3. The Pluralist Theory of Democracy

The Pluralist Theory, in contrast, is based on the principle of 'pluralism'. It views the society as essentially pluralistic in institutional framework and in its power structure as well. As a result, in it political power is fragmented and dispersed among the various branches of government. That political power is shared between the state and the numerous private groups and individuals.

Both the Elitists- Pluralists and Marxists agree on one thing that power rests in the hands of a minority. As a result, the majority of members of the society are excluded from the power structure. The former (i.e., Elitists-Pluralists) maintain that power is not concentrated but is shared among all sections of the people. The sharing is done through different organizations as are formed to articulate their interests. These associations and groups make regular and intense efforts to influence the policies and decisions of the government.

The chief theorists of pluralistic democracy are Robert Dahl, Sartori, Berelson, H. Eckstein, V. Presthus, F. Haunter, Lipset and R.E. Agger. Emphasizing the importance of pluralism Emile Durkheim writes, "Collective activity is always too complex to be able to be expressed through the single and unique organ of the state. A nation can be maintained only if, between the state and the individual, there is interrelated a whole series of secondary groups near enough to the individuals to attract them strongly in their sphere of action and drag them, in this way, into the general current of social life".

Lipset advocates his view of pluralist democracy in his book *Political Man.* Robert Dahl explains his pluralist theory of democracy in his book *Who Governs*? Dahl says, "there are several places where decisions are being made by industrialists, merchants, trade unions, farmers' associations, consumers, politicians, voters and many other groups and associations with a view to influencing policy-making by government".

However, some groups may be more influential than others, though it may not be easy to measure the different degrees of this influence exactly.

Dahl admits that formation of elites is quite natural even in a democratic society but it would be wrong to see them as a power elite and the ruling class. Dahl's conclusion is based on his empirical survey of New Haven. His finding is that the city is governed by a combination of elites in the cultural and economic fields. However, none of these competing elites can be described as a ruling elite.

Arnold M. Rose agrees with Dahl's pluralist democracy. According to Rose the society consists of many elites representing different interests. These economic and political elites do not work as allies forming a single ruling elite. He rejects the hypothesis of unified power elite and advocates in its place a "multi-influence hypothesis".

While M. Duverger defines pluralist democracy "as a plurality of decision centers", for V. Presthus, "it is a socio-political system in which the power of the state is shared with a large number of private groups, interest organizations, and individuals represented by such organizations.... Pluralism is a system in which political power is fragmented among the branches of government. It is moreover shared between the state and the multitude of private groups and individuals".

**Characteristics of the Pluralist Theory of Democracy**

The following are the main characteristics of the Pluralist Theory of Democracy:

1. The main focus of the Pluralist Theory is on the "power structure" of societies, that powers are fragmented and dispersed. The leadership is not necessarily confined to an elite or to competing elites nor is there anything like the power elite or the ruling class. The state has to share its powers with several political parties, interest groups, classes. Apart from being independent of the state, sometimes there may exist in a particular society, associations, private groups and individuals.
2. The Pluralist Theory warns against the dangers of concentration of political power at one centre – be it a political party, an elite or an organization. With the provision of separation of powers along with checks and balances at several points, no organ of the government or any organization is likely to emerge dominant having monopoly of power for a long time. There must be a limit on political powers of the state through a sharing of it with other political and non-political groups and associations in the society. This theory assumes that state too is an association like any other one in the society.
3. The major focus of the Pluralist Theory is on the "politics of consensus". It implies that all the organized groups in society should be taken into confidence while formulating public policy. Pluralist democracy rests on the premise of loyalty and obedience of the people to the laws of the state. It should be ensured through the process of prior consultation among various groups and individuals before a decision is taken. It assumes that any widening of gap between the rulers and people always endangers the very survival of a democratic system.
4. The Pluralist Theory considers periodical elections in a political system as an important element of the electoral process. It views it as the best means of eliciting public opinion on political issues of concern to the people.

The Pluralist Theory of Democracy is an amalgam of the "Classical Liberal Theory" and the "Elitist Theory" of Democracy. Its objective is to create an ideal democratic society. It will be a society where the individuals enjoy rights and freedoms without any let or hindrance from any agency from within or outside. It will provide the necessary congenial conditions that will enable individuals to participate in the political process of the state as well as develop their personality.

**Shortcomings of the Pluralist Theory of Democracy**

The Pluralist Theory of Democracy has some of the following shortcomings:

First, the Pluralist Theory undermines the ability and capacity of individuals to have a rational participation in the political process independent of their associations and organizations. The Theory tends to overemphasize the role and significance of groups and associations in a democratic polity.

Secondly, the 'politics of consensus' is a high sounding phrase in context of a conflict-ridden society. In such a society it is very difficult to arrive at decisions jointly in a spirit of mutuality and reconciliation. So is the task of formulating policies that may harmonize various conflicting interest of various groups, associations and organizations. It would become all the more difficult in situations where some of these groups represent the interests of the rich, while the others represent the interest of the poor. It is very often observed that the organizations of the rich are able to influence governmental policies and decisions while those of the poor are kept off from power centres. Thus in class-ridden societies, pluralism is seen to be confined only to a few organizations representing the rich alone.

Thirdly, pluralism gives rise to the "politics of pressure groups". It is an admitted fact that the various pressure groups are unable to rise above their narrow parochial interests. In pursuing them they are seen most often to indulge in unfair and illegal practices. As a result, the government is weakened and rendered incapable of formulating firm policies and effectively implementing them. Most of the time, the government per force has to function on basis of compromises, which over time tend to erode its credibility.

Finally, an elitist trend is very much evident in most organizations. Among those controlling various organizations such as political parties, interest groups, the pressure groups not only monopolize power and privilege but also are seen to neglect the interests of the rank and file. The net result is that in the process, the common man is neglected and forgotten. In reality, groups and associations serve only the interests of a coterie of people who largely consist of the leaders and organizers or their henchmen. This results in the decline of individualism and liberal democratic ethos. Its immediate effect is reflected in various organizations becoming an arena of domination, exploitation and corruption by these leaders.

Despite strong criticism of the Pluralist Theory of Democracy, it cannot be denied that the Theory has contributed in a positive way to the creation of consensus in political process, which is the hallmark of democratic polity.

**4. Participatory Democracy**

Participatory Democracy may be seen as a reaction against the Elitist Pluralist Theories of Democracy. The former counters the elitist view that the power of decision-making is the monopoly of certain elites or groups and the role of the masses is just the selection of elites once in a few years. The Participatory Democracy, has as its aim, to break this monopoly and distribute decision-making power more equitably. While subscribing to the principle of equality and majority rule, Participatory Democracy tends to extend this political equality by ensuring decision-making at grassroots. Cook and Morgan, mention two of its broad features:

(i) decentralization of authoritative decision-making in order to bring it (the decision-making) closer to the people affected by the decisions, and
(ii) direct involvement of common man in the decisions-making processes.

Participatory Democracy has much in common with the Classical Liberal Idea that democracy is a means of ensuring equal right to self-development along with its being a form of government. A participatory society cares much more for collective problems. It helps in the formation of politically active citizenry having a continuous interest in the governing process. It favours the idea of direct participation of citizens in the regulation of key institutions of society. It strongly believes that it will make political parties more open and accountable. It will also help to maintain an open institutional system. Besides it will ensure the possibility of experimentation with new political forms of participation.

Since Participatory Democracy aims to secure common man's participation in the decision-making processes, it may be worthwhile to ask: (i) why should there be a need for participation, and {ii) how to and how much should it be? The theorists of Participatory Democracy have tried to find answers to these questions.

The Participatory Democracy seeks to bring common man in the centerstage of the authoritative decision-making process. It believes that the true index of freedom is to be seen in the concrete liberties and opportunities available to the individual in the society to participate actively in the political and civic life. Pateman writes about the benefits of Participatory Democracy. According to him, "The Participatory Democracy fosters human development. It enhances a sense of political efficacy. It reduces the sense of estrangement from power centers. It nurtures a concern for collective problems. It contributes to the formation of an active citizenry capable of taking a much more acute interest in governmental affairs". Once people 'know that opportunities exist for effective participation in decision-making, and that participation is a worthwhile activity, they will definitely like to participate in it most enthusiastically'. McPherson supports the above view. He writes that liberty of the individual can be fully realized only with the direct participation of the people in the regulation of the affairs of the state.

Participatory Democracy may be viewed as everyman's revolt against the rule by the expert. It is based on the assumption that the best protection from tyranny is through the dispersal of power. It is only through Participatory Democracy that the individual can be rescued from apathy, ignorance and alienation.

## The Means and Extent of Participation

It is well accepted that participation in the affairs of the government is a prerequisite for self-development. Although various theorists differ regarding the means and extent of participation, there are a number of means of participation in modern democratic states. They may include voting in local or national elections, campaigning in the elections, active membership of a political party or a pressure group. Or they may include taking part in political demonstrations, industrial strikes, various forms of civil disobedience or in initiative, referendum, recall, etc. They may also include involvement in the implementation of social policies and various forms of community development programmes including women development, family planning, environment issues etc.

According to Poulantzas, participation of people in political affairs can be enhanced through two sets of changes: (i) by making the state more democratic *i.e.*, making parliament, the state bureaucracies and political parties more open and accountable, and (ii) launching new forms of struggles at local levels through factory-based politics, women's movements, ecological groups etc. In short, to make the society and the state effectively democratized. But how the two sets of changes are to be interrelated is a big question mark.

Owing to the enormous size and number of people inhabiting a state it is virtually impossible to involve all citizens in a face-to-face discussion every time a public issue arises. According to Macpherson, a substantial basis will be created for Participatory Democracy if (i) parties are democratized according to the principle of direct democracy, (ii) if there are genuinely participatory parties operating within the parliamentary structure, and (iii) if they are supplemented by fully-managed organizations in the workplace and local community. Only in such a political system the democratic value of 'equal right to self-development can be realized'. According to Carole Pateman, participation can be increased by extending democratic control over those institutions which affect the daily life of the people. But it is direct participation and control over immediate local issues, complemented by party and interest group competition in government spheres that can most realistically advance the principle of Participatory Democracy.

**Characteristics of Participatory Democracy**

In the light of the above discussion, some of the important characteristics of Participatory Democracy may be summarized as follows:

1. Democracy is not only a form of government but also a means of self-development. A participatory society fosters a sense of political efficacy. It stimulates a concern for collective problems. It creates the kind of citizenry who take continuous interest in the processes of governance.
2. In addition to representative institutions, a Participatory Democracy involves direct participation of citizens in the regulation of key institutions of society, both at work place and local community.
3. It (Participatory Democracy) wants to make the representatives directly accountable to the people. This is sought to be achieved though reorganized party system which is genuinely accountable to the parliamentary system.

4. It wants to maintain an open institutional system devising new forms of democratic control.
5. It wants to strengthen the poor resource-base of individuals and social groups by extending economic rights and policies involving distributive justice and redistribution of material resources.
6. It wants to loosen the hold of unaccountable bureaucratic power over both public and private spheres.

**Problematic Issues**

According to David Held, the Participatory Democracy shares difficulties associated with the previous Models of Democracy (Classical-Liberal, Elitist-Pluralist etc.). But still in many respects it represents an advance upon them. Yet many questions are left unanswered. Undeniably we learn to participate only by participating in political activities. Such participation helps foster an active and knowledgeable citizenship. Still it does not mean that an increased participation in itself will automatically bring a new revolution in human dcvclopmcnt. It is not ncccssary that people will generally become more democratic, cooperative and dedicated to the common good.

The Participatory Democracy rests on the belief that all people generally want to extend the sphere of control over their lives. However, it may be one thing to recognize a right, and altogether another to say that we must, irrespective of choice, participate in public life. There are many questions on which Participatory Theory is silent. It is not clear about the relation between liberty and equality; the limits on the part of the people to change and alter political circumstances; the extent of their willingness to participate in management of social and economic affairs; what if they refuse to become creatures of democratic reason as well as many more such questions.

According to Cook and Morgan, as a system of government also, Participatory Democracy has not been able to build a systematic theory. Participation of ordinary citizen in the decision-making process, both at local levels and national level, raises a number of issues which it has failed to adequately address at the theoretical level.

Some of these issues are :

(i) What may be an appropriate participatory unit for this kind of decision-making?
(ii) What should be its proper size and function?
(iii) Whether or not the involvement of a large number of citizens conducive to efficiency and competence of the decisions?
(iv) How to coordinate the decisions taken at the local levels with those taken at other levels and how they may be reconciled with the overall interest of the society at large? Such innumerable problems tend to pose a variety of obstacles in the implementation of Participatory Democracy in the true sense of the term.

## 5. The Marxian Theory of Democracy or Peoples Democracy

The Marxian Theory of Democracy is seen to emerge as a reaction against the evils of capitalism. It has as its basis the overall philosophy of Marxism. The nineteenth century, due to the problems created by the Industrial Revolution is seen to provide a fertile ground for the rise of various new theories of democracy. Out of them the most radical is the Theory of Democratic Socialism. It is the outcome of a growing realization by the workers that the extension of suffrage and other political rights has little effect in mitigating their sufferings or halting the ever-increasing economic inequality in the society.

Karl Marx attempts to relate the socialist practice to a historical and economic theory. He bases it on an interpretation of social evolution and critical analysis of the existing system of production and exchange. He tries to show how a socialist or democratic society which is built upon the capitalist foundation is unable to fulfil the great needs of society, namely economic security, social security and freedom of self-expression.

Marx has been a democratic republican for about two years (1842-1843) before he becomes a convert to communism. He has written many essays during this period analyzing the principal tenets of his liberal humanist and democratic philosophy. There is no recorded evidence to suggest that Marx ever abandons any of these basic beliefs about democracy and socialist philosophy. His defence of freedom of press and opposition to the Prussian institution of censorship is well known.

Marx's early critique of Prussian despotism is based on his concept of humanism. In his *Paris Manuscripts of 1844,* Marx makes an attempt to put forward his concept of true democracy. Here he describes democracy as a potent means to accomplish general human emancipation. He regards political freedom of bourgeois democracy only as a first step in the direction of man's total freedom. Even though on the whole he is contemptuous of the so-called rights of bourgeois democracy, yet he supports the rights of free expression, free assembly, free association and the like, coupled with universal suffrage thinking that they would enable the oppressed masses to organize and struggle for their emancipation.

After his conversion to communism, Marx develops his concept of bourgeois democracy by adding a class perspective to it. He feels convinced that democracy without socialism is inadequate and worthless. In a bourgeois democracy, it is the right of self-interest, or the organized self-interest of the bourgeois class that dominates and prevails as a whole.

Marx considers all forms of private property including bourgeois property as inconsistent with man's freedom in a true democracy. Even though bourgeois democracy abolishes property qualifications for voters and their representatives, but until private property and unequal possessions are abolished no true democracy can be realized. For true democracy means the negation of private property *i.e.,* the negation of all nonpolitical distinctions in actuality. It presupposes an end to class structure based on capitalist mode of production and distribution. It also presupposes an end of the alienated conditions of man characterized by wage labour, money, private property, class division with power of the state monopolized by the dominant class. To Marx, only a popular revolution can bring about social order based on true democracy having a basis in anti-class and anti-state. It means classless stateless exploitation-free social order for the true democracy to fruition and thrive.

Democracy, to Marx, is characterized by equality and abolition of classes. It is a form of state, a system of values and a form of society. The socialist democracy perceptibly differs from the bourgeois democracy in that its most crucial attribute is the capitalist economic system in which the ownership of means of production is vested in the capitalist class. The other important attribute of bourgeois democracy is the existence of private property, profit motive in personal ownership of capital, free competition, free market and the like. Moreover, in such a democracy the whole society is seen divided into two classes—the exploiters and the exploited. The capitalists or those controlling and owning the means of production are also the ones who control and dominate the state apparatus.

The Marxists claim that while their democracy is genuine, the bourgeois democracy is "fake". The latter, (bourgeois democracy) comes to be established on ruins of feudalism after protracted struggle of bourgeoisie against the feudal socioeconomic system and political organization. As against this, the socialist democracy comes into being as a reaction against the evils of capitalism and sordid exploitation in a bourgeois democracy. The bourgeois democracy exists only for the rich and the propertied. The latter use the state machinery in their own interests and against the interests of the exploited classes.

Although on the face of it, the bourgeois democracy maintains the instruments, institutions and infrastructure of a conventional democracy, but they are but devices to deceive and hoodwink the masses. Their object is to make them believe that the powers of the state belong to them. In reality, the political power in bourgeois democracy is controlled by the bourgeois minority. As against this, in a social democracy the government not only truly belongs to the majority but also really serves the interest of the majority. Social Democracy thus is, Marxists believe, a continuous process which will not stop till the goal of the stateless and classless society is realized.

Marxists reject the legitimacy of elections in bourgeois democracies on the ground that the ideologies shot into limelight during elections only serve the interests of the richer sections of the society. Freedom here is not meant to be enjoyed by all since bourgeois democracy under capitalism is "curtailed, poor , false." It is a democracy for the rich and insignificant minority of the capitalists and not for the poor. The restrictions imposed on suffrage, right of assembly and other areas squeeze out only the poor from politics. This is how they are restrained from taking an active part in the democratic process. A true democracy implies the role of majority, equality of all citizens and the existence of democratic rights and freedoms which are possible only in a Marxian democracy.

The theory of dictatorship of the proletariat forms an integral part of the Marxist Democracy, claimed to be a higher form of democracy than Bourgeois Democracy. After overthrow of the capitalist system the dictatorship of the proletariat comes to control all political power. Its object is to help the poor majority against the rich minority. It has to be continued until all exploitation rooted in class divisions comes to an end. The dictatorship of the proletariat represents an important phase and a step towards the realization of the communist society when the state will ultimately 'wither away'.

During the dictatorship of the proletariat, the state will be retained with all its repressive attributes with a view to effecting the transition from capitalism to communism. For, the repression under proletarian dictatorship and the earlier repression under dictatorship of the bourgeoisie have differed in a fundamental sense. Earlier, it is the minority that is seen to oppress and exploit the majority, now it is the majority that is oppressing and exploiting the minority. As a consequence, It is this dictatorship of the proletariat that will result in a new order of the Socialist Democracy in which the vast majority of people enjoy larger rights and liberties than they ever have had even in the best of bourgeois democracies.

However, the Marxists claim, in the transitional period between the evolution and 'the withering away of the state', the old state will continue to exist. The coercive power of the state will be used to nip in the bud all counterrevolutionary moves. It will be used to completely liquidate the last vestiges and remnants of capitalist resistance. The proletariat will use its dictatorship to wrest by decree all capital from the control of bourgeoisie and to concentrate all instruments of production in hands of the state.

Revolutionary dictatorship of the proletariat thus represents historical epoch of transition from capitalism to socialism and from socialism to communism. Thus, according to Marx, Engels and Lenin, there are two phases in the development of socialism into communism. The first is the socialist phase wherein the available consumer goods are to be distributed among the members of the society according to the principle of human needs. Only in a communist society, when the resistance of the capitalists has been completely broken, the capitalists have disappeared, division into classes has ended and the state has ceased to exist, then alone it will become possible to speak of freedom and the realization of complete democracy without any exception. In such a democracy people will gradually become accustomed to observing the elementary rules of social life that have been known for centuries. They will become accustomed to observing them without force or without compulsion. Also they would have learnt to do so without subordination as well as without the special apparatus for compulsion which is called the state. The expression 'the state will wither away' indicates both the gradual and the spontaneous nature of the progress from socialism to communism.

## Attack on the Marxist Theory of Democracy

The Marxist Theory of Democracy has been attacked by writers of various schools of thought – the 'Liberals', the 'Revisionists', the 'Anarchists', etc. on the following grounds:

1. The Liberals view the socialist democracy as a negation of true democracy because democracy is a government of the whole people of the society and not of one group pitted against another dominating and exploiting it. The socialist democracy, the Marxists explain, represents the interest of one class only. True democracy, according to the liberals, besides being the rule of majority implies a limited constitutional government, free competition, free economy, individual rights and liberties and so on.
2. There is no denying the fact that liberties, freedom and rights – individual social, economic and political – are the essence of democracy. The Marxists accept it in principle, but in actual practice deny many of the individual and political rights and liberties of the individuals. They neither give the people the right to criticize the government nor do they allow or tolerate any dissent. In this respect socialist democracy is fundamentally flawed and can not be called democracy in the real sense of the term.
3. In a socialist democracy, elections are a mere ritual as no opposition is allowed, no alternative party is permitted, people have no choice in electing candidates. The existence of different political parties, which distinguishes a democratic system is conspicuous by its absence in a socialist democracy. There is only one political party which dominates the system and no other political arty is allowed to compete under it.
4. Marx does agree that the transition to socialist democracy can be effected through established constitutional, peaceful means. But there are Marxists who believe in violence and revolution as the chief instrument of structural transformation in the society. In many cultures this excessive emphasis on violence is viewed with disfavour.
5. In a socialist democracy there neither is decentralization of power nor separation of powers between different branches of government. This gives rise to centralizing and despotic tendencies. The judiciary is also neither impartial nor independent in such a system. It thus fails to protect and safeguard the rights and freedoms of the people. The Marxists claim that in the final stage of communist society even 'democracy' will also come to an end, as it shall not be needed. This can be an invitation to a fresh variety of despotic rule. Moreover the prophecy has also not been proved correct.
6. The concept of 'dictatorship of the proletariat' has also been criticized from many angles. It is seen to imply loss of all liberties, a totalitarian and authoritarian rule and violation of human rights and dignity. This may prove much more dangerous and inimical to the freedom of the people than even the individual dictatorship. Viewed thus, the plea of revolution in proletarian

dictatorship is most undemocratic being not compatible with democracy. It runs counter to Marx's view that socialism can be achieved through peaceful parliamentary means. Instead of taking recourse to violence and revolution for the people, the transition to social democracy can be effected through the use of elections, pressure groups and other democratic instruments at their disposal. This can also enable the government to adopt welfare measures. Taking cue from these ideas of Communist Parties in Western Europe the doctrine of "Euro-Communism" had been evolved. It aimed to bring about socialist democracy through methods of parliamentary democracy.

7. The Marxist democracies as practiced in the different countries of the world have had little respect for political freedoms of individuals, their rights and civil liberties. The political choices are severely restricted. The political power is monopolized by a small minority in ruling positions. The system is characterized by intense centralization and bureaucratization. The proletariat dictatorships has thus degenerated into party dictatorship and ultimately to one man rule.

In spite of all the above criticisms, the importance of 'Socialist Democracy' cannot be belittled. It goes to the credit of the Marxists that they have popularized 'Economic Democracy'. But 'Economic Democracy' in the Marxist sense, does not presuppose Political Democracy: it replaces it. Political Democracy is only a superstructure of bourgeois and capitalist oppressions whereas the Economic Democracy is the substructure on which all political systems are reared. The primary goal of the economic democracy is redistribution of wealth and equalization of economic opportunities. Many writers agree that in proletarian democracy there has been much more social and economic equality than in liberal democracies. In the former, the gap between the rich and the poor has also been minimized.

There is a growing realization that the acceptance of small measures of capitalist innovations in socialist system will in the long run make socialist democracies more stable and viable, and thus providing decent, dignified and comfortable living to the masses.

### Other Marxist Writers on Democracy

An eminent Marxist thinker, Edward Bernstein, challenges Marx's analysis of capitalism. He questions the Marxian thesis that socialist revolution and the dictatorship of the proletariat are the inevitable steps in the transition from socialism to communism. Bernstein holds that political democracy and liberal freedoms as they extend to the working class almost render unnecessary the need of a militant class struggle. As a result this may at best bring crude communism.

Another writer, Karl Kautsky, even while defending the basic tenets of Marxism challenges the interpretation given by Lenin, especially concerning the Marxist Democracy. In his view Dictatorship of the Proletariat (DP) is a higher order of social democracy. In this his (Kautskys) emphasis is on democracy more than socialism and he seeks to achieve socialism through democratic means.

Another Marxist thinker, Rosa Luxemburg also criticizes Lenin for his antidemocratic policies such as suppression of free political life, establishing the dictatorship not of the masses but of the party over the masses. (Rosa) endorses Lenin's viewpoint that the party should seize power but she rejects that it should maintain itself by terror and denial of all normal forms of political freedom and regimentation. Even though democratic institutions are not perfect but to abolish them would be the worst alternative. For, it would paralyse the political life of the masses. The absence of unlimited democracy, a free public opinion, freedom of election and the press, the right to hold meetings and form associations, would turn the dictatorship of the proletariat into the dictatorship of the clique. Rosa declares, the proletarian dictatorship is not a matter of abolishing democracy but its correct application. For this the masses will have to participate actively in political life and work to shape the new order. Socialism and freedom, to her, are inseparable.

After the first world war and the collapse of the Second International, the concept of proletarian democracy becomes a subject of intense debate. It gives rise to a variety of Marxist versions on the nature of democracy. The devastation of the economy after the war spurred by the rise of welfare state in Europe necessitates certain structural changes in the capitalist economy. The working class in these countries instead of playing the role of agents of revolution view themselves as a part of the capitalist system. As a result, several European communist parties quietly abandon the goal of revolution and socialist democracy. During the second world war, the communist parties of some European countries are also seen to come round to accepting constitutionalism, parliamentary democracy, electoral process and representative institutions of bourgeois democracy.

Thus the Western Marxist Theorists come to believe that the socialist transformation in the advanced capitalist societies can only be realized by using the bourgeois democratic institutions. It means that socialism can be brought about by peaceful means such as through introduction of parliamentary democracy, multiparty system, civil liberties, right of freedom of expression and trade union activities. Democratic features are not to be seen as the monopoly of the bourgeois regimes but a part of the Enlightenment Tradition. The revolutionary methods of seizure of power by the proletariat are no longer seen necessary in the advanced capitalist societies.

The fact is that the historical experience of the dictatorship of the proletariat has not gone well with the concept of proletarian democracy as Marx and Engles envisage. To the latter the establishment of a proletarian state and society is a transition to true democracy. In the new system men, free from the fetter of capitalism would learn to organize production for the common good. But revolution in Russia fails to achieve this goal. For, the proletarian state as set up by Lenin and later further developed by Stalin becomes a distortion of the Marxian Theory. Under Lenin the concept of dictatorship of the proletariat gets transformed into a minority, *i.e.,* 'government of a small number' and under Stalin's leadership it becomes a means of autocracy and reign of terror. The 1936 Constitution even as it admits the exclusive domination of the Communist Party, it restricts membership which never allows it to become a mass party. Rather the party becomes less proletarian and less democratic and indeed a centralized bureaucracy.

However, this lack of political and civil liberties and the establishment of state socialism or 'socialism from above' becomes the target of criticism from many Marxist writers and Soviet dissidents such as Edward Kardelj, S. Stjanovic, Roy Medvedev, and many more. S. Stjanovic, for example, attacks the undemocratic nature of the Soviet socialist system because he sees the role of the working class in the government missing. These writers are intrigued to see the continuous increase in the power of the state, the party developing into a new class and a bureaucratic socialist society. Guided by the same logic Roy Medevdev calls for decentralization of power, freedom of expression and freedom to form other political parties, democratization of social life, functioning of the party on democratic lines, safeguards to the opinion of minorities and dissidents, freedom of press etc. as the ways to achieve true social democracy.

The answer to the question, whether the communist sates are democratic, will depend upon what meaning one attaches to democracy. According to Macperson, if democracy is defined in the narrow sense, that is a system of choosing and authorizing government, then the communist states being the vanguard states are governments for the people but not governments by the people. Again the vanguard state can be deemed democratic if there is full intra-party democracy and the party membership is open. Judged in this light, these states can not be called democratic. But if a broader meaning of democracy is taken, denoting an ideal of human equality, an equality that can be realized only in a classless society, then the communist states can be classed as democratic. The fact is that Marx's negative critique of bourgeois democracy does not match with a viable alternative with pragmatic positive connotations.

Admittedly in conclusion we may say that the Marxist Theory not only has broadened the area perceived as political but also extended its democracy to encompass the economic and social domains, thereby pursuing a much fuller democracy than what the Liberal Theory has had visualized.

## Representative Democracy or the Decline of Democracy

In recent decades, democracy has degenerated into a mere "power game." Its cause may be located in representative democracy. Over time, as Jefferson puts it, "the guardians have become the despots" and political representatives a separate "class" in themselves. With it there have occurred decline in democratic values as well as the quality of governance.

Today due to massive advancement of communication and information technologies democratic structures and processes are getting transformed in a big way. Ordinary workers are increasingly getting transformed into "knowledge workers," as well as "knowledge citizens." Glassman predicts that the combination of television connectedness to events, and leaders, candidates, and issues, as also interactive talk-back by viewers, instant referenda on local and national issues etc., may produce a new form of democracy. It will indeed be a 'mass-mediated direct democracy', which will be very different in structure and process from representative parliamentary democracy.

The current Models of Representative Democracy are guided by the following assumptions:

1. Not every citizen is competent to deliberate and decide on all matters of governance.
2. Not every citizen can spare the time required to attend to matters of governance.
3. The representatives not only can devote more time but also can acquire greater expertise in dealing with complexities of governance.
4. The representatives are expected to bring to bear a certain wider perspective on issues that affect larger groups than their electors. In this sense, they are not, and should not be, mere agents of their electors.
5. The time a citizen may devote to matters of governance, will depend on the relevance of the issues under debate to his or her own life and occupation. If the issues are relevant, they would find the time. In such matters of immediate concern to the citizens direct democracy is preferable to representative democracy.

For successfully rooting of democracy to local milieu three conditions may be fulfilled:

1. The need for a well thought-out and comprehensive political reform, and not an isolated, or administrative experiment.
2. A strategy to thwart the devolution of powers that will surely be made by the bureaucratic and political vested interests in the current system.
3. The local jurisdictions must have the exclusive responsibility for whatever tasks are assigned to them.

This requires devising such structures of decentralized governance for certain well-defined functions, so that through them, the citizens are able to govern themselves and, when necessary, act through elected representatives. The measure of true success in making representatives accessible to the people and making them act strictly as their agents may be derived from Jefferson's concept of "ward republics". In this context, not direct democracy but citizen's democracy can be a model.

Thus, there is need to work out ways concerning the issue of representative versus direct democracy. One way of doing this is by delimiting those areas where direct or near direct participation of the citizens is both feasible and desirable.

## Democracy and Human Rights

The Universal Declaration of Human Rights as adopted by the United Nations in

1948 incorporates not only traditional civil and political rights, but also social and economic rights. Even though almost every nation has encompassed civil and political rights in its Constitution, called "Fundamental Rights", but quite often the social and economic rights have been left out from its framework and left awaiting indefinitely their formalization as well as implementation.

The concept of Human Rights has evolved over time. Initially, the focus has been on Civil Rights which consist of freedom of speech, religion, movement, etc. But it is around the late nineteenth and early twentieth century that attention shifts to Political Rights like exercising franchise and participating in elected government. Further advances in Human Rights lead to the modern welfare state in which the poor and disadvantaged become "entitled" to certain benefits. In the next stage of evolution. the citizens are able to achieve their full potential by taking advantage of the explosion of knowledge brought about by the Media and the Internet.

Undeniably Social and Economic Rights cannot be divorced from Civil and Political Rights and even Socioeconomic Rights. This is because some of the Social and Economic Rights are very much needed for the exercise of Civil and Political Rights.

Fabre offers the following reasons for not incorporating Social and Economic Rights in the Constitution:

1. These rights cannot be specified in such a way as to provide guidance to the government and to the institution in charge of protecting them.
2. The judges will not be able to assess governmental policies on the basis of individual cases that reflect such policies only in a very piecemeal way.
3. The judges are not equipped with the necessary expertise to adjudicate the cases. The suggested solution is that the level of resources required to meet the Social and Economic Rights should be specified in the Constitution.

John Rawls has his own reservations on the subject. He lays down two criteria which need be satisfied before these rights are permitted to be included in the form of provisions reflecting distributive justice in the Constitution:

1. Principles specifying fair distribution must, so far as possible, be stated in terms that allow us publicly to verify whether they are satisfied.
2. Principles should be reasonably simple in that their basis can be explained in ways citizens may be assumed to understand in the light of ideas available in the public political culture.

Rawls suggests that the provision of basic minimum needs to all the citizens is a "constitutional essential".

Genuine equality of opportunity in a democracy is a must for a fuller political development. Equal opportunity is to get on in life in every sense of the term. It is to participate in the democratic process and to participate in the economic activities. It is to have social interactions and to receive education and so on. It must also examine the backward linkages, since inequalities at successive stages have their own cascading effect.

Equality of opportunity connotes "level playing field" before the game starts. And the skills relevant to such participation need be given to all citizens before that date. The state has a full stake in the capacity-building of its citizens.

Education is a sure means to build human capital as well as an increase its productivity. Right education helps leveling down the existing inequalities between individuals. Merely enabling the markets to function freely without building up the human capital and capabilities will lead only to an increasing gap between the info-rich and info-poor, developed and the less developed.

Overemphasis on income poverty and income inequality only goes to reveal the neglect of key variables like employment, ill health, lack of education and social education. In this context, "the basic needs provision approach" is of vital importance for both democracy and economic efficiency. This requires that the citizens are provided certain essential "capabilities".

## Democratic Theory Revisited: Some New Versions

The Liberal Democratic Theory has been recast in an empirical mould by many scholars. The first to do so is Joseph A. Schumpeter in his famous work *Capitalism Socialism and Democracy* published in 1942. This is subsequently restated by Robert A. Dahl in *A Preface to Democratic Theory.* Both these writers are seen to make scathing criticism of what they call the Traditional or Classical Theory of Democracy, or the Liberal–Democratic Theory. This theory has been traced back variously but generally to John Stuart Mill, T.H. Green, Earnest Barker and A.D. Lindsay. The Traditional Classical Theory gives democracy moral dimension. It perceives democracy as developmental, intended for the improvement of mankind. The Schumpeter-Dahl Axis, on the contrary, treats democracy as a mechanism. The latter considers it crucial to maintain an equilibrium.

C.B. Mcpherson, however, points out that the Pluralist-Empirical Concept of Democracy has been quite inadequate as a general theory of democracy and has done considerable harm to the Traditional Theory of Democracy.

The Pluralist Theory of Democracy as propounded by Robert Dahl, Sartori and other Behaviorists represents a reversal of the original nineteenth century Liberal Democratic Theory. It may be viewed as a departure from the later truly Classical Theory of Democracy. However, both in the Classical Concept of Democracy and the Liberal-Democratic Theory, democracy is seen as a means by which all men in a society can enjoy and develop their human capacities. The proponents of the empirical theory reject all this as irrelevant. They view democracy as simply a means by which men can register their wants as political consumers in the political market. As Schumpeter observes, "We now take the view that the role of the people is to produce a government, or else an intermediate body which in turn will produce a national executive not government. And we define the democratic method as that institutional arrangement for arriving at political decisions in which individuals acquire the power to decide by means of a competitive struggle for the people's vote."

Sartori also proposes a similar theory of democracy but with certain variations. He defines democracy as "an Elective Polyarchy" but adds that it should not be described as an "Egalitarian Polyarchy". He says that democracy is "apolitical system in which the influence of the majority is assured by elective and competitive minorities to whom it is entrusted." Robert Dahl, however, believes that minority rule is implied in the notion of democracy as "Elective Polyarchy."

Macpherson is equally critical of the Contemporary Pluralist Theory of Democracy. According to Macpherson, "The Schumpeter-Dahl axis is based on the implicit postulate that man is essentially a consumer of utilities and it proceeds by assuming that any realistic and honest liberal-democratic theory will treat men so. The point is of course that where and when and in so far as men do behave as consumers rather than experts, democracy is reduced to a means of letting people have some indirect say in 'who get what, when and how'. It is in such cases the Schumpeter-Dahl model makes very good sense. The Traditional Liberal-Democratic Theory also faces a similar dilemma. While it has always asserted a nobler democratic concept of man, it has also been accepted a model of society which entails that men behave as consumers."

Macpherson rejects the Empirical Theory of Democracy as inadequate. He tries to develop a new Normative Theory of Democracy by relating his theory of democratic politics to a vision of the contemporary human condition. He suggests some ways of moving from the existing competitive social order to a future society marked by the enhancement of creative freedom.

Macperson's theory of democracy is based on a humanist vision. It aims at putting an end to human alienation and exploitation. As he puts it, the most fundamental change in the Political Theory of Western Democracy which is made possible by technological change is the rejection of the concept of man as essentially an infinite consumer and infinite appropriator. The technological revolution in the west, thus, offers the possibility of people discarding the market concept of the essence of man, and replacing it by a morally preferable concept.

## CONCLUSION

In the history of Western Political Thought, the term 'Democracy' has often changed its meaning. It has been enriched by varied meanings over the ages. Democracy, however, has been transformed into a noble ideal after undergoing many mutations. Liberal Version of Democracy is seen to pave the way for experimenting a different kind of democracy *viz.* Proletarian Democracy or People's Democracy. The socialist countries which emerged in Europe and Asia were seen to reject the liberal democratic pattern of political development. This is how the concept of democracy has been changing from age to age, country to country. It will continue to change in future too with the changes of ideology and value-systems of peoples and societies.

PART III

# Western Thought
# Thinkers and Themes

# 14

# ARISTOTLE ON CITIZENSHIP

Aristotle's *Politics* is an investigation of how people live in political communities. It is both a practical study of the nature of real states and a theoretical exploration of the form of the best possible state. At the centre of both aspects of the work is the phenomenon of the *polis*, the self-sufficient political community, the state. At the heart of the state is the concept of the citizen. For, 'the state is an aggregate of citizens' (*Politics* I: ii, 59).

Aristotle follows the same method as he uses while studying other 'natural' objects. He seeks to analyze the state by examining its constituent parts. Those parts in the context of *polis* are the citizens of the state. It is the exercise of the responsibilities of citizenship which give the state its existence. Any explanation of the significance attached to citizenship in Political Theory must therefore examine both the basis of citizenship as the type of human function and the relationship between the fulfillment of that function and the phenomenon of the state.

Aristotle (384-322 B.C.) begins his political investigation with three claims:

First, man is a 'political animal' with a natural impulse towards association with others;

Second, the state 'exists by nature' as a result of that human impulse (*Politics* I: ii, 59); and

Third, there are certain human faculties, such as the ability to reason over matters of good and evil, and justice (*Politics* I: ii, 60).

These human faculties can only flourish in the context of a political association, the expression of which distinguishes man, the political animal, from other nonpolitical animals. Clearly, if the origins of the state are so deeply rooted in the fundamentals of human nature, and the qualities of citizenship are in turn at the heart of the nature of the state, then the origins of the human role of citizenship must also lie deep within human nature.

Aristotle in the *Politics* gives support to this view:

". . . men have a desire for life together, even when they have no need for each other's help . . . The good life is indeed a chief end, both communally and individually; but they form and continue to maintain a political association for the sake of life itself." (*Politics* III: vi, 187)

It is through political association that man's deep impulse towards community finds expression, and it is through citizenship that political association is enabled to function.

Aristotle is the greatest advocate-pioneer of the concept of the citizenship. He lived most of the times in Athens as a resident alien and deprived of citizenship rights by virtue of his Macedonian nationality. He, conceives the city-state (*polis*) as natural and proper form for the sake of good life. His concept of citizenship consists not in a mere residence in a geographically defined locality, but in having a share in the regime, the right of participation, that is, holding offices. He argues that the nature of citizenship changes according to the change of constitution. Hence the best form of civil virtue is variable. It is a relationship between the individual and the state by which the individual owes allegiance and the latter provides protection.

Aristotle's predecessor Plato, provides absolute authority to the guardians. But it is Aristotle who develops the citizenship and restores it to the centre of an ideal government. Ruling requires the special virtue of possessing practical wisdom, whereas being ruled requires "correct opinion".

## What is citizenship

The Greek city-states have among its inhabitant— citizens slaves, women, foreign resident and plebeian. Since man, to Aristotle, is a political animal, he can realize his full potential only in a *polis*, by participating in its affairs. For Aristotle, citizen is the one who enjoys the right of sharing in deliberative or judicial office.

Before Aristotle underlines who is a citizen, he clarifies what citizenship is not.

1. Mere residence in a *polis* does not make a person a citizen. That aliens and slaves too reside along with citizens in the same city.
2. Also the enjoyment of legal rights of suing or being sued and enjoying protection at home does not constitute citizenship because slaves also enjoy these facilities.
3. Descent from the citizen's parents also is not a condition enough to run for citizenship because the question here arises whether the parent is a citizen or not.

For Aristotle, the only rational way to define a citizen can be in terms of function and these are his participation in judicial power and public offices. Hence citizen, is one 'who has the power to take part in the deliberative or judicial administration of any state, and generally speaking, a state is a body of citizens sufficing for the purpose of life'.

In the Greek city-states, people are elected as juror by rotation to serve on popular courts. The term of assembly is for small duration and every citizen can serve on it. The assembly consists of the whole body of citizens who meet at least once a year. They can participate in the exercise of sovereign or supreme power. Citizenship in the Greek city-state, thus, means not merely participation in the election of the legislators, jurors or the executive authorities, but also it entitles direct or active share in the exercise of the deliberative and judicial functions. Thus in the Greek city-state citizenship means participation in the exercise of sovereignty which resides in the exercise of legislative and judicial functions.

According to Aristotle, to be good and virtuous requires the actual exercise of capacities to rule. He pinpoints notions which disqualify a citizen, *i.e.,* not to be a citizen. The alien and slaves despite the fact they reside in the city are not citizens. The enjoyment of legal rights such as enjoying protection at home do not constitute citizenship because these facilities are also available to slaves.

So, Aristotle defines the term citizenship in a particular time-situation on the basis of functions. The functions that make a person a citizen involve participation in judicial functions and public offices. In Aristotle's view, a citizen is one who has the power to take part in the deliberative or judicial administration of any state. Generally speaking, the state is a body of citizens sufficing for the purpose of life. The purpose of citizen is the salvation of the community.

The fundamental conception of Aristotle, that the community, the city-state, the political organization, even the state, is prior to man and the political man is prior to social man is always a subject of controversy. By upholding concept of man as a political animal he justifies that, man can only be a man in the political organization that is called state. The experiment of the new born babies and leaving them in the jungle with all necessary facilities like food, shelter, results in imbibing of animal character, away from the society. Here, for Aristotle, the society and the state is always the same. But the question of putting the community prior to the man, the state prior to the society, the political man prior to the social man, is always more of a point of controversy than a systematic explanation.

Aristotle's citizenship is not always the same in all forms of governments. It is dynamic in a sense that all people who are in participatory system of city-states are always the same. His empirical evidence reveals that there is no consistent rule of citizenship, there is no unanimity, no agreement as to who constitutes a citizen.

Both the origins of Aristotle's concept of citizenship and the nature of the functions which Aristotle wishes the citizen to fulfil influence the criteria which he establishes for the possession of citizenship. At the beginning of the *Politics*, in *book I*, he claims that 'the real difference between man and other animals is that humans alone have perception of good and evil, just and unjust, etc. It is the sharing of a common view in these matters that makes a household and a state' (Politics I: ii, 60).

Furthermore, 'whatever is incapable of participating in the association which we call the state . . . is not a part of the state at all' (*Politics* I: ii, 61). Those who are incapable of sharing a perception of justice, good and evil, those who cannot participate in the processes of discussion, deliberation and decision which lie at the heart of the human political association, cannot be admitted to the citizen body. This category of noncitizens includes those people who are best suited to the role of slaves, and women. They are, in his view, intelligent and able to reason, but have a tendency to let passion overcome their rational powers.

Aristotle excludes both manual and menial workers from the definition of citizenship. The logic of exclusion is that, the participation in both deliberative and judicial functions of the state demands a high degree of moral and intellectual excellence, which he calls as virtue. The virtue is not found in all inhabitants like slaves, women, aliens, merchants and labourers. The slaves do not have the deliberative faculty, nor do the women have this virtue. The resident aliens also cannot be citizens because they are the citizens of some other state.

Aristotle draws a clear difference/distinction between men and other animals on the basis of the endowment of rationality. For, rationality enables men to distinguish what is good and bad, just and unjust, right and wrong. With this faculty they can share a common view in matters of household and state. He (Aristotle) however excludes that category of men who though possess the power of rationality, but are guided by the passion. As against them, the citizens who have time for thinking of the state, who have a common conception of good and bad, work to them is not a means to an end but an end itself. Aristotle draws a distinction between the citizens and manual and menial workers. Although the works of manual and menial workers are productive to support the whole state but they are a means to an end rather than an end in itself. Hence, Aristotle finds it no more absurd to exclude the lower classes or the plebeians from citizenship than to exclude the slaves, women and freemen. What the lower classes have in common with slaves and freemen is the fact that all its members are necessary to the existence of the state though they are not a part of it. Furthermore, according to Aristotle, citizens must not lead the life of a mechanic or tradesman, for, such life is ignoble and inimical to virtue. Neither must they be husbandmen since leisure is necessary both for the development of virtue and the performance of political duties.

## Leisure and the Citizen

It is worth pointing out that Aristotle presumes that in most cases those who participate actively in ruling themselves seem to enjoy leisure and not have their time dominated by private commitments. In *Politics* Book III, Chapter IV, Aristotle essentially says that full-time workers cannot be citizens, even though they are useful to the state.

In the cultivation of virtue in citizens, education has a great role. It must make them capable of using leisure well. This is difficult: virtue comes readily to the fore when there is dire need or an external threat (war), but not so easily when people are at ease.

To Aristotle, the essence of citizenship lies in administrative partnership. He is clear that the citizens must not live in a mechanical or commercial life because, such life is not noble and militates against virtue. The citizens, the legislators and statesmen should possess virtue, so as to guide the state for the attainment of the common good. They may create the conditions by which the people can abide by the laws.

Aristotle compares the individual relationship with the city to the relationship of a part of the body to the whole body. The destruction of the whole body will also mean the destruction of each of its parts. If the whole body is destroyed there will not be a foot or a hand. The hand cannot survive without its attachment with the functioning body, so too an individual cannot survive without being attached to a city-state. Here, Aristotle lays emphasis over the whole than the parts because the whole is greater than the parts. Thus the individual needs the city-state rather than the city-state needs the man.

The political responsibilities of citizenship can hardly be greater, but for Aristotle, they are entirely in accordance with nature. Citizenship is nothing less than the fullest fulfillment of human potential in terms of the 'good life'. In this respect, as throughout Aristotle's *Politics*, he explains the essence of citizenship in active participation. The citizen is not merely an inhabitant of the state, nor simply a member of a politically privileged class but he is the essence of the state's ability to achieve the greatest measure of happiness and virtue as a community. For this, the citizen must have the leisure to devote himself to the educative cultural pursuits which facilitate his understanding of virtue. For this reason, Aristotle is clear that 'the citizens must not live in mechanical or commercial life. Such a life is not noble, and it militates against virtue' (*Politics* VII: ix, 415).

Thus there is more to the state and its role as an association serving the common interests of its people and fulfilling the human desire for community. In Aristotle's teleological political vision, the state has a purpose of letting its citizens to enjoy the greatest degree of happiness, and acquire fullest measure of virtue. The 'best state' will fulfil this purpose. It will permit all citizens to obtain the possession of *arête*, goodness, and *phronesis*, practical wisdom.

In the *Ethics*, Aristotle writes '. . . the end of Political Science is the highest good; and the chief concern of this science is to imbue the citizens with certain qualities, namely virtue and the desire to do fine deeds' (*Ethics*, I: ix, 81).

In the *politics* he makes the same point relating specifically to the form of the 'best state'. As he observes: 'our object is to find the best constitution, and that means the one whereby state will be best ordered, and . . . we call a state best ordered in which the possibilities for happiness are greatest' (*Politics* VII: xiii, 428).

The statesman must have knowledge of virtue if he is to guide the state towards the same, for, 'the true statesman is thought of as a man who has taken special pains to study the nature of virtue for he wants to make his fellow-citizens good and law-abiding people.'

Furthermore, 'legislators make their citizens good by habituation; this is the intention of every legislator, and those who do not carry it out fail of their object. This is what makes the difference between a good Constitution and a bad one' (*Ethics* II: i, 92).

If the citizens are to respond to the aims of the state in this respect, they too must have a knowledge of virtue. The laws and the education system must be shaped in such a way as to ensure that they are capable of attaining the ultimate goodness, happiness and virtue.

## Distinction between Good Man and Good Citizen

Aristotle argues that a distinction has to be made between the good man and the good citizen: The requirements of citizenship change as Constitutions change. Hence the best form of civic virtue is variable. But the virtue of the good man is not variable. So you can be a good citizen but not a good man. The key distinction to be made is that the virtue of a good man is characterized by ruling, but of a citizen by ruling and being ruled in turn. Ruling requires the special virtue of possessing practical wisdom. Being ruled requires "correct opinion." In so far as a particular Constitution allows for a person to participate in ruling, it may be possible for civic virtue and virtue itself to overlap, however.

This distinction between the good person and the good citizen can get muddied if we think only in terms of democracies. It does not help that the definition of citizen used by Aristotle in this discussion appears to be a more colloquial definition rather than the formal definition he has offered earlier. To better illustrate the distinction, an extreme example like Apartheid South Africa may be helpful: As a person of color in Apartheid South Africa, you are a good "citizen" insofar as you submit yourself to the rule of law under the Apartheid Regime. But in being governed over in this way, you fail to exercise the capacity to rule which is characteristic of the good, virtuous man. For Aristotle, being good and virtuous requires the actual exercise of these capacities to rule. A perhaps more soft way of putting it is that an Apartheid Regime may conceivably have succeeded in generating human beings who act in a way as to preserve its Constitution, but it cannot possibly have succeeded in generating human beings who are "good". A good virtuous citizen is a fully flourishing human being as such, precisely because it prevents many from exercising the capacity to rule.

## The Central Point: Importance of Citizenship

The centrality of Aristotalian citizenship is based on the principle of man's impulsive nature. It is embedded in his concept of gregariousness which implies that isolation results in loss of purpose and achievement of desired goals. The city-state, for Aristotle, comes to exist from the very day of the family, where male and female develop the first partnership. The fundamental principles of Aristotle's citizenship are as follows:

(a) All residents are not citizens and citizens are based on the principle of virtue to participate in public affairs;
(b) by participation in the city-state, through it in various political activities the concept of 'common good' is realized; and

(c) the number of people competent to share in this are also limited.

The citizens are expected to fulfill the functions of politicians, administrators, judges and soldiers. Aristotle's citizens body corresponds only to Plato's two classes of guardians: The producers of wealth are mere instruments and not members of the state. By dividing the population into citizens and noncitizens Plato sacrifices the unity of all for the sufficiency of the few. Aristotle's concept of city-state though contains all the members living in the society but *polis* means the citizens who are guided by the virtue of 'common good' and participate in the deliberative and judicial activities of the state.

## The General Theory of Constitution and Citizenship

Aristotle's concept of citizenship starts from the whole organization of the city-state and the role of the ruler. Since the city-state, is by nature, a collective entity, so are the different levels and layers of citizenship. Citizens are distinguished from other inhabitants, such as residents, inhabitants, resident aliens and slaves, and even children and seniors are not unqualified citizens. Aristotle defines the citizen as a person who has a right (*exousia*) to participate in the deliberative and judicial office. In Athens, for example, the citizen has to attend the political office, the assembly, the council, the other bodies and to sit in the juries. The Athenian system of citizenship differs from the modern representative democracy. In the latter case the citizens are directly involved in government. Although, full citizenship tends to be restricted in the Greek city-state (with women, slaves, foreigners and some others being excluded), the citizens are more deeply enfranchised because they are directly involved in governing.

Aristotle defines the Constitution as a way of organizing the offices of the city-state, particularly the sovereign office. He defines the Constitution as the sovereign body which means the different forms of government on the basis of the number of people and the exercise of the power. The basic assumption of Aristotle is that man is a political animal by nature who naturally wants to live together. The city comes into being historically because of the fact that there is partnership between persons who cannot live without one another.

There are two pairs of people in this form:

(a) The male-female, for the sake of reproduction, procreation, progeny, the continuance of the society-based on need; mutually beneficial.
(b) The naturally ruling and the ruled, on account of preservation; here he is referring to slavery.

Slavery is a kind of partnership where both the naturally ruling master and naturally ruled slave help each other to develop/preserve themselves. Slavery is a kind of partnership which benefits both master and slave in material production and preservation.

Both the pairs of natural partnership help and support the household. This household exists for the purpose of meeting the needs of daily life such as food, shelter, clothing and so forth. This way the whole city-state which has been the extension of family has been created, based on the principle of natural partnership, self sufficiency and mutually beneficial. So, Aristotle rightly points out that 'the city-state is nothing but individual writ-large.'

Aristotle notes that if, then, nature makes nothing that is incomplete or purposeless, nature must necessarily have needed all of these *i.e.,* all plants and animals for the sake of human life and human beings. It reflects that there are many hierarchies in nature, as well as beliefs. Those who are lower in the natural hierarchy should answer the command of those who are in the higher. Aristotle returns to the household rule. He takes up the question of the proper form of rule, over women and children. The relation of male to female is, by nature, a relation of superior to inferior and ruler to ruled. The basis is that the slave lacks the deliberative element, the female has it but lacks authority, the child has it but is incompetent.

Some have suggested that it does not mean that women's reason is inferior to that of men. In fact women have the ability to make men do what they want, either because of some innate psychological characteristics such as they are not aggressive and assertive enough. A part reason is the prevailing Greek culture at that period of time. Others argue that in case of women, emotions are ultimately more influential in determining their behaviour than the reason. Besides women are not allowed to enter all areas of public life like writing, philosophy, plays, novels and speeches. This denial to participate in the sphere of all activity results in lack of knowledge and skills which then are advanced as evidence to reinforce the original belief that they are inferior.

## CONCLUSION

Aristotle's concept of citizenship is thus based on the harmonious cooperation of all abilities and skills of the individuals to perform the duty *i.e.,* on the basis of production partnership-preservation partnership to make the city-state to be self-sufficient, self-sustaining and beneficial to all. The concept of citizenship of Aristotle is based on the principle of nature, the organization, whole being, developmental being *i.e.,* those that are superior to the lower being, and thus having the authority to guide and control. The whole purpose of citizenship is to organize the city-state based on the nature of the whole, its mutuality and its exclusion to the human nature.

In sum, citizenship, for Aristotle, is a bond forged by the intimacy of participation of those limited number of men in public affairs. It is neither a right to be claimed nor a status to be conferred on anybody outside the established ranks of the class. The citizen is expected to fulfill the function of a politician, juror or administrator or soldier, in being in the privileged status of the ruling group of the city-states and involving effective participation in the deliberative and judicial exercise of power.

# 15

# LOCKE ON NATURAL RIGHTS AND PROPERTY

## Locke's Political Philosophy

John Locke (1632-1704), is among the most influential political philosophers of the locke 17th century. In his *Two Treatises of Government*, he defends the claim that men are by nature free and equal. His view tuns counter to the claim that God has made all people naturally subject to a monarch. He argues that people have rights, such as the right to life, liberty, and property. That they exist independent of the laws of any particular society.

Locke uses the claim that men are naturally free and equal as part justification for understanding legitimate political government as a result of a social contract. Here people in state of nature conditionally transfer some of their rights to the government in order to better insure the stable, comfortable enjoyment of their lives, liberty, and property. For Locke, the government exists by the consent of the people, in order to protect the rights of the people and promote the public good. Therefore the government that fails to do so can be resisted and replaced with a new government. Locke is thus an exponent of defending the right of revolution. He also defends the principle of majority rule and the separation of legislative and executive powers.

### 1. The Law of Nature

The most central concept in Locke's Political Philosophy is his theory of natural law and natural rights. The natural law concept has existed long before Locke. It has existed as a way of expressing the idea that there are certain moral truths that apply to all people, regardless of the particular place where they live or the agreements they have made. Locke sees most important early distinction between laws that are by nature, and thus generally applicable, and those that are conventional and operate only in those places where the particular convention has been established. This distinction is sometimes formulated as the difference between natural law and positive law.

Natural law is also distinct from divine law. In the Christian tradition, divine law is what God has directly revealed through prophets and other inspired writers.

Natural law can be discovered by reason alone. It applies to all people. In contrast to natural law, divine law, is revealed only though God's special revelation. It applies only to those to whom it is revealed and whom God specifically indicates are to be bound by it. Apart from this Locke also thinks that natural law can be known through reason and special revelation. He sees no contradiction in God playing a part in the argument, so long as the relevant aspects of God's character can be discovered by reason alone. In Locke's theory, divine law and natural law are consistent. They can overlap in content, but they are not coextensive.

In the century before Locke, the language of natural rights also gains prominence through the writings of such thinkers as Grotius, Hobbes and Puffendorf. Whereas natural law emphasizes duties, natural rights normally emphasize privileges or claims to which an individual is entitled. There is considerable disagreement as to how these factors are to be understood in relation to each other in Locke's theory.

Leo Strauss, and many of his followers, take rights to be paramount. They go so far as to portray Locke's position as essentially similar to that of Hobbes. They point out that Locke defends a hedonist theory of human motivation and he therefore must agree with Hobbes about the essentially self-interested nature of human beings. Locke, they claim, only recognizes natural law obligations in those situations where our own preservation is not in conflict. He further emphatically states that our right to preserve ourselves trumps any duties we may have.

In emphasizing the right to life, liberty, and property, locke is primarily making a point about the duties we have toward other people such as duties not to kill, enslave, or steal. Most scholars also argue that Locke recognizes a general duty to assist with a view to the preservation of mankind. This includes a duty of charity to those who have no other way to procure their subsistence. So duties are primary in Locke because rights exist to insure that we are able to fulfill our duties.

### 2. State of Nature

Locke's concept of the state of nature has been interpreted by commentators in a variety of ways. At first glance it seems quite simple. For Locke it is "want [lack] of a common judge, with authority, puts all persons in a state of nature". Also , "Men living according to reason, without a common superior on earth, to judge between them, is properly the state of nature." (*Two Treatises* 2.19) Apart from the above, yet another Locke's definition is that, 'state of nature exists wherever there is no legitimate political authority able to judge disputes and where people live according to the law of reason.' On this account, the state of nature is distinct from political society where a legitimate government exists, and from a state of war where men fail to abide by the law of reason.

### 3. On Natural Rights

A contemporary of Hobbes and Rousseau, John Locke's theory of social contract enriches the liberal, democratic and constitutional tradition. He charts the transition from the natural to the civil society. In his view the state exists to protect the natural rights of life, liberty and property. That the state and law are the result of a contract consciously concluded between the ruler and the people. The theory refers to two contracts: One in the state of nature which exists before the contract, and the other contract through which society and the state come into being. It is through the social contract that Locke evolves his famous theory of individual Rights of Life, Liberty and Property and a Constitutional Government.

Locke refers to three natural rights of man–Right to Life, Right to Liberty, and Right to Estate (Property). The *first* natural right is the 'Right to Life' *i.e.,* right to make use of those things that are necessary or useful to his being or serviceable for his subsistence. It is also called right to preservation of one's life and hence to the means of subsistence. The Right to Life and Means of Life is deduced from the need of a strong God-planted desire in every man to preserve his life and being.

Locke's *Second Treatise* opens with a natural Right to Liberty i.e., freedom from the arbitrary will of others. It is a right to be interfered with, except when one has transgressed natural law. It is a right to freedom of the people. It is a right to order their action and dispose of their possessions as they think fit within the bounds the law of nature, without depending upon the will of another man. Initially, it is called freedom and later, a right. From, this is derived the right to execute the law of nature, which includes the right to punish the crime and take reparation. Negatively this right is deduced from the intention of the creator and positively from the need for self-preservation. This freedom from the arbitrary power is necessary to man's preservation. He cannot part with it but by what forfeits his preservation and life together. The only limitation upon this Right to Freedom is the Law of Nature. It teaches that 'no one ought to harm another in his life, liberty, health and possession'.

Then follows the Right to Property which, according to Locke, connotes 'a Right to exclude others from it; to use, enjoy, consume and exchange it'. This Right exists prior to the civil society and government. It is not dependent on the consent of the civil society and government. Nor is it dependent on the consent of others.

In fact the Right to Property is derived from the Right of Self-preservation and Property in one's own person. As Locke observes, the labour of his body and the work of his hands are his property. But in order to leave enough for others since all have an equal right to subsistence, to that extent the Right to Property is limited. It entails leaving enough for others.

## 4. Nature of Natural Rights

With regard to The Theory of Natural Rights two questions may be asked: (i) what is the source of natural rights and (ii) how these rights are to be enforced. Locke believes that all men are born with certain inherent rights. Locke views these rights as the gift of God. It is these rights derived from natural law that give men title to their lives, their liberties and estates. Since according to Locke, rights exist in the state of nature, men are entitled to them under any circumstances—whether they live under a government or not.

In the state of nature, if a right is a claim against the neighbour after the coming into being of the civil society and the state, it becomes a claim against the state *i.e.*, the state is expected to respect the rights of the individual. While the power to make laws and to maintain peace and order is vested in the state, it will not be correct on the part of the individual to give up his natural rights to the state because they are the gift of God to men and shall last till the end of their lives. In fact, even voluntarily giving up his rights well implies that an individual is stripping himself of the attributes he needs if he is to be a man at all. And the state that deprives man of his rights is creating conditions which will render its citizens to be something less than human.

Locke asserts that a man's natural rights inhere in his personality. In this sense they are immutable from the day of his birth and nontransferable throughout his lifetime. He defines natural rights as theoretical freedoms which men ought to have and which the state of nature recognizes as well.

But no agency exists in the state of nature to secure and enforce these natural rights to ensure that all men enjoy them. Hence it becomes necessary to set up an agency with political power. This agency then is expected to lay down conditions for the enforcement of natural rights that all men should enjoy them. Thus, Locke wants the state not only to give legal recognition to these rights but also to use its enforcement machinery to secure the enforcement of these legal rights which are nothing but natural rights made official. Once men have quit the state of nature, the duty to legislate both effectively and morally shall devolve on the state.

According to Hacker, these rights belong only to the individual. Being rights of the individual all individuals without exception hold them. Political power is there to make laws, mete out penalties, regulate and preserve property and defend its citizens from external attack. Having power to do all these things does not imply that the government has a 'right' in a similar or related sense as what belongs to the individual and the way he acts. One thing is clear, it is the right of the individual citizen that binds the state and limits its activities. If the state does not put up its own power and its legal authority to enforce the natural rights, then the individual can invoke his power and authority to safeguard and preserve freedoms that naturally belong to him. In the new situation, the citizen can revolt against the government in order to change it. But this right to revolt should not be a minority action because the contract is based on the consent of the majority.

In brief, the Theory of Natural Rights has the following assumptions:

(i) Natural Rights are Rights to Life, Liberty and Property. They are the birthrights of the individual and are nontransferable throughout his lifetime.

(ii) The individual independent of society or the state has these rights. He has them, as equal rights in the state of nature. Except by his own consent no one has the power to tinker with them or to transfer the same to the political authority of another body or collectivity.

(iii) The primary function of government is to maintain and safeguard the Natural Rights.

(iv) The limit on the authority of government is set by the Natural Rights. It is imperative that government should protect and preserve them. If it fails to protect these rights it loses its legitimacy and can be changed.

Locke, thus, provides a clearer enunciation of natural rights of man than what a Hobbes or a Rousseau does. He presents these rights as effective rights of the individual, the rights like property and inheritance which others have a natural obligation to respect. By using natural rights, Locke makes out a case for limited government and a right to revolution. He gives premium to individual's enterprise, opinion and belief against the religious orthodoxy and tradition.

According to Macpherson, historically, natural rights have been a theory of the rising middle class. It was used to assert the authority of the individual's conscience in the field of economy. It was also intended to defend individual's property against authoritarian interference and serve as an ideology of radical movements. Locke's inspiration is very much behind the American Declaration of Independence in 1776, in statements like these: 'All men are created equal and are endowed with certain rights by their creator such as life, liberty and pursuit of happiness'. Locke's influence can also be traced to the French Declaration of the Rights of Man in its reference to certain 'natural imprescriptible and inalienable rights of man'.

However, over time the doctrine of natural rights suffers decline. Edmund Burke questioning the whole idea of speculative rights insists that the basis of rights can only be customs and sentiments of society and not abstract reason. The whole idea of rights as prior to and against the state is also rejected by the utilitarians who hold that only law can confer rights which can be enforced. The natural rights theory also invites criticism of political philosophers because it divorces individual's interest from the society. By separating his claims from the basis upon which rights stand, it cuts its very roots. The assumption behind the theory that it is possible to have rights and obligation independent of society is an erroneous view to take. For the rights originate only in the society and in the context of social relationships and it is in this that their justification lies.

## Locke's Views on Property

The Theory of Property is largely a liberal construct. It is enunciates and makes popular in the philosophies of liberal persuasion, particularly in John Locke and Adam Smith. Along with Adam Smith, Locke is the first to assert and justify a natural individual right to property. He regards it as central to his theory of civil society and government. According to Locke, 'The great and chief aim of men's uniting into a commonwealth and putting themselves under government is the preservation of property'. He pleads for according its possession and benefit to all citizens. He advocates doing so though not in equal proportion but broadly in such measure as it can play a meaningful role in men's lives. He makes a spirited defence of private property as an institution against the then prevailing notions of property.

Plato, long before Locke, maintains that property obscures man's reasoning power and this he uses as a reason to bar the Guardians to possess it. Yet while giving his approval to property he cautions that any class, which becomes too wealthy, will constitute a threat to political stability. St. Thomas Aquinas does not accept that property is sanctioned by the natural law. He claims that it is an 'addition' enforced by human legislation. Hobbes, while conceding the right to own property to citizens. He vests absolute power in the sovereign to regulate it. Also, Locke while rejecting all existing theories, develops his own theory of property. He founds it on the natural rights basis. He thus paves the way for liberal capitalist right to private property.

In seeking valid reasons for justification of property Locke poses two questions:

(i) why we may have property at all, and

(ii) how property can justify privileged position?

Among many reasons, the most valid one, Locke gives, is that property ownership offers the essentials of a good life. He offers the following justifications for his Theory of Property.

**First,** God has put men on this earth and given them the right to make use of this earth's resources and to develop the appropriate means to use them for the greatest good of all. This is done by providing men the possession of the land material, the means and incentives that they turn earth into usable commodity.

**Second,** what justification, Locke gives, is called labour theory of value or labour theory of property right. It enjoins that every person has property in his own person and nobody has any right to it but what he provides himself. The labour of his body and the work of his hands are properly his. Therefore, whatsoever he removes out of the natural state with which he has mixed his labour and joins to it something that is his own, he makes it his property.

**Third,** the right to property is a natural right. This is what men possess at birth and prior to government. Property is justified because the law of nature so ordains. Locke asserts that government can and should recognize this right by embodying it in statutory form so that even if a government is dissolved or abolished, that right remains with each individual. In the state of nature equality does not prevail in matters of the ownership of property. So on conclusion of the contract as the state comes to be formed, the government then should give legal recognition to property. Also it should give legal recognition to the pattern of property distribution, which has existed prior to the contract. Also the very fact that citizens have given their consent to the creation of a money economy : they have fulfilled one of the core functions of the government, *i.e.,* to establish a currency and to ensure its stability. Since the basis of property is popular consent, if an outside agency wishes to invade men's property this must be done by persuading public first. It must explain to them why such an encroachment on their property is demanded. They must provide the rationale behind this move.

**Fourth,** man is an entrepreneurial animal having an acquisitive nature. He is always after seeking material comfort and security. Whenever he finds something with which he can enrich himself, he will do so. This acquisitive element in human nature leads him to acquire, develop and make use of property. This is Locke's yet another justification of property or land ownership.

**Fifth,** property adds an additional dimension to man's stature. It renders him larger and stronger than his fellows. It protects him from the depredations on his person and gives security. It lets him develop finer aspects of his personality. Property invests the individual with a tangible sense of identity; it satisfies the individualist urge in him.

**Finally,** property links an owner with posterity. Due to the law of inheritance, he can pass on to his children whatever he has earned, owned and accumulated in his lifetime. Being extension of his personality, property bestows upon him further security and knowledge that even death cannot extinguish the work with which his labour is mixed.

In short, Locke justifies property as man's natural right, the product of individual effort and initiative. Equating property with liberty, Locke sees no man fully free unless he has right to property and he owns something. By linking property with human labour, equating it with orderly, peaceful relations among the individuals, as well as good life of the citizen and autonomy of the individual, Locke raises the Theory of Property to new heights.

Locke does not find an answer to how much property a person may fairly claim for himself. While he projects property as a natural right of the individual prior to the civil Society and the state, he argues that in the state of nature this is a limited right but it becomes an absolute right later.

In the state of nature, Locke spells out three limitation in the right to property:

(i) Sufficiency limitation *i.e.,* the individual can appropriate only as much as he needs leaving enough for others since each man has a right to his preservation,

(ii) Spoilage limitation *i.e.,* only as much property he may appropriate as he can make use of; God makes nothing that man should spoil or destroy, and

(iii) Labour limitation *i.e.,* the rightful appropriation is limited to the amount a man can procure with his own labour.

However, Locke proceeds to show how later the introduction of money by mutual consent removes the limitations enumerated above :

**First,** the Spoilage Limitation is removed with the introduction of money and precious metals like gold and silver that do not spoil. By getting not spoilt it may be possible to rightfully accumulate them unlimitedly. Similarly, this limit also does not apply to immovable property or to land itself. With more land than he himself can use and which is at his disposal, its produce he can exchange with gold and silver, and hoard it without spoilage or injury to anybody. As consequences of this, whether this act will lead to inequality bothers him not because he associates this unequal possession by mutual consent even in the state of nature with its money exchange value.

**Second,** Sufficiency Limitation connotes that every appropriation must leave enough for others. Though this be initially valid it does not hold good as money for exchange gets currency. The matter of consent for the use of money is also the consent to its consequences.

Locke's plea is that greater production of the appropriated land more than makes up for the lack of land available to others. In fact it actually increases the amount that is left for others, leaving enough for good living of others.

To the plea that God gives the world to all men in common, Locke adds his own justification of giving it to the industrious and the rational for use. Elaborating it further he states that the hard work and industriousness of the individual can justify unequal and unlimited accumulation of property.

This is how Locke justifies appropriation of property more than required on two counts :

1. The necessary consequences of money and
2. That standard of those without land are higher than those who have it.

**Third,** the Labour Limitation is removed by the plea that everyman has property in his own person. It means that a man's labour is unquestionably his own property which he may freely sell for wages. The labour so sold therefore becomes the property of the buyer who may appropriate the produce of that labour as he wills. Thus proceeding from the common assumption that the earth and the fruits are given by God originally to mankind for their common use, Locke sheds one by one all the limitations with which unlimited right of capitalist appropriation has hitherto been handicapped.

## CONCLUSION

According to Macpherson, Locke uses the Theory of Property to justify capitalism. He defends it on grounds of individual initiative and his personal labour. He upholds and protects the productive capacities of a new system of commercial and industrial capitalism against the restrictive traditions of the feudal state. With him, property becomes a fundamental right which under capitalism is seen as inalienable private and exclusive possession so as to be marketable.

If property is a natural right, a reward of one's labour, what brings security and provides an opportunity to develop one's personality, it is quite natural that it will give a taste of meaningful freedom. Here Locke is not concerned with the lot of those who do not own property. Rather he is seen to be guided by a facile assumption that all would be men of property and none need to be the loser. Appropriation of property by one will be matched by better standard of living by the other.

Locke's view is challenged by the latter-day thinkers like Rousseau, Green, Marx etc. who do not share his optimism. They demand a more equitable distribution of property, its abolition or distributive justice, taking into account its social and psychological consequences. But all of them view property as an institution, having political and economic fallouts in all societies.

# 16

# ROUSSEAU ON INEQUALITY

Jean-Jacques Rousseau (1712-1778), lived and wrote during what is arguably the headiest period in the intellectual history of France—the Enlightenment. He was one of the brightest lights of that intellectual movement. He contributed articles to the *Encyclopedie* of Diderot, and participated in the salons in Paris, where the great intellectual questions of his day were being pursued.

### Rousseau on Inequality

Rousseau raises the clarion of 'liberty, equality, and fraternity' which inspires the French Revolution. A staunch critic of the modern concept of political and economic progress, he supports direct democracy as a model of political governance. What Europe called 'progress', he firmly holds, has been purchased at the cost of social inequality, violent exploitative morality, degrading domination of the indigenous people. In his book *Origin and Foundation of Inequality among Men*, he enumerates the factors for the origin of inequality. In his other significant work *Social Contract* he delineates the human society based upon 'liberty, equality and fraternity'.

### 1. Equality Vs Inequality

Making a distinction between natural or physical inequality and the moral-political inequality, Rousseau underlines that the natural inequality is established by nature. It consists of natural human differences such as those of age, health, bodily strength, qualities of mind and soul.

The other one, *i.e.,* the moral political inequality, he sees having its origin in social institutions and built on the privileges of wealth, honour and power. It has its basis in convention and the consent of men.

The two types of inequalities differ with each other. They point to similar-different and equal-unequal relations. The natural inequality among human beings is something self-evident, whereas social inequality is a consequence of social and political forces which have the effect of debasing some and elevating others. Such inequalities owe their existence to artificial gradation in society based on distinctions of privileges, caste, race, ethnicity, riches etc.

## 2. Origin of Inequality

Rousseau, in his book *Discourses on the Origin and Foundation of Inequality among Men* (1754), raises a number of questions such as—what is man's condition in the state of nature? How does inequality enter human society? What are its consequences on men and society? What role does civilization play perpetuating inequality? etc.

Rousseau envisions that the state of nature consists of two stages : The first one he calls the golden age in which man lives as a noble and lonely savage wandering in the forests without industry, without speech, alien to war and peace, neither helping nor needing help from others. He leads then a life, —free, equal and self-sufficient. He is seen caring only for his necessities and disregarding everything else. He is neither social nor antisocial but asocial. He is oblivious of what is good or bad, right or wrong, true or false. Unrestrained by the laws of society or convention he pursues his life in privacy and peace. The state of noble savage is that of peaceful ignorance. It is far away from the din of civilization. It is a free, equal and self-sufficient life.

However, this idyllic paradise-like life does not last long. As the population increases and property comes into being, there arises germs of civilization. Commenting on the emergence of property Rousseau writes: "The first man who having enclosed a piece of ground, bethinks himself as saying 'this is mine' and finds people simple enough to believe him to be the real founder of property and, civil society. The origin of property, though a chance occurrence, can not be undone because man who claims title to property soon assumes the role of employer. Its immediate effect is that earlier where two natural men once have stood on the plane of equality, they now stand as superior and inferior. Thus the great institution of inequality with its origin in private property is born".

In the *Second Discourse*, Rousseau provides another account *i.e.,* geography and accident are the root causes of the fall of man from nature. Some men begin to live along the sides of rivers and others continue to remain in forests retaining their primitive innocence. Natural catastrophes like earthquakes do disrupt habitual ways of living. Natural calamities call for the help of others. This leads to the notion of interdependence. During this period of forced temporary unions, pity and love undergo modifications and this sense gives way to deliberative and reflective faculties.

Again, Rousseau ascribes the rise of inequality also to the rise of agriculture, the discovery of metals and ploughing of a piece of land. The last one fosters the feeling, 'he who cultivates the land must own it.' This also makes men develop a habit of living together. With it comes family as a distinct social institution. But it is the introduction of property that gives rise to thousand quarrels and conflicts among men and their families.

Thus from the moment private property is introduced, and when one man begins to need help of another, from that moment it appears advantageous to have enough provisions for two instead of one; equality then disappears. In the changed environment, Rousseau graphically narrates that work becomes indispensable and vast forests become smiling fields. Man has to water these fields with the sweat of his brow. Slavery and misery are here soon seen to germinate and grow up with the crops.

The introduction of private property brings with it the division of labour. With it man's natural mental qualities come into action. This leads to the development of his memory, imagination, wit, strength, skill and talent. With it also develops his sense of egoism, selfishness, competition, cheating, trickery, rivalry, usurpation, and robbery. Rousseau points to these as the first evil effects of property and the inseparable attendants of growing inequality. Such a horrible state of society forces men, particularly the rich, to reflect on the wretched situation. They conceive the 'profoundest plan' to employ in their favour the forces of those who attack them. In Rousseau's words, "just as the man who puts up the fence creates the civil society, now a new pioneer comes along to suggest, that society cannot exist without political authority. This is the origin of law which binds new fetters on the poor and gives new powers to the rich. They irretrievably destroy natural liberty, eternally fix the law of property and inequality. They convert usurpation into unalterable right. They, for the advantage of a few ambitious individuals, subject all mankind to perpetual labour slavery and wretchedness."

It may be deduced from the above narrative that both the society and the state thus created are not the legitimate institutions. They arise because men are persuaded to believe that they need a common power to secure what will pass as justice and to establish what will look like peace. Men are so blinded by their lust for material comfort that they are moved by their desire to rise above the heads of their fellowmen. This makes them unable to ask profound political questions. It is a social framework based on property and inequality and a state founded on coercion which are seen to take over and overwhelm them.

Providing an overview of the development of inequality, Rousseau sees it grow in three stages:

(i) Establishment of laws and right to property, creating rich and poor in the society,
(ii) institution of magistracy, creating powerful and weak, and
(iii) conversion of arbitrary power into legitimate power, creating thus master and slaves.

### 3. Consequences of Inequality

Apart from the social and psychological consequences when property and inequality come, men become interdependent. They begin to obey the rules of conduct which are seen as necessary for social life. The central organizing principle of society thus becomes property. It also becomes the guiding force for human behaviour.

Besides, the social system based on private property, according to Rousseau, sets an egoistic standard of success. This standard comes to be implanted among all individuals. A race starts to own property, to be superior to other men. This gives rise to a situation that for a successful man there must be a man who is a failure, and for the one who gains public esteem, there must be one who fails to achieve it. The relations between man and man cease to be based on love, spontaneity or generosity. Rather all men are set to assume the role of either exploiters or exploited.

With inequality also comes corruption. It magnifies vanity of the propertied. As its evil effect it makes the poor subservient to the rich. Differences crop up between men. They have the effect of exalting some and debasing others. It creates a situation pleasing for some and hurtful and humiliating to others.

Rousseau sees in inequality an obstacle to political freedom. For those who have to depend on others for their livelihood will not follow their own judgement politically. This also weakens man's devotion to the community. It makes it less likely to accord with the General Will.

It is a well-acknowledged fact that the more equal be the members of a community, as Rousseau puts it, the deeper is their sense of belonging to it. So also the stronger is their love of justice and quicker their sympathy for the neighbour. But when inequality is strong, the rich and the socially exalted look upon the community as their own. The poor in contrast, feel themselves as the victims of the community and their devotion to it is weakened.

Rousseau asserts that what people call progress is of no value. It is because inequality renders it futile by striking a wedge between men, dividing the society into the propertied and propertyless.

In raising inequality out of equality, says Rousseau, men have not only built a towering mountain but also alongside it, a bottomless pit. All the inequality which now prevails owes its strength and growth to the development of man's innate faculties and the advancement of the human mind. Those who sit aside the mountain created by man's intelligence and skill are very fearful that they will tumble into gaping abyss at its foot. And those in the lower depths scramble over each other to attain the success and avoid the stigma of failure by which societies judge all men. For Rousseau, such progress has no use.

In the state of nature there is hardly any inequality. All inequality in fact is the direct result of the establishment of property, civil society and law. The so-called progress has taken the man away from the natural conditions, robbing him of natural liberty and equality.

Now one may ask what should we do in order to get back the natural liberty and equality? Should we abolish the civil society with all its progress, culture and property and make a return to the original state of nature or should a new society be formed through a social contract where man can be made as naturally equal and free as he was before? Rousseau rejects the first alternative and suggests the formation of a new society by entering into a Social Contract where each one of us places in common his person and his whole power under the supreme direction of the General Will. In return every member is received back as an indivisible part of the whole.

The purpose of the Social Contract is to create a society, which rather than authorizing inequalities based on property will promote equality based on the inherent identity of all men. Rousseau considers this as the foremost task of politics to bring out what is best and natural in every human being. To achieve this object, the democratic state based on General Will in which every individual has a share, is the only way to reconcile social existence with the political authority.

But even though Rousseau finds in the emergence of property as the primary cause of inequality, he does not recommend the abolition of property in the new state. Rather he wants the law and the state to ensure enough property for every individual so that even the poorest of them are independent of the rich. For Rousseau, freedom is only secure among the equals. Men are equal not when they have the same income but when each is economically his own master and no man is more dependent for his livelihood on another than the other on him.

The right to property is therefore sacred. But unlike Locke, Rousseau maintains that right of every man is not the product of his labour but only of so much property as will secure his independence. However, the sovereign community is made up of citizens who are men of independent property owners.

However, Rousseau realizes that unlimited right to property is a source and continuing means of exploitation. Only a limited right is justifiable. In fact he envisages a society of independent producers and not a society dependent on the division of wage-earners, land and capital owners.

Also property as a limited right is justifiable if it is consistent with the sovereignty of the General Will. A truly democratic society, for Rousseau, is a society governed by the General Will. It requires such an equality of property where no citizen shall be wealthy enough to buy another or poor enough to be forced to sell himself. However, Rousseau does not exclude hierarchy of rich and poor in society so long as distinction in ranks springs from the seniority of services rendered to the community and is not based on the vanity of wealth.

## CONCLUSION

In fine, this is Rousseau's remedy in today's globalized world when disparities between the North and South have increased manifold and the human society, whether of the developed or developing world is growing increasingly inegalitarian, exploitative and oppressive. In such a world there is dire need to abide by the criteria that Rousseau gives: '(Society) requires such an equality of property where no citizen shall be wealthy enough to buy another or poor enough to be forced to sell himself'.

# 17

# MILL ON LIBERTY AND DEMOCRACY

John Stuart Mill, an English utilitarian, liberal, democratic philosopher of the nineteenth century, through his writings, introduces humanistic and democratic values in the earlier liberal theory.

Mill's essay, *On Liberty* (1859) is one of the finest and the most moving essay on liberty. It makes an eloquent and powerful plea for liberty of thought and expression. It offers a defence not merely against the state interference but also against the pressures of the society, public opinion and religious orthodoxy on the affairs of the individual.

## What is Liberty?

Mill's espousal of the cause of liberty is inspired by the Greek idea of self-development. He considers it a privilege of every human being to use and interpret experience in his own way. He wants man to choose between alternatives to let his moral faculties come into play. He wants different persons to be allowed to lead life differently. For, he views variety as the basis for freedom.

The liberty, which Mill seeks to defend, is the liberty of the individual to develop, enrich and expand his personality. He lays down the conditions for the curtailment of liberty of the individual. He states one very simple principle: "the sole end for which mankind are warranted, individually or collectively, in interfering with the liberty of action of any of their member is self-protection. That the only purpose for which power can be rightfully exercised over any member of a civilized community against his will is to prevent harm to others. His own good, either physical or moral, is not sufficient warrant."

Elaborating the above principle Mill continues to argue that an individual cannot rightfully be compelled to do or forbear because it will be better for him to do so, or to make him happier. Nor should it be done because in the opinion of others, to do so would be wise or even right. These are good reasons, he says, for remonstrating with him or reasoning with him. But they are not good enough reasons for compelling him or visiting him with any evil in case he does otherwise. The only part of the conduct of anyone for which he is amenable to society is that which concerns others.

In the part, which merely concerns him, his independence is of right absolute. As Mill puts it: "over himself, over his body and mind, the individual is sovereign . . . the only freedom which deserves the name is that of pursing his own good in his own way so long as he does not attempt to deprive others of their effort to obtain it".

## Nature of Liberty

From the above statement of Mill on Liberty, certain principles can be inferred: First, Mill's liberty is of the individual. He regards individual as sovereign over his mind and body. He must therefore be left free in all that concerns him alone. In this sphere, society has no right to impose any restraints on the individual because all restraints are evil.

In this context, Mill divides the activities of the individual in two parts: *self-regarding* and *other-regarding* activities. The self-regarding ones may include those matters, which affect the individual himself, having no concern with others. He advocates freedom of the individual in doing those things, which affect him alone, whereas he favours imposing restrictions on such of his actions as have a bearing on others. He does not give society any right to use force or compulsion in regard to matters, which concern the individual alone and exclude others from their pale.

In the self-regarding functions Mill includes:

(i) the inward domain of consciousness demanding liberty of conscience in the most comprehensive sense, liberty of thought and feeling; absolute freedom of opinion and sentiment on all subjects, practical or speculative, scientific and moral or theological,

(ii) liberty of tastes and pursuits, of framing a plan of our life to suit our own character of doing things so long as we do not hurt others, and

(iii) liberty of combination among individuals, freedom to unite for any purpose not involving harm to others.

Mill defends individual's freedom from the state. He disagrees with those who believe that the state has a legitimate and positive role to promote the welfare of the people. His reservations are also about democracy based on the full democratic franchise. He favours extending only conditional support to such government.

Mill asserts that the phrases like 'self-government or power of the people' do not express the truth. The will of the people practically means the will of the most numerous and the most active part of the people *i.e.,* the majority. He fears that this majority may lead to 'tyranny of the majority' where the liberty of the minority may be lost. The advent of democracy, he holds, does not mean that the liberty of the individual will be protected. Rather majority may take away the liberty of the minority. Hence the liberty of the individual is in need of protection from the democratic state as well.

Similarly, Mill joins issues with those who are willing to put curbs on the individual liberty for the sake of the strong state. The worth of the state, in his view, is no more than the worth of the individuals who compose it. A state which dwarfs its men, according to Mill, in order that they may be more docile instruments in its hands even for beneficial purposes will find, that with small men no great things can really be accomplished. He continues to argue further that 'the perfection of machinery to which it has sacrificed everything will in the end avail nothing for want of the vital-power which, in order that the machine might work smoothly, it has preferred to banish.'

Mill denies that the evolution of government from tyranny to popular self-rule will occur automatically and he finds the solution in liberty. At the same time he warns that social tyranny may be more formidable than many kinds of political oppressions. For, social tyranny leaves fewer means of escape as it penetrates deep into the details of life. Hence protection against political tyranny must be supplemented by protection against the tyranny of prevailing opinion and feeling.

Mill sees the great obstacle to individual expression in the opposition of the society, also the barrier to free expression, whether in words and in deeds. He sees greater danger in the society turning itself a tyrant—collectively over the separate individuals who compose it. For the means of tyrannizing are not restricted to the acts which it may do by the hands of its political functionaries. By executing its own mandate against the wrong man, the society may practice a social tyranny much more formidable than hitherto known or faced by man.

Mill gives special importance to the liberty of the individual against the tyranny of prevailing opinion, sentiment and feeling. He denies that any government or society has right to suppress an opinion even if the support of the public be on their side. Such a power being illegitimate, even the best government has no more right to it than the worst.

The unconventional opinion held by the lone dissenter, Mill continues to argue, can be either right or wrong or partly right and partly wrong. If it is right, the suppression of it by the community will blot out the truth and mankind as a whole would suffer in consequence. Suppression or denial of its truth will mean that those who do so are claiming infallibility on behalf of the whole mankind. They are arrogating to themselves the monopoly of judgment by excluding every other person from the means of judging its truth. It amounts to assuming that their certainty is the same thing as absolute certainty.

Similarly all silencing of discussion is an assumption of their infallibility. In this connection his famous dictum is worth citing: 'if all mankind minus one were of one opinion and only one person were of the contrary opinion, then he, if he had the power, would be justified in silencing mankind'.

Thus Mill advocates completely unhampered and free discussion. He does not believe in the 'pleasant falsehood' that truth inevitably triumphs over persecution. He is well aware of the fact that history teems with instances of truth put down by persecution. In support of this he cites numerous examples of religious persecutions.

Mill gives the following three reasons against suppression of freedom of opinion and discussion. They are:

(i) Any opinion we seek to silence may be true and in silencing it we assume our own infallibility,

(ii) though the silenced opinion we may assume to be wholly erroneous, it may be partly true, and because the prevailing opinion on any subject is rarely the complete truth, it is only by the collision of adverse opinion that the remainder of the truth may shine out, and

(iii) even if the prevailing opinion be the complete truth, if it were not exposed to the challenge of free discussion, it will inevitably become dogma, prejudice and formula.

## Arguments in Defence of Liberty

Mill's arguments in defence of liberty rest upon a negative concept of freedom. He objects to the control over what he describes as the 'self-regarding' activities of an individual. For him, all restraint is an evil. He sees the individual not responsible to the society for his actions since they concern none but himself.

Mill's view rests on the premise that freedom consists in the absence of restraints; the best thing for the individual is that he should be left free to 'pursue his good in his own way'. There should be no fetters on the liberty of the individual and his person. In relation to individual he considers both society and state as antithesis. His concern is to give the individual an area within which he can act unobstructed by others. Though in the later phase, he does rise above this negative concept of liberty, he arrives at a deeper and more spiritual interpretation of it. Yet he is not able to divest himself of its negative conntation in fullness.

For Mill, the chief end is not the production of the greatest amount of happiness but the development of human personality in its richest diversity. It involves an improvement in the character of human beings and the general state of society. For he is well aware that unhappiness can not be eradicated by merely tinkering with government but achieving a thoroughgoing reform of the entire system.

Unlike Bentham, Mill is afraid of 'the tyranny of the majority over minority.' He is anxious to protect the interference of the state in the life of the individual. He wants to protect the minority against 'the tyranny of the majority' and the pressure of public opinion. In his other great work on Representative Government, Mill suggests measures for limiting the powers of the rulers. He lays great emphasis on the value of education and culture.

To summarize the discussion, for Mill, there are two ways that a person's liberty can be impeded:

1. public opinion
2. state intervention through laws and their interpretation.

In both cases, the danger is what Mill calls "the tyranny of the majority". For this reason, a democratic government must limit its own powers.

## Liberty of Thought and Discussion

A central issue of every polity is freedom of expression. It means freedom of thought, and consequently, of speech and writing. Does this infringe on other people's freedom to avoid unpalatable ideas or to have their opinions attacked? Here the cases of Socrates and Christ are relevant.

Mill suggests three considerations for making liberty a fact of life:

1. Open discussion is a requirement for democracy.
2. Practice of open discussion promotes openness which is essential for democracy.
3. Even if ideas that are wrong are presented, open discussion is better than suppressing them.

However, Mill adds the proviso that the discussion be temperate and fair, though the limits of this are hard to define.

Mill suggests three reasons to limit the interference of the government:

1. Individuals often know best their own interests and they are best placed to manage them. These interests are more a matter of political economy, and not directly a liberty issue.
2. Even in cases in which the government may do the job better, it is best to have the individuals manage things themselves so that they may learn and expect to take responsibility. This is not directly a matter of liberty, but it encourages habits of mind of independence and of responsibility that are required for a free people. Furthermore, it permits many experiments of various kinds of welfare by individuals. The government can act as a repository for the information and techniques.
3. On restricting the power of government he holds that the more it does the more powerful it becomes and the more dependent are people on it as a matter of habit or attitude. This has direct consequences for liberty.

For finding a proper balance between government interference and individual freedom. Mill wants to investigate the legitimate grounds for infringing upon an individual's liberty. He is particularly concerned with how to protect individual liberty in a democracy— that is, how to protect the liberty of the minority from "the tyranny of the majority." While investigating the moral foundation for the principle he points to the distinction of the Self Regarding and Other Regarding acts.

Mill gives three arguments for why we should never silence an opinion no matter how few accept it:

1. We can never be sure that the opinion we are endeavouring to stifle is a false opinion. All silencing of discussion is an assumption of infallibility. Yet we are not infallible.

2. However unwillingly a person who has a strong opinion may admit the possibility that his opinion may be false, he ought to be moved by the consideration that however true it may be if it is not fully, frequently, and fearlessly discussed, it will be held as a dead dogma, not a living truth.
3. Though the silenced opinion be an error, it may, and very commonly does, contain a portion of truth. Since the general or prevailing opinion on any subject is rarely or never the whole truth, it is only by the collision of adverse opinions that the remainder of the truth has any chance of being supplied.

Mill further justifies liberty of thought and discussion on the following counts:

(i) Even if the received opinion be not only true, but the whole truth; unless it is supposed to be, and actually is, vigorously and earnestly contested, it will, by most of those who receive it, be held in the manner of prejudice, with little comprehension or feeling of its rational grounds.

(ii) Also the meaning of 'the to-be-silenced-doctrine or opinion' itself will be in danger of being lost or enfeebled, and deprived of its vital effect on the character and conduct of the people, if subsequently found to be true.

## Critical Assessment

Mill's concept of liberty has certain limitations which are summarized as below:

**First,** as he himself admits, his concept of liberty applies only to human beings in the maturity of their faculties and not to children or young persons below certain age and more importantly 'the backward peoples or races'. In their case he sees paternal despotism as the legitimate form of government.

**Second,** while Mill thinks that absolute and unfettered freedom of thought and expression is a necessary condition, if mankind is to develop the personality which is the end of civilization. But he does not accord equal importance to absolute liberty in the field of action. This freedom of action is only to the extent that it does not do any harm to others. This position is inherently sound. For it will be dangerous to give the same degree of unlimited freedom to the individual in the sphere of action as well as in the realm of thinking.

**Third,** giving the free play to individuality is likely to lead to inequality among men. Rule by the majority that Bentham regards as the best, Mill rejects. According to Mill, only finer type of men are entitled to become the leaders of mankind. It is such people who should guide the less original and more imitative of the people by persuasion instead of running roughshod over them. Thus, there exists, in Mill's thought a tension between liberty and equality in essential terms.

**Fourth,** Barker calls Mill 'a prophet of an empty liberty and an abstract individual'. While praising Mill's concept of liberty as free play for that spiritual originality with all its individual vigour and manifold diversity, he believes that this alone can not constitute the basis of a rich, balanced and developed society.

Barker laments that Mill continues to cling to the individualistic concept of society, which constitutes a part of his intellectual inheritance. Also he (Mill) is unable to formulate the idea of a social whole. This alone can enable us to establish the right relation between the individual and the state.

Moreover, the dividing line between self regarding and other regarding actions of the individual remains very thin and artificial. However the later generation of liberal writers like Green, Hobhouse, Lindsay, Laski, and Barker etc. do not accept this distinction as valid.

In sum, Mill's essay on liberty will continue to be a beacon for posterity because of the emphasis he lays on liberty. For him, all social and political progress depends largely on the potentialities of the individual and his free choice. Any increase in the power of the state, irrespective of its form, is antithetical to the liberty of the individual. According to him the most valuable element in human life is spontaneous choice. Anything that is done by a compulsory power diminishes the scope of that choice and thus infringes liberty.

In addition to the above his plea for freedom of speech, thought and expression to all men as a hallmark of a free society and an every evolving culture and civilization comes to be hailed as the sheet-anchor of the liberal philosophy.

## Mill's Views on Democracy

Liberalism and democracy have great affinity with each other. They are seen to grow together in an environment in which the state is seen to free itself from the absolute power of the kings and religious traditions. If liberalism symbolizes the ideas of liberty, equality, rights and justice, democracy is the means to achieve these ends. Though one can find the traces of democracy in ancient India and in the Greek city-states and in recent times in the writings of Thomas Moore, Hobbes, Locke etc., but it is in the nineteenth century that writers like Bentham, James Mill, Tocqueville, J. S. Mill are seen to pave the way for developed democratic idea as well as democratic institutions.

Bentham finds justification of democracy on utilitarian grounds. He argues that individuals require protection from the governors as well as from each other. They need assurance that those who govern pursue policies that are in consonance with the interests of the individual. He finds the solution for this in representative democracy, constitutional government, regular elections, and majority rule. Besides he recommends laissez faire capitalist economy and universal franchise for men as the best protector of individual rights.

However, it is J. S. Mill who defends a concept of democratic politics, supportive of individuality, representative government, efficient administration and noninterference of government in the economic affairs. Extending Bentham's views further, Mill emphasizes the moral worth of democracy when he sees democracy as a means of improvement and development of mankind as a whole. Machperson calls his model of democracy as 'Developmental Democracy'.

Mill's book *Representative Government*, advocates the constitutional reforms by which the goal of good government can be realized. It also reflects on how best to avoid evils in the representative government. In Constitution he sees a means of bringing the general standard of intelligence and honesty existing in the community. In it he finds the individual intellect and virtue of its wisest members, more directly to bear upon the government. He favours investing it with greater influence than it may be possible under any other mode of organization. He views government as a purposeful enterprise. It is designed to educate the citizens. It seeks to develop human potentialities and to elevate the quality of governance. He considers political education as meaningful if every citizen is encouraged to participate in the process of self-government.

Mill strongly believes that only popular participation can impart legitimacy to government. For this citizens need to choose their own rulers and bring their influence to bear on the character and direction of public policy. Popular participation can better achieve this goal.

According to Mill no exclusive class or elite is capable of promoting political interest other than its own. Only if men are allowed to govern themselves they will begin to think of themselves and for themselves as individuals. In his view, liberal democracy or representative governmental is important because it is an effective means for the free development of individuality.

Democracy, according to Mill, draws people in the operation of government by giving them a right to vote. If they exercise it judiciously, it can bring a fall in government. He emphasizes the importance of participation in political life such as voting, involvement in local administration and jury service for creating a direct interest in developing citizenry.

Democracy, for Mill, is the only system of government which can provide protection to the interests of all in a community. Democracy is also an educational process. It helps develop in men interests of their own and develop their personality. In a democracy, political education is universal. In other systems, this education is limited only to the privileged class. In political participation, Mill sees a continuing lesson in the moral life. He considers it as a means of intellectual education. He sees it conductive to the full development of the capacities of the individual.

## Representative Democracy

However to achieve optimum political participation, Mill does not adopt Rousseau's model of direct democracy. Rather Mill wants the creation of certain institutions of government whereby the democratic theory is transformed into democratic practice. In representatively democracy he finds the solution.

By representative government Mill means, the whole people or some numerous portion of them, exercise through deputies periodically elected by themselves the ultimate controlling power. Besides a representative system, provision of freedom of speech, press and assembly provides a powerful mechanism whereby government can be watched and controlled. Electoral competition enables to harness leadership qualities for the maximum benefit of all. The benefit of popular control and efficiency can only be attained by the representative democracy. For it combines in it accountability with professionalism and expertise as well as it has the advantages of bureaucratic government without its disadvantages.

Mill makes a distinction between false and true democracy: The democracy of numbers which is the degeneracy of all governments is false democracy. Its principle of 'everyone to count for one and no one for more than one' is based on the wrong belief that any man is as good as any other. It also ignores the obvious differences of intelligence and virtue between men. This belief is also detrimental to moral and intellectual excellence of mankind.

A true democracy, in contrast, gives due weightage to all the different elements of society. It thus obviates the undue preponderance of any one component. In a true democracy, representation is given to every or any section not disproportionately but proportionately. A majority of the electors will always have a majority of the representatives, and a minority of the electors will always have a minority of the representatives. Man for man they will be as fully represented as the majority unless, there is a government of inequality and privilege. According to Mill, "Democracy is not the best form of government unless it can be so organized that no class, not even the most numerous, shall be able to reduce all but itself to political insignificance and from its preminent position it may direct the course of legislature and administration by its exclusive class interest."

### Views on Political Reforms and Representative Democracy

Mill suggests a number of political reforms to improve the quality and content of democratic governance. The foremost reform he suggests is how not to leave the choice of representatives into the hands of ignorant and indiscriminating masses. It is also how best to minimize the danger to government by collective mediocrity. He rejects Bentham's idea of universal adult franchise and direct popular control of administration.

Mill also voices his reservation against annual elections to parliament and the notion of delegation. He is very much conscious about the general ignorance and incapacity, as also insufficient mental qualifications in the legislature. His greater fear is the danger of its being influenced by interests not identical with the general welfare of the community.

Even as Mill accepts popular participation in the elections as an essential means of human development, he does not favour the idea of universal adult franchise or the principle of one-man-one-vote. He is fearful that with the working class being in majority, this one-man-one-vote principle may lead to legislation in the interest of one particular class at the expense of other classes as well as of posterity. He therefore suggests proportional representation and plural voting. Through proportional representation he hopes to give proper weightage to the right qualities needed in a candidate. He believes that this will, to some extent, ward off the evil effects of the numerical superiority of the ignorant masses. Plural voting is meant for the members of the smaller of the two classes whereby neither of them should outweigh the other and impose class legislation.

Thus all what Mill suggests means that while everyone should have one vote, some should have several votes. This is the rationale why he recommends plural vote for some people and the exclusion of it for others. For example, he recommends two or more votes for those who have already attained superior quality through education or property. He believes that only wiser and better men should have a claim to superior weight. He also supports women franchise.

## Critique of Representative Democracy and Political Reforms

However, Mill's views on representative democracy and political reforms are flawed. They are not in consonance with the modern political culture and ethos. He excludes certain classes from political participation such as people receiving poor relief, bankrupts, illiterates, those not paying taxes etc. Besides he seeks to limit the right to vote to those who pay something towards the taxes. His reason for doing so is that those who pay no taxes but have the power to dispose of other people's money by their vote, have every motive to be lavish and not to economize in course of governance. He considers it hurtful that the constitution of the country should declare ignorance to be entitled to as much political power as knowledge.

Mill rejects Bentham's plea for direct control of administration by the elected parliament. For, with the expansion of the activities of the government, Mill thinks, the representatives of the people do not have the adequate fitness to govern. He wants such a system in place which has not only efficiency but at the same time also popular control and self-criticism. The task of formulating a rational public policy cannot be left to amateurs or semiprofessionals. Since drafting of effective legislation is a complicated business, it requires superior intellect, broad experience and disciplined study. Both party leaders and heads of executive departments who have to run the actual government should have both the training and resources to make and carry out public policy. The elected representatives should know the limits of their competence and the semiprofessionals should delegate the responsibility of governing to the professionals.

Mill considers it wrong to subject men of higher intelligence to the control of men of lower capacity. The parliament should be content to watch and control the government. It should compel a full exposition and justification of all measures which anyone considers questionable. It should censure the professionals if they abuse their trust, or to expel them from office. The representatives should not be permitted to dictate in detail to those who are in charge of the administration.

In addition, for Mill, parliament should act as nation's committee of grievances and its congress of opinion. The chief weapon in their armory is words, especially what representative talk is a vital component of self-government. Their views represent the opinion of some important body of persons in the nation in whom people have reposed their confidence. In a democracy representatives talk has to be free to be the best means for effective political change and for enlisting citizens in the government process. According to Mill, parliament apart from being a great forum for the never-ending political conversation, should ensure that this conversation will be rational in substance. Thus both democracy and rationality should be evidenced in the government process.

## CONCLUSION

Though the entire thrust of Mill's writings is democratic, it may not be correct to rank him as a full egalitarian. He stands for a society of individuals more humanly developed which he thinks is possible only in a democracy. However, he considers democracy as a system to be flawed and pin points the dangers into which it is likely to fall. He insists that despite all shortcomings democracy remains the best form of government wherever it is possible.

As a democrat, Mill strongly believes, that government is ideally the best in which sovereignty or supreme controlling power is vested in the entire aggregate of the community. Besides, in such a system every citizen has a voice in the expression of the sovereign will and opportunity to participate in the discharge of some public function.

Besides, Mill believes that democracy makes a man happier and better. It helps cultivate values and worth of human personality. He insists on the development of the individual as the goal of government. Further what makes democracy better than monarchy and aristocracy is its influence upon human character. It is democracy that makes people self-reliant and capable of standing up for their rights. While highlighting merits of democracy Mill laments the shortcomings of democracy such as people's illiteracy, their apathy, ignorance, backwardness and so forth. He not only expresses his concern over the tyranny of the majority but also for the rights of the minority. As a liberal economist, he stands for the competitive market economy, private property and laissez faire economy. His model of democracy is designed to maximize liberty of citizens. It aims to secure for them property and a thriving capitalist economy. Thus Mill upholds a strong state and a flourishing capitalist society with liberty of the individual occupying the centerpiece.

# 18

# MARX ON STATE

## Bourgeois State

According to Lenin, no question has been more confused by bourgeois sociologists than that of the state, because no other question is as vital to the interests of the ruling classes. They picture the state as some kind of supernatural force given to man by providence since time immemorial. They see it supposedly having no class character. Rather they view it merely an innocuous "instrument of order" or an "arbiter" called upon to resolve disputes which may arise between people regardless of their class affiliation. Such a "theory" of the state serves to justify the privileges of the bourgeoisie, the existence of exploitation, and capitalism. Judged in this light true scientific explanation of the origin of the state, its essence and its role in society's life is possible only under Marxism-Leninism.

## Origin of the State: The Marxist Perspective

Politics and state, according to Marx, are but part of the superstructure. The substructure of it is the economic system of society. Engels gives a clear exposition of the Marxist theory of the origin of the state in his famous book *The origin of the Family, Private Property and the State(1884).*

For Engles, the state owes its origin to historical materialism. He sees state as a product of society at a certain stage of development. The origin of the state is associated with the division of society into classes. The conflicting economic interests lead to struggle of classes. State emerges as an organization of the possessing class for its protection against the non-possessing class. The state is merely an instrument of exploitation. The dominant class uses to maintain and perpetuate its class hegemony.

The state, according to Engles, is neither a natural institution (Aristotle), nor a creature of contract (Hobbes, Locke and Rousseau), nor a boon from God (theory of divine origin), nor the image and reality of reason (Hegel), but a necessity at a specific historical moment. When the society becomes entangled in an insoluble contradiction with itself, the need for power seemingly standing above society arises.

The power (state) becomes necessary to keep antagonisms and class struggles within the bounds of order. Moderating the conflict is its role. In spite of acting as a shock absorber in the interest of the dominant class, the state fails to end the struggle.

Thus state comes into being only with the emergence of classes; it has not existed from all eternity. The primitive communal society has been a stateless society. With the cleavage of society into classes and owing to the fact of this cleavage the state becomes a necessity. For example, the state of antiquity was a slave-owning state; its purpose was to hold down the slaves. The feudal state was the organ of nobility designed to hold down the peasants, serfs and bondsmen. The modern representative state is an instrument of exploitation of wage labour by capital. But if society becomes classless, due to development of socialistic mode of production, so do argue Marxists, the state will inevitably fall and wither away automatically.

Gramsci examines the relationship between base (substructure) and superstructure and concludes that state originates through the struggle of three types of social forces: (a) *which provide leadership,* (b) *against whom struggle is waged and* (c) *some auxiliaries or allied forces which lend active or passive consent to the leaders.*

In short, for Gramsci, the state comes into being through domination and hegemony. The state suppresses some enemies. It dominates antagonistic groups. It tends to liquidate, or to subjugate them perhaps even by armed force. But indeed it maintains its supremacy by means of intellectual and moral leadership. It gets the consent of people by creating false consciousness. It does so through its superior means of propaganda or ideological apparatus at its command. Thus the state in modern times has founded 'hegemonic rule' through domination and intellectual and moral leadership. Therefore a revolution to be successful must break the hegemony and ideological basis of the state at the same time. Gramsci assigns this task to 'organic intellectuals' and party organization.

Marxist theory of the origin of the state thus is a revolutionary philosophy of change. It envisages the suppression of the bourgeois state by a socialist revolution. It is spearheaded by the leadership of the organized working class who will forcibly capture the state power and establish a 'dictatorship of the proletariat'.

According to Engels, the bourgeois state does not wither away, but is abolished by the proletariat in the course of the revolution. What withers away after this revolution is the proletarian state or semi-state. In the meanwhile, the proletarian state establishes a classless society by building a socialist economy. It achieves this affective by abolishing private property and creating a non-alienated social man and an exploitation-free social order.

Thus as against the liberals of myriad hues Marxists demonstrate that the state is not something introduced into society from the outside. It is indeed a product of society's internal development i.e., the state comes into being by changes in material production. The succession of one mode of production by another causes a change in the state system.

Marxists argue that the state has not always existed in history. Primitive society which had no private property and no classes had no state either. Naturally, there were certain social functions, but they were performed by men chosen by all of society which had the right to dismiss these people at any time and to appoint others. In those distant times relations between people were regulated by public opinion. But the further development of the productive forces result in the disintegration of primitive society. Accordingly private property appear, accompanied by classes—slaves and slave-owners. It becomes necessary to protect private property, the rule and security of its owners, and this brings the state into being. However the birth of the state and its further development are accompanied by a fierce class struggle.

According to Marxism, the state is a product of class society. It arises with the appearance of classes and it will vanish, wither away with the disappearance of classes. But this will happen only under communism.

## The Essence of the State

In an antagonistic class society the state is a political instrument. It is a machine or a coercive apparatus for maintaining the rule of one class over another. The class dominating economically, *i.e.,* possessing the means of production, acquires in the state a powerful instrument for the subjection of the oppressed and exploited. The state has thus a clearly defined class character. Being the principal component of the superstructure founded on the economic basis of socicty, the state takes every measure to strengthen and protect this basis.

## Features of the State

The main feature of a state is the existence of public (social) authority representing the interests of the class which dominates economically and not of the entire population. This authority rests on the army, and the police, jails etc. In primitive society all the people are armed, but in a society divided into hostile classes, the armed forces are in the hands of the ruling class. They are used to suppress the people, to subordinate them to a handful of exploiters. Representative bodies (parliaments), the huge bureaucratic administrative machine with a whole army of officials, intelligence agencies, the courts, procurator's offices and prisons—all are used for the same purpose. All of them combined make up the political authority of the exploiting state.

As class contradictions deepen and the class struggle intensifies, the state machine expands. This process is particularly intensive in contemporary capitalist society where the state machine and the armed forces have grown to an unprecedented size.

While in primitive society people settled in consanguineous groups, in a modern state the population is grouped territorially; *i.e.,* in districts, counties, states, regions, etc. Territorial settlement is a result of the development of production, the increasing division of labour and the growth of trade and commodity exchange.

## The State in an Exploiting Society

The state in any exploiting society, (slave-owning, feudal, or capitalist) is designed to protect the interests of the ruling class both within the country, in relations with other classes, and outside, in relations with other states. There are therefore two main trends or functions in the activities of a state: internal and external. The internal function is the main one and the external function determines all the foreign affairs of a state.

Let us examine these functions:

The internal function of a state is to suppress the working people, to subordinate them to the small group of oppressors. This reflects the class nature of the "state and is expressed in its internal policy, the struggle against the oppressed classes". The first exploiting state is the slave-owning state. It is later succeeded by the feudal state. This in turn is superseded by the capitalist state. In spite of certain differences, all the three have one task in common: to keep the people in check and to crush their attempt to emancipate themselves from exploitation. The slave-owning state uses armed force to put down the slaves who rise against their masters. The feudal state forcibly binds the peasants to the landlord's estate and cruelly punishes those who refuse to toil for the landlord. The numerous peasant uprisings have ended in blood baths. The capitalist state, although it likes to parade in democratic garb, is also a machine for the subjection of the working people. Its real purpose is to protect private capitalist property, maintain wage-slavery and crush the revolutionary movement of the proletariat.

The external function of the exploiting state is to seize foreign territories or defend its own land from attack. This is reflected in its relations with other states and is expressed in its foreign policy. Foreign policy of a state stems from home policy and is a continuation of the latter. The reactionary, predatory foreign policy of contemporary imperialism is a natural supplement to its home policy of suppressing the working class and all other progressive forces.

## Types of the State and Forms of Rule

States differ according to the class they serve and the economic basis on which they arise. Four types of state are known in history: slave-owning, feudal, capitalist and socialist. In contrast to the first three, which defend the interests of the exploiters, the socialist state is a state of a new type, a genuine state of the people. Each type of state has its intrinsic form of government, *i.e.,* order, organization of rule by the dominant class. The form of government depends on the concrete historical conditions in each country, on the balance of the class forces and external conditions. However diverse the forms of government, however much they may change, the type of state, its class nature, remains unaltered. It continues to be within the framework of the given economic system. Lenin notes that a slave-owning society has different forms of government: a monarchy—the rule of one man, the emperor, the monarch; a republic–elective rule; aristocracy-the rule of a relatively small minority; democracy–the rule of the majority. In spite of these differences, the state in the slave-owning era, as Lenin writes, is a state of the slave-owners. Feudal society too presents a similar picture. A monarchy is the most widespread form of government in the feudal state, but at times it also appears in other forms, for example, a republic. Whatever the form, the feudal state serves as an instrument for suppressing the serfs and the artisans.

Diversity of form is also true of the liberal state. Most frequently this state appears as a republic. Under capitalism, the monarchic form seldom exists and the rule of the monarch is in one way or another restricted by the Constitution. In the imperialist era the bourgeoisie also makes use of fascist dictatorship. The unlimited power of the bourgeoisie is exercised in favour of the bourgeois or the dominant ruling class even in a so-called liberal state. With society's development the types and forms of the state change.

Liberal ideologists are fond of talking about the progressive role of the bourgeois state. They claim that only this state has brought the people full freedom; it is the highest type of democracy, genuine democracy. Today reformists are particularly vociferous in this respect. They portray the bourgeois state as a force standing above classes, equally restraining both labour and capital.

The capitalist state, they assert, has ceased to be the organ of only one class, *i.e.,* the capitalist class; now it serves all classes in society. There is, however, no evidence to support this statement, though it is correct that at the dawn of capitalism the bourgeois state does in fact possess some progressive features. It does help to introduce and develop capitalist production relations, which are more advanced than feudal relations. But the fact is that even in its heyday, however, the bourgeois state has not been a democracy far all. Yet despite the restricted nature of bourgeois democracy, it affords the working class far more favourable conditions than open dictatorships do for waging a successful struggle against the bourgeoisie, to establish the dictatorship of the proletariat and for socialism. That is why the working class in the capitalist countries heads all the progressive forces. Its purpose is to persistently combat the onslaught of the reactionaries. It is to fight for democracy and curtailment of monopoly rule.

## Dictatorship of the Proletariat

According to Marxists, the proletariat has the great historical mission of destroying capitalism and building a classless communist society. Yet this new society will not grow out of capitalism directly and at once. Between capitalism and socialism "lies the period of the revolutionary transformation of the one into the other. Corresponding to this is also a political transition period in which the state can be nothing but the revolutionary dictatorship of the proletarian".

The dictatorship of the proletariat arises as a result of the successful socialist revolution and through demolition of the bourgeois state machine. It is a qualitatively new type of state. It differs radically from the previous states in regard to its class nature, the forms of state organization and the role it is destined to play. All the preceding types of state have been but tools of the exploiting classes used for the subjection of the working people. They have been designed to reinforce the system of exploitation and to perpetuate the division of society into oppressors and oppressed. The dictatorship of the proletariat, however, is the rule of the working class which, together with all the other working people, destroys capitalism and builds a new society without antagonistic classes and exploitation.

In short, the theory of the dictatorship of the proletariat is the crux of Marxism. Only dictatorship, the undivided power of the proletariat, enables the proletariat to put an end to capitalism and build socialism. It is only natural, therefore, that the question of the dictatorship of the proletariat has always been, and remains, the pivot of the struggle against reformism and revisionism.

## Functions of the Proletarian State

Lenin calls the dictatorship of the proletariat the touchstone for testing the real understanding and recognition of Marxism. The state of the dictatorship of the proletariat is a state which exists in the period of the transition from capitalism to socialism. This period is characterized by a multi-structural economy and the bitter class struggle between the proletariat and the bourgeoisie. The crucial task facing the proletariat at that time is to break down the resistance of the bourgeoisie, and together with all the working people, to build socialism. This task determines the functions of the proletarian state.

One of the main domestic functions of the proletarian state in the transition period is the function of suppressing the exploiting classes, the bourgeoisie in the first place. Deprived of its political domination the bourgeoisie in any country cannot reconcile itself to its defeat and the loss of power and privileges, and therefore viciously resists the victorious proletariat. The suppression of the bourgeoisie, however, is not an aim in itself for the proletariat. Its main aim is to build socialism, to create a new, socialist economy. What makes this task so difficult is that the socialist revolution begins when there are no ready-made economic forms of socialism. It is the task of the dictatorship of the proletariat, of the proletarian state, to organize the economic life of society. For this they need to take immediate steps to build up a new type of economy superior to capitalism, *i.e.*, the economy of socialism.

In short, the task of the proletarian state is to secure socialism's economic victory over capitalism and thus attain a higher level of the social organization of labour than under capitalism. Once the basic means of production have been nationalized the proletarian state immediately should take over command position in the economy and organize its planned, science-based management. As socialism progresses the economic and organizational function of the state gains in scope and with the victory of socialism, will embrace literally all branches of the national economy.

Yet socialist construction is not confined to the establishment of a socialist economy. It calls for a steadfast growth of the awareness and culture of the people. Further it requires the obliteration of the survivals of the past in their consciousness. Thus to achieve the goal of socialist revolution it is only natural, therefore, that the education of the working people, particularly the semi-proletarian strata and the peasantry, in the spirit of socialism is to be continued. Besides along with the promotion of their general education and professional and cultural level the other key tasks of the proletarian state are to wage a relentless war against those who have been the exploiters for centuries. They have been enslaving the working people and in every way suppressing their striving for culture and knowledge. Therefore, to let the transition to socialism be smooth and easy socialist revolution is the only way.

In the phase of the dictatorship of the proletariat, the proletarian state acts as the chief guide and instrument of the cultural revolution which is an important element of the socialist revolution. The role played by the state in promoting cultural development and the education of the working people is due to its cultural and educational function.

In the sphere of foreign policy the activity of the proletarian state will be characterized by the function of the struggle for peace between the peoples, and the function of the country's defence against imperialist aggression. While persistently working for peace, the state under the dictatorship of the proletariat will constantly strengthen the country's defence and its armed forces as well.

Both liberal and reformist political commentators shout from the rooftops about "universal democracy", "democracy for all". They find this to be existing in the capitalist world. They uphold this "pure" bourgeois democracy in contrast to the dictatorship of the proletariat. This they see as a bureaucratic, undemocratic rule. But in reality, the Marxists assert, the very opposite is the case. The bourgeois democracy, is merely a screen for the omnipotence of the moneybags and for the actual lack of rights of the working people. The aim of bourgeois democracy is to perpetuate the capitalist system. It is to ensure the exploitation of the millions of working people by the negligible minority of the rich.

For the Marxists only the proletarian state is truly democratic. The dictatorship of the proletariat is a qualitatively new type of democracy. This, as Lenin writes, is democracy for the overwhelming majority of the people. It secures the exclusion of the exploiters and oppressors from this democracy. In the process of its development it increasingly turns into socialist democracy of the whole people. This is a qualitatively new type of democracy under the dictatorship of the proletariat and it stems from its very nature, its aims and purposes. Only in a firm alliance with all the working people and the democratic forces, of course with support of the masses the proletariat can organize themselves into a disciplined force capable breaking down the resistance of the exploiting classes. This is how they will retain power, build socialism and bring the people to a life of happiness.

The alliance of the working class, the non-proletariat sections of town and country, above all the peasants, they all constitute the basis, or the supreme principle of the dictatorship of the proletariat. It will embody the fullest and all-round expression of the genuine democracy of the proletarian state.

A primary distinction of proletarian democracy is that it not only proclaims the rights of the working people, but it also provides the conditions for the people to exercise them. Under the dictatorship of the proletariat the working people possess not formal rights, as exist in a bourgeois state, but they actually govern the country and directly, or through their representatives, manage its entire economic, political and cultural life.

The proletarian state guarantees the exercise of democratic rights by providing the corresponding material facilities. The working people own all the means of production, This enables them to manage the country's economy and to exercise their right to work. Their hold over schools, universities, scientific and cultural institutions, health and holiday homes give them the opportunity to exercise their rights to education and also to rest and leisure. The working people have at their disposal print shops, stocks of paper, radio stations, the best buildings, etc. This enables them to enjoy freedom of the press, speech, assembly, freedom of organization, etc.

The working people actively take part in the political life of the country and in state affairs. They do so through their wide participation in various state bodies, in numerous committees and commissions. Also they participate through their own social organizations. In a word, proletarian democracy, as Lenin asserts, is a million times more democratic than any bourgeois democracy.

### From the Socialist State to State of the Whole People

A distinctive feature of the state of the whole people is that it does not have to perform the function of suppressing the exploiting classes because they have ceased to exist as a result of the victory of socialism. This, however, does not mean that the working class has completely withdrawn from the class struggle. In fact it continues to wage its class struggle in close unity with the co-opted peasantry and the working intelligentsia against international imperialism.

Furthermore, relying on the support of all working people, on their consciousness and organization, the state takes recourse to necessary measures of coercion with regard to persons who violate the laws, standards and principles of socialist society.

Dictatorship of the proletariat and the state of the whole people are not qualitatively different types of states. In point of fact they are stages in the development of a socialist type state. The state of the whole people continues to further the cause of the dictatorship of the proletariat. It brings in place all needed institutions and organizations to build communist society. Its social basis is the working class, the collective-farm peasantry and the intelligentsia, but above all the working class. The last one is the most advanced, organized and conscious force of socialist society. It plays the leading role in the socialist revolution. The state of the whole people raises to a new height that what is the main content of proletarian dictatorship *viz,* socialist democracy. It preserves and develops the basic functions of the dictatorship of the proletariat, with the exception of the function of suppressing exploiters.

It follows that the socialist state invariably safeguards people's rights and freedoms and socialist laws. The state is particularly concerned with safeguarding socialist property, "the economic foundation of socialism, whose all-round development and consolidation is vital for successful communist construction."

Owing to rapid economic growth, the managerial function of a modern state have become much more complex and multiform. In the transition period from capitalism to socialism this function of the state is designed to ensure the economic victory of the socialist forces over the capitalist forces in the country,

However the immediate task of building of socialism is transformed to build the material and technical base of communism. It is charged to transform socialist relations into communist relations and thus further improve the well-being of the people. In the process the state comes to play an increasing role in controlling the measure of labour and the measure of consumption.

The foreign policy function of the proletarian state broadens in the period of the gradual transition from socialism to communism due to the serious changes occurring in the international situation, especially the strengthening and development of the fraternal cooperation with the socialist countries. Such is the new function which the working class people have to perform to lend credibility and support to the emerging socialist system.

Another new function is to support the struggle of the peoples for liberation from colonial and neocolonial oppression.

At the same time the proletarian state needs to strengthen the country's defensive capacity in every way. It is because, as long as imperialism which is pregnant with the threat of aggressive wars exists, a socialist country cannot feel complacent. It is imperative that it should be insured against the possibility of aggression.

## The Withering Away of the State

The necessity of strengthening and developing the socialist state does not mean that it will exist for ever. Needless to say, public functions similar to those performed by the state today in the sphere of economic and cultural management will be preserved under communism as well. But they will be modified and perfected as society develops. Their character and the ways in which they are carried out will be different from those under socialism. The state bodies will lose the political character as society moves towards communism. With time they will merge with society and become organs of public self-government. It is through them that all members of society will be able to participate in economic and cultural management. The distinction between the society and the state will be effaced. The state will wither away.

It would be incorrect, however, to imagine that the withering away of the state and the transformation of state administration into public self-government under communism will take place suddenly and all at once. The withering away of the state is a long, gradual process covering an entire historical epoch. For a certain period elements of state administration and public self-government will coexist and intertwine. A time will come when the need for the state will disappear.

It will come about only when society becomes fully mature for self-government, *i.e.,* under developed communism. The state will be able to wither away completely when society adopts the rule: 'From each according to his ability, to each according to his needs'. The stage will come when people have become so accustomed to observing the fundamental rules of social intercourse and when their labour has become so productive that they will voluntarily work according to their ability.

## CONCLUSION

In fine, the internal condition for the withering away of the state is the building of developed communist society. But there have to be external conditions too for the state to wither away, namely the victory and consolidation of socialism on the international scene. When speaking about the withering away of the state it is necessary to take the international situation into account. If communism triumphs in one or another country or a group of countries, but armed imperialist predators continue to exist in the world, then the communist society will definitely retain the state function of defending the country. This function will become obsolete only when the threat of an attack by imperialist forces disappears for ever.

# PART IV

# Indian Thought: Thinkers and Themes

# 19

# KAUTILYA ON STATE

## Origin of the State

Chanakya (c.350 – c.275 BC), also known as Kautilya or Vishnugupta, was born in Pataliputra, Magadh (modern Bihar). He later moved to Taxila, in Gandhar province (now in Pakistan). He was a professor (*Acharya*) of Political Science at the Takshashila University. He later became the Prime Minister of the Emperor Chandragupta Maurya.

Kautilya is indeed one of the earliest known political thinkers, economists and king-makers. He envisions the first Indian empire by unification of the then numerous kingdoms in the Indian subcontinent. He is the man who provides the impetus for fights and resistance against the Greek conqueror, Alexander. His foresight and wide knowledge of the art of governance coupled with politics of expediency comes to help found the might Mauryan Empire in India.

Arthashastra, the treatise on the science and art of governance and the practice of economic management was written by Kautilya in the 4th century before Christ. It consists of 15 Chapter, 380 Shlokas and 4968 Sutras. Kautilya wrote this treatise for his swamy (the king) Chandragupta Maurya but was intended to act as a guide for "those who govern". It contains all components to establish a strong state. The king is enabled to preserve the integrity and solidarity of the State.

## The End of the State

But what is the end of the state? This question is, indeed, the pivot on which Political Thought has revolved from ancient times to this day. For Plato, the state is a macrocosm in which the individual can find his proper place and perform the duties for which he is best fitted. To Aristotle, the purpose of the state is mainly ethical. The state is 'a community of equals, aiming at the best life possible.'

Hobbes regards the purpose of the State to maintain order and protect the right of property. Locke believes that the end of Government is the preservation of 'lives, liberties and estates'. For Rousseau, the state is a 'social contract' to fulfil the 'general will'.

Hegel considers the state as the greatest reality. "The existence of the state," writes Hegel, "is the movement of God in the world". "It is the absolute power on earth; it is its own end and object.'

In Bentham's view, 'the State exists to secure the greatest good of the greatest number'. Herbert Spencer looks upon the state as 'a joint-stock protection company for mutual assurance.' John Stuart Mill passionately advocates the liberty of the individual and considers it as the sacred duty of the state.

Marx expects the state to 'wither away' after establishing a 'classless society'. For Professor Laski the state is 'a fellowship of men. Its aim is 'enrichment of common life'. Bernard Shaw projects the aim of a state to be 'the greatest available welfare for the whole population and not for a class.'

H.G. Wells envisages the establishment of a world state, in which 'the freedom, health and happiness of every individual are protected by a universal law based on a restatement of the rights of man.'

For Kautilya too the basic principle or the primary duty of the king or the state is the happiness and welfare of the people. 'In the happiness of his subjects lies his happiness; in their welfare his welfare'.

## Functions of the State

For Kautilya the elements of sovereign state are the king, the minister, the country, the fort, the treasury, the army and its ally, and the enemy. A good king is described as born of a high family. He is godly, virtuous, courageous, truthful, grateful, ambitious, enthusiastic. He is not addicted to procrastination. He is powerful in controlling neighbor kings. He is resolute, with a good assembly, having a taste for discipline. He is endowed with a sharp intellect and memory. He is trained in various arts. He is dignified. He has foresight capable of discerning the need for war. He is not haughty and is free of passions and bad habits. He is observing traditional customs.

The acquisition of wealth and its security is dependent on peace and industry. Kautilya defines three kinds of strength:

1. The ability to deliberate, being intellectual strength,
2. a prosperous treasury, being strength of sovereignty, and
3. martial power, being physical strength.

The traditional six forms of state policy are: peace, war, neutrality, marching (preparing), alliance, and the double policy of making peace with one and waging war against another.

Although Kautilya is not reluctant to use warfare, at least he does recognize that if the situation is equal, peace is preferable. For, war involves loss of power and wealth, leads to evil and sin. Kautilya uses rational calculations of self-interest in deciding whether to march against enemies.

Kautilya believes that peace dependent on honesty or an oath is more immutable in this world and the next than that based on security or a hostage which is for this world only. Kautilya thinks that he and those who know the interdependence of the six forms of policy can play at pleasure with kings bound round with chains skillfully devised by themselves; but those chains based on human violence and suffering bind such kings and advisors and cause untold misery.

Kautilya values wealth most of all, for with money one can buy treasure and an army. Kautilya has been compared to Machiavelli. For Kautilya like Machiavelli also believes that the skill of intrigue is more important than enthusiasm and power when invading another country. He coldly calculates whether the expected profit will outweigh the loss of trained men and diminution of gold and grains, when deciding whether to march against enemies. By conciliation and gifts the conqueror should use corporations (mercenaries) against an enemy. But if they oppose him, he should sow seeds of dissension among them and secretly punish them. He may also use rewards for those who help him fulfill his promises to his people.

Kautilya does believe that the king should follow the will of the people. To Kautilya, whoever acts against the will of the people will also become unreliable. He should adopt the same mode of life, the same dress, language and customs, as those of the people. He should follow the people in their faith with which they celebrate their national, religious and congregational festivals or amusements.

Kautilya recommends that spies be used to persuade the local leaders of the hurt to be inflicted on enemies in contrast to the good treatment they might receive from their conqueror. He advises the extensive use of spies even in the guise of ascetic holy men. Various descriptions of magical potions and superstitions he gives are based on traditional folklore.

Economic and political functions of the state as found in Arthashastra are centered around the following areas: Life, role, excellence and qualities of a king; upright kingdoms; faithful citizens; the functions of governments; the duties of ministers, ambassadors, secretaries etc; planning and good process of decision-making; employment and the beauty of work; wealth and its role; a good army and the role of soldiers; agriculture and its importance; the various problems of the state like poverty, famine, crimes etc.

**1. Life, Excellence, Qualities and Duties of a King:** According to Kautilya, "The king who is well educated and disciplined in sciences, devoted to good government of his subjects, and bent on doing good to all people will enjoy the earth unopposed". A saintly king shakes off the aggregate of the six enemies like: lust, anger, greed, vanity, haughtiness and overjoy. He acquires wisdom, and restrains himself from the organs of senses. He is disciplined, maintains his subjects; employs good ministers for assistance; and keeps away from unrighteous transactions'

Kautilya discusses at length a king's schedule of work for each day. If a king is energetic, his subjects will be equally energetic, says Kautilya. He wants that a king should keep a time table/programme, each day. If he is accessible to people, he may be sure to avoid confusion and public disaffection. He should keep company with priests and teachers. He must believe in the dictum: "In the happiness of his subjects lies his happiness, in their welfare his welfare…the king therefore should ever be active and discharge his duties; for the root of wealth is activity, and of evil its reverse. By his good activities, a king can achieve his desired ends and abundance of wealth"

Referring to the qualities a king should have, Kautilya writes:

"Born of a high family, godly, possessed of valor, seeing through the medium of aged persons, virtuous, truthful, not of a contradictory nature, grateful, having large aims, highly enthusiastic, not addicted to procrastination, powerful to control his neighboring kings, of resolute mind, having an assembly of ministers of no mean quality, and possessed of a taste for discipline". These are the qualities of an inviting nature.

Again King's other qualities include, "inquiry, hearing, perception, retention in memory, reflection, deliberation, inference and steadfast adherence to conclusions, *i.e.,* the qualities of the intellect. Valor, determination of purpose, quickness, and probity are the aspects of a king's enthusiasm. He should be possessed of a sharp intellect, strong memory, and keen mind; energetic, powerful, trained in all kinds of arts, and free from vice".

Kautilya holds that a blind king is better than an erring king, because a blind king can be made by his supporters to adhere to whatever line of policy he ought to take. But an erring king who is bent upon doing what is against the science of Statecraft, brings about destruction to himself and to his kingdom by misadministration.

**2. Planning:** While talking about planning, Kautilya observes that king should plan his administrative measures after due deliberations in a well-formed council. The subject matter of the council should be entirely secret. Kautilya also refers to the duties of government superintendent in detail. Kautilya touches upon every possible area of administration starting from "formation of villages" and "division of land", to the duties of the superintendents of respective departments. Kautilya describes in detail the plan of how a fort should be built and a blueprint of a city within the fort.

**3. On Employment of Ministers and Others:** According to Kautilya Sovereignty (*rajatva*) is possible only with assistance. A single wheel can never move. Therefore, a king should employ ministers and councilors and listen to their advice. At the head of affairs there is a small body of elder statesmen, whom the king is advised to choose with the utmost care. The size of this privy council (*mantri-parishad*) varies. Men whose ability is inferred from their capacity shown in work, should be, having taken into consideration the place and time where and when they have to work, should be appointed as ministerial officers. The king should examine the character of ministers. He should ascertain their loyalty and disloyalty by temptations and through spies.

Kautilya makes it clear that those who are possessed of foresight, wise, of strong memory, bold, eloquent, skilful, intelligent, possessed of enthusiasm, dignity and endurance, pure in character, affable, firm in loyal devotion, also free from procrastination and fickle mindedness, and free from such qualities as excite hatred and enmity, should be appointed as ministers, councilors and priests.

**4. On Upright Government:** The elements of Government according to Kautilya, are 'the king, ministers, the country, the fort, the treasury, the army and the friends.' Excepting the enemy, these seven elements are said to be the limb-like elements of sovereignty.

"A wise king can make even the poor and miserable elements of his kingdom happy and prosperous; but a wicked king will surely destroy the most prosperous and loyal elements of his kingdom." "A wise king, trained in politics will, though he possesses a small territory, conquer the whole earth with the help of the best-fitted elements of his sovereignty, and never be defeated".

Kautilya claims: "acquisition and security of property are dependent upon peace and industry. Efforts to achieve the results of works undertaken are industry (*vyayama*). Absence of disturbance to the enjoyment of the results achieved from work is peace. The application of the sixfold royal policy is the source of peace and industry.

**5. Secret Service and Law:** Employing spies seems to have been common and part of royal administration in the ancient times. Kautilya too enjoins, " the king should create spies under the guise of a fraudulent disciple—a recluse, a householder, a merchant, an ascetic, a classmate, a firebrand, a poisoner, and a mendicant woman. Of these spies, those who are of good family, loyal, reliable, well trained shall be sent by the king to espy in other parts of his country (wandering spies) the movements of his ministers, priests, commanders of army" etc. Perhaps the least pleasant feature of political life in Arthasastra time was the espionage. The spy would enable a king to keep a finger on the pulse of public opinion.

Concerning law and justice Arthasastra says, "in cities and at places where districts meet, there will be three members acquainted with sacred law and three ministers of the king carrying out the administration of justice."

Ancient kings, it appears from Arthasastra, feared revenge and assassins. Against such possibilities they had a network of spies. They had arrangements for authorities in various districts and villages to know all comings and goings. People who were considered dangerous to the king and his rule would disappear without trace. King kept food tasters to avoid being poisoned.

**6. On Envoy/Ambassador:** Concerning qualities of envoys and ambassadors, Kautilya says, "The envoys and ambassadors shall make friendship with the enemy's officers etc. They will carry out their mission even at the cost of their own lives. Envoys and messengers are mouthpieces of the king. They will not care for the might of the enemy. They shall avoid liquor and women, and they will ascertain through spies the loyalty or disloyalty of the people of the enemy. They must be friendly to all and put on brightness in tone, face etc".

**7. On King's Secretaries and Courtiers:** Referring to the conduct of courtiers, Kautilya says, "A courtier possesses enough experience of the world and its affairs.

He will sit by the side of, and close to the king. He shall avoid speaking slyly; he shall never make false statements; he shall never interrupt the king while speaking; he shall tell the king both what is good and pleasing." "He shall avoid evil aspersions against others, not ascribe evil to others; he shall forgive evil done to himself and have as much forbearance as the earth". "When employed, he, the courtier shall follow the king in his pursuits after hunting, gambling, drinking, and sexual pleasures. Ever attending upon the king, he shall, by flattery, endeavor to arrest his fall into evil habits and save him from the intrigues, plots, and deceptions of enemies. He shall also endeavor to read the mind and appearance of the king. He shall show the net revenue after all kinds of expenditures are met with. He shall also show the exact particulars of whatever work he does".

**8. On well being of Kingdom:** Kautilaya speaks about the elements of kingdom and seeks protection of artisans, merchants, remedies against natural calamities, punishment of the wicked, detection of youth of criminal tendency, protection of all types of government departments, atonement for violating justice etc. It deals with categories of violations – both human and natural, and protection against them. These are the aggregates of a prosperous and peaceful kingdom.

**9. On Fort/Fortress:** Discussing the importance of forts and fortresses in the kingdom, Kautilya advocates that "on all four quarters of the boundaries of the kingdom, defensive fortifications against enemies shall be constructed: a water fortification, a mountainous fortification, a desert fortification and a forest fortification." He describes the demarcation of the ground inside the fort and the buildings within. "The fort shall contain twelve gates, provided with both a land and water and a secret passage".

This section gives a detailed account of what should be where, like king's palace, the apartment of gods, treasury, storehouse, houses, hospitals, shops, manufactories, guilds and corporations, roads, animals etc.

**10. On Wealth:** Kautilya holds that "wealth, wealth alone is important, in as much as charity and desire depend upon wealth for their realization.". Wealth, virtue and enjoyment form the aggregates of the three kinds of wealth. Of these, it is better to secure the first. While describing different kinds of wealth, Arthasastra mentions "wealth which, when obtained, increases the enemy's prosperity, or which causes loss of men or money, is dangerous wealth; wealth which causes fear from one's people is provocative wealth" etc.

**11. On Good Army:** Kautilya writes at length about army and its role. According to him, "the king himself should supervise the army". The army is one of the seven elements of sovereignty. Kautilya describes the various kinds of army in a kingdom. The army should be arrayed on a favourable position, facing other than the south quarter, with its back turned to the sun, and capable to rush as it stands. "The kshatriya caste is the best for army". His minister and priest should encourage the army. Astrologers and other followers of the king should infuse spirit into his army by pointing out the impregnable nature of the array of his army, his power to associate with gods, and his omniscience. Stationing the army so as to stand abreast is called a staff-like array (*danda*). Stationing the army in a line so that one may follow the other is called a snake-like array (*bhoga*). Stationing the army so as to face all the directions is called a circle-like array (*mandala*).

**12. On Agriculture:** Concerning the importance of agriculture to a Kingdom, Kautilya holds, 'The king should protect agriculture from oppressive fines and taxes, and cattle from thieves . . . and disease'. He must protect his citizens, and peasants in particular who are the ultimate source of prosperity. He further states, "there must be cultivable land, pasture land, well developed forests".

While describing the duties of the superintendent of agriculture, he explains how the superintendent shall ensure cultivation of state land, raise wet and dry crops and supervise harvests etc. " Lands may be confiscated from those who do not cultivate them, and given to others". For Kautilya the destruction of crops is worse since it is the labour that is destroyed thereby. Absence of rain is worse than too much rain.

**13. On Social Evils and other Problems:** Kautilya speaks about various social issues and problems that the king should give special care: 'They concern those orphans who are to be fed by the state and are put to study science and the duties of the various orders of religious life etc shall be employed as classmate spies'. The king should provide the orphans, the aged, the infirm, the afflicted, and the helpless with maintenance. He should also provide subsistence to helpless women when they are carrying and also to the children they give birth to.

Kautilya also sees the issues from people's welfare angle. For instance, "when, without making provision for the maintenance of his wife and children, any person embraces asceticism, he shall be punished; likewise any person who converts a woman to asceticism".

Kautilya discusses vices and calamities in detail. He describes the calamities of the elements of sovereignty; troubles of the king and of his kingdom; troubles of ministers; troubles of the army; troubles of the treasury; troubles of men (vices like gambling, drinking, addiction to women etc). He advises, "in order to avoid internal troubles, the king should keep under his control the powers of finance and army". "Of what kind the king's character is, of the same kind will be the character of his people".

**14. Characteristics of Enemy:** Kautilya explains at length all the wisdom relating to war. He advocates under certain circumstances going straightaway against the stronger enemy first, so that a subsequent engagement against the 'assailable' enemy may not be necessary. Kautilya describes the attitudes and behaviour of weak kings towards a strong monarchy. One example is, "The king should always make peace with an equal or superior king, and crush down an inferior." In other words, aggrandizement is human nature, and that a power superior in strength should launch a war against an inferior, and that war keeps a nation's blood circulation regular.

**15. On Citizenship:** Kautilya narrates the respective duties of four castes and of the four orders of religious life as determined by the three Vedas (*Sama, Rik and Yajus*). "Harmlessness, truthfulness, purity, freedom from spite, abstinence from cruelty, and forgiveness are duties common to all. The observance of one's own duty leads one to *Svarga* and infinite bliss (*Anantya*). When it is violated, the world will come to an end owing to confusion of castes and duties. Hence, the king shall never allow people to swerve from their duties. For whoever upholds his own duty, ever adhering to the customs of Aryas, and following the rules of caste and divisions of religious life, will surely be happy, both here and hereafter. For the world, when maintained in accordance with injunctions of the triple Vedas, will surely progress, but never perish. Kautilya concludes, this people (*loka*), consisting of four castes and four orders of religious life, when governed by the king with his scepter, will keep to their respective paths. They will ever devotedly adhere to their respective duties and occupations.

Kautilya, and following him other ancient authorities, agree that the ruler is the most important. He is the first, of the seven elements. Kautilya states that the King is the State. It is the King who appoints the ministers and superintendents. He takes measures of relief against calamities of other *Prakritis*; that the *Prakritis* bear the character with which the King stamps them. Hence the King occupies the position of preeminence. He is a perennial, never exhausting centre of power.

## Saptang Theory

The seven limbs as enumerated by Kautilya represent all the four essential features of the state: Territory, Population, Unity and Organization. Territory and population are covered by *Janapada*. There is no *Janapada* since without people. The two other elements, unity and organization, are provided by *Swami*, an independent sovereign and *amatya*, the organization through which sovereignty is exercised over the *Janapada* territory and its people. *Swamy* denotes that the territory of which he is a lord is an independent political entity. The *Swamy* is called *Sakyasamanta*, powerful enough to repel an attack by a neighbouring state. *Durga, Kosha* and *Danda* are additional means through which authority of the sovereign is made more effective and invincible.

The King heads the list of seven constituent elements of the state. The King occupies a place of pivotal importance in the body politic. A chapter entitled 'The Aggregate of the Calamities of the Elements of the State' is devoted to explain the importance of the King. After discussing relative gravity of calamity befalling different constituent elements of the state, Kautilya asserts that for their progress and downfall, the other elements depend upon the King. In this contexts, Kautilya offers a detailed list of qualities with which the King should be endowed and for this special emphasis is placed on education and training of the ruler.

First there is a list of the qualities that win the heart of the people or that inspire their confidence in the King. The qualities enumerated make him approachable and accessible: The king comes from a noble family, he is godly, spirited, comforting the aged, virtuous, truthful, unfailing in his promises, grateful, taking broad views, highly enthusiastic, not given to procrastination, firm in mind, desirous of self-discipline, having a large council of ministers. These are called *Abhigamika gunas* (inviting qualities).

Next Kautilya mentions the *dhigunas* or *Prajnagunas*, intellectual qualities such as ability to learn, understand and reflect and discuss. Under the quality known as *Utsahaguna* are included bravery, quickness of decision, assiduity etc.

Then there follows a long list of qualities that go to make up personal endowment (*atmasampat*) and they are: sharp intellect and keen mind, freedom from vices, dignity, capacity to take remedial measures against dangers, foresight; readiness in respect of place and time, freedom from passion, anger, greed, obstinacy, fickleness and haste, observance of customs as taught by aged persons.

Kautilya for the first time formulates an integrated scheme of education, for the simultaneous development of the King's intellect and character. The ruler of unrighteous character cannot rely on the loyalty and support of his subjects: "Which enemy is to be marched against" asks Kautilaya. His instant answer is, "a powerful enemy with wicked character should be marched against, for when he is attacked, his subjects will not help him, but rather put him down or go to the side of the conqueror. But when the enemy of virtuous character is attacked, his subjects will help him or die with him."

Thus Kautilya emphasizes the importance of the personal character of the King. He indeed sees King's capacity for righteous deportment as basis to beneficial administration. A King of unrighteous character and of vicious habits will, even though he is an emperor, fall a prey either to the fury of his own subjects or to that of his enemies. But a wise King trained in politics (*dandaniti*) and possessing a good character, though ruler of a small territory will conquer the whole earth with the help of his *prakritis* (the elements of the state).

According to Kautilya, the King is the guardian of law, not its maker. Royal decree has an independent validity of its own. It must prevail against equity (*dharma*) (*Vyavshara*) private contract and (*charitra*) usage. Kautilya also exalts reason (*nyay*) above the prescription of texts (*sastra*) in case of a conflict between the two. These statements that Kautilya makes at the head of section on the administration of justice in the Arthashastra clearly point to an attempt on his part to evolve a new norm in civil law. In the establishment of this civil law, royal authority would be actively exerted both directly by the King himself and indirectly by the judgment and rulings of higher officials of the state delivered in the name of the King.

The foremost duty of a King is protection of the people. Kautilya says people overcome by anarchy (*Matsyanyaya*) make Manu, son of Vivasvat, Sun-god, their King. They agree to pay one sixth of produce. Pleased by this, the King takes the responsibility of maintaining security and safety of their subject. The protection of people is therefore the prime duty of the King.

By protection here is meant primarily the protection of the person and property of the subjects. *Kantakashodhana* is concerned with the protection of the people from antisocial elements like deceitful artisans, traders etc., who by their hole and corner policy cause inconvenience and financial loss to the society. Also the people have to be protected from natural calamities such as fire and flood.

Protection of *Svadharma* is another duty of the state or for that matter, of the King. The King must ensure that people of different castes and order can perform their duties without any obstruction. But they are not to transgress the laws of the realm.

The duties of the King include ensuring *Yogakshema* to the subjects. The word *Yogakshema* means, acquisition of what has not been acquired (*yoga*), and preservation of what has been acquired (*Kshema*). Both the terms may be taken to mean security of possession. In fact *Yogakshema* in Kautilya has a wider connotation. It implies the material welfare, prosperity and happiness of the people. To achieve these objects the state is to undertake colonization of virgin land (*shunyanivesah*), build dams (*setubandha*), tanks and other irrigational projects. It has to, secure pastures (*vraja*) for cattle, open trade routes and ensure safety on them as well as working of mines etc. When the subjects are struck down by natural calamities it is the King who should take care of them like a father.

It is the duty of the state to maintain minors, aged persons and those in distress, when they have no one to look after them. The maintenance of the families of soldiers who have died in battle is also a charge upon the State.

The protection and welfare of the people is possible only through the proper exercise of the coercive authority of the State (*Danda*). With the help of the *Danda*, the ruler is to prevent might from proving right. It is *Danda* that enables the weak in holding their own against the strong. In the absence of *Danda, matsyanyaya* (anarchy) will prevail. But use of *Danda* requires great care. Only a just use of *Danda* can secure the protection of the subjects. The unjust use of this coercive power by the ruler might lead to serious consequences, including revolt of the subjects against the ruler.

Administration of justice is one of the most important functions of the King who is known as the fountainhead of justice (*dharmapravartaka*). In meting out justice the King should make no distinction between his son and the enemy. Punishment is to be meted out according to the gravity of the offence. In the capital the King is to administer justice in person. He has to appoint Judges at important centers (*Janapada Sandhi*), frontier post (*Sangrahana*), headquarters of ten villages, *dronamukha,* the headquarter of 400 villages and the *Sthaniya,* the chief city among eight hundred villages.

Kautilya says, "Kingship is possible only with assistance". Therefore the need of ministers. In this connection, in *Arthashastra,* there accur three words *mantri, amatya* and *sachiva*. *Amatya* is rather a general word for higher bureaucracy. The highest category of the *amatya* is the *mantrins*. Only those who came out successful in all the four tests (*upadha*) are appointed as *mantrins*. They form the topmost strata of the administrative bureaucracy. The King deliberates over the policy of the state with three or four ministers. It is consultation with them that enables the King to decide a definite action (*Arthanischaya*). The priest or *Purohita* is another important member to be consulted.

Beside the small body of counselors or advisers, the King must have a regular council of ministers, the *Mantriparisad*. Kautilya also recommends a large body of council of ministers *Akshudraparisad*. Since the King has to transact such vast administrative business, he should do this along with his whole council of ministers. For example, the King is not to give interview to an ambassador without being attended by the council of ministers. In case of any urgent business cropping up, the King should summon both his counselors (*Mantrins*) and his council of ministers (Mantriparishad). The King ought to act in accordance with the decision of his council of ministers or whatever is conducive to secure the object (*Karyasudhikaram*).

The council of ministers is largely responsible for shaping the policy of the government on such matters as are given below:

(1) Means of undertaking works including expedition into enemy's territory.
(2) Gathering of resources in men and material in relation to external and internal policy of the kingdom.
(3) Use of discrimination with regard to *Desa* and *Kala i.e.,* place and time.
(4) Means of averting possible dangers and calamities arising from his own state and that of enemy's state.
(5) Results arising from such works undertaken (*karyasiddhi*).
(6) The council may further resolve to take new works, to complete the works undertaken and to improve works already executed.

Kautilya says that all administrative measures are to be preceded by sound deliberation in a well formed council. If the majority view is not likely to help him achieve his object, the King is free to reject such view and follow a course that will help him achieve his object. The *mantirparisad* is neither a cabinet in a constitutional monarchy nor a sovereign parliament. Its function is to advise the King and assist him in the formulation and execution of the policy.

The text here does not set any constitutional limit on the power of the King. What checks are thought of are indirect. In the first place, his (the King's) training in *Dandaniti* is expected to impress upon him that it is his own interest to make use of his power with judiciousness. He may perform his duties in accordance with Vedic way of life. This will serve to make him behave with moderation. The preceptor or *purohita,* though he has no power to enforce his will, will constantly remind the King of his duty. Furthermore preceptors or ministers should also restrain the king when he is seen to be doing something harmful. But this will not be a constitutional check, but only a sort of moral pressure. However the most effective check on the ruler's behaviour will be the fear of losing the throne. For oppressive rule is bound to lead to discontent among the subjects. This may lead them to rise in revolt against a tyrant King and bring about his overthrow or ouster.

A remarkable feature of administration discussed in the Arthashastra is the extensive network of spies used for a variety of purpose. The text mentions two types of spies—*Samastha* the establishment, the members of which are generally stationed in a single headquarter and the other *Sanchara* the (roving ones) or the wandering spies. They are the ones who move from place to place as their service may require. The spies are disguised as a student, a farmer, a merchant, a bogus ascetic, a nun etc. They collect informations and what ever information is collected by them is communicated to *Samaharta* or then on to the King.

These secret agents are used for detecting corruption among state servants. For it is recognized that despite all care is taken in the appointment of officers, cases of embezzlement of state funds may still often occur. Several ways of embezzlement are enumerated by Kautilya. Spies are also used to find out what the people think of the king. This helps the king to feel the pulse of the nation.

The state servants, particularly high officers are likely to be disloyal and may even turn traitors. Likewise officers may become susceptible to seduction because they are disgruntled. Suitable efforts are to be made to win over disgruntled officers so that they may not go over to the enemy state.

Kautilya rightly remarks that all undertakings depend upon *Kosha i.e.,* finance. In the discussion on the relative importance of the *prakritis i.e.,* the seven elements of the state, he expresses the view that the treasury is more important than the army. The latter can be raised and maintained only with the help of a well filled treasury. Besides it helps the pursuit of *dharma* and *kama*. Sound finances are essential for any state.

Agriculture yields the most important part of revenue. The state therefore is entitled to the produce of the crown land and one sixth of the produce of other land. *Shulka* or custom duty is levied not only on export or import, but also on indigenous products. The rates of excise vary from one sixth to one twentieth, except on foreign goods which are charged at the rate of one fifth of their value. When the goods are brought along the water ways they have to pay duties and other charges at the port. The state also maintains a fleet on its own that is to be out on hire to traders and fishermen.

The main heads of revenue may be summarized as follows:

(1) Share of the produce of land;
(2) other dues and cess on the land including irrigation charges and taxes on houses in town;
(3) income from crown land, from forests, from mines and manufacturers;
(4) the custom at the frontiers, and octroi tolls and ferry dues in the interior levied upon merchandise in transport;
(5) profits of coinage and gains from trade operation carried on by the government;

(6) fees for license of various kinds to be taken out by artisans, craftsmen, professionals, and traders;
(7) fines levied in the law courts, and
(8) miscellaneous receipts like presents, escheats of ownerless property and share in the treasure trove. In times of emergency benevolence (*pranaya*) are resorted to and the rich are compelled to pay considerable amount to the state under one pretext or the other.

When for some reason such as costly military adventure, the treasury gets depleted, efforts become necessary for its replenishment. Among measures what Kautilya mentions, some of the more significant ones are listed below:

(1) A levy on agriculturist ranging from one fourth to one third of stock with them
(2) Farmers are induced to grow crops as directed by the state. A levy on traders ranging 50 *panas* on dealer silver etc. to 5 *panas* on dealers of vegetable cooked food etc. is made. Even actors, singers are to pay half of their income and brothels are to augment the state treasury through the earnings of beautiful young maids;
(3) If these measures do not suffice, contributions should be requested for specific undertakings, and people should be pressed to contribute to their utmost capacity of; and
(4) rich men should be asked to pay according to their means conferring on them titles, decorations and other honors in return.

## Mandala Theory

The foreign policy of the state is summed up in the formula of *sadgunya* or the sixfold policy. This policy is associated with the theory of *rajmandala,* the circle states. The *mandala* theory is set in relation to a king who is *Vijigishu*. A *Vijigishu* is a King who is endowed with good qualities. His elements of the state are in good condition. An *ari* (actual or potential enemy) is a king who is immediate neighbour. It is assumed that an immediate neighbour is most likely to be an *ari*. A *mitra* (ally) is he who is separated from the *Vijigishu* by the intervention of the Kingdom of an enemy (*ari*). *Ari mitra* is enemy's ally with territory beyond that of *mitra Miramitra*, the ally of *Vijigishu's* ally in the territory beyond that of territory of *mitra Mitramitra*; the ally of *Vijigishu's* ally in the territory beyond that of *Arimitra*. *Arimitramitra* the ally of enemy's ally *parsnigraha* is the enemy in the rear of *Vijighishu.*

Kautilya relates the theory of *Mandalas* to the theory of three *Shaktis* and six fold policy *Sadgunya.* Success depends upon how the King is able to put each of his *Shaktis* to their utmost. These three *Shaktis* are: *Mantra Shaki* the power of counsel, *i.e., Mantra Prabhushakti* that of material resources and *Utshshakti*, that of King's energy.

The circle of twelve states gives rise to the employment of six fold policy *Sadgunya* expressed in the following two ways:

(1) *Sandhi*, making an agreement of making treaty or policy of peace
(2) *Vigraha* – taking up a hostile attitude or a policy of hostility, the policy of *Yana i.e.,* preparing for launching an attack on one's enemy.

1. The *Vijigishu* should conclude peace when he finds himself weaker than the enemy.
2. He should wage war when he finds himself to be in the stronger position.
3. He should take to neutrality when he thinks that no enemy can hurt him nor is he himself strong enough to destroy the enemy.
4. He should march against the enemy if he is very strong.
5. He should take to refuge when he is weak.
6. He should adopt dual policy in a situation when he finds that he is in need of extraneous help.

Kautilya explains the conditions justifying severally the application of six type of policy towards the attainment of progress. He details a number of contingencies in which King may expediently use different methods to achieve his ends. He may promote his own productive work at the expense of those of his enemy or strengthen his own political as well as military position to the detriment of the enemy. The basic principle to serve as a guide is that while progress should be fundamental objective of all types of foreign policy, the particular type should be so selected as to ensure the maximum advantage for the King. "The purpose of all policies is to grow stronger in the long run, than the enemy."

By a judicious use of the six fold policy, the King should endeavour to pass from a condition of deterioration to that of stagnation and then to that of progress. The purpose of all policy is to secure an increase in one's power at the cost of natural enemy. This increase in power has to be a preliminary to the realization of the ambition to conquer the world. The six-fold policy is to be solely guided by this consideration. The interest of one's own state is to be the supreme criterion. It is expediency which should help to decide as to which policy will be more advantageous under the circumstances. The appropriate use of six measures may enable a *Vijigishu* to play with other Kings just as he pleases. Besides the six-fold policy there is also mention of four *upayas* or expedients, *sama, dama, bheda* and *danda*. It is said that the first two should be pursued to subjugate a weak King and the last two to vanquish the strong one.

Thus the Saptang Theory as propounded by Kautilya remains his monumental contribution to the science of politics and administration. It contains all the elements that may contribute to good governance.

## CONCLUSION

A realist to the core, Kautilya realizes that every nation acts to maximize its own interests and power. Alliances are only good so long as they appear in the best interest of both parties. However, as soon as the balance of power shifts allies may become enemies… and enemies may become allies. Since this is the natural order and to be expected, it is, therefore, only reasonable of the king to maintain his own kingdom's best interest at heart when dealing with foreign powers, be they friend or foe.

One retains an ally, not because of goodwill or a moral obligation, but due to one's strength. It is by the use of strength that one can advance both one's own self-interest as well as that of an ally. When one has an army, one's ally remains friendly, or the enemy becomes friendly.

The fact that countries act in their own self-interest is a timeless principle. Treaties are intended for states of equal power. Having an ally is good. But alliances only last as long as they are in the ally's self-interest.

There may be an abrupt change in the strength of any kingdom. It may be due to number of unforeseen events, such as famine or earthquake. And should a kingdom be weakened by calamity, it will become a ripe field for conquest. This renders even times of peace into potential portents to erupt into warfare. Therefore, it is only right that the king should be in a state of perpetual preparedness to meet any such eventuality. In the world of conflictual international politics, it is only natural that nations will interact with one another through dissension and force in which no conquest is unjust.

Kautilya firmly believes in a just king as a true conqueror. It is indeed such a king who carries out his duties and rules according to the law. He protects his people, hands down only just pronouncements, and applies the rules equally to "his son or his enemy". It is such a king who will "conquer the world up to its four ends".

The statecraft outlined in the Arthashastra is aimed entirely at conquering one's enemy and his territory, bringing more wealth to the kingdom, allowing the king to raise more armies and conquering more territory with the ultimate goal of conquering the world. To accomplish this will depend on the correct appraisal of the strength of the enemy as well as strength and weakness of various neighbours.

Naturally, if conquering weaker enemies is the chief end, wealth is the key to raise successful armies. This means a method of paying for weapons, chariots, and elephants, as well as keeping the soldiers well-fed, well-paid, and happy. It does not mean the purchasing of mercenaries for defence or for war because they are seen as unreliable. However to tackle stronger enemies, there is the outlet of diplomacy which must be given a fair trial.

The goal of Kautilya's science is power. For him, "power is strength" and "strength changes the mind." The more powerful a king becomes, the more likely it will be that he can affect not only the views and actions, but possibly loyalties of those with whom he deals–both subjects and enemies.

The first and foremost goal of the king must be to destroy his enemies and protect his own people, to bring his subjects the "three goods of life", namely material gain, spiritual good, and pleasure. In the happiness of his subjects lies the king's happiness, in their welfare his welfare. He shall not consider as good only that which pleases him but treats as beneficial to him whatever pleases his subjects.

About the same time, around centuries before Christ, there have been the renowned Greek philosophers like Thales, Plato and Aristotle, and Chinese philosopher, Confucius and Indian sage Kautilya.

Kautilya's *Arthasastra* is oriented to practical politics. In the classical Hindu view of personal evolution, there are four aims or ends in life:

1. *Artha* (accumulation of material wealth and family, implying all the strategies of survival, all the diplomacy of private and public politics and the manipulation of power and wealth);
2. *Kama* (the quest for pleasure and love);
3. *Dharma* (the laws of moral action and religious rituals); and
4. *Moksha* (spiritual release, redemption and transcendence).

The Arthasastra is devoted to the first aim in life, that is science of property and material success. This success includes political and diplomatic strategy. It aims at according to Kautilya, uniting all kingdoms under one king, Chandragupta. Apart from this principal concern Kautilya seems to have had little time for other aspects of life. His book has no *Dharma*. It is totalitarian and secular in nature. It is pragmatic in the sense that there is no permanent friend or enemy in politics – " my enemy's enemy is my friend". It maintains that royal ordinance can rightly override all other sources of law, which is disagreed by many theorists.

Some of the modern ideas of organization, planning, administration, management and bureaucracy are found elegantly enshrined in some sections of the Arthasastra. The State, in Kautilya's days, has been primarily the king, and so, kingship is dealt with in substantial detail: the qualitative aspects of a king's personality and leadership such as education, training for leadership and personal conduct. While most of their precepts primarily apply to king's handling of projects, finance and warfare, many of the instructions on normal life's requirements will apply equally to educated and virtuous people of today.

# 20

# GANDHI ON SWARAJ

Widely acclaimed as one of the most original and influential political thinkers and activists of the 20th century, Mohandas Karam Chand Gandhi (1861-1948) never wrote a systematic political or philosophical work in the mode of Thomas Hobbes or Hegel. The pamphlets and books he wrote are extremely diverse in topics. They cover a range of topics from, a critique of modern civilization, the place of religion in human life, the meaning of nonviolence, social and economic programs, even health issues etc. These works are constructed upon a series of concepts such as Satyagraha, Swaraj, Sarvodaya, Truth, Means and Ends and many others. Gandhi elaborates and weaves these concepts into thematic strands. The interconnections are related to his life and action. They are presented in a way that the pieces fit together. If they fall short of creating a comprehensive and systematic whole, they at least develop into a profound reflection on the nature of civilization, politics, society and religion.

Years before Gandhi becomes the great leader of the Indian independence movement and hailed by Tagore as the Mahatma, Gandhi had clearly elaborated his idea of a Truth-seeking civilization. In a booklet titled *Hind Swaraj*, translated in English as *Indian Home Rule* written on a trip back from London to South Africa in November of 1909 , Gandhi formulates his devastating critique of modern civilization as a mode of life under which "the nations of Europe are becoming degraded and ruined day by day".

### Critique of Modern Civilization: Towards Swaraj

From Gandhi's point of view, modern (western) civilization exemplifies the fact that "people living in it make bodily welfare the object of life". What is basically lacking in this civilization is any sense of morality, religiosity, duty and self-restraint as qualities of the soul.

Writing in *Hind Swaraj*, Gandhi makes it plain that this civilization takes note neither of morality nor of religion. Its votaries calmly state that their business is not to teach religion. Some even consider religion to be a superstitious growth. In their view, though the civilization seeks to increase bodily comforts, it fails miserably even in doing this. Gandhi calls this civilization irreligious. He laments that it has taken such a hold on the people in Europe that those who are in it appear to be half mad.

Gandhi's critique of modern civilization does overlook many of its strengths: its scientific and critical spirit of inquiry; its human control over the natural world; its organizational capacity etc. This is to say that Gandhi, far from rejecting the liberative contribution of modernity in *Hind Swaraj,* seeks to integrate these positive elements with a liberating reinterpretation of tradition. His critique of modern civilization embodies his rejection of colonialism and industrialism. His apprehension about rationality is truncated by materialism. He tries to translate modernity into a comprehensible world, where it is possible to find a moral foundation as opposed to the moral inadequacy of western civilization as model for free India.

Gandhi, thus, defines civilization primarily as a moral enterprise. In his words: "Civilization is that mode of conduct which points out to man the path of duty. Performance of duty and observance of morality are convertible terms. To observe morality is to attain mastery over our mind and our passions. So doing, we know ourselves". By defining civilization in moral terms, Gandhi not only sets himself against the very basic ethos of the modern West which is deeply embedded, according to him, on the two principles of 'might is right' and 'survival of the fittest', but also guides his readers toward a new definition of the concept of Swaraj.

To Gandhi, Swaraj does not mean simply replacing British rule with Indian rule. It is "much more than simply wanting English rule without the Englishman; wanting the tiger's nature but not the tiger" Political independence, to him, is not an end in itself. Swaraj is above all about individual autonomy. It involves self-respect, self-restraint and maturity.

Gandhi appeals to individual Indians to free themselves mentally and through character development from internal and external colonization. If this transformation occurs, then Swaraj as an experience of self-rule and self-discipline will come automatically. In other words, his aim is to revitalize the idea of civilization as dharma, meaning a sense of order. It is a quality of the soul and duty toward other human beings. This can be done through a redefinition of self-government as self-actualization.

Gandhi's remarks on the individual experience of Swaraj are very significant. This is how Gandhi formulates the ideal of Swaraj: "Do not consider this Swaraj to be like a dream. There is no idea of sitting still. The Swaraj that I wish to picture before you and me is such that, after we have once realized it, we will endeavor to the end of our lifetime to persuade others to do likewise. But such Swaraj has to be experienced by each one for himself".

For Gandhi, if civilization is dharma, Swaraj is an experience of truth. Under Swaraj, a community lives by its own truth. It conducts its affairs in the light of its traditions and values, while remaining alert to their limitations. Seen in this light, Swaraj means the capacity for self-government as an experience. It starts at the bottom and not at the top. Gandhi calls this experience as deliberative democracy. It may be seen as a process of enforcing civic engagement and empowering civil society vis-à-vis the state. But there is no empowerment of citizenship and democracy without the idea of self-actualization.

What Gandhi criticizes in modern civilization is the process of reduction of self-restraint and self-actualization to self-interest. Therefore, to value human freedom only as the freedom to pursue one's self-interest lacks moral and spiritual depth. It creates a life devoid of meaning and truth. He reasons why the achievements of modern civilization have turned into forces of evil. His answer is that the spirit of truth is turned into falsehood by modernity. The dharmic nature of civilization has been swept aside, with the diminished passion for search for truth. For Gandhi the truth is actually the spirit of search for truth. When it comes to his own life, he sees it as 'An Experiment with Truth'. He never claims any finality about his conclusions, but keeps an open mind regarding them. This is why Gandhi compares Swaraj to a house with its windows and doors open. Quoting the Rigvedic prayer he says: "May the noble winds from all over the world blow into my house".

## Gandhi's Concept of Swaraj

So, Swaraj, to Gandhi, means essentially "being open to others". At the same time it means building a character for oneself, by living one's life as a moral project. In other words, individuals's autonomy consists in being honest to one's moral commitments and not being governed only by one's instincts.

For Gandhi, freedom is not only a right but mainly a duty. "Real rights are a result of performance of duty", says Gandhi. All rights to be deserved and preserved come from duty well done.

Fundamental rights can only be those rights, the exercise of which is not only in the interest of the citizens but that of the whole world...Rights cannot be divorced from duties. This is how Satyagraha is born, when striving to decide what one's duty is. In this sense, Swaraj is not just a state of self-proclamation of freedom but a state of moral living, a total commitment to truth.

True freedom, for Gandhi, is not merely the freedom to do what one desires, but also the ability to ensure that what one chooses is the result of a sense of duty and self-knowledge. This choice is done not as a "freedom from restraints" but as "freedom through restraints". In fact, it is a self-imposed restraint. It is nothing but self-regulation, self-discipline and self-governance. Therefore, Swaraj is not only freedom from coercion and domination, it is also self-regulation through self-restraint.

Hence, self-restraint forms an indispensable part of Gandhi's concept of Swaraj. This also explains the reason of his disapproval of a restraint-free civilization. So does his rejection of all what compels an individual to be the slave of his instincts.

A true civilization is thus a state of self-transcendence through self-restraint. It is the essence of Swaraj as well. It's a process of making mistakes and unmaking them. In other words, freedom should provide conditions of growth of an individual with the civilizing process resulting from an inner reform of the individual. As for the outward independence, it is a yardstick to measure the freedom of self within. There can be no outward self-rule without the experience of truth. And there is no experience of truth without self-realization and moral freedom.

## Swaraj as Swadeshi and Sarvodaya

The true Swaraj is the reign of moral freedom. It is the conquest of the demands of the senses for the realization of the higher self. This means Swaraj is the realization of the higher self. It is not only self-sufficiency and self-reliance, what Gandhi calls Swadeshi, but is also the service of all. The spirit of Swadeshi is duty and responsibility toward the community. The major accent of it is on the idea of national self-reliance through economic and political expressions such as developing homespun cloth and boycotting foreign cloths. In the spinning wheel Gandhi sees the symbol of self-reliance. In its daily use he sees India's desire for self-determination.

Gandhi insists that our attention should first be given to our own indigenous resources and culture. For he regards self-reliance as the basis of self-rule. In this context he also points to the significance of Swadeshi in the quest for Swaraj. Thus the concept self-reliance, Swadeshi and Swaraj are interrelated. They are all rooted in a common tradition. Yet, he emphasizes the need to remain alert to their limitations, especially corruptions that have set in this tradition. Therefore, he does not countenance a self-governed and a self-realized culture which does not participate in a dialogue with other cultures. Swaraj, to him, is thus a means of translating the self-governance into a larger human community.

Gandhi talks at length about Sarvodaya. He sets out to use and refine this concept of Sarvodaya after reading Ruskin's *Unto This Last* in South Africa. Sarvodaya means "the welfare of all". It is a concept opposed to the utilitarian principle "greatest good of the greatest number". He summarizes the idea of Sarvodaya in Ruskinian contents such as: the good of the individual is contained in the good of all; all men have the same right to earn a living from their labor; and a life of labor where one works with one's hands is a life worth living. His concern for the welfare of all is revealed most clearly in his treatment of the untouchables and women in India.

For Gandhi, a community which can get rid of all its violence and illegitimate possessions can share its resources, both natural and human, with the rest of humanity. Once describing his ideal for a free India, he notes, "I want the freedom of my country so that other countries may learn something from my free country, so that the resources of my country might be utilized for the benefit of mankind…" Freedom and independence in the Indian context involves, for Gandhi, not only dedication to the well-being of India, but also commitment to the service of humanity.

Gandhi puts premium on the duty of humans in the making of a humane society that will be in balance with the order of the universe. He asserts that the essential nature of an individual is to seek self-realization and spiritual elevation. And this essential search for self-realization and truth can only be through the pursuit of dharma. Dharma, as the very name connotes means a set of principles and codes of conduct that enable an individual, society, or a civilization to attain their true nature. As a result, dharma is not only the real nature of our actions but also the ground which supports or upholds these actions. It is the permanent universal truth. Therefore, practising one's dharma as a duty is to contribute to cosmic order. Keeping these definitions in mind, dharma may be defined as the ethico-moral order of the universe. It is the righteous path of performing one's duty. This disinterested Karma or duty when realized, leads one gradually towards the goal of full liberation. On this issue, Gandhi is closely inspired by the ancient Vedic culture with its unique meaning of Swaraj.

Swaraj is perfect freedom from all bondage. Gandhi equates it with moksha or liberation. Swaraj is attainable by degrees and every advance needs be measured against the highest ethico-normative ideals. Swaraj on the individual level entails self-awareness. It is indeed a matter of conscious choice. It has to be an intelligent and responsible choice. The satyagrahi or the one who holds fast to truth, should become actor rather than reactor. There is no Swaraj so long as there is the fear of death. Swaraj requires cultivation of the capacity for dispassionate self-assessment, and ceaseless self-purification. It involves continuous self- restraint and progressive self-realization. It is connected with the sense of ever-growing Swadeshi or Self-reliance.

In terms of Gandhi's metaphysics, the individual and national Swaraj are inseparable. Self-rule by the same yardstick is incompatible with every form of exploitation. Any demand of Swaraj implies Swaraj not for oneself alone, but for his neighbour, too. Swaraj is the basic characteristic of the free individual. It is also the basis for communitarian Swaraj. This is not only the foundation for national Swaraj, but also complete roadmap of leading us to a world dedicated to Satya and Ahimsa. It has a potential, thus, to become the basis of global Swaraj, a universal Ramarajya or Golden Age.

Swaraj entails both Self-rule and Self-reliance. Each unit in this expanding circle needs to stand on its own moral worth and lend strength to the others. Instead of centralized government, Swaraj can be realized only in a decentralized confederation of village republics. This confederational structure will be composed of innumerable villages, ever-widening, never-ascending circles. Life in them will not be a pyramid with the apex sustained by the bottom. But it will be an oceanic circle whose centre will be the individual who is always ready to perish for the village and the latter *i.e.,* the village ready to perish for the circle of villages, till at last the whole becomes one life composed of individuals. Such individuals by nature will never be aggressive in their arrogance. They will ever be humble and always willing to share the majesty of the oceanic circle of which they are integral units.

With such a structure in place, the outermost circumference *i.e.,* the world federation of autonomous village republics will not wield power to crush the inner circle. Rather it will give strength to all within and derive its own strength from it. Despite this picture of Global Village Swaraj being something Utopian, Gandhi argues, if Euclid's point, in true conceptual terms is incapable of being drawn by human agency, still it has an imperishable value for the building blocks of the universe, in the same way, India needs to emulate this true picture, though never realizable in its completeness.

The struggle for independence, or National Swaraj, Gandhi views, from the broader perspective of Ideal Swaraj. It is not through independence for its own sake, but only through National Self-rule that India can become an active champion of international cooperation and global interdependence. Enslavement of millions by the British Raj, he notes, has the effect of preventing them from making a vital contribution to the Universal Swaraj of humanity.

Gandhi insists that any continuance of alien rule is demoralizing to the ruled. While the oppressed endure indirect complicity with imperial iniquity, their own legitimate aspirations persistently are seen getting frustrated. Thus not merely political independence but authentic Swaraj, he observes, can originate only at the individual and village level. If individual Swaraj involves a constant process of self-purification, National Swaraj requires national self-purification. The latter goal involves the removal of social abuses, the elimination of economic exploitation, and the transcendence of religious differences. Swaraj, as Gandhi sees it, involves the inauguration of spiritual rebirth. It can be achieved through the radical reconstruction of internal structures, and the comprehensive reform of an entire social system. While denouncing imperial rule, he also identifies the weaknesses and shortcomings that Indians themselves will have to overcome in order to realize true Swaraj.

## Swadeshi and Swaraj

For Gandhi, Swadeshi is Self-reliance and an integral component of Swaraj. To him, Satya and Ahimsa can be taken as absolute values. Just as Ahimsa is logically dependent upon Satya, so does Swadeshi follow logically from Swaraj. Swaraj is derived from Satya. It implies that Self-rule is the expression of the intrinsic truth of the individual. Since Swadeshi being rooted in Ahimsa, complete nonviolence will therefore require full Self-reliance.

As a validating principle Swaraj comes prior to Swadeshi, though in daily practice it is Swadeshi that provides the measure of realized Swaraj. Swaraj, according to Gandhi, thus is both the individual and national goal, and Swadeshi is collective strength.

Self-reliance too does not connote any romantic notion of 'rugged individualism'. Rather it is an active force which expresses itself in phrases like 'self-help' and 'self-dependence'. Gandhi has preference for the English term 'self-reliance' because it is suggestive of an effort to do what one can for oneself, while leaving plenty of elbow room for mutual assistance. In Swaraj, therefore, ethical self-transformation and working for the welfare of all become one.

Similarly, for Gandhi, the freedom of the satyagrahi reflects utter unselfishness and altruism. It is the selfless service (anasakti yoga) as enjoined by the Bhagavad Gita. It means serving the needs of others effectively which ought to nurture the essential nature of the self. Although this is essentially a religious perspective it can be translated into an economic programme. It means our producing as much as possible for local consumption, and bartering the rest for necessities. In this connection, Gandhi's injunction is: obtain essential goods, only what is strictly required. He rejects consumer economics because he is convinced that it encourages mass poverty and it is also a social disease. Thus Swadeshi, to him, is 'patriotism' in a political context and 'dharma' in a moral context. Fusing these two contexts, new dimensions are seen in both. Swadeshi is seen as service, simultaneously confirming benefits not only on ourselves but also on our families, our country and the world.

In the protracted struggle for Swaraj, Gandhi's continuous emphasis is on the principle of the Swadeshi, Constructive Programme, the revitalization of Panchayats, the development of indigenous institutions of New Education or *Nai Talim*, and the emergence of village industries through the use of the spinning wheel or charkha. He is willing to defend each of these programmes on its own merits. But he is convinced that Indian Swaraj shall have no lasting foundation without the systematic application of Swadeshi.

The principle of nonviolence, and application of Swadeshi need be examined in relation to the principle of Satya or Truth. This is essential for periodic self-correction and mental purgation. Specific means of attaining Swadeshi must likewise be examined and assessed in terms of their fidelity to the ideal of Swaraj. Viewed in this light, the pursuit of Swaraj through Swadeshi, for Gandhi, is a matter of individual judgment. It is based upon appeals to conscience and experience. He firmly believes that Swaraj through Swadeshi can come about only if every aspect of life is given adequate attention. All attempts to divide life into separate and discrete compartments have to be avoided by all means.

## Sarvodaya and Swaraj

Gandhi's concept of Satya as the end and, Ahimsa as the means, enables him to develop his philosophy of Satyagraha and Sarvodaya. They are the crucial levers for non- violent social transformation. Though he delineates no plan for social transformation, his ideal of Ramarajya remains at the heart of his political vision. He realizes that Ahimsa will eventually win global acceptance as a universal criterion of civilized life. It is a force behind the magical power of millions striving for a common cause. This gives the masses a clear, if intuitive, sense of direction towards the goals of Swaraj. It symbolizes individual emancipation as well as national and global independence.

Sarvodaya is based upon the principle of diffusion of power. It is yoked to a firm recognition of the moral priority of social virtue over sectional interest. Competition must make way for concord. It must enable us to fulfill a spiritual requirement in a civilized world. It has to become a revolutionary enterprise which will eventually benefit all humanity. The individual seeker and society as a whole has to enrich itself and the macrocosm through mutual responsiveness and responsibility. In practical terms, the axis of social life calls for a critical shift from an aggressive emphasis on rights to an active concern and obligation towards his fellowmen. All material and psychological exploitation that causes poverty and dehumanization has to come to an end. For this the constructive innovativeness of the technological age, need replace soulless mechanization and trivial gadgetry.

Gandhi advocates the development of a true science of economics. It has to be based upon the principle of Sarvodaya. It will be directed towards an intelligent regulation of the flow of wealth in terms of justice. In fiscal terms he defines Swaraj as "a just wage for a worker that which will secure him the same labour, when he needs it, as he has put in for us today". It is this which can let Swaraj to grow into all-fulfilling Sarvodya.

Gandhi rejects every form of exploitation. He views all human beings as equal sacrificers for the welfare of all based on Swaraj. He lays down this as the basis for a just redistribution of wealth. This principle is consistent with the sacrificial moral order (*rita*) of the cosmos. To achieve an egalitarian order, in the true Swaraj all men and women must act as trustees, rather than as owners of their resources. They ought to consider themselves as the partners of all their fellowbeings in society. Every individual needs to weigh his or her circumstances in the court of conscience according to the criteria of truth and nonviolence and the obligations of Sarvodaya.

Such a radical redefinition of both the means and ends of production can bring about a fundamental reform of society. It can at the same time also reverse the rising tide of personal expectations which has become the bane of predatory consumerism today.

Gandhi's advice to political workers is to immerse themselves in the Constructive Programme and to engage in "Bread Labour". They should always be willing to sacrifice their comforts in the service of *daridranarayan*, God in the form of the poor. He terms this the path of universal service. It involves the practice of a nonviolent socialism or Sarvodaya rooted in a sense of mutual trust among all classes of society. In his Swaraj all members of the individual body are equal. In it the prince and the peasant, the wealthy and the poor, the employer and the employee are all on the same level.

### State Power Versus Enlightened Anarchy

Gandhi shows deep concern for the entrenched tendency of State Power to degenerate into active violence. He is deeply concerned lest human beings should lose their humanity and in the process lose their souls. This may happen if individual were to abdicate his or her moral responsibility for the sake of the Leviathan. For Gandhi, the onus of responsibility for human life and universal welfare rests with the conscience of individuals. It will be a dangerous delusion to suppose that a human being can relinquish any portion of this responsibility in the name of social contract or legal sovereignty, tacit consent or rule of law. Man being a moral agent, it will be wrong for him to give unconditional consent, for any reason, to the general body of laws, pronouncements and programmes of any political institution. The freedom of the individual to serve the cause of universal welfare (Sarvodaya) must be preserved against the claims of state authority. Only this will preserve the regenerative influence of truth- force.

The ultimate political ideal for Gandhi is Swaraj. It is interpreted by some writers as a state of enlightened anarchy. It is a state in which each person is his own ruler. But the goal of stateless society in today's world of oligopoly and institutionalized violence is but a distant dream. Authentic progress towards Swaraj will depend upon the resolves of men and women of courageous compassion and calm determination who are constantly searching within themselves the seeds of wisdom and strength. Progress towards the goal of Swaraj is thus an endless journey. It is like Euclid's straight line. Though it has no breadth and no one has yet succeeded in drawing such a line and no one ever will, still, as Gandhi asserts, we can progress in geometry only by postulating such a line. This is true of every ideal.... The only way is for those who believe in it to set the example. He firmly believes, once the inward source of one's strength is touched, the long journey of individual and social regeneration will begin and culminate in the fullness of Swaraj of the individual and the society as a whole.

Gandhi very much wants to inculcate a sense of self-respect, self-confidence and self-reliance among the people to promote the power of decision-making in them. He wants every individual to acquire the capacity to resist the abuse of power. As Gandhi observes, although he does not want to be reborn, yet if he has to be, he should be born an untouchable so that he may endeavor to free himself and them from that miserable condition. Removal of Untouchability, Khadi and Hindu-Muslim Unity—form the essential ingredients of Indian Swaraj. Already in 1920, Gandhi categorically rejects "any religious doctrine that does not appeal to reason and is in conflict with morality." He abhors blind following and parochialism of every kind. His morality consists "not in following the beaten track but in finding the true path for ourselves and in fearlessly following it."

In every type of exploitation Gandhi sees the essence of violence. So he insists on the sharing not only of political power and social respect, but also of economic opportunity. In a free India, says Gandhi, the poor must enjoy the same power as the rich who must understand that their desires above and beyond the bare necessities are to be accommodated only after the essential needs of the poor are satisfied. He warns that a violent and bloody revolution will be a certainty one day unless there is a voluntary abdication of consumerism. He pleads for sharing for the common good, of riches and the power that riches give.

Gandhi argues that the socio-spiritual underpinnings of British political, economic, bureaucratic, legal, military, and educational institutions are inherently unjust, exploitative and alienating. Therefore as Pinto explicates in *Hind Swaraj*, Gandhi's chief focus is on the moral inadequacy of western civilization, especially its industrialism, as the model for free India. He rejects the deeply embedded principles of 'might is right' and 'survival of the fittest.'

Gandhi's call for Swaraj represents a genuine attempt to regain control of the 'self', our self-respect, self-responsibility, and capacities for self-realization. It has to be a struggle for liberation from institutions of dehumanization. It will be Swaraj when we learn to rule ourselves. The real goal of the freedom struggle, for him, is not only to secure political *Azadi* (independence) from Britain, but rather to gain true Swaraj (liberation and self-rule).

## Contemporary Relevance of Swaraj

How is Gandhi's concept of Swaraj relevant for us today? While it is easy to get caught up in the symptoms of our many crises which include the brutal violence, the enormous inequities, the extinction of cultures and languages, the degradation of the environment, it is equally important, if not more, to understand their roots. We must creatively analyze the content and the consequences of our current economic, political, social, and educational systems, without reverting to a romanticized past of pristine traditions. From these critical reflections, we must generate new spaces, systems, and processes. They are based on moral and holistic visions of human potential and human progress capable of leading man to the fullness of freedom. A visionary, he considers decentralized, direct democracy as key to peace. He believes that power resides in the individual and in self-rule.

Gandhi's concept of Swaraj is integral to three parallel action-reflection agendas for the 21st century: it retains the potential to extricate us from this multilayered crises in which man is caught today. Swaraj for humanity as a whole involves decolonization of the mind, critical traditionalism, and constructive regeneration.

Gandhi in his first order ideal is opposed to the State as a coercive agency. For it comprises means such as the military, police, prisons, courts, tax collectors, and bureaucrats. The State, to him, is concentrated violence. As he puts it: "In so far as the State represents violence in a concentrated and organized form, the State is a soulless machine. It can never be weaned from violence to which it owes its very existence."

Gandhi believes that 'the greatest good of all' can be realized only in the classless, stateless democracy. He differentiates between direct democracy and representative democracy. He rejects the latter. He looks with suspicion the centralizing power of western democracies which feed into violence. He thinks that in decentralization lies the key to world peace.

All the political power that is concentrated in the State, Gandhi asserts, can be devolved down to every last individual. When power will come to reside in the people, they can use it at any time. Gandhi says, "In such a state (of affairs), everyone is his own ruler. He rules himself in such a manner that he is never a hindrance to his neighbor." By reforming enough individuals and communities, he hopes society at large will also change. His concept of Swaraj elucidates intrinsic connection between the individual and society.

Gandhi's Swaraj translated into "self-rule" or "autonomy" entails a condition where every individual will take steps towards self-rule in their lives. Only then India will naturally move towards self-rule and manifest as a nation. He insists that everyone will have to take Swaraj for himself. If people become free, India becomes free. But true realization of Swaraj will be only when we learn to rule ourselves.

## Gram Swaraj to Global Village

Gandhi is critical of the liberal democratic tradition on three counts: First, it reifies the political self of man from his social self. Second, it contributes to objectification and technocratisation of the political realm. Thirdly, it results in the accentuation of man's alienation in the name of his people's political rights.

Gandhi's alternative to the western participatory democracy is a critique of the positivist disjunction between means and ends. This he spells out in clear detail in *Hind Swaraj*. Commenting on the West Minster Model, Gandhi writes: "A superficial study of British history has made us think that all power percolates to the people from parliaments. The truth is that power resides in the people and it is entrusted for the time being to those whom they may choose as their representatives. Let us not push the mandal theory to ridiculous extremes and become slaves to resolutions of majorities. Swaraj will be an absurdity if individuals have to surrender their judgement to majority. The very essence of democracy is that every person represents all the varied interests which compose the nation. It is true that it does not exclude, and should not exclude, special representation of special interests, but such representation is not its test. It is a sign of its imperfection". Again, "True democracy cannot be worked by twenty men sitting at the Centre. It has to be worked from below by the people of every village".

Without discounting the necessity of a Central Government to administer some areas, Gandhi stresses that it need not and ought not be patterned after the accepted Western form of democracy. What he objects to is the Central Government administration becoming the bearer of the alienated political rights of the citizens. Under his plan, the state will be there to carry out the will of the people, not to dictate to them or force them to do its will. Not unaware of the danger of full democracy turning into mobocracy, he declares, there can be no real democracy until the power is shared by all. To the argument that most people do not understand the complicated machinery of the Government, his answer is that every citizen silently, but none the less certainly sustains the Government of the day in the ways of which he has no knowledge.

Gandhi believes that real Swaraj will come not by the acquisition of authority by a few but by the acquisition of the capacity by all to resist authority when it is abused. Swaraj is to be attained by educating the masses to a sense of their capacity to regulate and control authority. While conceding the need for a Central Government administration, Gandhi wants it to be structured not as a pyramid but as an oceanic circle. In this type of set up which is to be composed of innumerable villages, there will be ever widening, never ascending circles. Life will not be a pyramid with the apex sustained by the bottom. But it will be an oceanic circle; its center will be the individual. He will always be ready to perish for the village, till at last the whole becomes one life composed of individuals. Such individuals will never be aggressive in their arrogance but ever humble. They will share the majesty of the oceanic circle of which they are integral units.

Gandhi's life-long-mission was to build a healthy and strong India based on the village system. He writes in 1936: "I would say that if the village perished, India will perish too. It will be no more India. Her own mission in the world will get lost". But he does not close his eyes to the obnoxious existential realities of Indian villages. This is very much evident from vivid descriptions of appalling conditions of Indian villages in his writings. "Instead of having peaceful hamlets dotting the land, we have dung heaps. The approach to many villages is not a refreshing experience. Often one would like to shut one's eyes and stuff one's nose. Such is the surrounding dirt and offending smell", he admits. However this state of affairs is not to be an irredeemable situation. This will very much be transformed by the villagers themselves, provided proper help and guidance are extended to them". To this end Gandhi offers a blueprint of one world based on Village Swaraj.

In Gandhi's Village Swaraj, the building blocks are: Trusteeship, Swadeshi, Full Employment, Bread labour, Self-sufficiency, Decentralization, Cooperation, Equality etc. This model village presents a comprehensive picture, encompassing the economic, political, social and educational dimensions. It includes meticulous details which incorporate in it a wide variety of practical things–cattle keeping, medical care, hygiene and sanitation, compost manure, eradication of untouchability, provision of basic education, cropping patterns and irrigation practices, indeed all those things which are crucial to building a peaceful village life.

Gandhi's vision of Village Swaraj is not anchored on the modern (Indian-industrial) notion of development but on the post-modern insistence on quality of life. It is very much alive to the harrowing experience of the evils wrought by modern urban industrialism. With the foresight of a prophet, Gandhi anticipates it quite early in his career. Hence his emphasis is on simple living on the pattern of village life wherein quality is the crux. Gandhi writes: "My ideal village will contain intelligent human beings. They will not live in dirt and drunkenness as animals. There will be neither plague, nor cholera, nor smallpox, nor one will be idle. No one will wallow in luxury. Every one will have to complete his quota of manual labour".

The model village of Gandhi is to be a settlement of a thousand souls. The programmatic blueprint among other will have the following broad features:

Education will be compulsory upto the basic course. As far as possible, every activity will be conducted on the cooperative basis. There will be no castes such as we have today with their graded untouchability. Nonviolence with its technique, satyagraha and noncooperation will be the sanction of the village community. The Government of the village will be conducted by the panchyat of five persons annually elected by the adult villagers.

Conceived as a basic unit, the village is also to be postulated as a link in the strong chain of society. It will 'be composed of innumberable villages with ever-widening, never ascending circles'. Life will not be 'a pyramid with the apex sustained by the bottom, but an oceanic circle whose center will be individual'. He will always be ready to perish for the village, the latter ready to perish for the circle of villages, till at last the whole becomes one life. Therefore, 'the outermost circumference would give strength to all within and would derive its own strength from it.'

In the final analysis, for Gandhi, the unit of society is a village or call it a manageable small group of people who will, in the ideal, be self-sufficient in the matter of their vital requirements as a unit and bound together in bonds of mutual cooperation and interdependence.

Gandhi's concept of Village Republic has been criticized broadly on two counts: (i) he conceives the village as an insulated system and that (ii) he opts for rural primitivism in utter disregard of the tremendous advantages that can accrue to humanity through the advance in technology. However, both these accusations are based on a widely prevailing ignorance about his position in this regard.

In Gandhi's scheme, interdependence goes with independence. It is based on man's social nature which distinguishes him from the brute creation. If it is man's privilege to be independent, it is equally his duty to be interdependent.

Gandhi considers it possible to reconstruct one village so that villages collectively, not villages individually, will become self-contained. Since in no circumstances can it be possible to produce all the things we need, so though our aim is complete self sufficiency, we shall have to get from outside the village what we cannot produce in the village. We shall have to produce more of what we can in order thereby to obtain in exchange what we are unable to produce.

Gandhi is clear that man is not born to live in isolation but is essentially a social animal independent and interdependent. Thus when he speaks of villages collectively striving for a self-contained system, he is advocating integrated area development. Similarly, having ruled out the possibility of complete self-sufficiency, he recognizes the need for regional specialization and exchange of goods between regions—a notion akin to balanced regional development.

The accusation that Gandhi opts for village primitivism is farther from truth. In one of his utterances in 1936, he clarifies his position thus: "There would be no objection to villagers using even the most modern machines and tools they can make and can afford to use". It implies that only a technologically developed village will have modern machines and only economically advanced villages can afford them. Thus he does not object to the villages being technologically or economically advanced but to villages being exploited by cities. He is keen to save the villages "from catching the infection of industrialism", though he does not object to heavy industries. "I do visualize electricity, ship building, iron works, machine making and the like, existing side by side with village handicrafts", says Gandhi. In his view, while hitherto industrialization has been so planned as to destroy the village crafts, in the state of the future, it will subserve the villages and their crafts. The coexistence between the city and village is possible only if a sane policy which permits a balance between them is pursued. Gandhian scheme very much provides for it. For Gandhi clarifies that: "under his scheme, nothing will be allowed to be produced by the cities which can equally well be produced by villages. The proper function of cities is to serve as clearing houses for village products". Viewed in this light, the accusation that villages will not be in a position to produce sophisticated high quality goods under Gandhian scheme equally flows from ignorance. He writes in 1937: "When our villages are fully developed there will be no dearth in them of men with high degree of skill and artistic talent. There will be village poets, village artists, village architects, linguists and research workers. In short, there will be nothing in life worth having which will not be had in villages". To dismiss such a high quality village life as primitive is a travesty of truth.

Much of what Gandhi stands for is nothing but modern, in being rational to the core. Negatively speaking, it is an onslaught against the exploitative tendency inherent in industrialism and domination by urbanism. In positive terms, it may be seen as an attempt to establish a nonviolent social order from which exploitation is completely eliminated. In this context, Gandhi writes as early in 1934: "For the city dwellers, the villages have become untouchable. He does not know them, he will not live in them, and if he finds himself in a village, he will want to reproduce the city life there". Gandhi wants the village people to fight against this superiority complex on the part of the urbanite by becoming self-reliant and autonomous. For that villages have to be self-contained before they are enabled to cater to the needs of the city dwellers.

However, in Gandhi's scheme of conflict resolution, even a confrontation has to necessarily lead to the conversion or change of heart of the oppressor. He is convinced that the citizens must realize the duty of making an adequate return to the villages for the strength and sustenance which they derive from them, instead of selfishly exploiting them. It is only then that the healthy and moral relationship between the city and village will spring up.

Gandhi very well knows the difficulties involved in bringing about a transformation in a positive direction of achieving a balanced relationship between the city and the village. Today the cities dominate and drain the villages of their lifeblood. To Gandhi, the exploiting of the villages is itself organized violence. Since Swaraj can be built only on nonviolence, for this the villages have to be given their proper place. Nonviolent society cannot be built on a factory civilization, but it can be built on self-contained villages. Rural economy has to eschew exploitation altogether because exploitation is the essence of violence. The nearest approach to civilization based on nonviolence, he notes, is the erstwhile village republic of India.

Gandhi enumerates various factors in a rural context which facilitate the building up a nonviolent social order:

First, it is possible to evolve a nonviolent occupational structure fundamentally free from violence involving no exploitation or envy of others. When a man is content to own only so much land as he can till with his own labour, he cannot exploit others. For example, some early handicrafts are seen to exclude exploitation and slavery as also a peasant way of life which is conducive to a nonviolent society.

Second, village life promotes the Swadeshi Spirit which restricts us to use and service our immediate surroundings to the exclusion of the more remote, be it in religion, polity or economy. This necessarily inculcates a spirit of independence and self reliance.

Third, in the milieu of the rural setup, everyone is encouraged to perform physical labour, which is a great social leveler. Return to the village life means a definite, voluntary recognition of the duty of bread labour and all it connotes. This notion of compulsory bread labour is indeed a measure having revolutionary vitality for social transformation.

Finally the principle of trusteeship has greater applicability in the context of the land-based economy of villages. Invoking the traditional injunction, 'all land belongs to Gopal' that is the community, Gandhi wants land to be collectively owned and managed. He advises the Zamindars to give their tenants fixity of tenure, take a lively interest in their welfare, provide well-managed schools for their children, night-schools for the adults, hospitals and dispensaries for the sick. The tenets must look after the sanitation of villages in a variety of ways. They (Zamindars) must make them feel that they are their true friends taking only a fixed commission for their manifold services. Thus Gandhi advises the Zamindars that they should be the trustees and trusted friends of the entire village community. In this way they can help facilitate the emergence of a nonviolent society.

One notices a certain theory gap mainly concerning in the nature of individual group relationship in Gandhian scheme of village life. The individual Gandhi thinks is of supreme consideration. No society can possibly be built on a denial of individual freedom. It is contrary to the very nature of man. But individual freedom ought not to be exercised for personal ends. Quite the contrary, individual freedom alone equips a man for the service of society. Unrestricted individualism, Gandhi asserts, is the law of the beast of jungle. Therefore man must learn to strike a mean between individual freedom and social restraints. In this connection he hopes that individual being pure, he should sacrifice himself for the family–and at last the nation and for all. This hope of Gandhi is in consonance with his notion of oceanic circle. The individual is expected to be in permanent readiness to sacrifice himself at the altar of society, yet retaining his freedom which is an essential prerequisite to serve the society. 'If the individual ceases to count, what is left of society'? Gandhi asks. Individual freedom alone can make a man voluntarily surrender himself completely to the service of the society. If it is wrested from him, he becomes an automation and society is ruined.

From the foregoing discussion, it follows:

(1) The interest of the individual and the group are harmonious,
(2) individual autonomy and other regarding or altruistic orientation can coexist, and
(3) the balance between individual freedom and social restraint can be achieved.

These propositions have at their heart the basic dilemma. This is how to translate them into empirical reality particularly in a village community. For, the village society is characterized by continuous face to face interaction in the midst of time-old ties of caste, kinship and territory. Such a community disregards individual interests, suppresses individual autonomy, freedom and initiative. To be able to pursue interests of the village as a whole, individuals should have the capacity to transcend their ties of family, kin, caste and class. Presumably altruistic orientation on the part of the individual is more prominent where narrow primordial ties are weak. The practice of social restraint becomes meaningful only when it leads to the well-being of a wider collectivity. The social milieu in a village society is seen to inhibit this tendency. That is the basic dilemma. On the one hand, the ideal village society emphasizes the value of primary groups and on the other hand, the need for the individual to shed primordial ties for developing independence, altruism and a service orientation to the community as a whole.

## Swaraj as Model Democracy

In Gandhi's model democracy every individual plays an effective role in the running of the community and country's affairs. It is not just a ritualistic one as is the case today in many countries where the only role of citizens is the casting of votes at regular intervals. Parliamentary democracy, to Gandhi, is just a starting point as it embodies a set of hard-won values. But his search is for the means to make society accept the values to live by. He does not consider it enough that institutions and rules be formed on the basis of those values and later on to revert back to mere ritualistic adherence. This would be sheer hypocrisy. Even while he criticizes the functioning of the democratic institutions as they prevail in Western world, he cherishes the democratic values that have inspired them. He acknowledges the importance of institutionalized values but only as a starting point. He wants these values to be practised in social life.

Gandhi is second to none in advocating the fundamental rights of citizens, provision of an independent judiciary and a free press. For him a healthy, well-informed and balanced criticism is the "Ozone of public life". When towards the end of 1921, restrictions are imposed on the rights of free speech and free association, he reacts vehemently calling for action in defence of the rights.

Gandhi envisages a scheme for indirect elections to the national legislature. Each village is to elect a representative and all such representatives will act as an electoral college for national legislature. In this connection, it has been argued that indirect elections are seen to be more open to corrupt influences because it is easier to manipulate the handful of members of an electoral college than the entire electorate numbering hundreds and thousands. But he favours the system in the context of awakened and dynamic participatory communities and not in the context of the sleeping ones waking up just for one day every three and five years. He wants to make the villages powerful bases of the democratic system. He is keen to see them as the vibrant nuclei that can catch the slightest vibrations in the atmosphere. As the American experience of the electoral college for the election of the President shows, he underlines, the members of the college are bound to honour the mandate given to them by their electors.

Gandhi does not favour the idea of an upper house as a check on the popularly elected lower one clarifying this point, he writes: "I have no fear of a popular legislature running away with itself and hastily passing some laws of which afterwards it will have to repent. I do not want to give a bad name to, and then hang the popular legislature".

Gandhi believes that in a democracy decision should be made by a majority vote and that the minority should be normally bound by the majority decision. At the Lahore session of the National Congress in 1929, where the historic resolution on complete independence was passed, an amendment to the resolution was lost by one vote only. Some supporters of the amendment requested Gandhi to accept it, going by the strength of the feeling in favour of it. But their reasoning did not find favour with him, and he clarified his position thus: "As regards an appeal to me to accept the amendment which has just been lost by a strength of one vote, let me remind you that we claim to work under a democratic constitution. One vote today has meant that the amendment has been lost, but one vote the other way could have easily meant the retention of the amendment. What you have to consider is whether the country would suffer by the loss of the amendment".

Gandhi's lifelong mission has been to bring the people into the political process in an effective manner. He does not want them to remain passive objects of manipulation by political vested interests. Rather he expects them to become the active agents of day-to-day political decisions and actions. His movements are also intended to create the necessary awareness essential for such a role. The decentralization of power is also not to be an imposition from above. But it has to be designed to building up of a non-violent popular power at the grass-root level in the communities that are fully equipped to assert themselves, irrespective of the attitude of the powers that be at the top. In fact such self-rule is to be part and parcel of his strategy of civil disobedience. Herein people are to refuse to pay taxes in a spirit of noncooperation with the authorities and to run their affairs in the village by themselves. This decentralization of power is to be buttressed by a decentralization of the economic setup. The aim should be to give the people a large measure of control over their economy.

The constructive programme is another potent weapon in the armoury of Gandhi's dynamic nonviolence. It provides a comprehensive spectrum of constructive and reformative test for village-based resurgent communities. Even though several villages did assert their autonomy during the civil disobedience movements, but due to the slow progress of the constructive activities these communities could not acquire a higher level of dynamism.

In 1942, on the eve of Quit India Movement, Gandhi came up with a comprehensive picture of self-governing village republics. Undoubtedly at his call hundreds and thousands of village communities all over India sprang to their feet to make a bid for freedom when the movement was to begin. He wanted to put before them a concrete programme of action to gain true Swaraj. Delineating his vision, Gandhi writes: "My idea of village Swaraj is that it is a complete republic, independent of its neighbours for its own vital wants and yet interdependent for many others in which dependence is a necessity. Thus every village's first concern will be to grow its own food crops and cotton for its cloth. It should have reserve for its cattle, recreation and play-grounds for adults and children. Then if there is more land available, it will grow useful money crops, but excluding ganja, tobacco, opium and the like. The village will maintain a village theatre, school and public hall. It will have its own water works, ensuring clear water supply. This can be done through controlled wells or tanks. Education will be compulsory upto the final basic course. As far as possible, every activity will be conducted on the cooperative basis. There will be no castes as we have today with their graded untouchability. Nonviolence with its technique of Satyagraha and noncooperative will be the sanction of the village community. There will be a compulsory service of village guards who will be selected by rotation from the register maintained by the village".

Furthermore, the government of the village will be conducted by a panchayat of five persons annually elected by the adult villagers, male and female, possessing minimum prescribed qualifications.

## CONCLUSION

According to Gandhi, a social order based on Ahimsa must be characterized by interdependence, harmony and this be of substantial but not of mechanical equality.

It should also be informed by the principle of Swadeshi. It simply means that the most effective organization of social, economic and political functions must follow the natural contours of the neighbourhood, that is, the primacy of the immediate community. The village in India, has been the primary unit of social, economic and political organization. The village republic, self reliant and vibrant, will also be, as far as possible, self-sufficient in food and clothing. Besides it will have all powers and institutions of self-government. It will be committed to perfect democracy based upon individual freedom. Decentralization will be the basis of the village republic; substantive equality, its basic characteristics; and participation by all, the essential mode of its functioning.

In sum, Gandhi's vision of Swaraj is composed of innumerable villages with ever-widening never-ascending circles. Here life will not be a pyramid with the apex sustained by the bottom. But it will be an oceanic circle, the centre of which will be the individual always ready to perish for the village. And the latter ready to perish for the circle of villages, till at last the whole becomes one life and where all share the majesty of the oceanic circle of which they all are integral units. This, in nutshell, is the Gandhian blueprint of the Global Swaraj.

# 21

# AMBEDKAR ON SOCIAL JUSTICE

### Dr. Ambedkar's Vision and Legacy

Dr. Babasahab Ambedkar (1891-1956) was one of the finest flowers of the twentieth century Renaissance. He was a towering personality whose striving for human freedom and dignity has been a glorious saga of modern India. He bequeathed to his people an abiding legacy, the implications of which deserve to be fully grasped.

Echoing his Master, Buddha, Ambedkar insists that a man can become great not owing to his royal birth but by being motivated by the dynamics of a social purpose and acting as 'the scourge and the scavenger of society'. He debunks the Hindu social organization based on Chaturvarna and the denial of rights to the Shudras who have been subjected to inhuman bondage for centuries. He lashes at Brahamanism because it has proved to be a bar to the establishment of an egalitarian society.

With an uncanny foresight, Dr. Ambedkar pinpoints the inapplicability of the Western pattern of democracy to India. His vision of democracy implies basic changes in the social and economic life of the people. He favours acceptance of these changes by the people without resorting to disruption and bloodshed. He envisages the removal of social and economic contradictions in the life of the Indian society. He wants political democracy to be accompanied by social democracy.

Dr. Ambedkar pleads for statutory safeguards to better the lot of the depressed, deprived and the downtrodden. He strives all his life crusading against discriminatory and dehumanizing tendencies in Indian society and to better the lot of Shudras, the 'wretched of the earth', to borrow a phrase of Fanon.

Ambedkar stands for a society based on the principles of liberty, equality and fraternity; the last one, he insists, is the most needed in order to ensure social endosmosis. A precondition to bring this about is a revolution in the thinking of the Hindus and the annihilation of the caste system. He is convinced that it is the caste system which has reduced the Shudras to the level of serfs, 'the hewers of wood and drawers of water'. He denounces the British Government for maintaining the policy of indifference towards the social reforms of the Hindu Society. He voices certain terms and conditions at the Round Table Conference and submits a

Memorandum to the Minorities Committee in which he demands that the majority rule must not perpetuate the present state of hereditary bondsmen on the class of untouchables. His chief concern has been to put into motion a series of measures that will end the exploitation of depressed classes. They will create in them a sense of dignity and honour, and a consciousness of equality and freedom.

Dr. Ambedkar popularizes the slogans, 'Tell the slave, he is slave and he will revolt', and 'Educate, Agitate and Organize': Besides, as the founding Father of the Indian Constitution, he makes the Constituent Assembly abolish untouchability and incorporate this provision in the schedule concerning Fundamental Rights.

Dr. Ambedkar has been seeking relentlessly to achieve social justice and equality for the oppressed and the suppressed humanity. All through he has been striving to wipe out the tear from the eye of the suffering by improving their lot through a reconstruction of the social and economic order. The liquidation of the hierarchical caste system and the restructuring of society on the basis of the abolition of all privileges of caste or status, in his view, will be a sure way of forging and fostering thc unity of thc nation. He wants to accomplish this silent revolution through abolishing untouchability and forced labour. He sets before his people the ideal of 'one man, one value, and one man, one vote'. He places all people equal before law, securing equal freedom of profession and equality of opportunity.

A valiant fighter against every kind of obscurantism, Ambedkar's lifelong mission has been to instill in the minds of the depressed classes a sense of dignity and self-reliance. He has been striving to free them from the tyranny of gods and the cretinizing codes of an iniquitous religion. He strongly pleads for forbidding the practice of animal sacrifice, piercing of the ear lobes and rolling on the ground and such other crude rituals and practices. The long oath of social solidarity he desires his associates and disciples to take embodies his strong commitment to values of rationality and humanism. His New Life Movement is not actuated by chauvinism and sectarianism as is sometimes made out, but by the deep understanding of the real India.

The objectives of the New Life Movement he spearheads are: (a) to free the untouchables from the thraldom of the Hindu and (b) to better the economic position of the untouchables. The demand for separate settlements is not a demand for separate states but providing places of habitation to the downtrodden, which he wants to be independent of the villages.

Dr. Ambedkar describes the village a sink of localism, a den of ignorance, narrow-mindedness and communalism. It is here that the Harijans are assaulted, dragged, injured, axed, gored, burnt alive and their woman-folk subjected to inhuman treatment; —a phenomena which has continued even after independence, inspite of statutory provisions and constitutional safeguards.

Dr. Ambedkar clearly foresees that even if a violent overthrow of the alien rule takes place, it will not have the effect of transforming the far more oppressive social order in India. That is why he labours hard to build up institutions and organizations like the Bahishkrit Hitkarina Sabha, Bhartiya Bahishkrit Samaj, Sevak Sangh, Samaj Samata Mandal, Samata Sainik Dal etc. This he does in order to 'educate, organize and agitate' the disinherited and the dispossessed by the caste Hindu for the realization of their legitimate rights. The Mahad Satyagraha for the right of drinking water and the Nasik Satyagraha for temple entry that he launches and leads are clear instances of the outstanding struggles of the untouchables for equal social rights. But after realizing that entry into temples can not solve their economic and social problems, Ambedkar thinks it better to eschew a religion which can not ensure equality even before God. Hence he embraces Buddhism in 1956 as a mark of protest because in his view Hinduism has failed to protect and promote the values of liberty, equality and fraternity among the castes and groups in Indian society which are so essential to create a human family composed of free individuals.

Dr. Ambedkar inspires the socially submerged classes to rise in revolt against socioeconomic thraldom and smash the centuries-old chains of slavery imposed on them by the Caste Hindu. He rouses the democratic awakening among them which has become a part of the general national consciousness. He pleads for the safeguards in the Constitution of India whereby adequate provision for the education, sanitation, recruitment in Public Services and other matters of social and political advancement are secured. He envisages the office of the Commissioner of Scheduled Castes and Tribes at the helm of framing the general policy of the Government.

It is interesting that Ambedkar opposes the idea of giving any special protection for the Scheduled Castes and the Scheduled Tribes in matter of admission to technical institutions because he fears that instead of removing their disabilities, it may perpetuate social aloofness. But he vigorously pleads for giving sufficient political power to them to influence legislative and executive action for the purpose of securing their welfare. He, therefore, proposes the inclusion of provisions in the electoral law to provide for adequate electoral representation and the right to elect their own men as their representatives.

Dr. Ambedkar stands for state socialism in the field of industry, agriculture ownership and method of cultivation. He wants to secure it by constitutional provisions which are unalterable by any act of Legislature and the Executive. He repeatedly proclaims that the aim and purpose of nationbuilding must be to ensure the economic security and political liberty of each individual. What is necessary is not merely to lay down a mechanism to enable people to capture power, but also to set before the nation the ideal of economic democracy.

Ambedkar wants the plank of state socialism to become a part of the constitutional law of the land and the legislature or the executive unable to alter or abandon it. He is at pains to locate the cohesive factors which will enable the creation of an integrated society reared on an associative mode of life. He repeatedly asserts that caste and democracy never go hand in hand. The caste system tends to perpetuate the communal majority instead of political majority and this ultimately cuts at the root of democracy. Whereas a political majority is changeable in its class composition, and grows or decreases in membership and influence, the course of politics among a communal majority is influenced only by those born into it. Unless the concept of socio-religious or ritual status gives way to secular status based on the principle of 'one man, one value, and one man, one vote', the practice of untouchability cannot be stopped. Mere reservation in Legislature and the Services cannot uplift the Scheduled Castes and Scheduled Tribes. What is needed is a total revolution of national psyche.

Dr. Ambedkar fully realizes the dangerous implications of fascism. He exhorts the working classes to fight against its twin manifestations—capitalism and imperialism. He emphasizes that unless the peasants and workers join together and secure political power by establishing their own government, they will not be able to abolish the various tyrannous systems and assert their legitimate human rights. He forewarns that in the absence of economic and social justice, political independence will not bring about either social solidarity or national integration. But he would stress the need to hold fast to constitutional methods for achieving social revolution. He forbids taking recourse to violent methods because they create chaos and anarchy, which in his view, are the breeding grounds of dictatorship.

An erudite scholar and a jurist of international repute, Dr. Ambedkar has left a rich legacy which shall remain a source of inspiration to men and women all the world over for a long time to come.

## What is Social Justice?

Social justice is a cardinal concept of human development. Its aim is to implement safeguards concerning interests of the weaker sections of society. It seeks to remove unjust imbalances between man and man. It wants to improve and emancipate lives of all citizens. Its prime concern is to let every man develop according to his or her own potentiality and merit. With this end it seeks to offer them adequate opportunities to participate in the power and wealth of the nation.

A look at the history and evolution of human society makes it amply evident that right from the beginning of man's social life, there have existed some sort of social disparity and injustice. It is the advancement of education and consequent increase of awareness, has taught us how best to organize and manage the society so that each and everyone can avail of all the available opportunities for their advancement on an equitable basis. For this, it is imperative that people's mutual sympathy and interdependence should become the basis of social justice. This will give the much-needed push to the movement towards equality. The institution to administer justice through a man-made social institution, Ambedkar avers, can help if it were armed with appropriate laws on social justice. It need be adequately equipped so that it may carefully ward off the past fallacies judiciously. It should be empowered not only to show the way to manage the present affairs but also humanely plan the future hopes for all the members of the society thereby paving the way for a just and exploitation-free society.

Social justice in its wider context stands for an egalitarian social order. It is opposed to every kind of injustice, violence, exploitation and suppression. It wages a war against all social evils. It strives for the removal of all inequalities, discriminations, untouchability, apartheid, slavery, forced labour, bonded labour etc. from the society. Social justice not only is promotive of the cause of the weak and the downtrodden, but also a force for reform to mend and restrain the activities of the strong and the rich.

## Dr. Ambedkar's Concept of Social Justice

The concept of social justice is enshrined in the preamble of the Indian constitution. The ideology contained in it has been evolved in the course of India's freedom struggle. Among the galaxy of leaders of the freedom movement Dr. B.R. Ambedkar stands out as a great champion of social justice. His whole life has been devoted to the cause of social justice. His lifelong mission has been to remove the disabilities of the depressed and deprived..

Dr. Ambedkar's concept of social justice is an all-inclusive concept. It aims to give every man a place of honour and dignity in the society. It is antithetical to any artificial discrimination and unnatural classification in society. It brooks no distinction between man and man, nor any discrimination based on caste, race, colour, class and ethnicity.

Dr. Ambedkar strongly believes that the concept of social justice is not a problem merely of distributing the material abundance among the people but basically it also implies a mode of life. Its basis is liberty and equality, mutual respect and regard for human essence which is ingrained in each and every human being. Above all it generates a feeling of fellowship and fraternity in them as equal members of society. In short, the measure of social justice is not merely material affluence and progress, but also human values that exist in abundance among the people.

Dr. Ambedkar has no place in his social philosophy for a world order in which the honour, power and prestige of one class is promoted and preserved at the cost of the rest of the people who are kept below the scale of human values and human development. He seeks to continue his fight for human liberation in various ways and at different levels, opening up every time a new dimension of social justice and social emancipation. Having known first hand the pangs of caste-based injustices, he is fully aware how unbearable can be its torture and humiliation, difficulties and disabilities, He therefore confronts the prevalent social injustices prevalent particularly in Hindu Society. He is resolved to unloosen their centuries-old stranglehold on the Indian society. Having pondered deeply over the nature and content of social justice he knows well that wherever there is exploitation and oppression, there exist injustice too. It is from this menace that the humankind needs be emancipated.

Dr. Ambedkar finds in liberty a great force in shaping human personality. The liberty he espouses is grounded in free expression of thought, belief, faith and worship. It is with this vision of liberty that man must express himself in various ways. Freedom provides the environment in which men can give vent to their creative energies resulting in the growth of art and literature. Freedom enables men to choose the best way to shape their destiny and cultivate and develop their personality.

Dr. Ambedkar believes that it is equality, which contributes to the mutual recognition of rights. It not only binds members of a society together but also acts as the chief social bond among the people. But it is fraternity that stands even above both. It is in-depth feeling which provides a sense of mutuality and accommodation in human relationships. It creates the right atmosphere whereby people can enjoy the values of liberty and equality.

Dr. Ambedkar has himself commented on what fraternity means. Fraternity, to him, is a sense of common brotherhood of all Indians, for all Indians. It is this principle of fraternity which gives unity and solidity to social life. Therefore, in no way can these principles of liberty, equality and fraternity be separated from each other in matters of dispensing social justice.

Dr. Ambedkar rejects the pernicious doctrines of Divine Laws as the cause and sustainer of social justice/injustice in human society. He does not find satisfying any kind of theological view of justice/injustice as preached by religious and theistic sects. For him the only thing real is the secular and moral aspect of social justice. He thinks it futile to hope to get justice in some other world while being inflicted and injured by the swords of social inequality and economic exploitation here and now in this world. And if there is no justice here and now in this world, says Ambedkar, by imperatives of any supposed Divine Law, how can it be possible elsewhere, in the imagined hereafter? For the same reason even as he holds in esteem the generosity of medieval Saints like Kabir, Nanak and others, he feels that equality before God is a very remote proposition to be realized, and may not have much meaning if it is not possible to achieve it in this world. He firmly believes that ideals of social justice are to be realized and enforced here and now itself. For this he wants proper provisions to be incorporated in the Constitution in order to protect the interests of the weak and the lowly. It is by the force of the Constitution and sovereign authority of the people behind it and not by any Divine Dispensation thus that the goal of social justice can be achieved.

According to Dr. Ambedkar "*Varnshram Dharm*" and God's grace can not be considered as the bases of the process of social justice. Its basis resides in the Constitution as manifested in rule of law, secular and socialist ethos, equality morality, fraternity etc. These, to him, are the essential elements of social justice.

Dr. Ambedkar explains the essence of social justice in extensive detail. He sees it embrace the unity and equality of all human beings. It entails expansion of human rights to all, respect for the equal worth of man and woman, and the protection of the weak and lowly. It involves mutual love, sympathy, tolerance and charity towards fellow beings. It signifies humane treatment in all cases, respect for the dignity of all citizens, the abolition of caste distinction and education and property for all. These are some of the important components of his concept of social justice.

Dr. Ambedkar lays emphasis on the need for fraternity of all in the Indian social situation. In his view the importance of fraternity is much more than political and economic justice. All kinds of justice, he opines, will automatically flow and follow from the practice of fraternity.

Why does fraternity, to him, so essential for the realization of social justice? Fraternity, for Ambedkar, is another name for fellow feeling. It consists in a sentiment which leads an individual to identify himself with the good of others. As a result the good of others becomes a thing naturally and necessarily to be attended to like any of the physical condition of our existence. It is this fellow feeling which can impel an individual to sacrifice his self interest for the common good.

Social justice, thus, is an inclusive category. It includes all sorts of justices in its scope. While social justice symbolizes the whole of social order, meaning the entire social system, other forms of justice stand for only one part of our social system. Whether it is a legal justice, economic or political justice, each one of these covers only one aspect and affects only a limited field of life. These myriad justices are no doubt necessary components of the social order but then, their implementation yields limited results. In fact they benefit only certain persons or sections of persons who are already well off. In comparison, social justice is a broad concept and is inclusive of all other types of justice. It provides for the common good, a place of dignity and honour for every man.

After independence when the new Constitution was being framed, Indian ruling elite consisting of Pandit Nehru, Dr. Rajandra Prasad, Dr. Ambedkar and a host of others, with an honest intention sought to translate the ideals of social justice and democracy in real Indian situation. Indian Constitution bears an ample testimony of this egalitarian and emancipatory endeavour.

Deeply committed to the upliftment of the oppressed people, Dr. Ambadekar's watchword to them has been: 'educate, organize, agitate.' For, according to him, politics can be a means to bring about the desired change in the socioeconomic life of the people and organizational structure of the society. His plunge into politics has therefore been aimed at inaugurating a social revolution for creating an egalitarian social order.

A votary of the righteous relationship between man and man and between man and woman, Dr. Ambedkar advocates the idea of woman empowerment and gender justice. His charisma impresses all sections of the depressed and oppressed including women and children. He has tirelessly worked for all those classes and groups who are in acute need of social justice in various fields of life.

Thus the main objective behind Dr. Ambedkar's view of social justice is to remove all man-made inequalities, every shade and variety of injustice through law, morality and public conscience. It is at his initiative that social justice as one of the noblest objectives was incorporated in the very Preamble of the Indian

Constitution. The various other constitutional provisions that are included in it aim at bringing about a just society. Their chief object is not only to help in the removal of imbalances in social, educational, economic and political life of the people but also to protect the right of the weak, aged, destitutes, women and children. By providing constitutional sanction, Dr. Ambedkar ensures to safeguard the interests of all the underprivileged and victims of injustice against the ruthless treatment that the propertied and socially high up classes have been meting out to them over the centuries.

Dr. Ambedkar's concept of social justice has a multi-dimensional form. It provides for a reasonable control and just distribution of the national economic surplus and advantage. It supports the principle of no economic exploitation, no social injustice and no political suppression of any kind on any section of society in the name of caste, sex, race, community and means of livelihood which all individuals are entitled according to their choice and liking. Every individual with talent must not be denied the opportunities to express himself in a creative manner.

## Social Justice through Democratic Constitutional Methods

Dr. Ambedkar's advice to politicians is that they utilize the hard-won political freedom fairly and honestly. They should strive for creating good harmonious and right relationship among the various classes of citizens in order to strengthen the rule of democracy. Responsibility for effective, non-exploitative and just governance rests on the shoulders of every citizen of this country. The task requires putting their heart and soul collectively for ushering a liberal, socialist order. It is not only that what the Constitution aims at, but also the promotion of integrated social justice requires each section of the society, including political parties to encourage and enlighten the people by their just conscience, righteous conduct and feelings of equality and fraternity. Once the people are enlightened it will mean the end of all fanaticism, violence, orthodoxy and communalism.

Dr Ambedkar hopes that the ideals of liberty, equality, fraternity and social justice as enshrined in the Indian Constitution together with the guaranteed fundamental rights to all citizens, and right incentives to the masses, supported by political parties and popular movements will help to achieve the goal of social justice.

Dr. Ambedkar favours applying constitutional methods such as nonviolent and legislative measures to achieve the ideal of social justice. In his social philosophy there is no place for violence or bloody revolution in pursuit of objectives and their implementation. Rather he encourages and enthuses all citizens to join in a common endeavour to achieve the goal of social justice, national unity, integration and brotherhood.

Dr. Ambedkar exemplifies in his life values and virtues of constitutionalism, social justice and democracy. He seeks to establish an egalitarian social order based on equality and social justice. He wishes to see it inform every sphere of Indian society. And to achieve this goal he remains committed to constitutional, peaceful and nonviolent methods of struggle. He does not favour causing any bickering and social dissension in society. He is indeed the role model for those in public life and a beacon to the future generations. He wants every Indian to feel duty-bound to carry forward the legacy of the freedom struggle and fulfill the unfinished agenda of socioeconomic revolution.

### Views on Caste System and Dalit Upliftment

Dr. Ambedkar draws inspiration from Mahatma Jotiba Phule. He is determined to complete the latter's (Jotiba's) life mission of emancipating the poor and downtrodden.

A revolutionary in the cause of the Dalit upliftment, Dr. Ambadekar has been a relentless fighter against untouchability and whatever is ugly and cruel in Hinduism, and Brahminism. He denounces the Hindu caste system as not only unjust but also immoral. His decision to embrace a new religion in the form of Neo-Buddhism, can be seen as symbolizing his unequivocal rejection of Hinduism.

Ambedkar launches a vehement attack on the multiform oppressions due to caste system and remains in the forefront of every battle against casteism and untouchability . He rejects both the prevalent approaches to reforming the caste system, namely, that of Dayananda Saraswati and of Mahatma Gandhi.

According to Dr. Ambedkar, society ought to be based on the four principal pillars of social justice—liberty, equality, human dignity and fraternity. If caste is to be annihilated, he declares, then its religious foundation, the Vedas and Shastras, will have to be destroyed first. He is convinced that faith in these scriptures is nothing but a legalized class ethic which favours the Brahmins. A breach in the system is not possible unless one is willing to apply the dynamite to the Vedas and Shastras. For they deny any part to reason, and to morality. Therefore it is imperative that first the religion of the Smritis needs be destroyed being the very basis of caste system.

Ambedkar joins issues with Gandhi concerning caste and its reform, especially his (Gandhi's) belief that the ancient Hindus have already achieved an ideal social system with the *Varna Vyavastha.* As Gandhi puts it, "the law of varna means that everyone will follow as a matter of dharma or duty the hereditary calling of his forefathers.... he will earn his livelihood by following that calling". As against Gandhi, Ambedkar believes that an ideal society has yet to be achieved in India. For him, the goal before the Indian nationals is not to make "Hinduism" or Hindu Society "shine forth" but to build a new, equal, free, open, non-hierarchical, modern India. Further it is wrong to say that the problem of the untouchables is a social problem i.e. in fact it is fundamentally a political problem of minority versus majority groups. He offers this as the rationale while launching a revolutionary movement for the liberation and advancement of the Dalits. With faith in the justice of his cause, Ambedkar declares on 20th July 1942 at Nagpur:" "With justice on our side,

I do not see how we can lose our battle. The battle is in the fullest sense spiritual. There is nothing material or sordid in it. For our struggle is for our freedom. My final word of advice to you is, 'educate, organize and agitate', have faith in yourselves and never lose hope."

Dr. Ambedkar's principal contribution is that he puts the untouchability issue at the centre stage of Indian politics. In Hinduism, he is convinced, the untouchables will never be able to obtain a respectable status and receive just treatment. There is no possibility for them to achieve either individual or group mobility within the Hindu social system. In this context, he therefore visualizes only two possibilities of their social emancipation: the political unity of untouchables and their mass conversion. Hence, in 1936 he speaks of conversion to another religion: "Though I have been born a Hindu, I shall not die as a Hindu". He makes a mention of conversion earlier in his address to the Yeola Conference of 1935. The conversion call of Ambedkar has had the effect of shaking the Hindu leadership from the roots. Several leaders approach him trying to persuade him not to go ahead with the idea. Ambedkar expresses surprise that the caste Hindus who have never shown fellow-feeling for untouchables then are pouring in large numbers to suddenly beseech them to stay within the folds of Hinduism. He wonders why do they now suddenly take such an interest in keeping the untouchables within the Hindu fold despite their having seen centuries of ill-treatment, humiliation and oppression at the hands of caste Hindus?

After long deliberation and a conscious choice in favour of Buddhism, Ambedkar takes his *diksha* (initiation) at Nagpur on the 14th October at 9:30 a.m. in the presence of five lakh Mahars, who all also get converted to Buddhism on that day. His embracing of Buddhism symbolizes a strong protest aimed at the caste Hindus who have done little to eradicate the evil of untouchability from the Indian society. For him, Swaraj or freedom does not mean anything until it puts an end to the slavery of the untouchables.

Thus, according to Dr. Ambedkar, untouchability is part of the caste system which is the very foundation on which Hindu religion stands. All great savants and seers of India have expressed their keenness to reform Hinduism, but they have failed because Hinduism is not amenable to reform so long as they favour retaining the system of caste. And if caste is touched the whole edifice of Hinduism will collapse, because Hinduism is nothing but caste. Gandhi's failure in this domain is also because he wants to abolish untouchability by retaining caste as it is. Caste in fact is an extension of untouchability with one caste (jati) being untouchable to the other. Dr. Ambedkar highlights these unpleasant facts of the Hindu social system as no one have ever done before him.

Dr. Ambedkar also picks holes in the Marxist Theory which claims that a person's actions are determined by his property relations, integrated property being predominantly a source of power. But this does not hold good in India, he says. Because here even the king, or the rich landlord is governed by the dictates of his priest even though the latter (priest) may be poorer than the king or the landlord. In India it is the caste that decides the social status and not the person's property. Therefore by and large upper castes of India also belong to the upper class. Viewed in this light, "caste" is the other name for "class". Despite the existence of many "poor people" among the upper castes, the fact is that in India economic status does not decide a person's social status which depends indeed on his birth. Marxists have ignored this basic fact because their leadership, he thinks, comes from the upper caste.

Dr. Ambedkar upholds the thesis that India is not yet a nation, but it is a nation in the making. His highlighting of nationality question is his major contribution to the discourse on identity, ethnicity, nation and nationalism. The "nationality question" with vociferous demands from the Indian society and polity, is seen to be making periodic eruptions in different parts of the country. A few examples include the nationality urges of the Kashmiris, Nagas, Gorkhas, Jharkhandis, Dalits, Mizos, Tamils and many others. To crush their legitimate aspirations with force in the name of national unity, will be senseless and prove counterproductive.

Dr. Ambedkar well realizes the imperative of fulfilling the nationality urges of these people in the interest of maintaining the unity of India. He is convinced that it can be preserved only if its diversity is recognized. He not only gives this warning but also rightly gets it incorporated in the Constitution of India.

## CONCLUSION

In fine according to Dr. Ambedkar caste system, as it has developed in India in the course of the past thousands of years, is a blot on the fair name of Hinduism. Besides it is a source of acute social disharmony and oppression of the lower castes by the upper castes. The problem gets further complicated by their economic distress and lack of education. Besides, their all-round backwardness further aggravates their misery. Despite the sociocultural efforts which social reformers have been trying from time to time, they have simply failed to eradicate the evil of caste-based discriminations, and their end is no where in sight. India's social revolution cannot take off unless the system of caste is rooted out from the Indian society. Nor will the goal of social justice be realized, for which Dr. Ambedkar has been waging a lifelong battle. This remains one of the greatest challenges before the statesmen and policy makers in free India.

# 22

# NEHRU AND LOHIA ON DEMOCRACY

## Nehru on Democracy: The Search for a New Model

Jawahar Lal Nehru is one of the outstanding leaders of the national movement and credited to be the maker of modern India. A great humanist, his faith in democracy emanates from his humanism. Democracy, with him, is not a dogma but a living faith. Democracy is a part and parcel of the human approach to the problems of individual and social life. It signifies harmonious living and a proper balance and adjustment among individuals and groups. It entails all-round development of individuals in society and equal opportunity for all men. Only democracy, he thinks, can achieve this ideal.

Democracy, for Nehru, is a multidimensional concept. It is not only political and economic, but something of the mind as well. True democracy is a way of life. It involves an atmosphere of tolerance and reasonableness. It implies an acceptance of free thought in matters of faith. It means the desire and capacity to live and let live. Political democracy remains incomplete without economic democracy. Political liberty without economic justice is a sham and hoax. It is not real democracy but only a counterfeit that passes for it.

Nehru looks upon collectivist version of democracy with suspicion. He will not ignore and sacrifice the individual for the good of society. His touchstone is how far any political or social theory enables the individual to rise above his petty self and thus think in terms of the good of all. He is quite clear that the good of the individual belonging to a privileged class can not lead to social good.

Nehru laments the process of deindividualisation and brutalization of the individual man. He ascribes it to capitalist good and neck-breaking speed of modern living. As a consequence the individual is getting merged in the crowd. He is critical how modern man is being subjected to myriad stresses and strains of highly industrialized and urbanized set up. The crowd dominates the individual. It lets him give way to unreason when he is a part of the crowd. To save the individual from this crowd which turns him into a brute, a democratic society is the answer. Only such a society can provide the individual with the conditions of creative development.

Nehru is not an elitist. He has immense faith in the power of the people. He is keen to involve them in the great task of building a strong and prosperous India. No polity, however democratic in its political structure, he believes, can be a full democracy unless it is based on the goodwill and strength of the people. He constantly reminds the people that they are partners in the vast undertaking of running a nation, partners in government, and partners in industry.

Nehru is against every kind of authoritarianism. He is convinced that authoritarian system fails to give full opportunity to the individual for his development. Both fascism and communism, in so far as they are based on the power of the state and social groups, are totalitarian concepts. Between fascism and communism, if he has to choose, he is prepared to accept the latter. He sees no middle road between fascism and communism. He considers the communist ideal any day better than fascism. Democracy, equality and removal of privileges are the imperatives of his philosophy. They are essential prerequisites of developing a socialist pattern of society through democratic and peaceful methods.

Nehru does not want people to work with the government or industry in a regimented manner. Democracy will cancel itself out if people are herded together in a totalitarian way. He sees a basic contradiction between democracy and capitalism. While democracy contributes to power of the many, capitalism gives power to the few. Without economic democracy, political democracy tends to promote monopoly and power concentration. He pins his hope on peaceful methods to bring about socioeconomic change. For this purpose he sees in adult suffrage a potent weapon. Ballot can prove even more potent than bullet, he asserts, to effect change in the polity.

Nehru does not want democracy to be reduced to static theories. For he believes that democracy is the most dynamic of the arts of government. He is quick to perceive that all institutions including the parliamentary institutions are ultimately the projections of people's character, thinking and aims. The extent to which they are strong and lasting depends on their being in accord with the people's character and thinking, otherwise they tend to break up.

Nehru's main contribution to the strengthening of democratic institutions lies in the fact that he introduces universal adult franchise. However, he is careful to point out that there can be 'no equality between the pauper who has a vote and the millionaire who has a vote'. Similarly there is no equality between the person who has tremendous educational advantages and the person who has none at all. But still he pleads for the enfranchisement of the entire people and the unrestricted growth of democratic institutions.

Nehru is convinced that the best school of democracy is democracy itself. In this context he emphasizes the role of popular franchise in the diffusion of political liberty. In his view, the growth of democracy depends on extension of franchise. His prescription is universal adult suffrage first, followed by education and a good standard of living. He considers universal franchise as the very basis of fuller democracy. It is the key to political liberty and political power to the masses. With universal franchise there is always the consciousness in the people that they are governing themselves. This consciousness is powerful enough to keep the government in line with public opinion. Since the government and governed inseparably constitute a democratic state, the problem like power is to be shared as common property in such a way that governmental responsibilities become more or less responsibilities of the people.

Nehru has a special preference for the parliamentary system of democratic government. He is aware that such a system calls for virtues like ability, devotion to work, a large measure of cooperation, self-discipline and restraint among the people.

Nehru is a great institution builder. He is a great champion of the freedom of expression. He pleads for a free and effective press. He considers the right to dissent as the basic prerequisite of a democratic polity. For building democracy at the grassroot, he introduces *Panchayat Raj* institutions at the village, block and district level. He wants to see them grow as alternative centers of power and as supportive forces to the urban centers of decision-making.

Nehru is a great teacher of democratic values and methods. He wishes to awaken the traditional and caste-ridden masses into the world of secularism, democracy and socialism. He wants to politicize the caste with a view to weaken its hold on social and political processes and institutions.

Acclaimed as one of the finest products of western liberalism, Nehru has been a prolific writer and a thoughtful speaker. He is deeply committed to the philosophy of democratic socialism. In his time there are seen to be broadly two models of democracy, —the Liberal Democratic Model and Marxist Model. Having imbibed the values of western liberalism during his long stay in England, Nehru became a votary of the Liberal Democratic Model. Major components of this Model are:

1. Constitutionalism
2. Representative government
3. Majority rule
4. Sovereignty of the people
5. Individual liberty, freedom of expression and limitations on government, rule of law
6. Liberty, equality, fraternity, social justice

Nehru adds a socialist dimension to the western liberal model of democracy. He gives primacy to human dignity, values of humanism, reason and science. His model lays emphasis on man's economic well-being, the reconstruction of society through science and technology. In it liberty and equality, —social, political and economic— go together. The legacy of socialism no doubt has had a profound influence on his thinking, however, he does question some of its antiliberal methods that are inimical to the growth of human personality.

## Democracy as Socio-Economic Equality

According to Nehru, democracy means both liberty and equality and that democracy can flourish only in an equal society. He is convinced that political, economic and social freedom go with equality and social justice. They can not be separated from each other. They are integral to democracy, by not mere possessing equality of vote but also economic and social equality in all crucial areas of life.

Nehru believes that democracy is a great leveler. No doubt people from birth onwards differ educationally, economically and in many other respects. He, therefore, advocates equality of opportunity for all. Its object is that all men lead good life and progress towards the goal of equality. In his view democracy must ensure removal of all disparities and special privileges if it is to become real mass democracy.

For Nehru, freedom and property, capitalism and democracy are antithetical to each other. In the Indian context he finds in caste the greatest hurdle to social equality. The caste system and what goes with it, he views as wholly incompatible, reactionary and a chief restrictive barrier to progress. There can be no equality in status and opportunity within its framework nor can there be political democracy and much less, economic democracy. Caste with its rigid hierarchical system allows little vertical mobility. Rather it signifies the very negation of social democracy as well as political democracy.

Thus, for Nehru, democracy means a system based on an egalitarian ethos and social philosophy. It involves the total transformation of the existing inegalitarian social structure and other existing inequalities in society based on private property and individual greed. Democracy has to grow to its full potential through consensus mutual adjustment and cooperative endeavour. Besides it need to ensure equal opportunity to all in order to develop the fuller self of the citizenry.

Nehru holds that democracy must go with social and economic justice. But to secure progress towards this ideal, a social order aiming at the welfare of the people is essential. It must ensure to all citizens adequate means of livelihood. Also it must ensure non-concentration of the material sources in a few hands as well as a proper control and distribution of these resources to various sections of the society. To achieve this goal he emphasizes the importance of socialism and planning. He confronts this dilemma of a modern complex society by securing social development through combining democracy with socialism. He seeks to realize it by and maintaining individual freedom and initiative with centralized social control and planning of economic life of the people, both at the national and international plane. He finds in democratic socialism the chief instrument of improving the conditions of the people. There is no place of violence, class war or revolution in his socialism, since it is to be realized through democratic means.

Nehru well realizes that without a well-planned economy, the goal of multifaceted development of a society of India's gigantic proportion will remain merely a dream. He, therefore, supports the idea of mixed economy in which socialist and capitalist principles are incorporated. Its success depends on what and how much of each will be necessary to ensure the enduring welfare of the people as well as maintain the optimum tempo of growth. It is under his direction the Planning Commission is established. Its objective is to make a proper assessment of the national resources and the extent of their utilization in a planned manner depending on the needs and necessities of the nation.

Nehru sees in Planning an inevitable advance towards socialist economy benefiting every section of the society within a democratic structure. He visualizes all future economic change in the direction of a democratically planned collectivism. However by it he does not mean an abolition of private economy and property but the public ownership of the basic and larger industrial establishments in India. This public cooperative control of the big industries, Nehru terms as democratic collectivism. As a system it requires careful and continuous planning and adaptation to the changing needs of the people.

In the context of endemic poverty and illiteracy prevailing in India, Nehru searches for a new model of democracy. He wants a model which will help overcome the dichotomy between political versus economic democracy. For this he makes a continuous effort to reach out for the ways to reconcile individual freedom with the demands of economic justice. He ponders over the dilemma of preserving individual freedom in the context of the rising wave of centralization as a consequence of advances in technology and industrialization and the other connected problem of national security. He, therefore, pleads for balancing the idea of freedom and equality and, if necessary, the curtailment of individual liberty in the interest of national security and the larger interest of the society and the nation.

In Nehru's model of democracy, majority rule has to make room for minority rights. Any curtailment of fundamental rights can only be done to fulfill the imperatives of social justice and ensure a happy synthesis of liberty and equality. His preference lies on the side of liberty of the individual because in his reckoning ultimately the individual alone counts. The individual is the root of mankind and the measure of all human progress. In his pursuit of socioeconomic democracy, Nehru like Gandhi therefore, at no stage forgets the individual who lies at the root of all progress. In his wellbeing alone lies the test for the true health of the polity and society.

In short, democracy, to Nehru, means not only social and economic equality but also a humanist perspective on individual and society. The main components of Nehru's democratic model can be summarized as follows:

1. The individual, his dignity, creativity and his happiness is the chief object of democratic governance.
2. Individual is the root of mankind and also the measure of all progress. As Nehru puts it, "I do believe that ultimately it is the individual that counts". The individual should be given full opportunity to develop. The only justification for governments to interfere in lives of the people is to realize the ultimate good. But Nehru is opposed to every type of authoritarianism because it cuts at the root of democratic way of life and is a denial of

individual's development. He has the same reasons for denouncing fascism and nazism because they both regard the individual as a means and not end. They treat him as subordinate to the state or having no existence apart from the state.

3. Nehru advocates the model of representative democracy based on the West Minster model as it has developed in Great Britain. The special features of this model as adopted in the Indian context include a written constitution, demarcating distinct spheres of action for its legislative, executive and judicial components, universal adult franchise, regular periodic elections, first-past-the-post system of majority rule and competitive political parties mobilizing public support to capture power and control the government.
4. Nehru finds in political equality the key to social and economic equality. He thinks that popular sovereignty can be ensured through vigilant people exercising their right to vote and taking active part in the political process. The extension of political equality and political development among the people, according to him, will hasten the implementation of the policies of social justice.
5. Nehru sees in the people the source of the ultimate authority of the government. He wants the people to express their general will through a web of well-connected popular institutions including an independent, impartial, high-powered election commission and a well-geared countrywide election machinery. By taking an active and intelligent interest in public affairs and in the electoral process, the people can exercise control on their chosen representatives and thus contribute to the development of democracy.
6. As against Gandhi and M. N. Roy's models of partyless democracy, Nehru is in favour of a democracy based on competing political parties. He believes that political parties provide not only forums for aggregation of demands and the free flow and exchange of varied ideas and information but also they offer divergent ideologies and perspectives on issues confronting the people there by setting up viable alternatives before the people to choose from. Nehru believes that only disciplined political parties can ensure efficient government and provide true representation to the people. Similarly, a strong opposition is desirable to keep watch on the acts of omission and commission by the government in power.

## LOHIA ON DEMOCRACY

### Theoretician and Strategist

Dr. Ram Manohar Lohia was one of the most controversial though provocatively original Indian thinker in Indian politics. He was steeled in the fire of Indian nationalist struggle. A contemporary of Nehru, Jayprakash Narayan, Acharya and Narendra Dev, Lohia played a great role in the freedom movement. He venerated Gandhi and in many respects he was close to him. Besides, he also admired Nehru.

He never made any compromises on principles. He solidly stood with Gandhi on the question of non-partitioning of India. He never forgave those whom he considered as 'the guilty men of India's partition'. Though there was much commonality in the thought of Nehru and Lohia, in the electoral politics they stood apart. They would not collaborate to build a modern vibrant strong India of their dreams. They both commanded the allegiance of the masses. They were their chosen leaders, yet they chose to stand apart in two opposing camps.

While between themselves Nehru and Lohia shared some common perspectives on democracy and socialism, but on many details of policies and programmes, they differed strongly. This resulted in the parting of their ways after independence.

In fact during Nehru's days of power, Lohia went to jail for more than twelve times. He spent a great part of his life in jails for having opposed the wrong policies of the government. Lohia excelled both as a theoretician and a strategist. He had firm grip on the organization, *i.e.*, the party machine which he made and unmade many times to translate his vision into reality.

### Beyond Capitalism and Communism: Quest for a Third Way

Lohia was a staunch critic of both capitalism and communism. His search was for the third way which he believed could be socialism. A keen student of international politics and the world forces that were shaping the destiny of peoples, he wanted to save humanity from tyranny and exploitation unleashed by capitalism and imperialism. The trampling of rights and liberties of people in communist regimes under one pretext or the other, gave a lie to their professions and practice. His deep commitment to values of human liberty and democracy did not let him accept basic denial of freedoms to the people whom he saw as the victims of statist oppression and inhuman treatment.

Lohia had been a witness to the great progress made by Soviet Union after the revolution. But he felt dissatisfied with the model of polity, as it developed both in Soviet Union and USA. He therefore started pondering over a new model of democracy that would suit India. Under his model of democracy both the feudal ownership and the industrial and capitalist ownership must come to an end. To achieve this goal he proposed agitation, protest, demonstration, gherao, and even civil disobedience as weapons to fight the menace of injustice, exploitation and corruption in the society.

Democracy, to Lohia, was the culmination of socialism and vice versa. If democracy was a means, socialism was an end. Socialism held a special fascination for him because it provided bread to the hungry and the starving. It had within it all the wherewithals to alleviate the suffering of teeming millions of India and put an end to their poverty, illiteracy and backwardness. Socialism, in this sense, was most suited to a country like India. In socialism he saw a progressive force that could save mankind from the prospect of massive disaster and destruction. The existing inegalitarian world order if went unchecked, he forewarned, would heap on the world unprecedented bloodshed and wars.

While upholding the doctrine of socialism, Lohia always stood for democracy as a political system. For him democracy was what suited the most to the needs of a country of the continental dimension like India. But, democracy to be meaningful to the people must reflect their expectations and aspirations and become a way of life with them. For this he wanted sovereign power to be cut into as tiny bits as possible. This could be the way to enable the common man in the village and township to understand political affairs and make intelligent use of them. The purpose of democracy is that people by themselves should become instruments of their own emancipation.

## Democracy: The Two Question Marks

Democracy, for Lohia, is to be understood as the rule of the people: It is a kind of government where the ruler and the ruled are lodged in one and the same person. He sees this unity of the ruler and the ruled in representative democracy where the people have the right to vote in order to elect their rulers. But concerning this type of democracy Lohia ask two questions: (i) whether the citizen is really sovereign and (ii) whether the citizen is free and ripe enough in intellect to make proper use of his vote? Admittedly only voters who are sovereign, free and mature in intellect, he believes, can make right choice in electing their rulers.

According to Lohia, the voters elect the legislature which frame the laws and to whom the executive is responsible. The legislature does not have control over the entire apparatus of the state such as army, police, judiciary, schools etc. The state though nominally sovereign has to perform more functions within the society, though its major concern is to protect the life and property of the people. Here its powers are limited by the laws of its own making and it would not destroy its own base.

The representative institutions are to Lohia, dependent on the capitalist system, with the real power lying in the hands of the industrialists, bankers and financiers. Justice too is also dependent on the laws of property. The ordinary citizen cannot hold his own in frontal opposition to the social system. He is not able to disrupt this social system even if he so desires.

According to Lohia, the democratic state is not entirely dependent upon an equal adult vote but moved by the power of privileges, either of birth or experience. These are seen to be entrenched in the upper house or in the judiciary and even in the legislature which is the creation of the voter. The last one *i.e.,* the legislature has to function still within an economic system which is highly unequal and unjust to the vast masses. Thus the voter inspite of his having been vested with the right to vote does not have much role in the running of democracy.

On the question whether the voter is free and ripe in intellect to make proper use of his vote, Lohia argues that representative institutions exist side by side with the system of education and culture. They are entirely unrepresentative and dictated by the same financiers and the ruling caste-class combine which limit the sovereignty of the adult voter. They own newspapers, subsidize the political parties and have a monopoly over higher education.

Lohia laments that the modern democracies are little interested in imparting freedom and maturity of mind to their citizens. Therefore the citizens are not free and mature enough to make proper use of their vote. In consequence in so far as the whole facade of democracy is made to function in the context of capitalist society, democracy as the rule of people, is contaminated and nullified by the rule of property. Since the state is also an instrument of the capitalist class, a democracy functioning within such a state and society can not result in the rule of the people.

Lohia equates democracy with 'temple of fire' which purges humanity of its dross. During the last two hundred years, democracy has waged a battle of freedom both against the feudal privileges and the rule of one nation over the other. It has challenged the privilege with equality, tyranny and force with consultative reason of equal citizenry, and serfdom with freedom. Pitted against foreign domination, democracy has brought into action the same passion for equality, reason, freedom and unity. Allthrough its struggles, Lohia has stood for a democracy which is based on the combination or unity of the rulers and the ruled on the one hand and destruction of inequality, injustice and reaction, on the other. Yet the fact that democracy has functioned within the capitalist system, it has proved helpless against the rule of property and privilege. The battle of democracy, he therefore asserts, has to be taken to its logical conclusion in today's context when the power of property and privilege has become manifold and formidable.

## Democracy as Method and Effort

Lohia views democracy both as a method and as an effort. The former, *i.e.,* democracy as a method, provides an opportunity for a peaceful social change, through universal adult franchise, representative institutions, discussion, dialogue and participation. It thus gives an opportunity to elect the rulers without any bloodshed and violence. Democracy as an effort, in contrast, continually aspires to put an end to all sorts of inequality, injustice, exploitation, discrimination, thereby paving the way to progressive rule of the people.

In its early phase, according to Lohia, the democratic effort is seen to enlist the base created by the capitalist society in its fight against the feudal order. It makes use of democratic liberties of the person, freedom of thought, expression, association and the representative institutions. Such use seeks to bring about a peaceable change in the existing feudal order. In fact these rights offer the minimum base of safety from where a citizen can attack the wrongs and injustices. They also limit the authority of the state and enable the citizens to express and organize themselves against the oppressive and exploitative system.

Again it is the representative institutions, Lohia continues to argue, that enable the citizens to deliberate and reason out political affairs. But since it is a rule based on property, it ignores the injustices and wrongs caused by the property base of society. As democracy is reduced to a method, it begins to be equated with representative institutions in the false belief that they will on their own establish the rule of the people. But the fact is that it proves helpless against the rule of property. In the circumstances the true character of the state is forgotten since democratic vote and the minimum civic liberties confuse men's mind and create an illusionary picture of the democratic state as an organic reflection of the entire nation. Though the democratic state is equated with the grant of liberties and settlement of disputes among different classes, however from the point of view of the propertyless sections, its weakness becomes apparent.

Referring to Britain, Lohia states that over one-tenth of the population has to live on a shrinking unemployment dole, insecure employment and fear of old age. Such a state of affairs only breaks and humiliates the individual rendering him devoid of that freedom and nobility which is the essence of democracy. The successive Reform Acts only achieve a victory of the democratic method. It is the capitalist ownership of the society which works the people's destiny and democracy is thought to consist of minimum governmental interference. The various welfare legislations such as factory acts, housing, education etc. only touch the surface of the capitalist abuse. Though democracy as a method restricts the use of violence in support of an alternative government, it increases the daily violence of capitalist ownership of society. Democratic effort to be real, Lohia emphasizes, must aspire to end this daily violence. However, for Marxists, such a democracy is deemed a bourgeois prejudice.

In the context of democracy as an effort, Lohia gives the example of Russia. After the revolution, he underlines, how the new Russian constitution enshrines certain distinct fundamental rights of the people such as right to work, to leisure, to maintenance in old age, illness, incapacitation and education. Giving at least a theoretical certainty to such democratic rights is indeed a great advance towards democracy. The Russian example brings out that there is need to extend the democratic method of civil liberties and representatives governments to include the right to a secure and stable economic existence.

Lohia concedes that the means to achieve this democratic effort in Russia are not always democratic and their ill-effects have become evident very soon. But any attempt to judge the Russian example on the touchstone of the democratic method alone neglecting the achievements and the extent of democratic effort will be wrong. The Russian example does reveal certain fundamental weaknesses of democracy as practised elsewhere, yet it does not make serious attempts to extend it in a direction not attempted before.

## Unity of Democratic Method and Democratic Effort—The Blueprint for a Socialist Democracy

According to Lohia, democracy of effort with its basis in reason, freedom and national unity is only possible within a socialist society. Even in the colonial countries, the message to end the property rule has reached the masses and they certainly do not look up to capitalism as the general doctrine of society. The postwar social democracy is another democratic attempt to take advantage of the social conditions for an alliance of the working class and other exploited classes against the rule of property. It is evident that society has come to a stage when the democratic method can negate the democratic effort and the mutual war between the two will end up in the disruption of democracy itself. In this context Lohia notes that the liberties of expression and organization are inadequate and they need to be supplemented with the strikes and struggles of the exploited classes. But he disapproves the use of violence in these struggles and wants it be strictly avoided. He is quick to perceive that at least theoretically, social conditions have created a broad front for socialism which can pave the way to the peaceful success of democracy. However, he feels that the adult vote is required to be reinforced by mass base and direct action if the gap between the democratic effort and democratic method, so vital to the success of democracy has to be bridged.

In the unity of democratic method and democratic effort is founded Lohia's blueprint of a socialist society. It is to be based upon the solid bedrock of democratic principles. It consists of the following broad principles:

(i) Maximum attainable equality and social justice
(ii) Social ownership of the means of production
(iii) Small unit technology
(iv) Four-pillar state
(v) A decent standard of living
(vi) World parliament and government

Lohia considers democracy and socialism as obverse and subverse of the same coin, having their roots in equality. A democratic society essentially has to be an equal society. For Lohia, equality entails such an 'ordering of social forces, as would balance a share in the toil of living with a share in its gains also i.e. the social forces would be arranged in such a way that 'each might get its due'. He terms this as 'the principle of immediacy' i.e. the maximum and immediate attainability relevant to the current situation in relation to the ideal.

The quest of equality remains a lifelong goal for Lohia. He rates it as 'high an aim of life as truth or beauty'. Without equality among the individuals, he emphasizes, there is little possibility for justice, human dignity, morality, brotherhood, freedom and universal welfare. He views inequality as a disuniting force. It creates dissensions among men and disunites them. In the century he lived, he has been a witness to the worst forms of inequality, but he has had a comforting hope that man has been fighting against these inequalities and injustices as he has never done before.

In this connection, Lohia refers to the *Sapta Kranti* (seven revolutions) which he finds taking place to further the goal of equality. He enumerates these revolutions as follows:

(i) Equality between men and women,
(ii) abolition of inequalities based on colour,
(iii) elimination of inequalities of birth and caste,
(iv) national freedom or ending of foreign influence,
(v) economic equality through increased production,
(vi) protecting the privacy of life from all collective encroachments, and
(vii) limitations on armaments.

Lohia roots inequality in man's predatory nature to privately own the gifts of nature and instruments of production for personal benefit and not for welfare of society as such. This in turn leads to economic exploitation. He finds this as the chief hurdle in the way of democracy and to overcome this hurdle he suggests a twofold solution:

(i) Destroy the attached merit to property in the minds of men, and
(ii) abolish private property in the means of production and establish ownership of the whole community.

Instead of big machines, Lohia is in favour of the use of 'small unit technology'. In this he is nearer to Gandhi than to Nehru who prefers heavy industry and the large scale factories because they produce in great number. Lohia's opposition to heavy industry is founded on the fear that if India takes to large scale technology, a hundred million people will be rendered jobless and need to be liquidated. The principal reason behind espousing the idea of small unit technology for Lohia, therefore, is that labour should have direct contact with the machine and he should master and adapt it to his needs and conditions. In addition, he feels, the villages and towns have abundant raw-material and the use of small unit technology will help the industry to be taken to village rather than villager to the industry. This will avoid the massive social dislocation due to industrialization which is a commonly witnessed phenomena.

The introduction of small unit technology will also serve the social aims of decentralization and democratization which are beyond large scale industry to attain. However, this does not mean that large scale industry should not exist at all. He concedes that large scale industry like railways, hydro electric projects are very much needed. But he makes an important policy proposal in this regard. While the large scale industry should be nationally owned, the small unit machines can be owned by the state and village governments as well as by 'peasant cooperatives'.

Furthermore along with the nationalization of large scale industry where it is most needed, Lohia also wants the disappearance of the all-powerful state, paving the way for *Chaukhamba Raj* (four pillar State). He argues that the state has hitherto been organized on two pillars: the Centre and the Province. But in order to provide wider participation to the people, it should be organized on four pillars—Village, District, Province and the Centre. He wants that each unit should be vested with autonomous power of action and decision on specified matters.

The four pillar state, Lohia states, should be both an executive and legislative arrangement. He wants it to extend to include the aspects of production, ownership, administration, planning, education and the like.

In his model of *Chaukhamba Raj*, the sovereign power of the state is to be so distributed that each little community lives the way of life that it chooses to do. It is expected to represent both the self sufficient village and the intelligent and vital village. This is his way of ensuring both economic and political decentralization to make democracy more participatory, responsive and representative.

Lohia distinguishes between 'decent standard of living' and the routine 'increased standard of living'. By decent standard of living he means a set of goods which form regular consumption of individual, whereas increased standard of living means continuous increase of goods. In contrast, a decent standard of living requires that these goods should be made available to all. In this system not only equal distribution of goods are to get priority, but also the fight between the have and have-nots is to be reduced to the most minimum level.

Lohia advocates the establishment of a world parliament vested with powers to enforce peace and promote economic development. He also pleads that an internal pool of capital resources is also required to be established which should 'take from each country according to its capacity and give to each country according to its needs'.

# 23

# PERIYAR ON IDENTITY

### Periyar : The Early Life

E.V.Ramaswami Naicker, popularly known as Periyar (Great Sage) (1879-1973), was born in 1879 in Erode of a respectable upper middle class family of artisans. He married at the age of 13, but after six years he donned the mantle of a sannyasi. He went on long travels as a religious mendicant all over the country. His visits to pilgrim centres, gave him an intimate knowledge of the evils of popular Hinduism. There he learnt first hand the exploitations of the masses by Brahmin priests.

Periyar saw in casteism the ugly face of Hinduism and wanted national reform of Hinduism. The movement he launched took a turn towards Racial consciousness and became a movement for Dravidian identity which aimed at defending the rights of the Dravidians against Aryan domination. He put the blame on the Aryans for introducing an unjust and oppressive social system in the country.

Periyar was quick enough to realize the implication of the new nationalists ideology which had the 'Aryan view of race'as it basis. He castigated the Indian elite for supporting this as a new model to understand caste with Brahmins, Kshatriyas and Vaishyas as the descendants of the invading Aryans and the Shudras and untouchables as the native conquered inhabitants. Acceptance of the new ideology to claim "Aryan" descent meant claiming "twice-born" status and to be dubbed as "Dravidian" or "Non-Aryan" was almost equivalent to denigrating a person as a "Shudra".

At twelve, the child Periyar joined his father's business to assist him. As he was picking up business and shaping well, he started taking interest in public affairs. He emerged gradually as a person of importance in the town. In this the prestige enjoyed by his father also helped. After his father's death in 1911, public offices and positions of respectability started gravitating to him. He became the chairman of the District Devasthanam Committee; an honorary magistrate for 12 years; an elected chairman of the Erode Municipal Council. Between 1907 and 1919, Periyar held as many as twenty-nine offices of public importance. Whatever position he held, he fulfilled his responsibilities with utmost sincerity, dedication and efficiency. By nature he was drawn to public affairs touching upon the life of the common man. His concern for them was genuine, deep and abiding.

## Periyar and the Congress Party

From 1907 onwards, Periyar started taking increasing interest in the policies and programmes of the Congress party. He attended conferences and even took a leading part in organizing them. However, it was only in 1919 that he resigned his Chairmanship of the Municipality and entered active public life. From then on, till his demise in 1973, he worked with total dedication in the service of the people.

While there was no substantial change in the objectives of his struggle and direction of his journey, still there were a few milestones and turning points which deserve mention. First, his decision to resign public office and join the Congress Party in 1919; second, the issues leading to his leaving the Congress in 1925; third, the founding of the Self-Respect Movement in the same year; fourth, his participation in, and leadership of the Justice Party; fifth, the anti-Hindi agitation in 1938; sixth, the establishment of Dravidar Kazhagam (DK) in 1944; seventh, his second marriage with Maniammai in 1949; eighth, the split of the D.K. consequent on his marriage and the formation of the D.M.K. in 1949; and finally, the D.M.K. capturing power in Tamil Nadu in the 1967 election. These were some of the developments that had far-reaching consequences on his life. In fact each one of these developments for him was an occasion for redefining priorities and changing strategies. He was seen intensifying the struggle on one front and easing it on another. He was seen withdrawing support from some and offering support to some others. If he was seen gaining new associates, he was also parting company with old colleagues. But always he kept his focus on achieving certain basic social goals which he unrelentingly pursued throughout his public-life.

Periyar held offices in Tamil Nadu Congress as its President in 1923 and 1924, and as Secretary in 1925. Whether it was Prohibition, Non-Co-operation, or Promotion of *Khadi*, his involvement was complete and total. While many were content with preaching prohibition, he cut down 500 coconut trees used as toddy palms in his garden. Propagation of Khadi to Periyar meant carrying heavy loads for sale in the villages, even to the extent of impairing his shoulders. In all what he did, halfhearted effort went against his grain.

Events and experiences however, made him believe that the Congress leadership was not sufficiently determined to eradicate the caste system. He found the congress disinclined to end caste-based privileges, to take effective steps to ensure social justice and bring about equalization of opportunities. He felt disappointed and disillusioned by the attitude of Congress leaders, including Mahatma Gandhi, to the Vaikom Agitation for temple entry which Periyar led. So was it regarding the discrimination against Non-Brahmin inmates at the Chermadevi Gurukulam run with the support of the Congress. What finally drove him to part ways with the congress was the nonacceptance of the principle of communal representation for which he moved a resolution in more than one annual conference of the Tamil Nadu Congress. His abiding focus was on eradication of the caste-system. It was on abolition of social inequalities and promotion of equality of opportunities. In order to be free to pursue these goals, he left the Congress in 1925.

### Self Respect Movement

In 1925, Periyar organized the "Self-Respect Movement", designed as Dravidian Uplift Movement. It aimed to expose Brahmin tyranny and the deceptive methods they used to control all spheres of Hindu life. He attacked Hindu religion as a tool of Brahmin domination and an opiate by which the Brahmins had dulled and subdued the masses. "A Hindu according to the present concept may be a Dravidian, but a Dravidian in the real sense of the term cannot and shall not be a Hindu". As for example, Ravana, a Dravidian hero is represented as a demon in the north. In his preface to *The Ramayana: A True Reading*, he states that "the veneration of the story any longer in Tamil Nad is injurious and ignominious to the self-respect of the community and of the country". Periyar, thus resurrected the Dravidian identity as against the Indian identity which was seen to be one with Aryan identity.

Periyar's departure from the Congress and the formation of the Self Respect Movement, marked a decisive and momentous step in his life. His was, from then onwards, a career of revolt, reform, iconoclasm and incessant struggle. Till the end, he remained a crusader, uncompromising and unrelenting. His platform was one of social justice; equality of opportunities; humanism and dignity of man. It was a hectic life he lived, never dull, never routine, never one of rest and leisure. It was a life of intense activity, a succession of struggles. Each resembled a storm or an earthquake whose reverberations were felt throughout the length and breadth of Tamil Nadu.

### A Crusader for Dravidian Identity

Periyar intensified his demand for communal representation in education and employment. He viewed this measure as the Magna Carta for the weak and the downtrodden. On this issue he rallied the Non-Brahmins and organized the first provincial conference to articulate their claims. He also made common cause with the Justice Party, which formulated the communal G.O. in 1921, reiterated it in 1922 and 1924, and implemented it in concrete form in 1929.

Periyar lent his support to many other progressive measures taken by the Justice Party. These included the establishment of a large number of Primary Schools in villages, the denial of government grant to schools that practised discrimination against Harijan students and the abolition of the institution of Devadhasis or Temple Girls. As a result of his continuous collaboration with the Justice Party, Periyar was elected its President in 1938, even as he was in prison.

During the period between 1925 and 1935, Periyar started a number of Journals to carry his message to the people. They were *Kudi Arasu* in 1925; *Dravidan* in 1927, *Revolt* in English in 1928; *Puratchi* in 1933; *Pahuththarivu*, as a Weekly and

Daily in 1934 and *Pahuththarivu* as a Monthly in 1935. In 1937 he took over *Viduthalai*, a Daily started by the Justice Party.

In the elections of 1937, the Congress won with an overwhelming majority, and Rajaji became the head of the Government in the then Madras Presidency. The introduction of Hindi as a compulsory subject by Rajaji in 1938, and Periyar's historic agitation against the move, paved the way for discussions and demands in terms of separation. It culminated in the eventual emergence and strengthening of the Dravidian Movement.

What Periyar had begun as a fight against social inequalities such as casteism, the dominance of Brahmins in education and employment, and opposition to Hindi as a compulsory subject, gradually took a racial connotation. It came to be viewed as a North-South,and Aryan-Dravidian conflict, and the Movement for Assertion of Dravidian Identity.

For Periyar communal representation in education and employment was a principle dear to his heart. He believed that education and equalization of opportunities were the only two weapons to fight the humiliating inequalities and cruel iniquities heaped on the masses and perpetrated over millennia. He fulminated with anger and fury, and organized a state-wide agitation when communal G.O. of the then Madras State, for which he had pleaded and fought ceaselessly since 1921, and which was in operation from 1929, was struck down by the Madras High Court in 1950 as Ultra-vires the Constitution, and the judgement was upheld by the Supreme Court.

The widespread resentment in the Southern States, Periyar's leadership in rallying the forces for social justice, and for the protection of the weaker sections brought about the first amendment to the Indian Constitution in 1951, and the inclusion of the following clause:

*Article (15) (4): Nothing in this article or in clause (2) of article 29 shall prevent the State from making any special provision for the advancement of any socially and educationally backward classes of citizens or for the Scheduled Castes and the Scheduled Tribes.*

Even after independence, Periyar kept alive his opposition to Hindi and carried on a campaign of erasing Hindi letters from the name-boards of railway stations in 1952,1953 and 1954. He organized a movement, in 1953, to break the idols of Ganesha in important towns of Tamil Nadu. A major struggle he threatened to launch was the one to burn the National Flag to protest against moves on the part of the Government of India to impose Hindi. However, he suspended the agitation in deference to an assurance from Kamaraj that Hindi would not be a compulsory subject.

In 1957, Periyar organized an agitation to burn certain sections of the Constitution of India. He declared that the document was a tool to preserve and perpetuate the caste system and the caste-based iniquities and privileges. In all of his agitations and struggles, he consistently eschewed violence. He denounced in unequivocal language attempts at damaging property during protest marches and agitations. He was essentially in favour of respecting the law and viewed with great disfavour any attempt at disturbing the normal life of the community. He insisted on the observance of a code of conduct and adherence to certain norms even in organizing agitations and protests. However, speeches made by him in 1957, at Kulithalai and Pasupathipalayam, were found inflammatory. They were seen capable of inciting people to communal violence. Consequently Periyar underwent a prison term for six months in 1957-58.

The triumph of the D.M.K. in the 1967 elections, and the formation of Government by Anna, to Periyar, amounted to a defeat in a narrow sense, since he strongly supported Kamaraj and the Congress party in the elections. However, Anna in an unexpected move, called on Periyar and announced the dedication of his Government to him and all that he stood for by way of social reform, social justice and respect for human personality. It was a unique event in the history of democracy in that a radical reformer like Periyar, who denied God, condemned religion, and went against popular faith, had at long last, found himself accepted and acclaimed by the masses and the Government in power in his own life time. The period after 1967, for Periyar, was full of honours, recognition and mass expression of thankfulness. For his part, he continued to be active, carrying his message through numerous meetings and periodic writings, and registering his protests through agitations.

## A Nonconformist and Iconoclast

Periyar remained a fighter all through his life and fought his battles on many fronts. Though his formal education was modest, the opportunities he had listening to learned discourses of scholars and savants with which his parents were associated, his own reading in later years and his travels abroad and within the country gave him breadth of knowledge and depth of insight.

Periyar had the benefit of visiting foreign countries both in the East and in the West. During 1929-30, his travels took him to Singapore and Malaya; in 1931 he spent eleven months in Europe. He visited among other countries, Germany, the U.S.S.R., France and England. In 1954, he went to Burma to attend the 2500th anniversary celebration of the Buddha. The streak of rationalism was evident in him from his youth. The following observation by Periyar is significant:

"I have not believed in caste, or practised any religion since my youth. I might have put up appearances of conformity where obligatory. Similarly, I have had neither fear for, nor faith in, God. I would not have desisted from doing something I wanted to do, fearing God's anger or divine punishment; similarly I would not have done anything against my will to please or receive favours from God."

To prove to the masses that the idols of gods were nothing more than the stone or bronze they are made of, Periyar broke the idols of Ganesha, burnt pictures of

Rama and denigraded the various other Hindu objects of worship. He exposed claims of superhuman powers and ridiculed the Puranic stories. He carried the torch of knowledge, enquiry and logic to the humblest of villages and the lowliest of citizens. His mission till the end was to bring awakening to the common man. It was to encourage and motivate them to think on their own, and remove the shackles and chains of blind faith and superstition on their mind.

Periyar believed that education enfranchise, held the key to man's liberation from intellectual, economic, social and political bondage. Equalization of opportunities for education continued to be the cornerstone of his struggle from the beginning. The singlemost important issue on which he left the Congress was the principle of Communal Representation in education and employment.

In his long public life, Periyar might have made adjustments and shown accommodation. He might have reconciled with differences in policies here and there for the sake of certain larger interests; but he never made any compromise on Communal Representation. He never supported any party and allied with any leader who did not subscribe to this principle. He was convinced that there was no such thing as liberation for the ignorant: for freedom to them from one bondage would only mean submission to another. The ignorant would only change their masters and not shed them.

Admittedly Periyar had a great role to play in the resurgence of India in the twentieth century. He was indeed the pioneer and architect of the broad measures for equalization of opportunities in education and employment. Considering the caste system as the cancer of the Indian society he found nothing more important than putting an end to this abomination. He waged a relentless war against the caste system, especially against the practice of untouchability, and all its manifestations in the society. Temple-entry, abolition of caste-based discrimination in hotels and restaurants, inter-caste marriages, priesthood on the basis of preparation and not by birth, and the use of the language of the people for worship, instead of Sanskrit, were some of the positive measures he espoused and fought for throughout his life.

Periyar was a humanist to the core. He had no particular emotional attachment to any language or race. A rationalist and a theist he had no faith in any religion. He had no unquestioning commitment to any political philosophy. He judged and evaluated everything on the basis of its usefulness, functional efficiency and equity.

Periyar was convinced that casteism was identical with Hinduism and Hinduism meant Brahminism and supremacy of the Brahmins. Consequently, his espousal of a casteless society, and his crusade against the caste system and its pervasive influence, made him denounce Hinduism as the source of this evil. In Brahmins he saw the early authors and subtle perpetrators of this cancerous stratification.

Periyar maintained that the Hindu mythologies, Puranas, stories about gods, and the practices obtaining in Hindu temples, were nothing but clever innovations and strategies to integrate faith in God with acceptance of the caste system and a Brahmin dominated culture. He came down heavily on the Hindu Gods, mythologies, and rituals. He saw them all as an outrage on human dignity and an unpardonable crime on humanity. He lamented that an oppressive religion was being perpetrated over 3000 years and for the future also it is sought to be preserved in the name of rituals, tradition, culture and religion. He demonstrated his unreserved contempt and anger for the obsolete order. He was in a hurry to bring in a new order. He was keen to found a new society on reason, equity and dignity of humanity. It may be said that he was the willing and self-appointed champion of the causes of all those who were underprivileged, poor and the downtrodden.

## A Champion of the Cause of Women

Periyar's struggle for the cause of women had perhaps few parallels in the history of women's liberation movement in India. He condemned the practice of child marriage, widowhood, dowry, the male-domination, the myths and Puranas that weave stories extolling servility in women as virtue. He ridiculed, denounced and exposed them daily in public meetings, marriage ceremonies, political platforms and writings. He saw in the continuous occupation of women in bearing and bringing up children as the main cause of their confinement to the home and their complete dependence on men. He saw contraception as the most effective tool of women's liberation and he was the earliest to advocate family-planning. He introduced the concept of 'self-respect marriage' which laid emphasis on the equality of sexes. He looked at family life as one of partnership. He discarded all rituals that implied subordination of women to men.

In the Self Respect Movement that Periyar spearheaded, women played a prominent role. In the resolutions adopted in the conferences organized by him, those concerning the rights and privileges of women were given pride of place. He advocated, with feeling and forcefulness, widow remarriage. When his own niece became a widow in her youth, Periyar set an example by arranging for her remarriage, defying all his orthodox relatives.

At the Self Respect Conferences in 1929 and 1930, women's right to divorce and to have property was emphasized. It is but appropriate that the title of Periyar, though in occasional use earlier, was officially conferred on him only at a women's conference held in Madras, in November, 1938.

Periyar's interest in politics per se was really secondary. His main concern was social reform. For politics, he viewed, as the game of those who, among other things, aspired for power. But Periyar on his part was unwaveringly against fighting elections and capturing power. Since he resigned his Chairmanship of the Erode Municipality in 1919, till his death in 1973, he had stoutly refused to seek or accept any office of power. In 1940, and in 1942, he was twice asked to take up the Chief Ministership of the Madras Presidency; he declined, saying that acceptance of office would be an impediment to his struggle for reform. After he left the Congress, political interest in him revived only when he opposed Hindi and led the agitation against it.

## A Votary of Dravidian Identity

Periyar feared the domination of the North over the South in an independent India. He therefore advocated a separate political identity for Tamil Nadu though he used the term Dravidasthan. Since, political interest for him occupied a secondary place, he concentrated all his energies on struggle for social reform and social justice. He however kept up his relentless fight against the imposition of Hindi on the people of the South. He opposed the D.M.K. under Anna because he gave precedence to political issues over policies of social reform. But the split of the D.M.K. resulted in one concentrating on the social front and the other on essentially political issues. When the D.M.K. gave up the separation-demand, following the Chinese invasion, the emphasis came to be on autonomy for the States and on the Federal concept.

In general, the effort of the Dravidian Movement had been, and even today is, to claim for the Tamil language and culture, which are as ancient as, or perhaps even more ancient than *Sanskrit*, a recognition and an identity commensurate with their past. It is indeed a standing vindication of the cause Periyar continued to espouse all his life.

Periyar courted imprisonment more than ten times: three times in 1922; and in 1924, when he was in the Congress. Later he was arrested and imprisoned in 1938, 1948, 1949, 1950, 1957 and 1960. Agitation against Hindi, temple entry, resistance to discrimination on the basis of caste in hotels and restaurants, protest against certain provisions in the Constitution and attempt at burning the Constitution or the National Flag were among the main battles for which he was put behind bars.

Periyar was a rationalist with a difference. He was all the time a field-worker. His audience ranged from intellectuals to illiterate masses from the slums and remote villages. He took examples from their day-to-day practices, dealt with them in detail. He explained his viewpoint in a language intelligible to them. He exposed the patent follies in their faiths, beliefs and practices. He was not interested in the philosophical niceties of the many Hindu concepts. He considered them merely of theoretical interest worthy to be confined to academics, intellectuals and a limited number of persons in the upper strata of society. His concern was in what is believed and observed by the people in their day-to-day life. Religion in the Hindu society is one of rituals, ceremonies and observances and this he wanted to be changed. He stood for modernizing the society and bringing it in tune with the ideals and values relevant to the times.

Periyar kept an open mind at all times. He was refreshingly resilient in accepting and absorbing changes. While he was alert and responsive to new developments, he did not rely on any authority, ancient or modern, for his views. The opinions expressed and the measures advocated, were essentially the result of his own experience, reason, observation and contemplation.

In general, Periyar put on his shoulders the duly to fight against every form of oppression, confront every form of exploitation and counter every practice that hurt human dignity. He rejected every belief that inhibited human effort and human endeavour. For one like him whose philosophy was broad humanism, and whose objectives were human welfare and human progress, the question of hating any community really did not arise.

Periyar opposed the Brahmins when he found them oppressing the non-Brahmin community. He opposed and condemned the male members of the Brahmin and non-Brahmin communities alike, when he saw injustice being done to the womenfolk in general. He criticized no less bitterly the non-Brahmin caste-Hindus who ill-treated and humiliated the members of the scheduled caste. In general, he stood always on the side of the weaker sections of the community. He pleaded and fought for their cause, without being approached or asked.

There was an underlying current of purposiveness in his strategy and a direction in his journey. All his actions were in harmony with his objectives. He allowed no gap between what he preached and practised. It was not merely his writings and speeches that conveyed his message. His own life and work unmistakably radiated his convictions. There was no trace of hypocrisy in him, no duplicity in word and deed. His life was as transparent as crystal glass: there was nothing to hide, nothing to withhold.

Periyar identified himself indistinguishably with the masses. His time, effort and thought were totally devoted to the task of bringing about an awakening among them. All his moves were designed to set them thinking. In the 93rd year of his life, he travelled for 183 days and delivered 249 speeches. In the 94th year, he toured for 177 days and delivered 229 speeches. A life so active physically and mentally in so advanced an age is truly rare in human history.

## CONCLUSION

After 50 years of tireless striving, hard struggle and massive educational efforts through speeches, writings and demonstrations, Periyar left behind him a society vastly different from the one he inherited. It was indeed a society more alert, more questioning, less gullible, better educated, and more modern. In general it was closer to the take off point for a state of living that would be richer in all respects.

Unlike Ambedkar, Periyar actually remained a strong votary of socialism—what he termed *samadharma*—and an admirer of the Soviet Union. He also remained firm in his rejection of religion and his strong advocacy of rationalism, science and progress. And yet, his subject was neither the industrial proletariat nor the abstract unmarked citizen produced within a discourse of universal history. His search for the Self led him to an exercise analogous to that of Ambedkar's. He therefore produced a narrative of Indian history as one of the perennial struggle between the subjugated Dravidas and the subjugating Aryans. His search for national identity led him to the discovery of the Dravida Self, which he occasionally expanded to include the Sudras and the Atisudras of the North. It was indeed an untenable exercise in terms of the time-honoured canons in whose name the fight was being conducted. History, in this struggle, was not a scientific, objective reading of the past. In fact it was what it has always been, – a narrative already constituted by and therefore subordinate to the political demands of the present.

Despite Periyar's great appreciation of socialism, he, like Ambedkar, came into conflict with the communists and socialists. He argued that class divisions in Hindu society were inscribed within caste divisions. He agreed that Brahmins had lived of their intellectual capital and spiritual surplus. The non-Brahmins, on the contrary, had been denied easy access to either. They had to labour to live. He criticized the division of labour into intellectual and manual labour. He debunked the elaborate religious and cultural codes devised to validate this division.

According to the Self-Respecters, perspective has been fundamental to the problems of justice and equality in caste society The very existence of dalit politics, during the anticolonial struggle as well as in the present post-independence phase, is seen to continuously disturb and challenge the binaries of nationalism/imperialism and securlarism/communalism. It refuses to be incorporated into either term of the binary. However, the existence of these binaries effectively serves to prevent the emergence and inclusion of the dalit in the mainstream national discourse as subject and instead it seeks to stifle his voice. Thus the essentialisation of dalit identity in dalit accounts of their own history, has been a major attempt to reclaim dalit voice from the hegemonic Hindu nationalist discourse.

Thus on the question of identity, Dravida Identity in particular, Periyar's contribution was seminal and pioneering. By linking it with Dalit Identity including every depressed and deprived group, such as women and children, he developed the Dravida-Dalit Discourse into a powerful movement.

# PART V

# Introducing Political Argument

# 24

# DO PROTECTIVE DISCRIMINATION VIOLATE THE PRINCIPLE OF FAIRNESS?

### What is Protective Discrimination?

Progressive discrimination or affirmative action have remained among the most misunderstood and controversial social policy measures among conservatives and liberals alike. They recognize that injustices inherent to many political systems have affected the economic and social progress of discriminated groups. However, the debate centers on the question whether the state should employ policies that attempt to redress the wrongs of the past, even if these policies may be inherently discriminatory. Even proponents of affirmative action disagree over the most effective way to implement policy.

However there are currently two dominating policy models that persist in governments everywhere: The first and most contentious model is a direct quota system. Whichever governments have adopted these policies have imposed aggressive quantized reservation systems. It entails requiring a set number of positions to be reserved for members of a disadvantaged class. Often these reservations are seen to expand beyond the public sector, and affect private enterprise.

The second model concerns the adoption of the affirmative action polices which encourage a holistic approach. Its objective is to increase diversity while also maintaining the same quality of work.

Preferential policy programs using the term affirmative action exist throughout the world. Many affirmative action initiatives, have as their goal, the idea of rectifying past discriminatory policies inflicted on certain socially and economically disadvantaged individuals and groups in the course of history.

India has been in the forefront in adopting a very aggressive form of affirmative action based on a rigid reservation system. The system it has adopted directly uses quotas in order to attain diversity in the work force and in the educational system.

## India's Caste System

When analyzing policies in India it is essential to understand India's complex social structure, especially its ancient caste system. The origins of India's caste system can be found in the Hindu tradition. All Hindus born in India enter the caste system upon birth. Once an individual is born into a caste there is never an opportunity to escape one's caste classification. Invariably caste completely dictates an individual's position in society, defining one's job opportunities and economic status.

Indian caste system is known as *chaturvarna vayastha.* It consists of four major caste classifications viz. the Brahmins, or priestly caste, the Kshatriyas, or the warrior caste, the Vaishyas, or trading caste, and the Shudras, or servile caste. India's caste system has its origin in an ancient Hindu Vedic Legend in which the four groups emerged from a Primordial Being. According to this Legend, the Brahmins emerged from the mouth, the Kshatriyas, from the arms, the Vaishyas, from the thighs, and the Sudras, from the feet.

There is a fifth category that lies even outside the caste system. They are called untouchables, or the outcast. The untouchables are at the lowest rung of the Indian social system. As per the Legend they are not claimed by the Primordial Being. Untouchables, not classified, are regarded as impure and polluted. They are to be shunned and avoided by members of the caste system. In the Indian society untouchables have been the most discriminated and oppressed group since many centuries.

## British Policy of 'Divide and Rule': Towards Divisions in Indian Society

Since Indian society is naturally divided by the religious, linguistic, and regional variations, the British, therefore, called for separate political representation for each group. Behind the policy of separate political representation the British had two primary motivations. Apart from accentuating the differences among the Indian factions and ethnic groups they wanted to safeguard the interest of their Indian political allies, notably the Muslims, *i.e.,* to let them resolidify their weakening grip on India. The second reason was to weaken the social base of the Indian national movement by sharpening caste and ethnic cleavages and antagonisms which had remained dormant by then. By doing so they wanted to restrain the ambitions of the Indian political elite which was emerging as a force of national integration and Indian nationalism.

To counter the British policy of 'divide and rule', the Indian Nationalists sought to negotiate with untouchable leaders the terms of separate political representation. They pleaded that they would agree to give up the demand of separate electorates and in lieu of it they would get reserved seats within Congress. This is how reservation policies in India came to be mooted during the early phase of Indian nationalist struggle. However, reservation policies were further debated and developed in the Round Table Conferences of the 1930s. In these conferences discussion was focused on the induction of Indians in government along with ensuring political representation to each group within the Indian society.

The Conferences revealed the profound divisions and fissures within the Indian Society. This realization contributed to development and expansion of progressive discrimination policies. These conferences brought to the fore many of the contentious issues affecting disadvantaged minority groups in India. But the main focus of discussion remained on issues affecting the untouchables. Despite stalemate between the Indian National Congress and the minority factions at conferences over separate political representation or joint electorates, the solution to this was found in the preferential treatment policies. The Communal Award of 1932 was in fact India's first progressive discrimination policy initiative. As a result of it, Muslims and other minority groups got separate electorates. However, the greatest benefits accrued to the untouchables in that they were given voting rights, special electorates, and reserved seats in the Congress. These policies were maintained after India became independent, and eventually they were incorporated into the Constitution. They were further expanded to include many different disadvantaged classes, and groups within the Indian society. This had a bearing on the government policies on employment and higher education.

India's progressive discrimination policies are based on the classification system established by the British. They divided the Indian population into several groups of castes and tribes. They then used these classifications to identify groups entitled for positive discrimination. The lower castes and tribes were called scheduled castes and scheduled tribes. As per the national statistics, the Scheduled Castes, 15% of the population, are reserved 15% of the seats in congress, 15% of the positions in the public workforce, and 15% of the admissions into Universities. The untouchables or dalits come under this category. The Scheduled Tribes, comprising about 7.5% of the population, they are given reservation on the basis of an equal proportion of positions. These tribes have remained separated from society in very far-flung rural areas, in the mountains, or in the jungles.

The latest group finally to receive benefits under the progressive discrimination scheme have been those groups included in the classification of Other Backward Classes. This is the largest group in India and accounts for over 50% of India's population. It includes Varnas, Shudras and untouchables (non-Hindu). This group though the largest within the Indian society has been granted only 27% of the reservations.

The "other backward classes" in the Constitution of India find a mention in one of the directive principles of state policy which enjoins that some measures may also be adopted for the benefit of other backward classes. It does not specify what these measures should be and who the other backward classes are. So Commissions were set up to find definitive answers to these questions.

These groups (OBC) are the intended beneficiaries of positive discrimination and are claimants to three main kinds of benefits: The first pertains to political reservation involving reservation of a certain number of seats in Parliament and in the state legislatures for members of the scheduled castes and the scheduled tribes, roughly in proportion to their strength in the population. At present political reservation in Parliament and in the state legislatures is only for the benefit of the scheduled castes and the scheduled tribes and not for the other backward classes. In their case political reservations are written into the Constitution of India and are mandatory. However, when the provisions were made mandatory in 1950, it was decided that this would apply only for ten years. But since then the Constitution has had to be amended every ten years to continue the benefit of political reservations for the scheduled castes and the scheduled tribes. As per the original idea it was hoped that at some future time the need for these special provisions will no longer exist. But this future time seems every time to be receding further and further away.

The second kind of reservation concerns job reservations. They apply mainly to government appointments at union and state level and also to organizations which are substantially funded by the government. They apply not only to the scheduled castes and the scheduled tribes but also to the other backward classes. Over the years visibly there have been an extension of job reservations for the benefit of the other backward classes and this has become the most contentious issue. It is widely debated whether the wholesale extension of job reservations for the other backward classes accords with the spirit of the Constitution or not. For the provision concerning job reservations, unlike political reservations are not mandatory; they are only enabling provisions saying that the state may take such measures as are necessary for the special benefit of the other backward classes.

Finally, there are reservations in education. They have also led to contention, for reservation exists not only in general arts and science courses but also in medical and engineering schools. It is the reservation in medical and engineering schools which has been very controversial. What is the problem with extending these reservations on such a very large scale? The logic of reservations or of positive discrimination is that special opportunities need be created for some people over and above the general provisions for equality of opportunity for all. Now, if this is done, then it does eat into the provision of equal opportunities for all. The question is one of balance and of reconciling several conflicting aims.

Dr. Ambedkar in his inimitable style explains that first, there is the aim of providing equal opportunity for all, irrespective of caste, creed and community. That is very important. The second aim is to create special opportunities for those sections of society which have been severely deprived and disadvantaged. But as he stresses these special opportunities should not be so extensive as to 'eat up' the general provision of equality of opportunity for all. To clarify his stand these were the words he used. And now many people feel that the extension of reservations to the other backward classes on such a large scale has carried the policy of reservations too far. In many ways now it threatens the more general principle of equality of opportunity irrespective of caste, creed and community, being the postulate inscribed into the Constitution of India. So, very broadly speaking, this is the framework within which the problem of positive discrimination or affirmative action in India has to be assessed.

## What is reservation?

Reservation, in India, is a policy by which a fixed number of slots in educational and government institutions are allotted to members of certain communities based on caste. The communities that are found eligible for reservation have historically been scheduled castes and scheduled tribes. Later on, there have been moves to expand the scope of reservation to include other backward castes (OBCs) as well.

Reservation is a form of affirmative action. It implies the allocation of fixed quotas based on caste. The system of reservation as introduced in India is far more pervasive and stringent than what is being practised in countries such as the United States.

## Reservation: Its Purpose and Rationale

The stated reason for the implementation of reservation is the advancement of socially and educationally backward classes of citizens. In this case they are the scheduled castes and scheduled tribes. They have been victims of thousands of years of discrimination by India's upper castes.

On India gaining independence, a special provision was made in the Constitution providing for certain special section like the scheduled castes and scheduled tribes (SCs and STs) a minimum representation in various fields. This provision made initially for ten years was supposed to have ended after a period of 10 years but the practice has been continued till today by the Government of India by taking recourse to periodically amending the Constitution. Further by continuing to increase quotas many state institutions have now come to reserve more than 50% of their seats.

In 1979, the Mandal Commission was established to assess the situation of the socially and educationally backward classes. The commission didn't have exact figures for sub-castes, known as the other backward classes (OBC), and used the 1930 census data to estimate the OBC population at 54%. Further it went to classify as many as 1257 communities as backward. In 1980, the commission submitted a report which recommended changes to the existing quotas, increasing them from 27% to 49.5%. The report was implemented in 1990 amid a great deal of controversy.

Ever since private companies, particularly the highly successful service companies in the IT sector have opposed the move. They argue that such quotas will negatively affect their competitiveness. The opponents of progressive discrimination advance the following arguments:

1. Quotas do not work. In most higher education institutions, quotas remain unfilled because of a lack of candidates. Students from tribal groups often

dropout well before they can reach university level. Clearly, the primary and secondary education systems are faulty. Moreover, it is often the richest among the backward castes that use - and reuse - the quotas. They do not let benefit those who need them the most.

2. Providing social opportunity is the state's responsibility and not of the private sector. By asking companies to provide reservation, the State is essentially shying away from its responsibility, of giving each citizen of India an equal education and an opportunity at social mobility.
3. In addition, quotas based on caste do not work in a society as complex as India. The situatuion gets complicated and especially in a situation where high caste groups can be poorer than low castes. And quotas do not provide incentives for lower castes to get out of the system, that is, for instance by disallowing people to use a quota more than once. Most of all, if discrimination against someone is bad, then so is discrimination in favor.
4. The better course will be that the Government should emphasize affirmative action and not reservations in education and private sector employment. In fact government educational institutions must be upgraded to attract good students and teachers. The private sector must create facilities to train SCs/STs to gain competencies, and jobs by their own merit.

Most political analysts agree that affirmative action is necessary in India primarily because of the society's caste-based hierarchical social organization. Inequality is built into its deepest structures. The vast majority of the people find themselves excluded from public life for centuries.

Contemporary social science research has firmly established that past discrimination which has got embedded deep in social structure can produce inequality of opportunity, indeed widen it, even when there's no present discrimination. Different initial points of privilege and disadvantage (based on birth) will generate hugely different outcomes for individuals.

Similarly, individual career achievements are determined not by talent or merit alone. In fact they are greatly influenced by the individual's membership or lack of a dominant, well-placed, educated group on the one hand and his/her access to "the right" social contacts, information about career options, role-models and mentors on the other. An upper caste boy or girl is much more likely to know about admissions to elite institutions and job options than a Dalit boy or girl.

Such inequality of opportunity cannot be reduced without creating the level-playing-field through progressive discrimination. The aim of such a policy is not only to promote individual betterment, but also to acknowledge historic injustices against a group and compensate them through quotas or preferences in job recruitment and in admissions to schools and colleges.

The philosophy behind affirmative action is that it is better to teach a man to fish, and be self-reliant. This will enable him to eat for life rather than give him a fish that he can eat for just a day. It is far easier, as a reforms measure, to simply mandate a quota and get populist approval than to implement root and branch education reforms in a country of the size of India with its myriad complexities. Successive governments have taken this simplistic approach to reforms over the years. They have done so ignoring the micro-details and hoping still that things will eventually get sorted out on their own.

### Pro-affirmative action arguments

The following arguments are cited to support affirmative action:

(i) Diversity is desirable and won't always occur if left to chance.
(ii) Students starting at a disadvantage need a boost.
(iii) Some stereotypes may never be broken without affirmative action.
(iv) Affirmative action is needed to compensate minorities for centuries of slavery or oppression.

### Anti-affirmative action arguments

The following arguments are cited to oppose affirmative action:

1. Affirmative action leads to reverse discrimation.
2. Affirmative action lowers the standards of accountability needed to push students or employees to perform better.
3. Affirmative action tends to result in a truly colour-blind society.
4. Affirmative action is condescending to minorities, enjoining the need for affirmative action to succeed.
5. Affirmative action demeans true minority achievements, *i.e.,* success is ascribed to affirmative actions rather than one's hard work and ability.

### Pro-reservation arguments

The advocates of the schemes of reservation advance the following pleas:

* That there is no adequate representation of oppressed classes in these institutes corresponding to their population.
* That due to historical and current oppression, it is not fair to expect the oppressed classes to compete with the so-called upper class students.
* That these measures can somehow help to undo centuries of oppression.
* That safeguards already exist to protect against exploitation by people who have a good economic background.
* That reservations have been present in states like Tamil Nadu for many years. They are reported to have produced good results in promoting social justice without compromising quality.
* That such affirmative action policies, without quotas, exist in other countries.
* That affirmative action is not against article 15 (Right to Equality) of the Constitution because Art. 15(4) says that government can take necessary steps for the upliftment of socially and educationally backward classes.

### Anti-reservation arguments

The opponents of reservation oppose reservation on the following ground:

* That allocating quotas on the basis of caste is a form of racial discrimination which is contrary to the right to equality.
* That as a consequence, of legislation for providing reservation for Christians and Muslim religious minorities in all government education institutions is also introduced, this will run counter to the ideas of secularism, and introducing a form of discrimination on the basis of religion.
* That most often, only the economically sound people, rather then the rich from the so-called lower castes make use most of the reserved seats. This tends to render the aim of the measure a total failure. Political parties know reservations are no way to improve the lot of the poor and the backward. But still they support the move because of self-interest.

Another plea the detractors take concerns the extension of reservation to the "creamy layer". The issue pertains to those who use the reservations over again to further their own family interests. Several studies about the OBC have brought out that they are quite comparable with the general caste in terms of annual per capita consumption expenditure, and the top strata of OBC most often stands even much ahead of the general caste in a host of consumption areas. They further argue:

* That the quality of these elite institutions may go down, once merit is compromised by reserving seats for certain caste-based communities.
* That there are no efforts made to give proper primary education to really deprived classes. This underscores the need to reserve seats for higher studies. The government schools in India have absolutely no comparison to the public schools in the developed countries. The truth is that only about 65% of the Indian population is literate, the *functional literacy* is even as low as only 34% of the population. The critics argue that "reservation" only in higher institutions and jobs, without improving primary and secondary education will not tackle the core issue.
* That the government is dividing people on the basis of castes for political advantages.
* That this may also result in prolonged reservation system indefinitely.
* That the caste system is being kept alive through these measures instead of advancing alternative innovative ideas which will make sure equal representation, making at the same time the caste system irrelevant. But the policy decisions taken by the ruling elite only fortify the caste system.
* That the autonomy of the educational institutes is threatened.
* That not everyone from the so-called upper class are rich, and not all from so called lower classes are poor.
* That this policy has a potential to cause huge unrest in the Indian society. Providing quotas on the basis of caste and not on the basis of merit will depress and demoralize many educated and deserving students.

* That this policy will also increase the phenomenon of Brain Drain from India. In consequence, the under graduates and graduates from the upper castes will start moving to foreign universities for higher education. This will be a great set back, having an adverse bearing on Indian education and economy.
* That multinational companies will be deterred by this action. As a result foreign investment in India may dry down, halting thus the growth of the Indian economy. Doubtless, urgent and people-friendly actions are needed to be taken to improve the lot of the poor and the downtrodden who have not benefited from various plans of development even after 60 years of India's independence. But care must be taken that the new measure of affirmative action being initiated may not seriously impair the economy's competitiveness in today's highly competitive world.
* That reservations in the private sector is a far cry. If even after providing so many facilities to reserved categories during education, if there is no adequate representation of them in the work force, there must be some problems with the education system. Universal primary education along with quality education at secondary and higher education levels deserve top priority.

**Some suggestions**

Some writers suggest the following policy changes in order to find a solution to the problem:

1. They hold that the backward classes enjoy overwhelming majority in fields like politics, administrative services, government jobs etc. It is a clear pointer that they have outprospered the forward classes, and grown into dominant castes. So any move to amend the Constitution to give them any further reservation in politics, services, education and private sector jobs will be a case of "tit for tat", a revenge for 3000 years of oppression.
2. According to them, the inequalities have fairly come down. Especially in Indian cities it is very difficult to separate individuals based on caste unless it is revealed. Younger generations come to know of their friends' social category only during the time of admissions to the higher education institutions. So the quota system, far from being a leveler, is likely to create a rift in different sections of the society. One wonders why extend and enforce an amendment to increase the current quota system when actually it should be the other way!
3. The current reservation system is based on 1931 census which gave details about percentage of Hindus, Muslims, Brahmins, SCs, STs, OBCs etc. With colonial rulers the motive to gather this information was not so much administrative convenience but "Divide and Rule". Since in 1941 no census was conducted, Indian reservation quota system for the OBCs is based on the projections of 1931 census. Thus both the Mandal Commission and the current

policy decisions are based on the 1931 census since free India's census only show the percentage of SCs, STs and religions and not OBC's.

4. People belonging to OBC's who are tax payers or children of tax payers should not be eligible for reservation. This will ensure that benefits reach the poorest of the poor and this way India will move towards social justice.
5. There should be proper monitoring of who take what benefits out of the facilities given or made available.
6. Emphasis should be on proper primary (and secondary) education to let people from the so-called lower strata of the society become natural competitors.
7. Emphasis should also be on increasing the number of higher education institutes including universities, IITs, medical and engineering institutes. For example, seven good engineering institutes for a country of one thousand million, aspiring to become an economic and political power in the world are not substantial by any reckoning.
8. Once a person gets a job from the quota it should not be extended to his/her children as it will make the community complacent. This will also amount to denial of opportunities to other more deserving candidates from the lower community. Essentially a shrinking population base that needs upliftment will happen by adopting this policy of excluding 'the creamy layers' from reservation policy.
9. Government should stop private medical colleges without adequate infrastructure and staff from imparting post graduate courses as they dilute the quality.
10. Time is ripe to do away with all other kind of formal reservations in India like near hundred percent reservation in posts of Hindu Temple priests, etc.
11. Current reservation proposals may be attractive to some but it is of little use to millions of people who are leading a very pathetic life in India, irrespective of caste. Right approach would be to provide them proper quality primary education and to minimize their drop out rate from schools. This will be one way to make them "natural competitors". Giving scholarships at the higher levels to the needy and deserving rather than forcing 50% reservation can prove far more effective means of their empowerment. A recent example of this approach is when backward class and village students from one of the most underdeveloped states like Bihar made it to IIT in the general category, the secret of it was proper guidance and economic help. However, the initiative came from private sector, not government effort.
12. Some suggest a time-bound programme, with greater emphasis on primary education and exclusion of 'the creamy layers' from reservation category.

# 25

# DEMOCRACY, GOVERNANCE AND ECONOMIC GROWTH

## Democracy and Economic Growth: The Debate

The debate on democracy and economic growth has raged for centuries. It is often linked to the legitimacy of democracy as a political regime. Francisco l. Rivera Bating offers a brilliant analysis of the two. He poses the following questions:

Is democracy associated with greater economic growth. Do increased political and civil rights lead to improved standards of living, compared to more authoritarian regimes?

The existing evidence on the links between democracy and economic growth, he says, does not provide a clear cut support of the idea that increased democracy causes growth.

Some early studies, found statistically significant effects of measures of political freedom on growth.

However, more recent studies have provided ambiguous results For instance, Barro (1996) concludes that the established links between democracy and growth are a result of the connections between democracy and other determinants of growth, such as human capital.

Similarly, Rodrik (1997), concludes that, after controlling for other variables, there does not seem to be a strong, determinate relationship between democracy and growth.

## The Linkages between Democracy and Governance

The existing literature offers various arguments that link democracy to both greater and lower quality of governance. First of all, by definition, democracies bring about regime change by ballot. They allow a peaceful and regular ouster of inept, inefficient and corrupt government administrations and bring in their place more efficient, successful regimes. Thus the quality of governance on average in a democracy is higher in the long-run.

On the contrary authoritarian regimes may randomly provide high-quality governance, but if they do not, they can only be changed by force, which may take much longer than under democratic institutions. As Amratya Sen observes: "In considering the effects of democracy relative to authoritarian regimes we have to consider the political incentives that operate on governments and on the persons and groups that are in office. The rulers have the incentive to listen to what people want, face their criticism and seek their support in elections."

Potentially there is the high cost of sustaining poor government policies under authoritarian regimes. Without a democratic voice, people have no control of the risks their governments assume. Without transparent political institutions and a free press they have no way to understand these risks. This may amount to taxation without representation. In fact, history is filled with examples of nondemocratic governments causing great harm to their citizens.

As against this line of argument there are a number of authors who hold that the proliferation of interest groups lobbying for power or for rents under democratic institutions may lead to policy gridlock. This may have the effect of preventing the major decisions to be taken that are otherwise required in the development process. About Singaporean growth which has been one of the most remarkable over the last 30 years, Lee Kuan Yew, the forner Prime Minister has argued, it would not have occurred without the stringent restrictions on political and civil rights under his regime. Some writers have also highlighted the successful experience of China in undertaking market reforms. They attribute it to the strong political will and the rulers' capacity to take hard well-thought out decisions on time in comparison to disorganized and distorted reforms in regimes, such as Russia.

In this connection some refer to the distortions in the working of the electoral democracies. This is displayed in their efforts to effectively promote grassroot participatory decision-making. The fact that electoral votes can be purchased may allow wealthy individuals or parties to control the electoral process in much the same way that an openly authoritarian regime would. Here what we confront is democracy in form but hiding inside it an authoritarian system.

Thus the introduction of democratic institutions in the form of more ample political rights, civil rights, and freedom of the press, among others, may or may not be associated with improved governance.

The index of quality of governance is itself the average of two indexes: First the quality of government institutions. This index is based on a comprehensive evaluation of each country's government institutions regarding: (1) *law and order,* (2) *bureaucratic quality*, (3) *corruption*, (4) *risk of expropriation*, *and* (5) *government repudiation of contracts*. Such an index is constructed with larger values connected to higher quality of government institutions.

The most vital element is the extent to which the country is open to international trade. It is seen that protectionist governments are more likely to engage in policies that distort prices and undermine the ability of the private sector to produce efficiently and innovate. This may be a direct outcome of not only the trade –and other—taxes and restrictions which the policymakers impose but also the indirect cause of the rent-seeking activities that are almost inevitably associated with the protectionist policies.

To measure the strength of democratic institutions we need to utilize the index of political rights. According to this measure, countries with broader political rights i.e. more democratic institutions enable people to participate freely in the political process. This entails the right of all adults to vote and compete for public office, and for elected representatives to have a decisive vote on public policies.

The index of political rights is based on a careful analysis of a country's political institutions. Based on this index, the strength of democratic institutions is to be measured. Those with higher values indicate stronger democratic institutions and those with lower values point to the features of authoritarian regimes.

There are, of course, a variety of social and economic forces that explain the quality of governance in a country. According to one analysis, as development occurs and economic activity expands, countries are able to provide greater resources to the public sector and thus allow governments to function more efficiently.

A wide dispersion of the population in a country on the other hand can make transportation and communications difficult. Also it can magnify ethnic divisions that can prevent an effective governance. Where the percentage of the population residing in an urban area is greater there will be positive correlation with the quality of governance.

Finally, the availability of an educated workforce can also improve the quality of governance.

## Model of Democracy, Governance and Endogenous Growth

The evidence indicates that where democracy is negatively connected to the quality of governance, it bristles with corruption. It has been noted that in democracies, citizens can vote officials out of office if they believe them to be corrupt. This gives politicians an incentive to stay honest and work for the interests of their constituents. The existence of more effective democratic institutions can also facilitate the activities of the press. This can monitor corruption by disseminating information on corrupt government officials to the public. This itself makes them accountable for whatever they do.

In a democracy, corrupt officials impose a tax on the profits made by firms and entrepreneurs engaged in the innovation, design and production of new goods in the economy. There is the requirement of license for each new goods invented in order to be produced. Government officials take bribes in order to grant their approval. Civil service income as wages they receive is negligible compared to the bribes. This in many cases inhibits foreign investment and leads to flight of capital and entrepreneurs to other countries. Corruption has thus a negative correlation with the quality of governance.

## Democracy and GDP Growth

China is the world's biggest country. India is the world's biggest democracy. Each accounts for one-sixth of the world's people. China's stunning growth in its gross domestic product has been sustained over a longer period. It has been averaging 8 percent or more a year now for more than two decades. Poverty in China (i.e. 16 percent) is half of that in India (*i.e.,* 35 percent). Even with people-friendly indicators like literacy, life expectancy, and maternal and infant mortality, China is seen faring much better than India.

Unlike China, India is a vibrant, but tumultuous democracy. Here governments are "hired and fired" by the people through periodic elections.

One is tempted to ask: Is India's slower economic growth a price of democracy? The answer is categorically 'No'. Democracy neither causes nor diminishes economic growth. A country's economic sluggishness is due to bad policies and not due to weaknesses inherent in democracy. So, in case of India it is due to factors like policies of economic autarky, import substitution and industrial licensing. Besides other factors may include fear of foreign investment, rejection of market principles etc. It is all these combined that may have resulted in a slow rate of growth.

The policies that India has been following during the last four decades have been the outcome of conscious choices made by the ruling elite. These have had nothing to do with liberal democracy per se. Likewise the governments, suspicion of foreign firms as multinational too has been a product of history. It goes back to the entry of the East India Company into India as a trader which served but a springboard for the colonization of the country by Britain.

Jawaharlal Nehru wanted the state to occupy the commanding heights of the economy. He saw in planning an the instrument of choice for economic growth. He envisaged all economic growth to be at the cost of a free-market price mechanism. This vision of planned development grew from an admiration of what at that time seemed to be impressive achievement by the Soviet Union. The latter (the Soviet Union) was soon emerging as one of the two superpowers in the world. This led him to make compromises with liberal democracy. In view of some economists, this perhaps contributed to the persistence of poverty, multiplication of wants and massive illiteracy.

Significantly enough, in the 90's the economic performance of both India and China changed dramatically without introduction of any change in their basic political systems. This change can be explained in their abandoning of their old socialist dogmas or this may be due to deregulating their economies by adopting market principles and engaging with the international economy. Since China did this much earlier, so its growth rate has been impressive and has continued for a longer period. Accordingly its share of world trade has also been more substantial than that of India.

In case of India, democracy cannot be called into account for their common failure before and their parallel success after economic reforms. Conversely drag on the economy can be seen in terms of such factors as corrupt politicians, police and judges. In addition there is the element of bureaucratic resistance to reforms as well as other inhibitive factors in case of India.

The same point illustrating the above contention can be stated more pointedly in respect of India. Although the political system or parliamentary democracy is the same all over India, still there has been great variation in economic performance among the different states. With democracy being common to all states the explanation for this uneven development and variance in performance cannot be found in the system of democracy. Rather the explanation lies in the mix of policies and quality of governance. Neither democracy nor economic growth nor poverty alleviation is self-generating and self-guaranteeing. In the absence of sustained annual growth of 7 percent or more for the next two to three decades India will end up redistributing poverty rather than creating wealth. The policy that seeks to pull the rich down and keep the country poor instead of uplifting the poor or solidifying the middle class, runs the risk of increasing the number of the rich only marginally but ending in aggravating the misery and suffering of the common people.

The market democracies are seen to have the best record of sustained prosperity. Both democracy and capitalism put faith in the ability of citizens to decide what is best for them economically and politically. For, they know that governments can be fallible and markets can often prove imperfect. It will always be a better bet to let the people decide and face the consequences of their choices. It is assumed that masses are endowed with an intrinsic capacity to learn from mistakes and success alike. Their will to learn and learn fast should get a fillip which is possible only in a democracy. Once they realize that they themselves are responsible for their economic and political futures, they have the capacity to take decisions which can be crucial and life-changing.

## Democracy and Economic Growth: The Changing View

Over time, views on the relationship between democracy and economic growth have changed:

i. In the 1960s and 1970s democracy and economic growth were often considered as competing concerns. Jagdish Bhagwati in 1966 is seen taking the position that the political economy of development poses a crucial choice between rapid (self-sustained) expansion and democratic process.
ii. More recently, scholars often come to more optimistic conclusions. As for example, Rodrik in recent empirical studies based on samples of more than 100 countries, suggests that there is little reason to believe democracy is conducive to lower growth over long time spans.

**Reasons why democracy may be good for economic growth:**

1 Democracies can claim legitimacy and public support. Only governments

with some legitimacy can implement and sustain policies that may bear high short-term costs which may be pre-requisites of economic growth.

2 Certain institutional characteristics of a democracy, like an independent legal system, are also very much necessary for a successful liberalization. As North puts it, well specified and enforced property rights are a necessary condition for economic growth. The entrepreneurs and foreign investors are only secure when political and civil rights are secure, otherwise arbitrary confiscation is always a threat.

3 Democracies may limit rent-seeking due to their system of checks and balances. As Rodrik argues that democratic *institutions*— political parties, elected representatives, free speech, and the like—can be seen as the ultimate institutions of conflict management. It is because they allow for differences among social groups to be resolved in a predictable, inclusive, and participatory manner.

**Reasons why democracy may inhibit economic growth**

The two major factors that can inhibit economic growth in a democracy are as follows:

(i) Democracy may lead to policies that hamper economic growth involving rich-to-poor redistribution, large public sector, high taxes due to majority voting.

(ii) In a democracy there may be excessive influence of interest groups which according to Olson will reduce flexibility of the economy.

**Reasons why an authoritarian regime may be good for economic growth**

* Only an authoritarian government is in a position to introduce and implement unpopular measures. Many a time electorates are seen to turn down economic reform even when it would benefit a majority of voters. Policies requiring a long-term perspective that they would be popular ex post and would prove to be beneficial in the end are often not implemented in a democratic regime.
* The demand for comprehensive state action entailing economic reform and massive state intervention in the economy requires strong state to achieve speedy and successful economic development
* Supporters of this view often refer to the experience of countries such as Chile, South Korea and Taiwan which had authoritarian regimes.

**Reason why an authoritarian regime may not be conducive to economic growth**

* It is often seen that autocrats may also be forced to follow opportunistic policies if their survival in office is threatened.

* All authoritarian regimes are not homogeneous. Some may be under bureaucratic elite, some may be under technocratic elite and some others may be under military elite. Where we find certain authoritarian regimes having a high economic growth we should try to know the nature of the elite controlling the government. This factor may explain the experience of several nondemocratic technocratic regimes such as those in South Korea and Taiwan. At the same time enough evidence is also available that there are many counter examples of leptocratic and/or inept authoritarian regimes whose rule has led to low economic growth rates.
* Authoritarian rule can also mean arbitrary and capricious rule. Its undue interference in individual, societal and political affairs may hinder economic growth.
* A strong state and an authoritarian state are not necessarily the same thing. For a democracy having good governance can be a stronger state than the one under an inept and administratively deficient autocrat.

**A model to measure the correlation of democracy and economic growth**

* Barros has developed an Economic Growth Model that covers three time periods (1965-75, 1975-85, 1985-90)
* Controls include: initial income, initial level of human capital (schooling, health), educational spending, fertility rate, government consumption, market distortions (black market premium, rule of law), investment, terms of trade.
* Democracy variables include political rights and civil liberties.
* Although not so significant, but positive effect is seen if some of the controls are not included while measuring the correlation between the two..

Evidently thus, a relationship between democracy and economic growth is nonlinear. At low levels of democracy, more political rights foster growth but it reaches a peak at middle level.

Viewed in this light it would be wrong to conclude that democracy has anything to do with slow economic growth. There may be other determinants such as human capital, bureaucratic openness, market-friendly rules and procedures etc. which can very well go with a democracy as well.

# 26

# IS CENSORSHIP JUSTIFIED?

## Meaning and Definition of Censorship

The term "censorship" comes from the Latin, *censere* and it means "to give as one's opinion, to assess." The Roman censors were magistrates. They took the census count and served as assessors and inspectors of morals and conduct. In contrast to the Roman definition, contemporary usage of censorship offers no agreed-upon definition of the term. Here are a few excerpts of definitions of "censorship" with varying views. They indicate the variety of approaches to this concept.

Censor, according to Merriam Webmaster's Dictionary means:

(a) An official who supervises conduct and morals;
(b) who examines materials (as publications or films) for objectionable matter;
(c) who reads communications (in times of war as letters) and deletes material considered harmful to the interests of his organization.

Censorship is the suppression of ideas and information that certain persons—individuals, groups or government officials—find objectionable or dangerous. Censors try to use the power of the state to impose their view of what is truthful and appropriate. They judge what is offensive and objectionable, for everyone else.

Censorship involves removing or keeping from public access expressive materials like books, magazines, films and videos, or works of art. Individuals and pressure groups identify materials to which they object and which they want to be censored. They pressure schools not to use them. They bid libraries not to shelf them. They forbid video stores to carry them. They direct publishers not to publish them, or art galleries to display them. Censorship also occurs when materials are restricted to particular audiences. The basis of it may be their age or other characteristics.

Censors pressure public institutions, like libraries, to suppress and remove from public access information they judge inappropriate or dangerous. Their chief concern is that no one else may have the chance to read or view the material and make up their own mind about it. The censor thus wants to prejudge materials for everyone.

In the context of a library censorship means the "the removal of material from open access by government authority."

Censorship, thus, connotes the following:

1. The denial of freedom of speech or freedom of the press.
2. The review of books, movies, etc., to prohibit publication and distribution, usually for reasons of morality or state security.
3. The official restriction of any expression believed to threaten the political, social, or moral order.
4. The prevention of publication, transmission, or exhibition of material considered undesirable for the general public to possess or be exposed to.

Censorship, entails according to Professor Chuck Stone, the cyclical suppression, banning, expurgation, or editing by an individual, institution, group or government. It refers to all those who enforce or influence its decision against members of the public — of any written or pictorial materials which that individual, institution, group or government deems obscene and "utterly without redeeming social value," as determined by "contemporary community standards."

Thus, from the above definitions it follows that censorship is a word of many meanings. In its broadest sense it refers to suppression of information, ideas, or artistic expression by anyone. It may be by government officials, church authorities, private pressure groups, or speakers, writers, and artists themselves.

Censorship may take place at any point in time. It may occur before an utterance, that is, prior to its widespread circulation. Or it may be enforced by punishment of communicators after dissemination of their messages, thereby deterring others from the like expression.

In its narrower, more legalistic sense, censorship means only the prevention by official government action of the circulation of messages already produced.

However, some writers "censor" themselves before putting words on paper, for fear of failing to sell their work. They are thus engaging in censorship in this narrower sense. Some even boycott sponsors of disliked television shows.

Again in modern times censorship also means: supervision and control of the information, and ideas circulated within a society.

In this sense censorship refers to the examination of media including books, periodicals, plays, motion pictures, and television and radio programs for the purpose of altering or suppressing parts, thought to be offensive. It is because of this that offensive material may be considered immoral or obscene, heretical or blasphemous, seditious or treasonable, or injurious to the national security.

## Cencorship and Mass Media

The mass media include television, the movies, and recordings. But the term can be extended to cover popular books and magazines and, now, the Internet as well. There are a few people who regard television and the movies as mere entertainment. Their view is that what we see and hear with such frequency is like water off a duck's back: it amuses, moves, or entrances but without in any way affecting us.

Censorship is not meant for such cases. However, there be those, who consider the influence of the mass media actual and malignant. Censorship or, more broadly, regulation may be meant for all of them.

The case for regulating the mass media today rests on several premises:

(i) The mass media are the prime educational force in the country;

(ii) that their effect is, by and large, pernicious running counter to the education of the young in schools, society and to the qualities required of mature citizens in a civilized republic; and

(iii) government alone, may have the power to block this descent into decadence.

In context of censorship we need now to face these and many more such questions:

(a) Is not prior restraint, or censorship in the strict sense, banned by the very idea of the freedom of the press?

(b) Would censorship of the movies, television, and recordings be constitutional?

(c) Can censorship be made responsible and consistent with the needs of liberal democratic government?

(d) Why should, what we see and hear be determined by some faceless bureaucrat?

(e) Will censorship not be misused and abused by politicians?

(f) Is censorship enough to correct the moral corruption that has already shown itself in our midst?

Truly speaking, freedom of the press which originally means the elimination of censorship is now under severe threat. This in many cases is due to the abuses of "the press". It is now thought in many informed quarters that the abuses consequent upon publication of books, pamphlets, handbills can be corrected by punishment subsequent to publication. The offending materials, which in any case circulated slowly, can be withdrawn from circulation. Contrasted with this, the movies, television, and recordings can be "published" once all over the country. It can be seen and heard by millions, young and old alike. That is what makes for the rare power of the mass media. Furthermore, the visual and auditory appeal of drama and music gives them a power totally different from that of printed matter. Equating these media with the press in its exact sense is off the mark. For the harm caused by printed material can be minimized after publication, but the harm caused by movies and television programs shown even once can be widespread and terrific.

In most instances, censors consist of sincerely concerned individuals or a body assigned this task. It is their strong belief that censorships can improve society and protect children. Above all, it can restore what the censors see as lost moral values.

### Relationship between Censorship and Intellectual Freedom

In voicing their opinions and concerns, would-be censors are seen exercising the same rights people seek to protect when they confront censorship. In making their criticisms known, people who object to certain ideas are seen exercising the same rights which those who created and disseminated the material to which they object had exercised. People's rights to voice opinions and then trying to persuade others to adopt those opinions is protected only if the rights of persons expressing ideas they despise are also protected. The truth is that the rights of both sides must be protected, or else neither will survive.

### How do Censors Justify their demands that Information be Suppressed?

Censors may sincerely believe that certain materials are offensive and harmful. They are violative of society's ethico-normative order and social values. This is the rationale why such stuff, hateful and destructive, should not be allowed to see the light of day. Censors and others concerned individuals or groups are worried lest younger or weaker people who are impressionable and vulnerable should be badly influenced by bad ideas, and should do bad things as a result. They see a very clear distinction between ideas that are right and morally uplifting, and ideas that are wrong and morally corrupting. They sincerely wish to ensure that society benefits from their perception and moral judgment. They are convinced that certain individuals and certain institutions, even society itself, will be endangered if particular ideas are allowed to be disseminated without restriction. What Censors often ignore is that, if they succeed in suppressing the ideas they don't like today, it will be used as a precedent to suppress even the correct ideas tomorrow.

### What are the most frequently Censored Materials?

Throughout history, books have been banned for many reasons. The reasons include political content, sexual expression, or language offensive to some people's racial, cultural, or ethnic background. Other considerations concern gender or sexuality, or political or religious beliefs. Still others that have often been censored include materials considered heretical, blasphemous, seditious, obscene or inappropriate for children.

Thus, to the question, who will do the censoring we need to recall that in monarchical days of old, the Censor was an individual appointed by the king. From his secret decisions there was no appeal. Today there are Boards of Censors as well as individual Censors in many of our states and cities. Their main business is to supervise movies and shows.

Formerly the Censors, often appointed, were relatively unknown individuals. Today, it should be possible to enlist some of our most distinguished citizens to serve as Censors. Now we realize that how central, rather than peripheral, this function really is.

However, undeniably today, we find a few hidden figures in movie studios and television networks, motivated primarily by profit, who decide what should be available for our viewing. With few exceptions, the viewer is offered a variety of bad alternatives. Whatever be their technical wizardry, but the fact is that for inch by inch, yard by yard, the mass media have lowered the standards of their productions. It is seen appealing increasingly to animal appetites. Once they are released, they give little quarter to the nobler elements of freedom and civilization.

The choice is that either we may have a rigorous censorship of the mass media, in conformity with responsible liberal democratic principles with Censors known to all and operating under law, or else we may be in for an accelerating descent into barbarism and destruction, sooner or later, of our so-called free society itself.

## Censorship: Differing Perspectives

In broad historical terms, censorship as the control of the information and ideas circulated within a society — has been a hallmark of dictatorships throughout history. In the 20th Century, Censorship is achieved through the examination of books, plays, films, television and radio programs, news reports, and other forms of communication. This is done for the purpose of altering or suppressing ideas found to be objectionable or offensive. The rationale for Censorship have varied over time. Some censors target materials deemed to be indecent or obscene; others do so if their find it heretical or blasphemous or seditious. Invariably this is seen to result in suppression of ideas under the guise of protecting three basic social institutions: the family, the orthodox religion, and the state.

Censorship and the ideology supporting it go back to ancient times. Every society has customs, taboos, or laws by which speech, dress, religious observance, and sexual expression are regulated. In Athens, where democracy is seen first to emerge, censorship has been well known as a means of enforcing the prevailing orthodoxy. Indeed, Plato is the first thinker to formulate a rationale for intellectual, religious, and artistic censorship. In his ideal state outlined in *Republic*, Official Censors would prohibit mothers and nurses from relating tales deemed bad or evil. Plato also proposes that unorthodox notions about God or the hereafter be treated as crimes and that formal procedures be established to suppress heresy. In his *Republic* poets have no place. Freedom of speech in Ancient Rome has been reserved for those in positions of authority. The poets Ovid and Juvenal are both banished. Authors of seditious writings are punished severely. The emperor Nero deports his critics and burns their books.

The Organized Church soon joins the state as an active Censor. The Biblical injunction, "Thou shalt not take the name of the Lord, thy God, in vain" is clearly an early attempt to set limits on what would be acceptable theological discourse. Likewise, "Thou shalt not make unto thee any graven image" becomes a basis to set limits on how the Divine may or may not be represented.

Unique historical considerations have also seen to contribute to censorship. Perhaps the best example is the hate speech law in Germany. It is illegal, under German law, to depict any kind of glorification of the Nazis or even to display the emblem of the Swastika.

In a global context, governments have used a powerful array of techniques and arguments to marshal support for their censorship efforts. One of the earliest has been the religious argument. Certain things are deemed to be offensive in the eyes of the Deity. These things vary from country to country, religion to religion, even sect to sect. They are mostly, though not always, sexual in nature. The commentaries on the nature of the impulse to be censorious towards sexual expression are too numerous in the classic texts. They point to the fact that the problem of governments and citizens reacting in this way is not a new one. What is new are the potential global consequences.

National security and defense follow the religious impulse as a rationale for suppression. Thus impulse to censor, in its more modern form, is obviously even more pervasive. And while the influence and hold of religion on secular affairs is muted and loosened in certain parts of the world, the power and influence of governments have been usually seen to be on the increase. It is difficult to think of any government that would forego the power to censor all media, not simply those that appear on line.

So many nations of the world today are considering the filtering system known as PICS (Platform for Internet Content Selections) as an answer to their concerns. In this context, the question of parental controls has become important. In many countries, the state justifies censorship with the claim that it is acting, "state as parent" or "state as Big Brother," This is how they justify their claim in imposing many of the restrictions on information distribution found today across the world.

Parental claims certainly have a place in the dialogue, but they offen can cut across meaningful lines of discourse as well. Despite the presence of a widespread and deadly worldwide epidemic (AIDS), there are parents who object to the teaching of safe sex models in public schools. Such objections pose an obvious problem: do their rights as the parents of their own children supersede the rights of all children in a classroom, library, or online community to have access to information that could save their lives? The legal precedents, which usually provide clear guidelines in such matters, are mixed here. Courts have ordered operations and vaccinations in the public health interest. But at the same time courts have also ruled that religious beliefs are a compelling answer to public concerns.

That question is of much greater import in respect of the restriction on so-called "obscene" or "pornographic" material online. This is probably the most pervasive type of censorship around the world. For, the behavior it seeks to limit is private and personal in the most fundamental way. "I know it when I see it," a U.S. Supreme Court Justice once said of obscene material. The judge perhaps unremittingly spoke a great truth. The fact is that different nations across the world have different thresholds for what they consider pornographic material.

The biggest current issue in terms of pornographic material is child pornography. People trafficking in such material, even in the United States, have little or no recourse to free speech or free expression claims. Yet, there is no uniform age of consent. Those limits are set by the states and they can vary by as much as six years. So what may be valid in one state may be a violation of law in another.

Balancing compelling national interests with compelling individual interests as well as competing national interests in the online world, is going to be the work of generations. In the past, nations were able to legislatively proscribe certain types of behavior. But the Internet pushes against national, or even, supranational borders in a way that no medium before it has ever done. The potential for expansion, or opening economic and political opportunities where there had been none before, is now beyond imagination. So, too, is the potential for its calamitous misuse, both by governments, individuals and corporations.

As is evident, freedom from censorship today is the exception in the world. The rule historically has been, and continues to be, repression and suppression of disfavored ideas. The one redeeming fact is that, in most parts of the world, the ideal of liberty is embraced at least theoretically, and no state openly claims a commitment to religious, intellectual, artistic, or political censorship. The universal appeal of free expression is reflected in the many covenants and declarations that have been passed in support of freedom and human rights. These include the UN Charter (1945), the UN Declaration of Human Rights (1948), the UN Covenants on Civil and Political Rights (1966) and on Economic, Social, and Cultural Rights (1966), the European Convention on Human Rights (1953), the Helsinki Final Act (1975), and the American Convention on Human Rights (1978). These documents give hope that the Internet might yet succeed in realizing its promise of providing a free and unencumbered flow of information throughout the world.

## Enlightenment and Freedom of Expression

The powerful bureaucratic system of pre-censorship practised in late Medieval Europe, was the target for John Milton in his much disputed speech *Areopagitica* to the Parliament of England in 1644. Here Milton vigorously opposed the Licensing Act passed by Parliament in 1643. In Milton's noble plea for freedom of the press, he also quoted Euripides. He did so to add the weight of the ancient struggle for free expression to his own arguments. Milton's strong advocacy in defence of free expression contributed to the final lapse of the Licensing Act in Britain in 1694. Milton's *Areopagitica* also became one of the most quoted documents on the freedom of expression. It also remains as much today a true beacon of enlightenment as it was when it was written.

The 17th and 18th centuries represented a time of reason. During this period the rights, such as liberty and dignity of the individual came into political focus and soon became subject to legislative protection. Sweden was the first country to abolish censorship and introduce a law guaranteeing freedom of the press in 1766. Then Denmark/Norway followed suit in 1770. Soon thereafter came the First Amendment of the Constitution of the United States (1787). It guaranteed freedom of speech as well as of the press. This was following by the much quoted statement by the French

National Assembly in 1789: *"The free communication of thought and opinion is one of the most precious rights of man; every citizen may therefore speak, write and print freely."*

Although censorship, as a frequently applied legislated instrument, lost ground during and after the 18th century in Europe, governments maintained legal frameworks curbing freedom of expression. The instruments included Acts of National Security, Criminal Acts on Obscenity or Blasphemy, or Laws on Libel.

## Censorship: The Press and Libraries

In the 18th century, the press in most of Europe was frequently subjected to strict censorship. The 19th century saw the emergence of an independent press. Censorship gradually was seen ceding to the demand for a free press.

Censorship in libraries was a result of the benevolent public concern for morality. Although government-instituted censorship had apparently been abandoned in most western countries during the 19th and most of the 20th century, public concern for offensive literature did not subside. Subsequently, public libraries were expected to act as the benevolent guardians of literature, particularly concerning books for young readers. This, in turn, gave teachers and librarians licence to censor a wide range of books in libraries under the pretext of protecting readers from morally destructive and offensive literature.

However, censorship of libraries is far from a recent practice. On the contrary, libraries have been the targets of censorship since ancient times. History is littered with the destruction of library collections or their becoming flaming pyres on all continents. The deliberate burning of a library is recorded in China as early as in 221 B.C. The huge libraries of Nalanda and Takshila also met the same fate. Although the destruction by fire of 400,000 rolls in the Bibliotheca Alexandrina in 47 B.C. was by all accounts accidental, the burning of the entire collection of the University of Oxford library in 1683 was on direct orders from the King. Even in the 20th century, the burning and destruction of libraries has been extensively applied by rulers, as a warning to subversives and a method of ethnic language purging. This is what took place quite recently in Sarajevo and Kosova. During the period 1990-99, all the libraries in Kosova were subjected to the burning or destruction of the Albanian–language collections.

Public book pyres were favoured by the Nazi–regime in Germany in the late 1930s as one of their many brutal methods of censorship. The destruction of libraries was systematically applied by the rulers of the USSR. It may be seen as infamous and perhaps the longest lasting and most extensive censorship in the 20th century.

## Censorship and USSR

The Russian empire, having a long tradition of strict censorship, was slow to undergo the changes that central European countries had passed a century before. Censorship reforms were started in a single decade of tolerance, from 1855 to 1865 during the reign of Tsar Alexander II. It was then that the transition was made from legislation on pre-censorship to the punitive system based on legal responsibility. During the decade, the press enjoyed greater freedom and more radical ideas were voiced. But soon enough censorship laws were reimposed in 1866. It had the effect of practically eliminating the basic ideas of the much wanted reform. With October Revolution (1917), a new long and extensive era of strict censorship began which lasted until the end of the 1980s.

Religion, regarded as gross and misleading superstition, was targeted only a few months after the revolution. In the spring of 1918, a decree was issued formally separating Church from State. It was followed by strict prohibitions imposed on religious bodies along with nationalization of all Church property.

In 1922, the central censorship office was established, known for short as Glavlit. Its aim was to purge the Soviet society of all expressions regarded as destructive to the new order and contagious to the minds of people. The Glavlit had absolute authority to subject the performing arts and all publications to preventive censorship. It was also armed with the power to suppress all political dissidence by shutting down "hostile" newspapers.

However, in the early 1920s during the time of Lenin and Trotsky, writers and artists were granted creative freedom. This was done on condition that they would observe the rule of not engaging in overt political dissent. Although the majority of intellectuals were opposed to the revolution, many artists and intellectuals supported the revolution's ideals of equality for all and freedom from slavery and poverty. Also Russian artists had embraced the ideals of the European Modernist Movement, already in 1915. They formed the visionary *Avant Garde* Aesthetic Movement, which survived until 1932. With advent of the Stalin regime the censorship system became all the more elaborate. The methods of purging became increasingly sinister. It only allowed authorized printing. It ordered banning of publications and it prevented import of foreign books.

## Censorship and Nazism

*"From these ashes will rise the phoenix of the new spirit"*, Gobbles optimistically declared of the massive funeral pyres of some 20 000 volumes of offensive books which were devoured by flames in Germany in 1933. Numerous book pyres were enthusiastically lit by the young members of the fanatical Nazi movement. In order to cleanse the minds of people and society, any book written by a Jewish author, or a communist or humanist, was fed to the flames. *"Where they have burned books, they will end in burning human beings"*, observed the German author Heinrich Heine. He was sadly proved right, by Nazi–Germany's gruesome mass extermination of people, including at least 6 million Jews, but also Romani, communists, dissidents, deviators from the ideal "Arian Race".

Hitler, the omnipotent Fürer of the Third Reich, also implemented the severe censorship. All countries occupied during World War II (1940-45) become victims of intolerable propaganda machine of the Nazi regime. In occupied countries, national newspapers, publishers and radios were taken over at once, or shut down. In countries such as Norway, strict censorship was put in place. Listening to "foreign" radio or producing, reading or disseminating 'illegal' newspapers was made punishable with death.

### Apartheid Censorship in South Africa

The Apartheid Regime in South Africa (1950-1994), in upholding their cruel policy of racism, resorted to severe censorship, torture and killings. In this respect, the prohibitive policies of the Apartheid Regime strongly resembles that of the USSR. The censorship affected every aspect of cultural, intellectual and educational life. Detailed information about all items censored has been carefully compiled by the South African publisher *Jacobsen*, in the "*Jacobsen's index of objectionable literature*" (1996). This admirable work has preserved for posterity all the details of the Apartheid madness.

### The Press in times of War

"*Truth is the first victim in a war*"—All through its 400 years history, the media has been the first hostage to be taken, either by occupying forces or by military dictators when overthrowing governments. As a rule, the press has been faced with the choices of gagging or closure. Many a respectable newspaper were simply taken over by or submitted to becoming the mouthpiece of the new rulers.

Some of the worst examples of rigid press censorship induced by military dictators in the 20th century were those of Spain (during Spanish Civil War 1936-39, Greece 1967 -1974, Chile 1973-1990 and Nigeria 1966-1999). Also Turkey, under the pretext of ensuring national security against "the enemy within" – the Kurd minority - still upholds strict censorship through the Anti–Terror Act of 1991, in spite of countless pleas from the international society.

### Pornography and the Regulation of Internet

More recently with internet resulting in the free flow of ideas, thoughts and opinions. guardians of public morals the seen to voice their concern about what was decent and obscene in the multitudinous information. As a result obscenity became the prime target of censorship.

As pornography became most widespread it forced the policy makers to find ways to save the young impressionable minds. With this end the most extreme form of censorship was sought to be used by taking recourse to regulations and law. The custodians of religious and other pressure groups were also pressed into service to fight this menace which had the potential to wreck a whole generation of the young and hence the future posterity. However, in retrospect, the state action in defence of morals was but a ruse to serve the interest of some influential members of the Polity who wanted to safeguard the society of certain ideas that were considered obscene and offensive. They set themselves as watchdogs targeting books, plays and movies, that they thought to be obscene. They strove to suppress them either through the state intervention or by themselves. But what is obscene and what it is not has been a matter of virulent debate. To find a way out, the society, state and the judiciary have been grappling with this problem quite for time. For example, on obscenity a judge pronounced that 'the test of obscenity is whether the tendency of the obscenity is to deprave and corrupt the mind of those whose mind is open, to such immoral influences and into whose hands a publication of this sort may fall, But later in another judgment, a distinction was made between what it termed as the 'fifth for filth sake' and 'a piece of literature'. The rationale it cited was that while the former type of publication had no message or inspiration, the latter type, in contrast, had 'an honest purpose and an honest thread of thought'. The banning of such works would be without any valid basis especially in that it dealt with the reality of life, love and sex. The Judge ruled that 'sex is not dirty or sin' and that 'the literary-moral-legal test ought not to be what is suitable for a 14 year old school girl to read.' Hence it follows it would serve no purpose to belittle good literary works, for, they are a source of valuable knowledge about the way people act, feel and think. It was such change of perspective that led to removing the ban on some great works of Rousseau, Voltaire, D.H. Lawrence and the like which had been earlier banned on the charge of obscenity.

### Is Censorship Justified ?

This is one topic that has been debated age after age. The debate has become more loud and strident with "the coming of age of media and the culture of the country". Censorship being a pretty dubious issue calls for certain set parameters which come from higher offices of law, that enforces what is ethically correct and conducive to the health or the society. The higher judiciary in India commenting on film censorship, has noted :

"Film censorship is seen necessary because a film motivates thought and action. It assures a high degree of attention and retention as compared to the printed word. The combination of act and speech, sight and sound in semi darkness of the theatre with elimination of all distracting ideas can have a strong impact on the minds of the viewers and can affect emotions. Therefore, a film has as much potential for evil as it has for good. It has an equal potential to instill or cultivate violent or good behaviour. It cannot be equated with other modes of communication. Censorship by prior restraint is, therefore, not only desirable but also necessary."

### Censorship in Indian Context

Censorship is not only applicable to the Indian media or industry, but also to most of the countries in the world. Censorship has its pros and cons, but probably, the advantages it provides generally just tilt the balance a bit more in its favor. Censorship regularizes what the audience gets in a way that no one in any case, is harmed or feels offended by the display.

The procedure for every kind of media product has a mention in the guidelines. It has to pass through a procedure that reveals the end product to suit one and all, whether these were the days of the completely susceptible Indian society where a kiss was shown by mere joining of two flowers or to the age, where a movie has gone much beyond a kiss. Should one assume that the society has come of age and so has the censorship! The censor board, generally headed by a renowned media personality with rounds of experience at the top, mostly sense behind him, it is not a mere gimmick. The censored part is not actually for the hack of it but appraising the pertinence of the content and a knowledge of how much and what would be accepted in a humane manner. Be it *Satyam Shivam Sundaram* in the yesteryears or *Da Vinci Code* recently, there has been something in every decision that goes through the Censor Board. The main task of the Board remains to look into the interest of the society which is not an easy task at any given point. Be it showcasing of vulgarity or violence, contempt of court or protruding religious violence, there is not a shortage of things, to be kept in mind that might just turn profit for one party into a ghastly treat for the viewers.

Everyone knows the hoopla made when Manisha Koirala starrer *Ek Choti Si Love Story*, was into trouble over the scenes found offensive and released the film with a cut in few scenes. If at that time probably the movie was released as it was, the retaliation of the enraged crowd would have been much more than what it was by just one fraternity.

However a recent example where the Censor Board acted a bit unreasonably was during the release of *Rang De Basanti*. When later it was specially screened for the defense ministry that it got clearance. The issue was about the showcasing of a corrupt defense ministry and their hang-ups with the corporate honchos. The movie however turned out to be a huge hit.

Many arguments have been given for and against censorship involving ideas written or spoken. To be censorable implies that the idea or scenes that constitute a genuine danger to the overall health of society are not valid and hence they should not be presented.

Censorship in this sense involves controlling the dangerous expression of ideas by those in authority. The authority in this context means all those successful practitioners of censorship in the form of religious head,, monarch, a dictator or even a democratic government. To them, political, economic and ideological means come handy to suppress the ideas dangerous to the status quo.

Some of the methods used for censorship consist of a ban on publications of books, comic etc. They may include blacklisting of controversial literary figures and the performing artists. It may also entail blocking their employment in media and communication, or it may make prior permission compulsory for movies, radio and TV programmes, etc. In this connection, the newspapers and the press in many democratic countries, are not censorable by way of prior restraint. Unless deliberative malice is proved in the courts it can not even be sued for libel. Even though the theoretical basis of censorship ill accords with the liberal tradition of individual liberty, censorship has been justified on the following counts:

### Arguments in Favour of Censorship

(i) The idea presented or about to be presented are explosive and dangerous by the standard laid down by those in power and thus worthy to be suppressed as well as fit for penal action. Such ideas may appear beautiful and appealing to the feelings and communal sentiments of some cultural/ social groups in a multiethnic multicultural society like India, but they can become sources of social disruption and disorder.

(ii) Author National basis to justify censorship goes back to Plato Republic. It rests on the belief that the minds of those who would fall victim to the ideas to be censored might not be capable of seeing the falsity inherent in them and hence be led astray by their siren voice. The moral obscenity and hardcore pornography call for strict censorship. For they can disrupt the normative order of the society and can prove dangerous to the health of the system. With the coming of internet the problem has become much more acute and has assumed a global proportion As a result a debate has ensued how to check this menace which has no frontiers.

It is well said that 'every idea is an incitement'. Or again, 'dissent not conformity is the key to progress'. What the society needs is free flow of ideas and it is censorship which seeks to impose fetters on it. Justice Oliver Wendel Holmes says, when censorship is exercised you are in the real overt action and not ideas. A line needs be drawn between the freedom of expression and the public order and morality. Censorship, to be a positive force for the good must strike a balance between the imperatives of free speech and expression and the society's ethico-normative order. Where and how such a line needs be drawn to secure the goal of good life and ordered liberty is the most point.

### UDHR: "Not to forget and never let it happen again"

When signing the Universal Declaration of Human Rights (UDHR) in 1948, the members of the newly established United Nations pledged to remember the millions of people murdered in Nazi Germany. But history has repeated itself, as in Rwanda in 1994 and the Yugoslav dominions in the I990s. And this has happened when yet, most member countries of the UN are signatories to the Declaration. During the year of international celebrations of the 50th Anniversary of the United Nations Declaration of Human Rights, independent human rights and freedom of expression organizations reported violations of freedom of expression in almost 120 countries.

The report noted the sordid fact that 118 journalists were imprisoned in 25 countries and 24 journalists were murdered. Numerous newspapers, publishers and broadcasters were subjected to banning, closure or violent attacks such as bombings. Currently, most of the serious attacks on freedom of expression are committed in countries in the Southern Hemisphere or former East Block Countries. Even today, more than half of the world's population still lacks an independent press.

The painful paradox of history's worst crimes is that they are continuing to repeat themselves. This can hardly be resolved creating a database such as the *Beacon for freedom of expression*, though it might provide another tool for enlightenment and actions by people, thus hopefully contributing to end the violations.

# 27

# SHOULD THE STATE INTERVENE IN THE INSTITUTION OF FAMILY?

## Family: The Cradle of Love, Life and Culture

A family may mean "two or more persons related by birth, marriage or adoption who reside in the same household." Of course, this definition cannot capture the richness of family life in India in which family entails three generations living together, tending the young and caring for the elderly.

Family is the most important form of human organization. Its basis is matrimony and kinship. It is a web of relationships between husband, wife, parents, children, brothers, sisters and other relatives. Family is the basic building block of all that is indispensable and enduring in human civilization. Family is the agency that ensures reproduction and socialization of man from cradle to the grave. As one economist once observed, "The real world is the world around the kitchen table, the world of the nursery, the world of the bedroom."

Throughout the ages the family has been viewed as the foundation of the social order. It is the bedrock of a nation, and the bastion of a civilization. Cicero speaks of the family as "the first society" and "the seedbed of the state." The Universal Declaration of Human Rights of the United Nations (UN) describes the family as "the natural and fundamental group unit of society."

The family is a universal and irreplaceable community. Its roots lie in human nature. It is the basis for all societies at all times. It is the cradle of life and love for each new generation. The family is the primary source of personal identity, self-esteem, and support for children. It is also the first and foremost school of life. It is uniquely suited to teach children integrity, character, morals, responsibility, service, and wisdom. As UN document states, "the family provides the natural framework for the emotional, financial, and material support essential to the growth and development of its members, particularly infants and children. . . . The family remains a vital means of preserving and transmitting cultural values".

These roles of transmitting culture and socializing children make the family indispensable to civil society. It is family that transforms helpless, dependent babies into responsible, independent adults and responsible citizens.

Family has been called 'the seedbed of virtue' and 'the bedrock of civil society'. President Theodore Roosevelt claimed that there is 'no finer factory of individual character than the family'. It is also the wellspring of citizenship.

## The Relationship of Marriage to the Family

Despite its recent decline, the institution of marriage remains central to family life. It is marriage that bring together two people in a lifelong bond. This bond not only creates a new family but also links existing families in a manner that invigorates and perpetuates both. Marriage results in abiding ties and a sense of belonging between the couple, their parents and extended kin, their anticipated children, and society at large.

Although men and women of full age have the right to marry and to found a family, "marriage is not so much about rights, but responsibilities". The married couple who create the family set a pattern of sacrifice, duty, and obligation that naturally flows into parental duties of raising and nurturing children.

## Modern Pressures on the Family

During the last century, families have faced unprecedented challenges, both political and cultural. On one side there have been ideologies that seek to supplant familial devotion with political devotion, to cultural trends that emphasize adult desires over children's needs.

By their very nature, totalitarian movements seek to subsume familial devotion to devotion to the state. Every totalitarian movement of the twentieth century, from Communism to Nazism, is seen to weaken the institution of family. They view family with suspicion. They overestimate the capacity of the state to "rescue" children who are living in precarious environments. As a result, these societies too often are seen to relying upon state-sponsored institutions to care for children. They often exclude families to have the responsibility of caring for their own children themselves, in their own homes.

In the last generation, by contrast, the pressures on the family have not come so much from political forces but from cultural changes in the West. By the late 1970s, some cultural voices are seen to start questioning the very utility of the family and marital commitment to the needs of children. As a result, at least in part, marriage rates have declined over the past five decades, while rates of divorce, unwed childbearing, and cohabitation have increased.

## The Family and the State

Given the important role that families play in society, it will be pertinent to ask: does the state have any role in supporting the family? To this question the answer is, yes. Government, within appropriate limits, should work to support and strengthen families. This support falls into three broad categories: (i) respecting the prerogatives of families, (ii) proactive support for healthy marriages, and (iii) supporting all families that need assistance.

To support families effectively, government must recognize that families exist apart from the state. The U.S. Declaration of Independence states that all human beings are endowed by their Creator with certain inalienable rights, in other words, rights that predate the state. The state can only recognize and acknowledge these rights. In the same manner, the family is a gift that the state should not deny or manipulate for its own purposes. The state must recognize and respect the family for what it is, as a matter of fundamental moral and natural law. By intruding on the prerogatives of the family or ignoring the decline of the family, the state shall only weaken its very foundation. The state's foremost obligation in this sphere is to respect, defend, and protect the family as an institution.

### State Intervention in the Family: Differing Dimensions and Perspectives

The question, whether state should interfere in the family became a live issue in the context of women liberation movement in Europe and America during 1960's and 70's. The movement came to be popularly known as Feminism due to its espousal of women issues. Gender inequality as manifest in many areas of social life became the object of criticism by feminist writers. They objected to discrimination of women in the home and in wage labour, in matters of sexuality, marriage and motherhood and in many other areas.

Gender difference works in every organization of the State. It works through the institution of Patriarchy which connotes male dominance over women in the society. Patriarchy is a system of male authority and an instrument of oppression of women. It is made worse through man's monopolistic access to resources within and outside the home and family.

The oppression of women has several dimensions – economic, sexual, cultural, ideological — and is secured in a variety of ways such as:

(i) Devaluation of women's work and achievement,
(ii) education deprivation,
(iii) discrimination in access to economic resources and political power,
(iv) ideological indoctrination that women are inferior to men, and
(v) social taboos, restraints and coercion.

For centuries in a male-dominated world marriage customs, conventions and laws have contributed to male hegemony. Legal reforms have not resulted in a substantial change in the status of women. This has led to a virulent debate among the various schools of Feminism about the role of the state in the institution of family. There are Liberal Feminists who are inclined to confine the family to the 'private sphere'. They do not countenance male oppression of women as a problem warranting state interference in the family. Alongwith Liberal Feminists there are the Radical

Feminists who look upon the family as the symbol of women's oppression. They favour state interference in securing the emancipation of the women as a class.

The idea of noninterference of the state in the family is rooted in the long tradition of the sanctity of the family. It is based on the *pater familias* doctrine. In terms of this doctrine, the family household is conceived as an extension of the personality of the *pater familias.* This doctrine considers 'intervening in a man's family affairs as an invasion of the personal private sphere'. It views familial relationships as 'private' and governed by 'natural instinct and sympathy'.

J.S. Mill, even as he considers women as equally capable of achievement in all spheres of life, still he likes to confine women's sphere to the domestic work. He defends this as 'the most suitable division of labour between the two persons'. John Rawls, while he considers the family as one of the social institutions worthy to be evaluated by the theory of justice, he finds the traditional family to be just. The measure of just distributions is, for Rawls, the household income, which accrues to head of the household. Thus he would not question justice within the family.

The Liberal Feminism accepts the distinction between the public and private spheres. But its primary focus is on equality in the public realm which excludes the family from its reckoning. The Liberal Feminism considers the family as the centre of the private sphere. It insists on the liberal right to privacy. It is encompassing and protective of the personal intimacies of the home such as the family, marriage, motherhood, procreation and child rearing. It views any plea of state interference in the family in the name of justice as the negation of the traditional liberal conception of the family as the centre of private life. The rationale being that private family falls outside both state and civil society.

There is an obvious imbalance in the amount of domestic chores performed by women in comparison to men. The solution that the Liberal Feminists offer is often individual and private and not public or political. It is that men and women should share the load equally. They look upon domestic violence as an aberration and not something all-pervasive, warranting interference by the state. However, marriage as an institution does need some reforms. But the family has the key to the spiritual transformation of man and society.

## Should the State Intervene in the Family?

As against the Liberal Feminists the Radical Feminists do not agree with the 'public' and 'private' distinction that the former make. In their view the battle for gender equality must not only contend against public discriminations but also cover domestic labour, women's devaluation of her work, and such other aspects of her personal sphere like domestic violence. They consider the right to family privacy as a hindrance to any type of reforms in women's domestic oppression. They are opposed to excluding the family from the state-initiated reforms designed to protect women's interest. They favour state intervention in order to protect women against numerous abuses to which she is subjected. They lament that in the name of privacy the numerous institutions within the society deprive women of their identity, autonomy, control and self-definition.

The Radical Feminists also question why domestic labour by women is not given public recognition and due evaluation. They argue that the devaluation of housework is tied to the broader devaluation of women's work. They believe that the struggle for increased respect to women can enhance respect for their contribution to the family. They view the domestic assault as a socioeconomic crime which needs be confronted at the political level. For the domestic assault is nothing but another instance of the misuse of power by men who think that they alone have the right to control the women and their lives, even if it be through violent means. The Radical Feminists therefore exhort women to liberate themselves from the scourge of gang rape, domestic violence, family splitting and the like. Marriage, to them, is not an involuntary state in which women can be treated chattel-like. They find the ultimate solution to this problem in women not marrying, and if they do, they should refuse to be monogamous. They need also shed trappings of marriage such as husband's last name, joint tax return or a wedding ring and the like.

But the Radical Feminists have now come to split into two camps on the question whether the family reform should involve women freeing themselves from their husband and children. On this point, a sizeable chunk of the Radical Feminists are seen refusing such a course. They consider it prudent not to bring in marriage, motherhood and family in the feminist discourse. But they are united on the need of a revolution to sweep away patriarchy as a system of women oppression in socioeconomic and other spheres.

## From Personal Sphere to Political Sphere

The Radical Feminists uphold the dictum, 'the personal is political' or 'women's body is women's right.' They see the family as the root cause of women's oppression and therefore they favour its abolition. Their slogan is now changed. They want that the family as personal sphere must now be opened to political change, by force if necessary. For this the state should enter the home to ensure gender justice.

The fact is that the state today is assuming myriad welfare functions. They include intervening in the family sphere and regulating the various family functions, such as making payment for the domestic work. Housekeeping is no longer a personal business of the family, but very much a matter of 'socioeconomic justice'. The state has a duty to take such remedial measures as providing salary to the housewives. In short, the state should not be kept away in the name of family autonomy, private or personal sphere. Both social justice and familial justice demand state intervention in the family. In no case the family should be left alone.

There is another school of 'Individualist Feminists' who oppose state intervention in the family on the basis of an ingenious plea that even when the Feminists and the state are seen working towards a common goal, truly speaking, each one is in fact pursuing a different goal. The state, to them, is a male from the feminists perspective and therefore, it is likely to use its power to protect the interest of men as a class. In this context, they maintain that woman is a 'self-owner' with the inalienable right to use her body and property in whatever peaceable manner she may choose to do. In short, women must retain full control of their own body and must not let it diminish through marriage. Furthermore, the state should have no domination over private sexual arrangements.

However, the Individual Feminists do agree that only a revolution can end the women's oppression within the family, but such a revolution should empower the individual women. What women most direly need is liberation and not state control. Both the family and marriage should be out of the political realm and limited to the private realm.

While the Liberal Feminists consider the family as the centre of private life, Radical Feminists view the family and marriage contract not as private one at all. It is through the family that patriarchy sustains itself. The state ought to thrust justice into an inherently oppressive condition of marriage and family life.

The Individualistic Feminists demand that the state must withdraw from family. The adults must work out their own definition of justice in the privacy of their own homes. They view the state as a partner in the everyday family life. The state gives legal sanction to marriage and divorce . The State should not only have controlling interest in the affairs of the family but it should also have a stake in eradicating the evils of marriage and family.

## State Intervention in Family: Arguments in Favour

The state should proactively strengthen the family for a number of reasons:

1. By shoring up the family as an institution, the state strengthens the foundation of civil society. When civil society is weak, citizens feel less connected to others. They feel more subject to the whims of a politicized and conflict-ridden world beyond their control.
2. The state should aim to strengthen families because stronger families mean higher levels of well-being among the rising generation. A significant number of today's children and youth are struggling. They suffer from unacceptably high levels of emotional stress and distress, behavioral problems, and mental illnesses etc. Even with all the added social and psychological services directed to the young, too many still remain anxious and depressed. These symptoms go with unacceptably high rates of suicide, domestic abuse, and a number of physical ailments. Children and youth desperately want and need loving families.

   Specifically, the proactive role of the state in strengthening the family means encouraging greater love and loyalty between all family members. It involves promoting loving, faithful, and healthy marriages. It also means encouraging increased connection and communication between parents and children. It entails encouraging both fathers and mothers in rearing children in a positive and healthy environment and in teaching them the values and morals essential to personal achievement and the good of society.

3. Finally, the state should support healthy marriages as well as also those that need assistance. Despite government policy to strengthen healthy marriages, many children still grow up in less-than-ideal situations. Research indicates that these children face increased risks for negative outcomes and are in greater need for social services. Therefore, the state is required to offer a variety of tangible social services to families in need. Some of the welfare programs should include cash assistance, food assistance, child-care services, and health care. Efforts should be made to ensure that all families are provided a minimum standard of living.

While such programs provide a safety net for many families and children, there are limits to government intervention. Social services cannot replace the natural, human relationships—especially those of involved mothers and fathers—that are ideal for children's development. Whether support is channeled through cash assistance, in-kind transfers, or social workers, these worthwhile endeavors can only supplement what children need most — the love and attention of their mother and father. No government program can replace families.

## Principles of Family Policy

As the well-being of children is fundamentally linked to the well-being of families, public policy should thus seek to support and strengthen families. The more the state takes step to strengthen the family, the more the state can help ensure better outcomes for children.

Each child has the greatest chance to realize his or her own worth. He can achieve his or her true potential, when he or she is raised within the context of a strong family. Therefore, public policy should support all families, because each and every child deserves support. At the same time, since marriage is so foundational to strong family life, public policy should seek to ensure that greater numbers of children grow up in a loving family with their own parents.

For example, children who grow up in dysfunctional families are more likely to be abused and neglected. Public policy should have a child welfare system to investigate potential instances of abuse and neglect. It should have a foster care system to take care of children who are abused and neglected. Further, if effective public policy can help couples to form and sustain healthy marriages, fewer children will be abused or neglected. It will reduce dependence on and need for child welfare services. Similar types of public policy can also impact nearly every social program from child protective services to child support enforcement, from antipoverty programs to services for runaway youth.

It is imperative that society must place the well-being of children first and foremost. This can be possible only by strengthening the family. It means that the government should prudently protect, promote, and nurture the dignity and worth of every person.

Following are the principles that ought to shape public policy in a way that honors and values the family:

**The need to create the conditions that allow families to thrive.**

Perhaps the most effective policy measures that support or strengthen the family are indirect ones. With their help the governments enable the family to thrive on its own and function autonomously. This principle finds support in the Universal Declaration of Human Rights, which enjoins: "No one shall be subjected to arbitrary interference with his privacy, family, home or correspondence."

Two indirect measures for strengthening the family are as follows:

1. Government ought to keep the tax burden on families as low as possible.
2. Governments ought to create the conditions whereby both parents do not feel pressured to be in the workplace just to make ends meet.

Therefore, parents should at least have the option to split their roles and functions in the family if they so choose. Along with it public policy should help to enable families with greater flexibility to address the needs of their children.

Also public policy should seek to strengthen the bonds connecting fathers to their children, while honoring the role of motherhood as an esteemed and respected institution in society.

**Guidelines to strengthen marriage and family.**

There are a number of guidelines that can inform government support for marriage. One is that healthy marriages are good for children; dysfunctional and abusive marriages are not. Hence, as a strategy for improving the well-being of children, government should promote healthy marriages.

Because each child has dignity and worth, government must support children and families regardless of family structure.

All children are unique gifts and have unique talents, each and every one of them deserves support and encouragement, regardless of their family arrangement because the family intersects so many areas of public policy.

The following should be viewed as illustrative ways on how the government should be seeking to strengthen the family:

For allowing the family to thrive perhaps the most effective initiatives can be significantly to lower the tax burden on the family. While families should be left free to make their own decisions in matters such as health care, education, home ownership, and workforce participation, greater freedom and flexibility need be ensured to let the family thrive as a vital social institution.

There is also need to take other initiatives to provide families a larger stake in decisions that affect both children and parents. Parents should be provided greater freedom in the choice of schools their children would like to attend, especially in the case where a school does not meet acceptable standards. Similarly they should be provided greater choices when it comes to prescription of drugs. Families should also be provided more choice and greater control over their healthcare needs.

### Supporting Healthy Marriages

Both work and marriage are keys to helping families escape poverty and welfare dependency. Couples should be given ample choices to gain access to services where they can acquire the skills and knowledge necessary to form and sustain healthy marriages. Civil society institutions should be encouraged to conduct public education campaigns about the importance of marriage. They should offer premarital education and marriage enrichment programs to help couples develop the skills and knowledge necessary to form and sustain healthy marriages. They should provide targeted outreach to troubled marriages so that couples do not have divorce as the only alternative when they are experiencing marital distress. An overall goal in all such efforts is to increase the proportion of children growing up in healthy married households.

### Strengthening Parenhood

Research indicates that children who grow up without involved fathers or mothers are significantly more likely to suffer emotional problems, perform poorly in school, engage in criminal activity, and indulge in drug abuse and alcohol. Even when fathers and mothers are physically present, they can be seen psychologically absent from the lives of their children. The role that responsible parents play in society can be pivotal. Government should provide them the right anxiety-free environment with ample facilities to creatively use their leisure in the company of their children.

Within the child support enforcement program, there is need to increase the involvement of noncustodial parents, usually fathers, with their children. While parents ought to fulfill their financial obligations to their children, parental contributions to children need extend far beyond just financial provision. Parents are to be seen more than paychecks. They are required to make valuable social, emotional and psychological contributions to their children's lives. Children want and deserve their parents' contributions and involvement, even when they do not live with them.

### Encouraging Abstinence until Marriage

To ensure that more children grow up with a mother and a father, there is need to encourage adolescents to postpone sexual activity until marriage and help to reduce the rates of adolescent pregnancies. Young people should be encouraged to better understand the value of waiting until they are "older" before becoming a parent, and the value of waiting until they are married. Family welfare campaigns and right education can go a long way in bringing forth, positive thinking, strong personality and character.

Good choices early in life pave the way for healthy families in the future. When children face a choice between self-restraint and self-destruction, there should be enough inner reserve of ideals and values promotive of good choices.

### Assisting Children in Need

Despite all family welfare programmes still there may be many children who will grow up without the involvement of both parents in their lives. These children include foster children waiting for adoption. They may be abandoned children or children who have experienced their parents' divorce and even the ones who are born into single parent families.

The prevalence of poverty, violence, drug abuse, and high crime environments can compound these problems. Those lacking in support of families should have more and more caring schools and other community institutions. In their absence they will have a tougher time developing the values and social skills necessary for successful relationships. They will be at higher risk to suffer from a range of behavioral, emotional, health and educational problems. These well let them more prone to commit the juvenile and even adult crimes than other children.

Mentors can significantly reduce the risk of negative outcomes for children. Their guidance can decrease the chances of engaging in self-destructive or violent behavior. Their wise and timely counsel can not only contribute to stability, but it may also have a profound, life-changing impact on the child. Mentoring relationships create continuing cycles of hope and promise. They not only provide positive influences for individual children, but also strengthen families and communities.

In addition, the state should strongly support increased funding to working parents to have adequate access to quality child care. Children from single-parent families are more likely to face a number of unique challenges. They need to be assured that the care of a loving mentor, a loving home, or the security of economic self-sufficiency can help mend matters.

### Valuing the Family: State and Civil Society

By promoting strong and healthy marriages, increasing connection and communication between parents and children, the civil society institutions can foster greater involvement of both fathers and mothers in rearing children in healthy and positive environments. They can help teach children values and morals essential to personal achievement and the common good.

Government is just one actor among many whose decisions may impact the health and well-being of families. To that extent government policy is limited in what it can do to strengthen families. But what it can do, it ought to do. An attempt need be made to place the family as a critical component of the public policy dialogue.

This may ensure greater involvement of future generations to gain promise and hope along with the best possible opportunities.

### The Agenda of Welfare State vis-a-vis the Family

The agenda of welfare state vis-a-vis the family here should include:

1. end state-mandated and state-controlled education, leaving the training and rearing of children up to their own parents or legal guardians;
2. abolish child-labor laws, again reasoning that parents or guardians are the best judges of their children's interests and welfare, vastly better than any combination of state bureaucrats;
3. dismantle the social security system, leaving protection or security in old age to be provided, once again, by individuals and their families;
4. there is a need to give priority in legal and policy discourse to children´s needs as distinct from parents' rights. The need is to operate on the basis that children´s needs and rights are paramount. This is particularly in the context of marriage and relationship breakdown when children may be particularly vulnerable;
5. joint parenting is centrally important for the well-being of children and should be an integral part of policy development;
6. the role of the state should be to support families and promote their general well-being ensuring at the same time access to appropriate services and supports;
7. the state interference in family life should be permitted where necessary to safeguard vulnerable members such as children, the elderly and people with disabilities;
8. family care should be promoted and supported with particular reference to vulnerable members within families – children, people with disabilities and dependent older persons; and
9. social services and supports for families and ongoing changes in family law should be planned and developed in tandem with constitutional reform.

## CONCLUSION

The family is "the natural, primary and fundamental group of society". The State guarantees should protect it. While the State pledges itself "to guard with special care the institution of marriage on which the family is founded and to protect it against attack", it is now widely accepted that the concept of 'family´ encompasses various sets of relationships and living arrangements. In addition to the family based on marriage, with or without children, there are a number of other family types, e.g., lone mothers or fathers widowed, separated or divorced, single parents usually a mother with one or more children, families brought up by grandparents and separated families who may live in two different households but who are still families.

The United Nations refers to the family as a basic social group composed of a married or unmarried couple and children, including adopted ones. The International Year of the Family, 1994, uses the term 'family' as an all-embracing, all-inclusive one. It covers a wide range of structures and functions. It has, as one of its aims, to recognize, support and empower diverse family forms. The European Court of Human Rights refers to ties and bonds "amounting to family life" such as those that exist between some couples who are neither married nor co-habiting. A definition of family should be capable of embracing diverse family forms, including grandparents and children, foster parents and children, lone parents, unmarried partners and children and even same sex parents and children.

## Family Care: How far State should go?

The fundamental theory of liberty upon which all governments repose faith excludes any general power of the state to standardize its children by forcing them to accept instruction from public teachers only. The child is not the mere creature of the state; those who nurture him and direct his destiny have the right, coupled with the high duty, to recognize and prepare him for additional obligations.

It is cardinal that the custody, care, and nurture of the child reside first in the parents, whose primary function and freedom include preparation for obligations that the state can neither supply nor hinder. And it is in recognition of this that these decisions have to be respected and the private realm of family life in which the state cannot enter should be strengthened.

Having focused on phenomenon in the child protection system, now a look at the governmental education system would be in place . The public education system, too, is becoming today an increasingly suspect institution from the point of view of family rights. A partial list of the trends that have been either implemented or proposed in public schools would include: aid-preventive explicit sex education, continuing through high school; school-based health clinics, providing contraceptive advice and devices, and abortion referrals; lengthening the school day and/or the school year; lowering the age of mandatory schooling.

The trend is towards a convergence of education policy and welfare policy, with the schools as all-purpose social service centers. In the "school of the future" proposed by some theories, it is hard to see what role is left for the parental home to play in a child's life, except that of providing meals and beds. In fact, even meals are slipping away from the domain of the home, as more and more schools provide breakfast as well as lunch. The logical end point, of course, is the system of ancient Sparta or Indian Gurukula with children living in government barracks or with all—caring educational centers. The main difference would be that the Spartan state did not seize the children at quite so early an age, as the Gurukula did.

The relationships between members of the family community are inspired and guided by the law of "free giving." It is respecting and fostering personal dignity in each and every one as the only basis for value. This 'free giving' takes the form of heartfelt acceptance, encounter, and dialogue, disinterested availability, generous service, and deep solidarity.

# BIBLIOGRAPHY

## Suggested Readings

Ahmad Iiyas, *The First Principles of Politics* (Allahabad, Allahabad Publishing House: 1957)
Alex Callinicos (Ed.) *Marxist Theory*, (Oxford, OUP, 1989).
An Admirer, *Periyar E.V. Ramaswami*, (Madras, D.K. Publication 1984).
Andrain Charles F. *Political Life Social Change: An Introduction to Political Science*, (California, Wadsworth Publishing Co., 1970).
Andrew Vincent, *Modern Political Ideologies*, (Oxford, Blackwell, 1992)
Anthony H. Birch. *The Concepts and Theories of Modern Democracy* (London, Routledge, 1993).
Arblaster Antony, *The Rise and Decline of Western Liberalism* (Oxford, Basil Blackwell, 1984)
Arora, N.D. and Awasthi, S.S. *Political Theory* (Har-Anand 2000)
Arora, N.D., *Theory of State*, (New Delhi, Social Science Research Publication, 1973).
Arora, V.K. and Rathore, L.R., *Ram Manohar Lohia and Socialism in India* (New Delhi, Deep and Deep, 1984)
Asirvatham Addi, *Political Theory*, (New Delhi, S. Chand & Co., 1988)
Barbalet, *Citizenship*, (Milton Keynes, Open University Press 1988).
Barry, Norman P., *On Classical Liberalism and Libertarianism* (New York: St. Martins Press, 1987)
Bellamy, R., *Theories and Concepts of Politics: An Introduction* (Manchester: Manchester University Press, 1993)
Benn and Peters, *Social Principles & Democratic State*, (London, George Allen and Unwin, 1975).
Berlin Isaih, *Four Essays on Liberty* (Oxford, O.U.P. 1975).
Berry Norman P., *Models of Political Theory* (London, Macmillan, 1989).
Bhatia, K.L., Hari Om, *Social Justice of B.R. Ambedkar* (New Delhi, Deep and Deep, 1995).
Blondel, J., *The Discipline of Politics* (London: Butter-worths, 1981)
Bottomore Tom, *Dictionary of Marxist Philosophy*, (Oxford, Basil Blackwell, 1985).
Bronilaw Greenek, *Civil Society and the Present Age*, (Internet).
Brown, Alan., *Modern Political Philosophy* (London: Penguin, 1986)
Bullock and Shock, *The Liberal Tradition*, (Oxford, the Clarendon Press, 1967)
Bultasky, F., *The Modern state and Politics*, (Moscow, Progress Publishers, 1978).
Callinicos, Alex; (ed) *Marxist Theory* (Oxford: OUP, 1989)
Cevitas, R (ed), *The Ideology of the New Left* (Cambridge: Polity, 1986)

Connolly, W., *Political Theory and Modernity* (Oxford: Blackwell, 1988)

Cook and Morgan, *Participatory Democracy*, (N.Y., Harper & Row, 1971).

Cornay, M., *State and Political Theory*, (N.Y., Princeton University Press, 1984).

David Held, *Models of Democracy*, (Cambridge, Polity Press, 1987).

D'Entreves, A.P., The Notion of State (Oxford, OUP, 1972).

David Held, *Political Theory Today*, (Cambridge, Polity Press, 1991).

Demokratizatsiya *Civil Society in the Post-communist Context: Linking Theoretical Concept and Social Transformation* (Internet).

Doctor Adi H., *Issues in Political Theory*, (New Delhi, Sterling Publishers, Pvt. Ltd., 1985).

Duncan, G., *Democratic Theory and Practice*, (Cambridge, OUP, 1983)

Dunleavy, P., and O'Leary, *Theories of the State: The Politics of Liberal Democracy* (London: Macmillan, 1987)

Dunn John, *Rethinking Modern Political Theory*, (Cambridge University Press, 1985)

Easton David, *Political System*, (Calcutta, Scientific, Book Agency, 1971).

Ebenstein W., *Great Political Thinkers*, (New Delhi, Oxford & IBH Publishing Co., 1960).

Frolov I., *Dictionary of Philosophy*, (Moscow, Progress Publishers, 1984).

Galbraith, J.K., *The Anatomy of Power*, (Boston, Hougthton Miffinn Co., 1983).

Ganguli, B.N., *Gandhi's Social Philosophy,* (Delhi, Vikas, 1973)

Garner James Wilford, *Political Science and Government,* (The World Press, Calcutta, 1951)

Giddens, A., *Central Problems in Social Theory*, (London, Macmillan, 1979)

Gopal S. (ed.) *Jawaharlal Nehru: An Anthology,* (New Delhi, Oxford University Press, 1980)

Gray John, *Liberalism*, (Milton Keynes, Open University Press, 1986).

Gray, H., *Liberalism: Essays in Political Philosophy*, (London: Routlege, 1989)

Greaves, H.R.G., *The Foundations of Political Theory*, (London, Bell and Sons. 2nd edition, 1966)

Hacker Andrew, *Political Theory*, (New York, Macmillan, 1968).

Halsey, A.H., 'T. *Marshall: past and present*'. Sociology, 18(1) 1984

Hayek, F.A., *The Road to Serfdom*, (Chicago, Chicago University Press, 1944).

Hobbes Thomas, *Leviathan* (ed. John Plamenatz), (Glasgow Louins, 1969).

Hobhouse, L.T., *Liberalism* (London, Witism and Sons, 1927).

Holden Barry, *The Nature of Democracy*, (London, Nelson; 1974).

Hsiao, K.S., *Political Pluralism A Study in Comparative Political Theory*, (London Kegan Paul, 1927).

J.L. Macfarlane, *The Theory and Practice of Human Rights*, (London, Maurice Tempel Smith, 1985).

John Dunn (ed.), *Contemporary Crisis of the Nation-state*, (Oxford, Blackwell 1991).

Kangle, R.P., *The Kautilya's Arthsastra, A Study Part III,* (Bombay, University of Bombay, 1965)

Kapoor, A.C. *Principles of Political Science* (Delhi, S. Chand & Co. 1963)

Koener Kink F., *Liberalism and Its Critics*, (London, Croom Helm, 1985).

Krishna Gopal, *Thought and Ideas of Gandhi, Nehru, Tagore and Ambedkar*, (New Delhi, Jawahar Publishers and Distributor, 1994).

Kymlicka, W., *Liberation, Community and Culture*, (Oxford: Cloredon, 1989)

Labedz Leopold, *Revisionism*, (London, George Allen and Unwin, 1962).

Laski, Harold, *A Grammer of Politics*, (London, George Allen and Unwin, 1951).

Leftwich, A., *What is Politics*, (London, Basil, Blackwell, 1984).
Leftwich, A. (ed.) *New Dimensions in Political Science* (Aldershot, Edward Elgar, 1990)
Lenin, *Selected Works*, (Moscow, Progress Publishers, 1971).
Lipson, Leslie, *The Great Issues of Politics* (Bombay, Jaico Publishing House, 1967).
Lloyd, C. (ed.), *Social Theory and Practical Practice* (Oxford: Clarendon, 1983)
Locke John, *Of Civil Government* (London, J.M. Dent and Sons Ltd. 1943).
Lohia Ram Manohar, *The Wheel of History*, (Hyderabad, Lohia Samiti, 1955)
Lubasz, H., (ed.) *The Development of the Modern State* (New York: Macmillan, 1964)
Maclver, R.M. *The Modern State*, (Oxford: OUP, 1926)
Macpherson, C.B., *Democratic Theory*, (Oxford, Clarendon Press, 1973).
Macpherson, C.B., *The Life and Times of Liberal Democracy* (Oxford: OUP, 1977)
Majumdar, Bimanlehari, *History of Political Thought from Ram Mohan to Dayananda (1821-84)* (Calcutta, 1934)
Marshal, T.H., *Citizenship and Social Class and Other Essays* (Cambridge: CUP, 1950)
Marx and Engles, *Selected Works* (Moscow, Progress Publishers, 1971).
Marx Karl, *Economic and Philosophical Manuscripts of 1844* (Moscow, Progress Publishers, 1974).
McElory Wendy, *Marriage and Family* (Internet).
Medvedev Roy, *On Socialist Democracy* (London, Macmillan, 1969).
Mehta, V.R., *Ideology, Modernization and Politics in India,* (New Delhi, Manohar, 1983)
Miliband, R., *The State in the Capitalist Society* (London: Quartet Books, 1973)
Mill, John Stuart, *On Liberty*, (London, Watts and Co., 1948).
Miller, D., and Siedentop, L. (ed), *The Nature of Political Theory* (Oxford: Clarendon, 1983)
Miller, David, *The Blackwell, Encyclopaedia of Political Thougt* (Oxford, Basil Blackwell, 1987).
Nageshewar Prasad, *Hind Swaraj: A Fresh Look* (New Delhi, Gandhi Peace Foundation, 1985).
Nickolls David, *Three Varieties of Pluralism* (London, Macmillan., 1974).
Pantham, Thomas and Deutch Kenneth, *Political Thought in Modern India*, (New Delhi, Sage, 1986).
Parekh, B.*Gandhi's Political Philosophy: A Critical Examination*, (Houndmills Macmillan, 1989).
Patil, V.T., *Studies in Nehru* (New Delhi, Sterling, 1987).
Paul Miller and Paul, (Ed)., *Liberty and Equality* (London, Basil Blackwell, 1985).
Paul, Millew, Paul and Ahran, *Marxism and Liberalism*, (Oxford, Basil Blackwell, 1986).
Pierson, C., *Marxist Theory and Democratic Politics* (Cambridge: Polity, 1986)
Plant, R., *Modern Political Thought* (Oxford: Blackwell, 1991)
Poggi, G., *The Development of the Modern State* (London: Hutchinson, 1978)
Poulantzas Nicos, *Political Power and Social Classes*, (London, Verso, 1978).
Raghavan, Iyer, *The Moral and Political Thought of Mahatma Gandhi*, (New Delhi, OUP, 1974).
Randhir Singh, *Reason, Revolution and Political Theory* (New Delhi, P.P.H. 1967).
Rao, K. Raghvendra, *Kautilya and the Secular State,* (Journal of the Karnataka University-7)
Rawls John, *A Theory of Justice* (London, OUP, 1972).

Richard G. Fod, *Gandhian Utopia*, (Boston, Boston Press, 1989)
Robert Goddin and Phillip Pettit, *A Companion to Contemporary Political Philosophy*, (London, Blackwell, 1993).
Robert Nozick, *Anarchy State and Utopia* Ed., Jeffrey Paul, (Oxford, Basil Blackwell, 1981).
Rousseau J.J., *The Social Contract*, ed., Henry J.Tozer (London, George Allen and Unwin, 1924).
Ryan Alan, *Property & Political Theory* (London, Basil Blackwell, 1984).
S.P.Verma, *Modern Political Theory*, (New Delhi, Vikas Publishing House 1994).
Sabine George, *A History of Political Theory* (London, George Harper and Co. Ltd., 1956).
Sandel, M., *Liberalism and Its critics* (Oxford: Basil Blackwell, 1989)
Sarangi, Prakash, *Liberal Theories of State:* Contemporary Perspectives (New Delhi: Sterling, 1996)
Sartori Giovanni, *Democratic Theory* (Calcutta, Oxford & I.B.H. 1965).
Scruton, Roger, *A Dictionary of Political Thought* (London, Macmillan, 1982).
Selucky Radoslav, *Marxism, Socialism and Democracy* (London, Macmillan, 1979).
Sibley Mulford, *Political Ideas and Ideologies* (Delhi, Surjeet Publications, 1981).
Spiro Herbert J., *Politics as the Master Science-From Plato to Mao* (New York, Harper & Saw 1970).
Tawney, R.H., *Equality* (London, George, Allen & Unwin, 1931).
Tawney, R.H., *The Acquisitive Society* (Bombay, Orient Longman, 1955).
Thakurdas Frank, *Recent English Political Theory* (Calcutta, The Minerva Associates, 1972).
Turner, Bryan, *Equality*, (London, Eills Horwood, 1986).
Turner, B.S., *Citizenship and Capitalism*, (London, Allen and Unwin, 1986)
Varma, *Modern Indian political Thought,* (Agra, 1971)
Veeramani, K., *Periyar and His Ideologies* (Madras, Periyar Self-Respect Propangada Institute, 1983).
Verma, Rajni Kant, *Lohia* (Allahabad, Rasim Prakashan, 1969).
Vermani, R.C. *An introduction to Political Theory & Political Thought* (Gitangali 2005)
Victor Passisnichenki, *Civil Society Concept: Prospect and Post-communist Challenge* (Internet).
Vincent, A.W., *Theories of the State* (Oxford: Basil Blackwell, 1987)
Vincent, Andrew, *Theories of the State* (Oxford: Basil Blackwell, 1987)
Wasby S., Political Science: *The Discipline and Its Dimensions* (Calcutta: Scientific Book Agency, 1972)
Wayper, G.L., *Political Thought* (London, English University Press, 1972).
Weisberg, H. (ed) *Political Science: The Science of Politics* (New York: Agathon, 1986)
White, Stephen K., *Political Theory of Post-Modernism* (Cambridge: CUP, 1991)
Wyliczanki, Josef, *An Encyclopaedic Dictionary of Marxism, Socialism and Communism* (New York, De Gruyter, 1981).
Will Kymillicka, *Contemporary Political Phiosophy-an Introduction*, (Oxford, Clarendon Press, 1990).
Wingrop Norman (ed.), *Liberal Democratic Theory and Its Critics* (London: Croom Helm, 1983).
Wolin, S.S., *Politics and Vision*, (London, George Allen and Unwin., 1961).

# INDEX